Nationalism, Modernism,
and Personal Rivalry in
Nineteenth-Century
Russian Music

Russian Music Studies

Malcolm Hamrick Brown, Series Editor

Professor of Music
Indiana University

Nationalism, Modernism, and Personal Rivalry in Nineteenth-Century Russian Music

by
Robert C. Ridenour

umi
RESEARCH PRESS

Produced and distributed by
UMI Research Press
an imprint of
University Microfilms International
Ann Arbor, Michigan 48106

A revision of the author's thesis,
Indiana University, 1977

Library of Congress Cataloging in Publication Data

Ridenour, Robert C
    Nationalism, modernism, and personal rivalry in
nineteenth-century Russian music.

    (Russian music studies)
    "A revision of the author's thesis, Indiana University,
1977."
    Bibliography: p.
    Includes index.
    1. Music—Russia—History and criticism. 2. Music—
History and criticism—19th century. I. Title. II. Series.
ML300.4.R5 1981   781.747   81-76
ISBN 0-8357-1162-5

Contents

Preface

In 1859 the famous piano virtuoso Anton Rubinstein and a group of his friends founded the Russian Musical Society in St. Petersburg. They proposed to foster symphonic and chamber music in Russia through an annual concert series and to raise the level of Russian music education by opening a conservatory patterned on Western European models. Such goals would seem unobjectionable, but the work of the Society met with strenuous opposition from a circle of young composers headed by Mily Balakirev and from the influential critic and composer Alexander Serov. The Balakirev group (including César Cui, Modest Musorgsky, Nikolai Rimsky-Korsakov, and Alexander Borodin, with critic Vladimir Stasov as aesthetic adviser) attacked Rubinstein and his Society in the press for being anti-Russian, founded the Free Music School as a rival to the Conservatory, and organized concerts of their own. Their competition with the Russian Musical Society subsided in 1867 when the Society invited Balakirev to conduct its annual concert series, but it broke out again with even more intensity when Balakirev was dismissed from that post in 1869. The renewed rivalry continued until Balakirev withdrew from the struggle and from all musical activity in the early 1870s, and his circle lost its original cohesion and exclusiveness. Serov occupied a more ambiguous position in the fray. He began the 1860s as an opponent of Rubinstein and a nominal ally of the Balakirev circle, then spent most of the period vilifying both sides in his voluminous critical writings, yet died in 1871 an honored and active member of the Russian Musical Society. Despite all his inconsistencies, however, as the composer of by far the most popular Russian operas produced during the 1860s, Serov was a force to be reckoned with in musical St. Petersburg.

This rivalry for leadership of Russian musical life, one of the most crucial chapters in the cultural history of modern Russia, has not received the attention it deserves from scholars. Most musicologists have shown more interest in the music produced in Russia in the 1860s than in the organization and functioning of Russian musical life. Professional historians have generally paid scant attention to the cultural history of modern Russia, including the musical rivalries of the 1860s. This has left the field, with a few notable recent exceptions,[1] to music-loving amateur historians, who lack the scholarly methods and critical judgment required for the task. As a result, the literature on Russian music in the mid-nineteenth century contains neither an adequate description of the musical rivalries in the 1860s nor a wholly satisfactory interpretation of them. The struggle that surrounded and gave impetus to the birth of professional music education in Russia and fostered the emergence of such composers as Tchaikovsky, Musorgsky, Rimsky-Korsakov, and Borodin—men who won international recognition for a Russian school of composition—has remained obscure.

The traditional view of the competition between the Balakirev circle and the Russian Musical Society (one that has been incorporated into most textbooks on music history and general Russian history[2]) sees the struggle as a nationalist reaction of patriotic Russian musicians to the cosmopolitan and Western-oriented Musical Society and Conservatory. Serov has usually been ignored in this interpretation since his vacillating role does not fit conveniently into the nationalist-Westernizer division, and his works are now little known. This explanation of the rivalry, besides failing to account for Serov's career, rests on inadequate study of the ideas and actions of all the participants as well as the questionable assumption that these men were motivated exclusively by selfless ideals. As the author of a pioneering study in the social history of music has written, our idealistic view of musicians "has been so completely dominated by the nineteenth-century conception of art as pure activity, occupying only the higher strata of its creator's consciousness and unaffected by such lower strata as those which reckon up the bills and consider the possibility of paying them, that we do not consider the composer's relationship to the musical world in which he must . . . secure performance and publication."[3] A strictly nationalist interpretation of the rivalries in Russian musical life in the 1860s stumbles over this very problem. Although such an interpretation seems consistent with certain publicly expressed ideals of the Balakirev group, it not only does not fit Serov's career but fails as well to explain much of the pragmatic behavior of the Balakirev circle.

I propose to move beyond the nationalist issue to examine other bases for the rivalry between the Balakirev group, Serov, and the Russian Musical Society. These include not only the broader aesthetic questions of "realism" and "modernism" in music but also such purely personal and practical considerations as individual loyalties or antagonisms, competition for positions of power and prestige in the musical world, and the desire to make music a financially and socially viable career. This study not only explores the ideas and ideals of its principal subjects but also their actions and interrelationships, as well as the structure and functioning of the musical life of St. Petersburg during the 1860s, the single most important period in the development of modern Russian musical culture.

The 1860s brought sweeping changes and unprecedented activity in all spheres of Russian life. The sudden intensification in musical activity after the Crimean War was part of a general trend toward reform and greater private initiative in public affairs following the stifling conservatism and repression of the last years of the reign of Nicholas I. The musical rivalries of the 1860s illustrate the vigor with which at least a portion of educated Russian society responded to the reforming spirit and apparent opportunities for personal advancement thrown open by the accession to the throne of Alexander II.

This book is a substantially revised version of my doctoral dissertation, defended in the Department of History, Indiana University, Bloomington. I wish to acknowledge the advice and support of my advisor, Barbara Jelavich, and of the other members of my research committee, Alexander Rabinowitch, Charles Jelavich, and Malcolm Brown. Special thanks are due Dr. Brown for his expert assistance in revising and polishing the final draft of this book. All dates in the text and references, unless specifically noted otherwise, are given according to the Old Style or Julian calendar in use in Russia until 1918. Throughout the nineteenth century this calendar lagged twelve days behind the New Style or Gregorian calendar used in the West. For convenience, the terms "music," "musical life," and "musical culture" are used to refer only to secular art music. Russia has a rich tradition of folk and church music, but these lie outside the scope of this study because the musicians in question concerned themselves almost exclusively with what is commonly called classical music. Library of Congress transliteration is used for direct quotes in Russian and for bibliographic references to Russian-language sources in the footnotes and in the bibliography, including all proper names relevant to those sources. In the main body of the text, well-known Russian proper names with commonly used spellings are given in their familiar form. Less well-known Russian proper names are transliterated in a manner that suggests their approximate pronunciation in Russian.

Robert C. Ridenour
Bloomington, Indiana
September 1980

Notes to the Preface

1. Such as Edward Garden, *Balakirev: A Critical Study of His Life and Music,* (New York: St. Martin's Press, 1967); David Brown, *Tchaikovsky: The Early Years 1840-1874* (New York: Norton, 1978); and Richard Taruskin, *Opera and Drama in Russia: The Preachment and Practice of Operatic Esthetics in the Eighteen Sixties* (Ann Arbor, Mich.: University Microfilms, 1976).

2. See, for example, Michael T. Florinsky, *Russia: A Short History* (New York: Macmillan, 1964), p. 381; Jesse D. Clarkson, *A History of Russia,* 2nd ed. (New York: Random House, 1969), p. 309; Paul Henry Lang, *Music in Western Civilization* (New York: Norton, 1941), pp. 948-55; Donald Jay Grout, *A History of Western Music,* 3rd ed. (New York: Norton, 1980), pp. 653-59.

3. Henry Raynor, *A Social History of Music: From the Middle Ages to Beethoven* (New York: Schocken Books, 1972), p. 11.

Chapter I

Musical Life in Mid-Nineteenth-Century
St. Petersburg

St. Petersburg was indisputably one of the great cities of the world in the mid-nineteenth century. It enjoyed prestige and power as the capital of the Russian Empire, the largest state in the world and one of the Great Powers of Europe, and displayed the wealth and grandeur of a particularly lavish nobility and royal court. Nevertheless, in its musical life St. Petersburg in 1860 was little more than an outpost—though a frequently spectacular one—of Western and Central European musical culture. When secular art music first appeared in Russian society in the seventeenth century, it arrived not as an organic outgrowth of the rich tradition of Russian folk and church music but as an import from the West. The following two centuries witnessed the gradual spread of a taste for operatic and concert music in Russia, the development of native musicians to supplement or replace foreign performers and teachers, and finally the emergence of native composers capable of making original contributions to the art.[1] But in 1860 Russia was still a colony of the West in the field of music.

It was in St. Petersburg that Western music had most firmly established itself in Russia, for the Russian capital in the 1850s could boast a rather extensive if unevenly developed musical life, including two opera companies and several concert societies. As with virtually all public activity in tsarist Russia, the dominant force directing all this musical activity was the government, in this case specifically the Imperial Theater Directorate, a department of the Ministry of the Imperial Court. This office controlled the two opera companies—one performing in Italian, the other in Russian—St. Petersburg's drama and ballet companies, and the Imperial theater in Moscow.[2] The Theater Directorate also exercised indirect control over all concerts in the capital because it enjoyed an official monopoly on public entertainments during the winter season, which lasted from September until the beginning of Lent, usually in March. On 1 February 1846 Nicholas I had commanded that all privately sponsored public concerts be forbidden during the theater season. Only during Lent, when the Imperial theaters closed, could private organizations or individuals arrange public concerts. Following repeated violations of this regulation and constant petitioning for exemptions, the tsar promulgated a new decree on 7 March 1854 requiring approval by the Imperial Theater Directorate of all public concerts. Two-and-a-half years later Alexander II forbade all petitions for exemption from this rule.[3] Thus, the Theater Directorate controlled the scheduling of all public musical entertainments in St. Petersburg. As a rule, it restricted all concerts to the Lenten season so as to insure that they would not compete with the Imperial opera companies.[4]

The pride of the Theater Directorate was St. Petersburg's Italian Opera. In fact, since the 1730s, when Empress Anna established the first permanent musical theater in Russia by hiring an Italian opera troupe for her court, opera had been the preferred musical entertainment of the Imperial family and the Russian aristocracy. During most of that period the Imperial court provided St. Petersburg with companies of illustrious foreign singers.[5] The tradition was broken in 1812 when Napoleon's invasion of Russia abruptly ended the tenure of the French ensemble then in favor in the Russian capital, leaving a fledgling Russian troupe as the sole Imperial opera ensemble;[6] but the policy of hiring a foreign opera company resumed three decades later. In 1843 the renowned Italian tenor Giovanni Rubini created such a sensation by his singing in St. Petersburg that the director of the Imperial theaters invited him to return for the 1843-44 season with an entire Italian troupe. For the next four decades a foreign opera company again dominated musical life in the Russian capital, overshadowing its rival Russian ensemble.[7] Not until the 1880s did the Italian Opera in St. Petersburg lose its privileged position, court association, and state subsidy.[8] Despite the patriotic fervor of Nicholas I and Alexander II, the Imperial Russian court supported a foreign opera company performing in Italian, to the detriment of the Russian troupe.

The Theater Directorate spent enormous sums to provide the Italian Opera an excellent orchestra, suitably impressive sets and costumes, and, above all, one of the finest groups of singers in all Europe, as memoirists of all musical tastes agree.[9] Some even claimed that Paris, the musical capital of the world in the mid-nineteenth century, did not surpass St. Petersburg in this respect. When the young Pyotr Tchaikovsky visited France in 1861, for example, he was impressed by the physical productions of the operas he saw in Paris but wrote that the performances were, "of course, much inferior to those in St. Petersburg."[10] An Italian diplomat stationed in St. Petersburg intermittently from 1856 to 1863 recorded in his diary that the Russian capital's *"Opera Italien* in winter, as Covent Garden in the summer, gives the finest performances in the world. The best artists are engaged at exorbitant fees . . . The staging of operas and ballets sometimes costs hundreds of thousands of francs."[11]

The Imperial theaters paid Giuseppe Verdi 20,000 rubles for *La Forza del Destino,* which received its world premiere in St. Petersburg in 1862, and provided the work with a spectacular production and a large cast of first-rate artists.[12] Salaries exceeding 10,000 rubles for the season were not at all uncommon for leading singers, and some made more than 20,000 rubles.[13] As a result of such expenditures, subsidized by the Ministry of the Imperial Court, St. Petersburg audiences heard nearly all the finest exponents of vocal culture that Western Europe produced, as even Soviet musicologists, who are highly critical of the "antinational" leanings of the Imperial theaters, are forced to admit.[14]

From September to March the Italian Opera performed four nights a week in the Grand Theater, St. Petersburg's finest.[15] Rossini, Bellini, Donizetti, Verdi, and Meyerbeer's French grand operas formed the basic repertory, along with occasional performances of Weber's *Der Freischütz,* sung in Italian as were all other works, Mozart's *Don Giovanni* and *Marriage of Figaro,* or an Italian novelty.[16] Admission prices were higher than for any other theater, but they did not discourage attendance. In fact, the Italian Opera was the most popular theater in St. Petersburg, especially in high society.[17] Many members of the Imperial family had permanent boxes, as did other socially prominent figures. So prized were boxes at the Italian Opera that subscriptions for them were usually acquired only by inheritance.[18] At a Monday evening performance, the most fashionable of the week, "one could see all of court, diplomatic, military, and official Petersburg" at the Italian Opera, according to one memoirist.[19] While this illustrious group filled the loges and parterre, attracted no doubt as much by fashion as by a passion for music, the upper balconies held the humbler opera lovers of the Russian capital: lesser officials, artists, and students.[20] The amphitheater, a broad, deep recess in the fifth balcony, even provided about a hundred seats for only twenty-five kopeks apiece. One former frequenter of these inexpensive seats later recalled that "from the middle places . . . you had a splendid view of the chandelier of the Grand Theater and also of the feet of the singers whenever they approached the footlights. From the side places, you could even see part of the stage. The sound was excellent."[21]

Leading singers with the Italian Opera enjoyed immense popularity and prestige in the Russian capital. In his memoirs, Pyotr Kropotkin recalled that when Madame Bosio, the company's prima donna in the late 1850s, fell ill,

thousands of people, chiefly of the youth, stood till late at night at the door of her hotel to get news of her. She was not beautiful, but seemed so much so when she sang that young men madly in love with her could be counted by the hundred; and when she died, she had a burial such as no one had ever had at St. Petersburg before.[22]

One witness of Bosio's interment in 1859 estimated the crowd at 200,000.[23] Her death elicited a poetic tribute by Nikolai Nekrasov and a ballad that became very popular in fashionable society. One of the most impressive monuments in all of the cemeteries of St. Petersburg was erected over her grave.[24] The Italian Opera's audience also adored star tenors such as Enrico Tamberlik. A frequenter of the theater in the 1850s later wrote that "a significant part of Petersburg society literally talked of nothing but Tamberlik."[25] Allowing for the obvious exaggerations in the above statements, it is still clear that the stars of the Italian Opera enjoyed enormous public attention and acclaim.

Like all audiences of that day, those attending the Italian Opera tended to be demonstrative in their likes and dislikes; prolonged applause and shouts for encores greeted their favorites, but whistling and catcalls awaited those who displeased them. Nor was it unheard of for members of the audience to make noisy exits during the performance.[26] On the whole, however, the audiences for the Italian Opera maintained a level of decorum in keeping with their high social status. Even the occupants of the less expensive seats could seem rather prim and correct,[27] and one critic reported with pride that the audience at the revival of Mozart's *Don Giovanni* during the 1859-60 season listened to the overture in silence and even applauded it. In earlier days, he remembered, audiences would only applaud the vocal acrobatics of star singers and generally talked through the overture.[28]

In the mid-nineteenth century St. Petersburg's Russian Opera, with native singers performing exclusively in Russian, could not match the high tone of the Italian Opera on either side of the footlights. The Imperial Theater Directorate, which controlled both troupes, considered the Russian one only an adjunct to its more illustrious rival opera theater.[29] Alexander Gedeonov, Director of the Imperial Theaters from 1833 to 1858, was notorious for his rude treatment of Russian artists.[30] The Russian company received relatively little material support, and its quality necessarily suffered. The Theatrical Regulations of 1827, which remained in force until the 1880s, forbade the Imperial theaters to pay any Russian singer or actor more than 1,143 rubles a year, and a full pension required over twenty years of service on the court stage—a long career for a singer.[31] In the 1860s the Theater Directorate evaded the restrictions on fees for Russian artists so that actual salaries of leading Russian singers sometimes reached five thousand rubles or more for a season,[32] but this fell far short of the ten to twenty thousand rubles routinely paid to leading soloists of the Italian Opera. Eduard Napravnik, assistant conductor for the Russian company in the early 1860s, recalled that the singers had good voices and were talented but lacked serious training, like the birds of the air. The orchestra, consisting almost entirely of foreigners and numbering around seventy men, was of adequate quality but neglected and without discipline. The chorus of eighty (who were paid very meagerly—240 rubles or, for a few, 300 or 360 rubles a year) was also undisciplined and neglected.[33]

In the 1850s the Russian Opera even lacked a suitable theater in which to perform. While the Italian company occupied the Grand Theater, St. Petersburg's best, the Russian troupe was relegated to a large stone building across the street originally constructed to house a circus.[34] Fire destroyed this structure in January 1859,[35] and for over a year the Russian Opera had to share the Alexandrinsky Theater with its resident drama company while the damaged building was rebuilt. Renamed the Mariinsky Theater, the permanent home of the Russian Opera reopened on 2 October 1860. In a curious display of generosity toward its second opera company, the Theater Directorate had provided a large and elaborately decorated theater for the underpaid singers and haphazard sets and costumes of the Russian Opera.[36]

In the mid-1850s the Russian Opera performed much less often than its Italian rival. During the 1854-55 season, for example, the Russian company gave only thirty-four performances while the Italian troupe presented eighty-three.[37] Toward the end of the decade the number of Russian performances increased steadily,[38] and in the 1860s, after the opening of the Mariinsky Theater, the Russian Opera regularly performed four times a week like its Italian counterpart.[39] In fact, in the 1860s the Russian company actually exceeded the number of performances by the Italian Opera because it reopened for several weeks following Lent.[40] This was not necessarily an advantage, however, for the closing of the Italian Opera before Lent marked the end of the social season, and the Russian Opera's performances after Easter attracted little attention.[41]

The Russian company, although composed of Russian singers performing in Russian, presented a repertory not strikingly different from the Italian Opera except for a few Russian works and some French and German comic operas. A report by the theater's chief "machinist" concerning the priorities for reconstructing the company's sets after they were all destroyed in the 1859 fire provides a good outline of the repertory and the relative importance of the works. Mikhail Glinka's *A Life for the Tsar* headed the list of eight operas set for immediate and full reconstruction. Also in this group were Glinka's *Ruslan and Liudmila,* Alexei Verstovsky's *Askold's Tomb,* and Alexander Dargomyzhsky's *Rusalka,* but these four were the only Russian compositions in the repertory. The remaining first-priority works were Weber's *Der Freischütz* and three French grand operas. The other ten works in the repertory, mainly light comedies by Auber and Flotow or mainstays of the Italian florid school, were to be presented with sets selected from those built for other operas or else were not to be performed at all.[42]

Considering the limited interest of its repertory and the indifferent standards of production and performance, it is not surprising that the Russian Opera in the 1850s drew an audience both smaller and less distinguished than did the Italian company. Although ticket prices were very low (a half ruble for a seat in the sixth row) attendance was still unimpressive. Ticket sales of a mere three or four hundred rubles were considered neither surprising nor catastrophic.[43] One visitor described the audiences as being composed of provincials, bureaucrats, officers, and students.[44] The Russian Opera generally had to rely for support on a small group of patriotic music-lovers and those who could not obtain or could not afford seats at the Italian Opera.

Although opera dominated the musical life of St. Petersburg in the mid-nineteenth century, the Theater Directorate permitted a variety of concerts during the Lenten season when operas were forbidden. The Russian capital had long been the most northeasterly point on the circuit of major European cities regularly visited by traveling recitalists, playing host to such renowned foreign artists as Robert and Clara Schumann, Franz Liszt, and Hector Berlioz, as well as many lesser lights of the European musical world.[45] During Lent these visiting musicians gave recitals or appeared in concerts with the theater orchestras, as did members of the two local opera companies. *Tableux vivants* usually accompanied the latter, providing the public with as close an approximation of opera as the law permitted during the weeks of abstinence before Easter.[46]

In addition to these performances that featured more-or-less illustrious soloists, the Lenten concert season also brought the Russian capital symphonic concerts sponsored by several organizations. The Philharmonic Society, St. Petersburg's oldest concert organization, was founded in 1802 to popularize serious choral and orchestral music and to raise money to support the widows and orphans of deceased musicians of the Imperial theaters. For nearly half a century it had organized two or three concerts a year with the choir of the Imperial Chapel and instrumentalists from the theater orchestras.[47] After 1850, however, the court chapel choir stopped participating in its concerts, and by 1860 its repertory had shifted to popular excerpts from Italian operas, interspersed with a few German symphonic works to give the programs a serious air. The Philharmonic Society was apparently concerned more with raising money for the theater musicians' pension fund than with elevating public musical taste.[48] It generally offered two or three concerts each year, but by 1860 its activity had become sporadic, with no concerts some years and as many as three in others.[49]

The Concert Society, established in 1850, was a more stable and serious organization. Its orchestra of select musicians from the Imperial theaters gave three concerts each Lenten season, assisted by the choir of the Imperial Chapel. Founded by Alexei Lvov, musical director of the court chapel, the

Concert Society numbered among its members several princes and many high military and civil officials.[50] Grand dukes and duchesses, even the emperor himself, attended its concerts.[51] A combination of high ticket prices (ten rubles for three concerts) and a small auditorium assured the Concert Society an exclusive audience.[52] Its programs enjoyed a reputation for seriousness and careful selection of soloists and repertory which relied heavily on Beethoven, Mendelssohn, and the eighteenth-century classics.[53]

Beginning in 1859 the Theater Directorate adopted the model of the Philharmonic and Concert societies and arranged its own series of Lenten concerts.[54] These took advantage of the ready availability of the Imperial theaters' orchestra, large chorus, and well-known soloists to present programs combining serious symphonic literature with overtures, choruses, and ensembles from popular operas. For example, each of the four concerts given in March 1860 included a symphony by Beethoven, another serious symphonic work, and several excerpts from operas by composers ranging from Rossini to Wagner and Glinka.[55] Thus, the concerts of the Theater Directorate fell somewhere between the earnest sobriety of the Concert Society's programs and the obvious appeal to popular taste of the Philharmonic Society's.

While all these concerts were restricted to the weeks of Lent, one concert series, the University concerts, managed to circumvent the Theater Directorate's monopoly on musical performances during the winter opera season. Officially entitled "Musical Exercises of the Students of St. Petersburg University," this annual series of ten Sunday afternoon concerts offered the Russian capital its only regular source of symphonic music outside the Lenten period. Apparently these performances escaped the ban on private concerts during the opera season because they took place at the University and in the afternoons. Alexander Fitztum, inspector of students at the University, organized the orchestra, drawing from the group of amateur musicians who regularly met in his home for Friday evenings of chamber music. University students then supplemented this core group, along with a few invited professional artists with their students.[56] The concerts were strictly and carefully organized, with programs for the entire season drawn up in advance. Each concert always included an overture and a symphony, and a soloist, usually instrumental, appeared between them.[57] The concerts were open to the public for a fee of one ruble, and Anton Rubinstein, who regularly attended these performances in the 1850s, occasionally taking part as conductor or pianist, recalled that there was rarely an empty seat in the auditorium of the University: "The public flocked in! Often whole crowds could be seen walking across the Neva River" [on the ice].[58]

In addition to the solo concerts of the Lenten season and the symphonic programs presented by the University, the Theater Directorate, and the

Philharmonic and Concert societies, St. Petersburg in the 1850s also offered concertgoers two other types of music. For the more serious music-lovers, there were chamber music concerts, a rarity before the 1850s but quite frequent by the end of the decade. A dozen such programs, usually featuring a string quartet, often with supporting artists, took place in the winter of 1858-59 alone.[59] At the opposite end of the musical spectrum were the summer concerts of light music in the parks on the outskirts of St. Petersburg and in the villages surrounding the city. From May to September the social life of the city moved to the suburbs, where the well-to-do owned summer homes and many other citizens spent Sunday afternoons enjoying the fresh air and coolness of the public gardens. A particularly strong attraction was the musical entertainment traditionally provided at the train station in each village. Most famous of all were the concerts at the Pavlovsk station, where the orchestra played waltzes and polkas under the direction of Europe's "Waltz King" himself, Johann Strauss, Jr., each summer from 1856 through 1865.[60] Other suburban stations supplemented their orchestras with such diversions as Scottish bellringers, a company of eight dancing Negroes, and an "unburnable man."[61] Although such entertainments offered little of interest to the serious music-lover, they indicate that interest in music, at least in its lighter forms, extended beyond the comparatively narrow circle of those who attended the opera or symphonic concerts.

Thus, St. Petersburg's public musical life in the mid-1850s offered an impressive range and variety of institutions but was unevenly developed. The Italian opera company of the Imperial theaters was as glittering as any in Europe, but its Russian counterpart lagged far behind not only in quality of performance and repertory but in official and public support as well. Still farther behind came public concerts. They were confined almost exclusively to the six-week Lenten season, and by far the majority of them were individual benefit concerts designed chiefly to display the talent of the featured soloist and to attract the fashionable public. St. Petersburg's three regular concert societies and the Theater Directorate together gave only about twenty symphonic concerts a year—ten by the University, three or four by the Theater Directorate, three by the concert Society, and two or three by the Philharmonic Society. The two opera companies, by contrast, performed approximately two hundred times each season.

The precedence of opera over concert music had long been characteristic of the musical life of Western European cities as well, at least where opera enjoyed the prestige and support of a royal court,[62] but by the 1850s the symphony concert also had come into its own as an independent focus for musical activity. By 1860 modern concert life as we know it, with fully professional orchestras presenting regular and frequent symphonic performances, was well on its way to consolidation in London, Paris, and

Vienna.[63] In St. Petersburg, however, the Concert Society, the only organization in the city presenting fully professional symphonic concerts without operatic excerpts, performed only three times a year and for a small, elite audience. The Philharmonic Society and the Theater Directorate's concerts gave as much emphasis to operatic as to symphonic music, and the University concerts relied on a mostly amateur orchestra. One student participant later remembered the performances of the fifty-member orchestra as "outstanding,"[64] but others have pointed out that the lack of rehearsal time (at best, one rehearsal preceded each concert, and sometimes the performances were actually read at sight) and the amateur or student status of most of the orchestral musicians produced unsatisfactory results.[65] In his memoirs, Anton Rubinstein admitted that in spite of all efforts the orchestra "played terribly . . . How was it possible to take money for such things?"[66] Thus, St. Petersburg's most regular source of concert music, which accounted for fully half of its annual symphonic concerts, was hardly an impressive institution for a major European capital.

Concert life in St. Petersburg suffered not only from the short concert season and the infrequency or questionable quality of regular symphonic performances but also from limitations in repertory. With few exceptions, the individual concerts that filled the Lenten season featured little more than the brilliant virtuosity of some foreign singer or instrumentalist tossing off the latest bravura showpieces.[67] Such performances had little musical significance and were more likely to be reviewed in the society columns of St. Petersburg's newspapers than by serious music critics.[68] The programs of the regular concert organizations included more serious repertory, but they were old-fashioned in their tastes, relying heavily on Mendelssohn, Beethoven, and Mozart.[69] The symphonies of Robert Schumann were only introduced to St. Petersburg at the end of the 1850s, over a decade after they had become standard works in Germany; the still more advanced works of Wagner and Liszt were even later in securing a place in the repertory.[70]

The greatest inequity in St. Petersburg's musical life in 1860 was not the predominance of the Italian over the Russian Opera or of operatic over instrumental music, however, but the almost complete domination of public musical activity by foreign music and musicians. The taste for concert and particularly operatic music was widespread among the upper levels of St. Petersburg society, and even the lesser ranks enjoyed Johann Strauss's waltzes and polkas, but nearly all the music to which they listened came from the West. The Italian Opera performed only foreign works, and the bulk of the Russian Opera's repertory also came from abroad. Nor were Russian compositions a regular part of St. Petersburg's symphonic concerts.

The strikingly small number of Russian operas—only four of eighteen works in 1860—in the repertory of the Russian Opera and the rarity of

Russian works on orchestral programs reflected, in part, a genuine shortage of talented and skilled Russian composers. Native musicians had begun producing operas for the Russian court and for private theaters maintained by some of the wealthiest landowners as early as the 1770s,[71] but despite claims by Soviet musicologists that they succeeded in creating a distinctive national genre of Russian comic opera by the end of the century,[72] the works that survive appear to be only more-or-less talented imitations of foreign models with occasional interpolations of Russian folk tunes. Not until the second quarter of the nineteenth century did Mikhail Glinka, a composer of talent and genuine originality, provide the Imperial theaters with the first important Russian operas—*A Life for the Tsar* in 1836 and *Ruslan and Liudmila* in 1842. Although both works, especially the earlier, betray strong foreign influences, even Western critics acknowledge their originality and their distinctive national character, which arises from the use of melodic contours, rhythms, and harmonies drawn from Russian folk music.[73] Unfortunately, Glinka's achievement was not matched by any of his compatriots before the 1850s. In the field of concert music the story was even less satisfactory, for Glinka's output of symphonic works was quite small, and no other Russian produced any important contribution in this area before the mid-nineteenth century.

St. Petersburg in 1860 depended on foreign sources not just for the bulk of its operatic and concert repertory but also for the performers of its music, whether of Russian or foreign composition. The most popular performing organization, the Italian Opera, not only featured foreign soloists, but its orchestra was also composed chiefly of foreigners. Even the orchestra of the Russian Opera, although its singers were Russian, was foreign for the most part.[74] The major concert societies relied at least in part on the foreign instrumentalists from the Imperial theaters for their orchestras, and foreign virtuosos were usually the leading attractions of the Lenten concert season.

Although many Russian nationalists at the time (and some scholars to this day) accepted as a matter of principle the inherent superiority of "national" art over any imported culture, the foreign domination of St. Petersburg's musical life did not necessarily affect its aesthetic quality adversely. In fact, the Russian capital in the mid-nineteenth century enjoyed performances by outstanding artists of some of the finest music ever written. But the leading role of music and musicians from abroad at all levels of St. Petersburg's musical life indicated that the Western secular art music first introduced in Russia nearly two centuries earlier had not yet struck firm roots in Russian culture. No matter how popular it might be in certain segments of Russian society, this music would remain something of a hothouse flower, artificially cultivated on Russian soil, as long as the country could not produce native musicians to staff its performing groups and provide them with a significant native repertory.

A fundamental reason for the shortage of Russian musicians was the inadequacy of musical education in Russia. St. Petersburg entered the 1860s without an institution of higher music education. Although a conservatory opened in Warsaw, then part of the Russian Empire, early in 1861,[75] the capital city, St. Petersburg, could claim no such institution. The only schools specializing in musical training were the Theater School, which trained musicians, mainly vocalists, exclusively for the Imperial theaters,[76] and the Imperial Chapel's academy, which prepared singers for the choir of the court chapel. In 1839 the Imperial Chapel began to offer its students lessons on orchestral instruments, but only in the late 1850s were its instrumental classes opened to persons not preparing for membership in the chapel choir.[77] Neither school taught more than the rudiments of music, plus vocal or instrumental technique.

Anyone aspiring to a career in music had either to go abroad or to study privately in St. Petersburg.[78] The Russian capital boasted a great many piano and voice instructors, the former mainly Germans and the latter usually Italians, but many were themselves poorly trained and musically ignorant.[79] One music critic complained in 1860 that "here, anyone who gets the idea in his head teaches music. He needs only to be a foreigner, preferably a German, to plunk the piano keys a bit, to wear spectacles—and that's that."[80] Even Petersburg's better piano and voice teachers provided training only in performance skills, not music history or theory. They could not offer a well-rounded music education. Lessons in music theory or composition were almost unknown in the Russian capital before 1860.[81] Thus, the few comprehensively trained native musicians resident in St. Petersburg in that period had either acquired their music education abroad or by private study, perhaps under the direction of a local musician or through their own resources. The difficulty of this procedure doubtless discouraged many Russians from pursuing serious musical study.

Limited professional opportunities for careers in music further restricted the number of Russian musicians. As seen earlier, the Imperial Opera paid its orchestral musicians and chorus members very poorly. Leading singers received more money, but only a few Russian soloists earned decent salaries, and they were always overshadowed by the more popular foreign stars at the Italian Opera. Much the same was true of instrumental virtuosos. Only the very finest Russian pianists and violinists could compete for public favor with Franz Liszt and the numerous lesser lights from abroad who visited St. Petersburg each Lent to give concerts. Nor was a Russian likely to succeed in Russia as a music teacher. St. Petersburg already had dozens of such teachers with the automatic advantage of being foreigners; any German who could "plunk the piano keys a bit" stood a better chance of acquiring pupils than all but the most accomplished Russian musicians. The only full-time public conducting posts open to Russians in St. Petersburg were as music director of the Imperial Chapel or the Russian Opera because the Italian company hired only foreign artists and the various concert societies needed no permanent conductors for their limited activities.

Finally, a Russian seriously interested in music could not rely on much success as a composer. The Theater Directorate and the leaders of St. Petersburg's concert societies made little effort to encourage the production of Russian works, and the Petersburg musical public showed no great inclination for them. In the 1856-57 opera season, for example, only twenty-three of eighty-four performances by the Russian Opera were of Russian compositions, while Flotow's *Martha* alone achieved eighteen.[82] Among Russian operas, only *Askold's Tomb* by Verstovsky and Glinka's *A Life for the Tsar* enjoyed frequent performances and considerable popularity; by 1855 the former claimed 116 performances in St. Petersburg since its first production there in 1841, and the latter had 105 since 1836.[83] Popularity did not necessarily guarantee favored treatment by the Theater Directorate, however, for in the winter of 1854-55 Glinka was shocked to discover that not a single costume or set for *A Life for the Tsar* had been renovated since its premiere nearly twenty years and over one hundred performances earlier.[84] The original St. Petersburg production of *Askold's Tomb* survived more than 150 performances before being destroyed in the theater fire of 1859.[85]

Other Russian operas were much less popular and fared even more poorly with the management. After a few seasons in the repertory in the early 1840s, Glinka's *Ruslan* waited nearly fifteen years to be revived, and then it disappeared again after six performances.[86] Dargomyzhsky's *Rusalka,* first produced in 1856, barely remained in the repertory, receiving only twenty-one performances in the eight years following its initial season.[87] The Theater Directorate tried other Russian operas now and then[88] but apparently made no concerted effort to seek out or encourage Russian composers. Even a figure of the stature of Anton Rubinstein, whose operas were produced in Vienna and Dresden as early as 1861, had to wait until the mid-1870s to hear one of his major works for the operatic stage produced in St. Petersburg.[89] Russian music was heard even less frequently at concerts in the Russian capital.

Thus, even Glinka, the best composer Russia had produced, could not surpass second-rank Western musicians in the esteem of his compatriots or the Theater Directorate, on whom performances of his operas depended. Moreover, Glinka's few orchestral works were rarely heard because St. Petersburg had few serious symphonic concerts, and those tended to program mainly classics of the German repertory. Neither Glinka nor Dargomyzhsky, the leading Russian composer in St. Petersburg after the death of Glinka, was ever able to live off the income from his compositions.[90] A Russian musician, whether composer, conductor, teacher, instrumentalist, or singer, had little chance of becoming famous or wealthy, even if he were the very best in his chosen field. Those who fell short of that standard had no chance of success at all.

Russians were further discouraged from pursuing careers in music by social pressures. Polite Russian society greatly enjoyed music, or at least pretended to, but had little respect for most professional musicians. Musical skills were widely cultivated in upper-class homes but only as a pleasant diversion. "Boys from well-to-do or wealthy homes," according to one memoirist, "were often given a taste of piano-playing, and girls from such homes were always taught to play," as one of the social graces necessary in a lady,[91] but music was not considered a suitable profession for a gentleman. As another memoirist wrote:

> To compose music "on the side" was considered not just a respectable pastime for a Russian nobleman, but actually almost a distinguishing characteristic of a certain level of culture . . . But along with this went the understanding that of course any nobleman would be in government service; exceptions were made only for those who owned sufficient serfs to be able to live nobly without any profession.[92]

Russian society expected knowledge of music in anyone with pretensions to culture or social status, but a professional musician, unless he was a famous virtuoso, lionized by the crowned heads of Europe, could count on scant social prestige.

Even the Russian legal system discriminated against professional musicians. By law, the rights and privileges of citizens of the Russian Empire varied according to their *chin* or rank. This in turn depended on their social class, education, and profession; but the classification system did not recognize professional musicians. As early as the eighteenth century, trained painters, sculptors, and actors could earn the title "free artist," which gave its holder exemption from the poll tax and military recruitment, and the right to live anywhere in the country,[93] but the government did not extend this privilege to musicians. A private music teacher or a composer who did not inherit gentry status or also pursue a profession recognized by Russian law would have no more legal rights or privileges than a peasant, regardless of his success as a musician. A music teacher in an academy or a musician with the court theater received only the status of a menial functionary in government service, while a gentry composer like Glinka was classed as a nobleman, not a musician.[94] Thus, only a nobleman could afford to devote himself entirely to music except as an employee of the Imperial theaters or a teacher in a state academy. Even members of the gentry were not entirely free to choose any musical profession because they would be required to renounce the special privileges of their noble rank as a condition for joining one of the companies of the Imperial theaters.[95] Thus, the Russian legal system further discouraged Russians from pursuing careers as musicians.

By 1860, then, the Western musical forms first introduced into Russia in the seventeenth century had gained a solid foothold in the social life of St. Petersburg. The upper classes, following the leadership of the Imperial court, had generally developed a taste for music, and inhabitants of at least moderate means could regularly attend public music programs. The city boasted two opera companies and several concert societies, plus dozens of benefit recitals and appearances by visiting virtuosos each season. The development of musical life in Russia was uneven, however, and the essentially Western music and musical institutions had been absorbed only partially into the native culture. Opera clearly overshadowed orchestral music, which in turn eclipsed chamber music. Foreign composers and performers overwhelmingly dominated all types of musical activity in the city. For lack of proper musical training and encouragement, Russia lacked sufficient native musicians to staff its orchestras and opera companies or to provide them with a significant native repertory. Finally, Russian law and society refused to grant the professional musician the social and legal status accorded other artists. As long as these conditions prevailed, St. Petersburg—and, indeed, the Russian Empire—could never be more than a musical colony of Western Europe.

Notes to Chapter I

1. The most thorough account in English of the history of Russian music before the mid-nineteenth century is Gerald R. Seaman's rather disappointing *History of Russian Music: Volume I, From Its Origins to Dargomyzhsky* (New York: Praeger, 1967). The reader of Russian is directed to the classic study, Nikolai Fedorovich Findeizen, *Ocherki po istorii muzyki v Rossii: S drevneishikh vremen do kontsa XVIII veka* [Essays on the history of music in Russia: from earliest times to the end of the eighteenth century], 2 vols. (Moscow: Muzykal'nyi sektor gosudarstvennogo izdatel'stva, 1928-1929) or to the most recent Soviet textbook, Ol'ga Evgen'evna Levasheva, Iurii Vsevolodovich Keldysh, and Aleksei Ivanovich Kandinskii, *Istoriia russkoi muzyki* [The history of Russian music], 2 vols. (Moscow: Muzyka, 1973-   ).

2. Erik Amburger, *Geschichte der Behördenorganisation Russlands von Peter dem grossen bis 1917* (Leiden: E.J. Brill, 1966), p. 102.

3. Sergei Taneev, "Publichnye kontserty i baly v stolitsakh" [Public concerts and balls in the capitals], *Russkii arkhiv* [The Russian archive] 23, pt. 2 (1885): 445-46.

4. Leopold Auer, *My Long Life in Music* (New York: Frederick A. Stokes, 1923), pp. 129-30.

5. M. Ivanov, "Pervoe desiatiletie postoiannogo ital'ianskogo teatra v Peterburge v XIX veka (1843-1853 gg.)" [The first decade of the permanent Italian theater in Petersburg in the nineteenth century (1843-1853)], *Ezhegodnik imperatorskikh teatrov* [Annual of the Imperial theaters], 1893-1894, appendix 2:55.

6. Abram Akimovich Gozenpud, *Muzykal'nyi teatr v Rossii ot istokov do Glinki* [Musical theater in Russia from its beginnings to Glinka] (Leningrad: Gosudarstvennoe muzykal'noe izdatel'stvo, 1959), pp. 335, 341.

7. A.I. Vol'f, *Khronika Peterburgskikh teatrov s kontsa 1826 do nachala 1855 goda* [A chronicle of the Petersburg theaters from the end of 1826 to the beginning of 1855], 2 vols. (St. Petersburg: R. Golike, 1877), 1:106-07.

8. Irina Ivanovna Onnore, "Odinnadtsat' let v teatre: Iz vospominanii artisticheskoi zhizni Iriny Ivanovny Onnore, byvshei pevitsy Imperatorskogo Moskovskogo teatra, nyne professora peniia v Peterburge" [Eleven years in the theater: from the memoirs of the artistic life of Irina Ivanovna Onnore, former singer at the Imperial Moscow Theater, now a professor of singing in Petersburg], *Russkaia starina* [Russian antiquities] 149 (1912):161.

9. Eduard Frantsevich Napravnik, *Avtobiograficheskie tvorcheskie materialy, dokumenty, pis'ma* [Autobiographical creative materials, documents, letters], ed. Iurii Vsevolodovich Keldysh (Leningrad: Gosudarstvennoe muzykal'noe izdatel'stvo, 1959), p. 39; Petr Boborykin, *Vospominaniia* [Memoirs], ed. E. Vilenskaia and L. Roitberg, 2 vols. (Moscow: Khudozhestvennaia literatura, 1965), 1:131; Tsezar Kiui, *Izbrannye stat'i* [Selected articles], ed. I.L. Gusin (Leningrad: Gosudarstvennoe muzykal'noe izdatel'stvo, 1952), p. 512; Modest Il'ich Chaikovskii, *Zhizn' Petra Il'icha Chaikovskogo* [The life of Pyotr Ilich Tchaikovsky], 3 vols. (Moscow: P. Iurgenson, 1900-1902), 1:126.

10. Letter to his father, 12 August 1861, in Petr Il'ich Chaikovskii, *Polnoe sobranie sochinenii* [Complete writings] (Moscow: Gosudarstvennoe muzykal'noe izdatel'stvo, 1959-   ), 5:69.

11. Quoted in Gustavo Marchesi, "The Years of *La Forza del Destino*," *Verdi* 4 (1961):321.

12. Aleksandr Vasil'evich Nikitenko, *Dnevnik* [Diary], ed. I.I. Aizenshtok, 3 vols. (Leningrad: Gosudarstvennoe izdatel'stvo khudozhestvennoi literatury, 1955-1956), 2:300-301; Marchesi, "The Years of *La Forza*," 5 (1962):1085.

13. *Severnaia pchela* [The northern bee] (St. Petersburg), 25 March 1863, p. 323.

14. Abram Akimovich Gozenpud, *Russkii opernyi teatr XIX veka* [The Russian opera theater in the nineteenth century], 3 vols. (Leningrad: Muzyka, 1969-1973), 2:149.

15. Napravnik, *Avtobiograficheskie materialy*, p. 39.

16. Kiui, *Izbrannye stat'i*, pp. 516-17; M.[S.] L[alaev], "Ital'ianskaia opera v Peterburge: Sezon 1861-1862 goda" [The Italian Opera in Petersburg: the season of 1861-1862], *Sovremennik* [The contemporary] (Sovremennoe obozrenie) 91 (January-February 1862):81; M.[S.] L[alaev], "Ital'ianskaia opera v Peterburge: Sezon 1862-1863 goda," *Sovremennik* (Sovremennoe obozrenie) 94 (January-February 1863):225.

17. Boborykin, *Vospominaniia*, 1:134; Feofil Matveevich Tolstoi [Rostislav], "K voprosu ob uprazdnenii, v vidakh ekonomicheskikh i patrioticheskikh ital'ianskoi opery i dramaticheskoi frantsuzskoi truppy" [On the question of abolishing the Italian Opera and the French drama troupe on economic and patriotic grounds], *Severnaia pchela*, 22 February 1863, p. 197.

18.	Auer, *My Long Life,* p. 176; Peter Kropotkin, *Memoirs of a Revolutionist* (New York: Horizon Press, 1968), p. 120; Konstantin Apollonovich Skal'kovskii, *Vospominaniia molodosti (Po moriu zhiteiskomu) 1843-1869* [Reminiscences of youth (on the sea of life) 1843-1869] (St. Petersburg: Tipografiia A.S. Suvorina, 1906), p. 98.

19.	Boborykin, *Vospominaniia,* 1:226.

20.	M.R[appaport], "Teatral'naia i muzykal'naia khronika" [Theater and music chronicle], *Syn otechestva* [Son of the fatherland] (St. Petersburg), 18 September 1860, p. 1184.

21.	Kiui, *Izbrannye stat'i,* p. 512.

22.	*Memoirs of a Revolutionist,* p. 119.

23.	Alexander Serov to M.P. Anastasieva, 7 April 1859, in Aleksandr Nikolaevich Serov, "Aleksandr Nikolaevich Serov: Materialy dlia ego biografii, 1820-1871" [Alexander Nikolaevich Serov: materials for his biography, 1820-1871], ed. Vladimir Vasil'evich Stasov, *Russkaia starina* 20 (1877):534.

24.	V.A. Bernatskii, "Iz zolotogo veka ital'ianskoi opery v Peterburge" [From the golden age of Italian opera in Petersburg], *Russkaia starina* 168 (1916): 21-22.

25.	Skal'kovskii, *Vospominaniia,* p. 113.

26.	See "Peterburgskaia zhizn' " [Petersburg life], *Sovremennik* (Sovremennoe obozrenie) 85 (January-February 1861):388, 390; Lalaev, "Ital'ianskaia opera, 1861-1862," pp. 52-53, 56.

27.	Boborykin, *Vospominaniia,* 1:131.

28.	Vladimir Fedorovich Odoevskii, *Muzykal'no-literaturnoe nasledie* [Musico-literary legacy], ed. G.B. Bernandt (Moscow: Gosudarstvennoe muzykal'noe izdatel'stvo, 1956), p. 248.

29.	Gozenpud, *Russkii opernyi teatr,* 2:7.

30.	Anton Grigor'evich Rubinshtein, "Avtobiograficheskie rasskazy (1829-1889)" [Autobiographical accounts (1829-1889)], in Lev Aronovich Barenboim, *Anton Grigor'evich Rubinshtein: Zhizn', artisticheskii put', tvorchestvo, muzykal'no-obshchestvennaia deiatel'nost'* [Anton Grigorievich Rubinstein: life, artistic course, creative work, musical-social activity], 2 vols. (Leningrad: Gosudarstvennoe muzykal'noe izdatel'stvo, 1957-1962), 1:412.

31.	Onnore, "Odinnadtsat' let v teatre," 149:160.

32.	*Ibid.,* 149:167; Dar'ia Mikhailovna Leonova, "Vospominaniia artistki imperatorskikh teatrov D.M. Leonovoi" [Memoirs of D.M. Leonova, artist of the Imperial theaters], *Istoricheskii vestnik* [Historical herald] 43 (1891):335, 342-43; Vladimir Vasil'evich Stasov, *Izbrannye sochineniia (Zhivopis', skul'ptura, muzyka)* [Selected writings (painting, sculpture, music)], ed. E.D. Stasova *et al.,* 3 vols. (Moscow: Iskusstvo, 1952), 1:203.

33.	*Avtobiograficheskie materialy,* p. 39.

34. Leonova, "Vospominaniia," 43:138; Kiui, *Izbrannye stat'i*, p. 517.

35. Vladimir Vasil'evich Stasov, *Izbrannye stat'i o muzyke* [Selected articles on music] (Leningrad: Gosudarstvennoe muzykal'noe izdatel'stvo, 1949), p. 146.

36. Gozenpud, *Russkii opernyi teatr*, 2:10.

37. Vol'f, *Khronika do 1855*, 2:211-13.

38. A.I. Vol'f, *Khronika peterburgskikh teatrov s kontsa 1855 do nachala 1881 goda* [A chronicle of the Petersburg theaters from the end of 1855 to the beginning of 1881] (St. Petersburg, 1884), pp. 108-10.

39. Napravnik, *Avtobiograficheskie materialy*, p. 39.

40. In 1862 the Russian Opera performed 114 times ("Russkaia opera v 1862 godu" [The Russian Opera in 1862], *Severnaia pchela*, 9 January 1863, p. 31), while the Italian Opera performed eighty to ninety times a year at about the same time (Lalaev, "Ital'ianskaia opera, 1862-1863," p. 225).

41. Aleksandr Sergeevich Dargomyzhskii, "Aleksandr Sergeevich Dargomyzhskii: Materialy dlia ego biografii, 1813-1869" [Alexander Sergeevich Dargomyzhsky: materials for his biography, 1813-1869], comp. Vladimir Vasil'evich Stasov, *Russkaia starina* 12 (1875):345.

42. Gozenpud, *Russkii opernyi teatr*, 2:11.

43. Kiui, *Izbrannye stat'i*, pp. 517-18.

44. Boborykin, *Vospominaniia*, 1:225.

45. Akademiia nauk SSSR. Institut istorii, *Ocherki istorii Leningrada* [Studies in the history of Leningrad], 6 vols. (Moscow: Izdatel'stvo Akademii nauk SSSR, 1955-1970), 1:777-78.

46. Boborykin, *Vospominaniia*, 1:227; Skal'kovskii, *Vospominaniia*, p. 98; "Peterburgskaia zhizn'," *Sovremennik* (Sovremennoe obozrenie) 73 (January-February 1859):414; 74 (March-April 1859):190-91, 335-36.

47. "Peterburgskoe filarmonicheskoe obshchestvo" [The Petersburg Philharmonic Society], *Entsiklopedicheskii muzykal'nyi slovar'* [The encyclopedic musical dictionary], 2nd ed. (Moscow, 1966), p. 390; Akademiia nauk SSSR, *Istoriia Leningrada*, 2:534; Levasheva, *Istoriia russkoi muzyki*, 1:220.

48. M.R[appaport], "Zametki i vesti iz artisticheskogo mira" [Notes and news from the artistic world], *Syn otechestva*, 20 November 1860, p. 1443 and 4 December 1860, p. 1506; Aleksandr Nikolaevich Serov, *Izbrannye stat'i* [Selected articles], ed. Georgii Khubov, 2 vols. (Moscow: Gosudarstvennoe muzykal'noe izdatel'stvo, 1950-1957), 1:552.

49. Editor's note in Kiui, *Izbrannye stat'i*, p. 562.

50.   Rubinshtein, "Avtobiograficheskie rasskazy," 1:410; Nikolai Fedorovich Findeizen, *Ocherk deiatel'nosti S.-Peterburgskogo otdeleniia imperatorskogo Russkogo Muzykal'-nogo Obshchestva (1859-1909)* [Studies on the work of the St. Petersburg branch of the Imperial Russian Musical Society (1859-1909)] (St. Petersburg: Tipografiia Glavnogo Upravleniia Udelov, 1909), p. 7.

51.   Mily Balakirev to his father, 28 February 1858, in Milii Alekseevich Balakirev, *Vospominaniia i pis'ma* [Memoirs and letters], ed. Emiliia Lazarevna Frid (Leningrad: Gosudarstvennoe muzykal'noe izdatel'stvo, 1962), p. 76.

52.   Findeizen, *Ocherk RMO*, p. 7; Rappaport, "Zametki i vesti, *Syn otechestva*, 20 November 1860, p. 1443.

53.   Stasov, *Izbrannye sochineniia*, 1:22, 27; Balakirev to his father, 28 February 1858, in Balakirev, *Vospominaniia*, p. 76.

54.   Rappaport, "Zametki i vesti," *Syn otechestva*, 20 November 1860, p. 1443.

55.   Serov, *Izbrannye stat'i*, 1:557-92.

56.   Vasilii Vasil'evich Bessel', "Moi vospominaniia ob Antone Grigor'eviche Rubinshteine" [My memoirs about Anton Grigorievich Rubinstein], *Russkaia starina* 94 (1898):351-52; M. Chaikovskii, *Zhizn' Chaikovskogo*, 1:124.

57.   Bessel', "Moi vospominaniia," p. 352.

58.   "Avtobiograficheskie rasskazy," 1:410.

59.   Findeizen, *Ocherk RMO*, p. 8.

60.   Akademiia nauk SSSR, *Istoriia Leningrada*, 2:598.

61.   "Peterburgskaia zhizn'," *Sovremennik* (Sovremennoe obozrenie) 81 (May-June 1860): 300-301.

62.   Henry Raynor, *A Social History of Music: From the Middle Ages to Beethoven* (New York: Schocken Books, 1972), p. 329.

63.   Percy M. Young, *The Concert Tradition: From the Middle Ages to the Twentieth Century* (London: Routledge and Kegan Paul, 1965), p. 234; William Weber, *Music and the Middle Class: The Social Structure of Concert Life in London, Paris and Vienna* (New York: Holmes & Meier Publishers, 1975), p. 3.

64.   Bessel', "Moi vospominaniia," p. 352.

65.   Napravnik, *Avtobiograficheskie materialy*, p. 38; Kiui, *Izbrannye stat'i*, p. 14; M. Chaikovskii, *Zhizn' Chaikovskogo*, 1:124.

66.   "Avtobiograficheskie rasskazy," 1:410.

67. Boborykin, *Vospominaniia,* 1:303.

68. See, for example, "Peterburgskaia zhizn'," *Sovremennik* (Sovremennoe obozrenie) 79 (January-February 1860):387.

69. César Cui, *La Musique en Russie* (Paris: Librairie Sandoz et Fischbacher, 1880; reprint ed., Leipzig: Zentralantiquariat der Deutschen demokratischen Republik, 1974), p. 147.

70. Vladimir Vasil'evich Stasov, *Selected Essays on Music,* trans. Florence Jonas (New York: Frederick A. Praeger, 1968), pp. 160-61.

71. Mikhail Semenovich Druskin, "Peterburg—Petrograd—Leningrad," *Sovetskaia muzyka* [Soviet music], July 1957, pp. 17-18.

72. See, for example, Tamara Nikolaevna Livanova, *Russkaia muzykal'naia kul'tura XVIII veka v ee sviazakh s literaturoi, teatrom i bytom: Issledovaniia i materialy* [Russian musical culture of the eighteenth century in connection with literature, theater and daily life: research and materials], 2 vols. (Moscow: Gosudarstvennoe muzykal'noe izdatel'stvo, 1952-1953), 2:163-81.

73. See, for example, Gerald Abraham in Michel D. Calvocoressi and Gerald Abraham, *Masters of Russian Music* (New York: Tudor Publishing Co., 1944), pp. 32, 47, and Michel D. Calvocoressi, *A Survey of Russian Music* (Middlesex, Eng.: Penguin Books, 1944; reprint ed., Westport, Conn.: Greenwood Press, 1974), pp. 36-37.

74. Rappaport, "Zametki i vesti," *Syn otechestva,* 6 November 1860, p. 1361.

75. Rappaport, "Teatral'naia i muzykal'naia khronika," *Syn otechestva,* 25 December 1860, p. 1601.

76. Findeizen, *Ocherk RMO,* p. 5.

77. "Leningradskaia gosudarstvennaia akademicheskaia kapella imeni M.I. Glinki" [The M.I. Glinka Leningrad State Academic Chorus], *Entsiklopedicheskii muzykal'nyi slovar',* p. 268; Rappaport, "Teatral'naia i muzykal'naia khronika," *Syn otechestva,* 25 December 1860, p. 1601.

78. Auer, *My Long Life,* p. 132; Stasov, *Selected Essays,* p. 81.

79. Odoevskii, *Muzykal'no-literaturnoe nasledie,* p. 249; S.N. Kruglikov, "Vospominaniia ob A.P. Borodine, zapisannye S.N. Kruglikovym" [Reminiscences about A. P. Borodin, recorded by S.N. Kruglikov], in *Muzykal'noe nasledstvo: Sborniki po istorii muzykal'noi kul'tury SSSR* [Musical legacy: collections on the history of musical culture in the U.S.S.R.], 4 vols. (Moscow: Gosudarstvennoe muzykal'noe izdatel'stvo, 1962-1976), 3:245.

80. Rappaport, "Teatral'naia i muzykal'naia khronika," *Syn otechestva,* 10 July 1860, p. 888.

81. Boborykin, *Vospominaniia,* 1:302-3; Rubinshtein, "Avtobiograficheskie rasskazy," 1:420.

82. Vol'f, *Khronika s 1855,* p. 110.

83. Vol'f, *Khronika do 1855,* 2:211.

84. Liudmila Ivanovna Shestakova, "Poslednie gody zhizni i konchina M.I. Glinki: Vospominaniia sestry ego, L.I. Shestakovoi, 1854-1857" [The last years of the life and the death of M.I. Glinka: memoirs of his sister, L.I. Shestakova, 1854-1857], *Russkaia starina* 2 (1870, 3rd ed.):414.

85. "Peterburgskoe obozrenie" [Petersburg review], *Severnaia pchela,* 28 January 1861, p. 91.

86. Vol'f, *Khronika s 1855,* pp. 112-13.

87. *Ibid.,* p. 110; Gozenpud, *Russkii opernyi teatr,* 2:110.

88. See the listing of the complete repertory of the Russian Opera, with dates of first performances, for the period from 1855 to 1881 in Vol'f, *Khronika s 1855,* pp. 142-43.

89. Rubinshtein, "Avtobiograficheskie rasskazy," 2:456. Two of his operas were performed, without success, in St. Petersburg in the early 1850s, but they were brief, immature works.

90. German Avgustovich Larosh, "Vospominaniia o P.I. Chaikovskom" [Memoirs about P.I. Tchaikovsky], in V.V. Protopopov, ed., *Vospominaniia o P.I. Chaikovskom* (Moscow: Gosudarstvennoe muzykal'noe izdatel'stvo, 1962), p. 36.

91. Boborykin, *Vospominaniia,* 1:302.

92. German Avgustovich Larosh, *Izbrannye stat'i* [Selected articles], ed. Abram Akimovich Gozenpud, 5 vols. (Leningrad: Muzyka, 1974-1978), 2:184.

93. Leningrad Conservatory, *100 let Leningradskoi konservatorii: Istoricheskii ocherk* [100 years of the Leningrad Conservatory: an historical survey] (Leningrad: Gosudarstvennoe muzykal'noe izdatel'stvo, 1962), p. 24.

94. Rubinshtein, "Avtobiograficheskie rasskazy," 1:417; Findeizen, *Ocherk RMO,* p. 9.

95. Aleksandr Ivanovich Rubets, "Vospominaniia o pervykh godakh Peterburgskoi konservatorii" [Memoirs about the first years of the St. Petersburg Conservatory], *Novoe vremia* [New time], 11 June 1912, p. 4.

Chapter II

Anton Rubinstein and the Work of the Russian Musical Society, 1859-1867

The decade of the 1860s marked a turning point in the development of music, as of so much else, in Russia. At a time when the emancipation of the serfs and other major reforms were altering the very foundations of the Russian social, economic, and political order, the musical world of St. Petersburg underwent a revolutionary transformation that changed forever the cultural life of the Russian Empire and eventually ended its colonial status in relation to the musical world of the West. No single event was more important in bringing about these remarkable changes than the founding of the Russian Musical Society, and no single individual played a greater role in them than the founder of the Society, Anton Rubinstein.

Anton Grigorievich Rubinstein was born on 16 November 1829 in a village on the Ukrainian-Bessarabian border. Both his father and his paternal grandfather were Jewish merchants, but the entire family joined the Orthodox Church in 1831 to escape the legal and social restrictions imposed on Jews in Russia. While he was still a small child, Rubinstein's family moved to Moscow.[1] There he began formal piano study at the age of eight with Alexander Villoing, a well-known pedagogue. He showed exceptional talent from the beginning and after five years of training was a finished pianist, who felt no need of further lessons.[2] He gave his first public concert in Moscow in 1839, when he was not yet ten years old, and its great success led to more appearances in Russia and a triumphant European concert tour, which lasted two and a half years and took him to all the major German cities, plus Paris, London, Warsaw, Prague, Amsterdam, and Stockholm.[3]

In 1844 Rubinstein's mother took Anton and his brother Nikolai, also a talented pianist, to Berlin for further musical training. There he studied composition with the famous music theorist Siegfried Dehn and fell under the influence of the leading musical figures in Germany in the 1840s, especially Felix Mendelssohn.[4] Although his lessons with Dehn lasted little over a year, they were sufficient to give such a musically gifted youth a firm grounding in the academic techniques of composition, and he soon began composing prolifically in all forms.[5] In the spring of 1846 Dehn himself testified in a letter of reference that both Anton and his brother Nikolai had completed a full analytical course in music theory, although neither had yet mastered strict counterpoint.[6] From Dehn, Rubinstein acquired not only technical knowledge of music but also a life-long devotion to the value of professional music education.

Young Anton's exposure to the music of Mendelssohn and Robert Schumann and his personal contacts with them (he spent much of his free time with the Mendelssohn family) shaped his musical predilections. For the rest of his life Rubinstein remained faithful in both his taste and his own compositions to the tradition of the German classics from Bach to Schumann.[7] He knew Liszt well and admired him greatly as a pianist and a person, but he confessed that he had no sympathy with the latter's admiration for Wagner and Berlioz.[8] He considered Wagner important only as a musical thinker, not as a creative artist, and denied that Liszt had any great talent for composition.[9] When Rubinstein dictated his memoirs in 1889 he went so far as to declare that he considered true music at an end, that "the last note in music was written by Chopin."[10]

Rubinstein's German training and musical conservatism also led him to resist on principle the introduction of national elements into serious music and thus to reject the tradition of Glinka, who had consciously sought to create a Russian school of composition. Writing in a Viennese music journal in 1855, Rubinstein stated his position unequivocally:

> M. I. Glinka, the most brilliant Russian composer, was the first to conceive and carry out the daring but unfortunate idea of writing a national opera. Proceeding from this viewpoint, he wrote two operas: *A Life for the Tsar* and *Ruslan and Liudmila.* Both are masterpieces of their kind, but unfortunately both also suffer from the fault discussed above—monotony. . . . National music exists, in the sense of folk songs and dances, but national opera, strickly speaking, does not.[11]

In his own music Rubinstein followed Mendelssohn and Schumann, completely eschewing the Russian style pioneered by Glinka. Only occasionally did he permit national or folk elements into his major works and then only in songs or dances interpolated in some of his operas to provide local color.[12]

Rubinstein's patriotism and attachment to his homeland are beyond doubt, but his Jewish background and foreign training seemingly prevented him from understanding Glinka's desire to write distinctively Russian music. He spent most of his life in Russia and considered himself a Russian, yet he was never completely assimilated. According to an acquaintance, Rubinstein frequently remarked that although he was a Russian citizen, Orthodox in his religion and desirous of living nowhere but Russia, he always felt that he did not quite belong in Russian society.[13] In fact, he never attained a perfect command of the Russian language. As a result of his birth into a Jewish family living in the borderlands of the Russian Empire and his extended travels in Western Europe during his formative years, Rubinstein spoke many languages; but, as one of his pupils in the 1860s noted, "he did not speak completely correctly in any of them. . . . In private conversation he could express himself very fluently in Russian . . but his grammar left much to be desired, and in an orderly exposition of a theoretical subject his weaknesses were much more evident."[14] Another acquaintance claimed that in diction, tone, and vocabulary, Anton Rubinstein sounded more like an émigré Russian or a student than a citizen of the Russian capital.[15]

The foreign travel and musical training that gave Anton Rubinstein his cosmopolitan musical tastes and his strange accent also made him very critical of the state of Russian musical life when he returned from abroad in 1848. In Western Europe he had seen the conservatories of Paris and other cities and attended or participated in orchestral concerts given by well-established concert societies in the French capital, Leipzig, London, and elsewhere. He knew personally such important musical figures as Mendelssohn and Schumann, who were not only talented composers but also successful professional musicians. In Petersburg, however, he found no institution of higher music education, no concert society able to provide a substantial annual series of professional performances, and only dilettante composers. "Art was in the hands of a few amateur-Maecenases, who enjoyed Italian opera more than anything and also composed music in that style," he wrote in his memoirs. "Musician-artists, people dedicated to art, did not exist at all."[16]

In 1855 Rubinstein discussed the weaknesses he found in Russian musical life in an article for the Viennese journal *Blätter für Theater, Musik und Kunst.* While generally putting the best possible light on the state of music in Russia, he pointed out the enormous preponderance of operatic over instrumental music and the impossibility of acquiring a full music education. He sang Glinka's praises, despite his disapproval of the latter's efforts to compose national operas, and even ranked Glinka among the finest composers in all of Europe; but he chided other leading Russian composers for their technical weaknesses and amateurishness. He complained, for example, that Verstovsky, the composer of *Askold's Tomb,* one of the most successful contemporary Russian operas, lacked the skills needed to create major works from his brilliant inspirations and that Alexander Varlamov, the most popular composer of Russian songs, had never studied music seriously.[17] In Rubinstein's view, true musicians must devote themselves exclusively to their art and completely master its technical aspects. The self-trained Russian composers could never hope to meet his standards.

Among all the inadequacies of Russian musical life, Rubinstein found the low social status granted musicians in the Russian capital particularly frustrating. In the elaborately structured Russian social hierarchy there was no legal rank for a practicing musician. In his memoirs he vividly recalled a personal experience of the late 1840s or early 1850s that impressed on him the need for legal recognition of the professional musician as a "free artist," the rank assigned qualified painters, sculptors, and actors since the eighteenth century. While attending services in order to receive communion during Holy Week, as required by the Orthodox Church, Rubinstein confronted the rigidity of the Russian legal class system in a particularly exasperating encounter:

> I had to give my name and rank, so they could be noted down in the confessional list. So the lector asks me:
> "Your name and occupation?"
> "Rubinstein. Artist."
> "Artist, what does that mean? Do you work in the theater?"
> I answer, "No."
> "Ah! perhaps you are a teacher in some institute?"
> "No," I answer.
> "Then you are in government service?"
> I repeat, "No, I am not in service." He is perplexed and I am perplexed.
> "Then just what are you anyway?"
> And so the interrogation continues for several minutes. Finally the happy idea comes to him to ask me who my father was.
> I say, "A merchant of the second guild."
> "So, it turns out, you are the son of a merchant of the second guild."[18]

It is easy to imagine the impact of this exchange on the young musician, already lauded all over Europe. The bald realization that his renown as a musician gave him no legal status in Russia, that he remained but a "son of a merchant of the second guild," must have deeply offended his self-esteem.

The personal affront coupled with general frustration over the quality of musical life in Russia prompted Rubinstein to contemplate founding a conservatory where professional musicians could be trained and receive the legal rank of "free artist." He actually worked out a proposal for such an institution in 1852, modeling it after the Imperial Academy of Fine Arts.[19] He was not motivated solely by a desire to improve the status of Russian music and musicians, however, for in October 1852 Rubinstein wrote his mother, "I am busy now with only one thing . . . a plan for a Music Academy. . . . This may have great consequences—for music in Russia and also for me."[20] The great consequences he expected for himself doubtless included not only the rank of "free artist" but also a permanent musical post in St. Petersburg.

Since his return to Russia in 1848 Rubinstein had been vainly seeking a way to make a career for himself in music as something other than a virtuoso pianist. His contacts with such serious musicians as Robert Schumann, a tireless opponent of the flashy but superficial performances of most leading pianists of the 1840s,[21] had produced in him a contempt for the role of pianistic showman. Unfortunately, Russia offered a serious artist few other opportunities to make a career. Rubinstein first placed his hopes in composition, undertaking to write an opera (the musical form most likely to achieve success in St. Petersburg) while living off the proceeds from piano lessons and occasional concerts.[22] In December 1850 he wrote his mother that he hoped the work, *Dmitri Donskoy,* would bring him fame as more than a virtuoso, so that he could give concerts, "not as a pianist playing operatic fantasias but as a composer performing his own symphonies, concertos, operas, trios, etc."[23] This plan failed, however, for he had to wait until the spring of 1852 for the premiere of his opera, and it was an utter failure, surviving only four performances before disappearing from the stage forever.[24] In the meantime Rubinstein had sought more than once a position as a conductor or accompanist with the Imperial theaters but with no success.[25]

Finally, early in the summer of 1852 Grand Duchess Elena Pavlovna, the widowed sister-in-law of Nicholas I and a passionate music-lover, invited Rubinstein to become permanent accompanist for her court and to take charge of her frequent musical soirées.[26] He accepted the post for financial reasons (he could live in the grand duchess's palace at no expense to himself),[27] but this was not the kind of career he most wanted. In August 1852 he wrote his mother that he lacked neither homage nor money but was overwhelmed with the luxurious style of living and hoped it would not last too long.[28] All the comforts of court life could not fulfill the ambitions of a gifted, serious-minded artist. Although his position in Elena Pavlovna's palace met his immediate financial needs, he was little more than a court retainer. It is easy to understand, then, how attractive he must have found the idea of establishing an advanced music school in St. Petersburg. Not only would the state of music in Russia be improved, but Rubinstein could make a prestigious career for himself as its founder and director as well. Thus, both ambition and idealism motivated Rubinstein's first effort to found a conservatory in Russia; he foresaw "great consequences" for himself no less than for Russia.

Unfortunately, Rubinstein's 1852 project for a Russian conservatory was premature. Not only was he only twenty-three years old, but also the last years of the reign of Nicholas I were marked by a political reaction and fear of private initiative that ruled out in advance such a proposal.[29] In February 1853 Rubinstein wrote his mother that his plan was "sleeping the sleep of the just because for many reasons it is difficult to carry out now."[30] With this project shelved and the failure of his second operatic effort a few weeks later,[31] Rubinstein had little hope of achieving the kind of career he wanted in St. Petersburg. Therefore, in the spring of 1854 he left Russia for Germany in the

hope of making a reputation that would allow him to return to his homeland
in triumph as a composer of European renown. By November 1854 he could
claim successful performances of his major works in important German cities:
"Now I have almost nothing more to do to make a name for myself; only time
and circumstances can help me advance." But he was not happy in Germany;
only his ambition and the knowledge that Russia offered no comparable
opportunities kept him there:

> If this ambition were not so dear to my heart I would cut my ties and return home, since
> you cannot imagine how unhappy I am, from a social point of view, in this country. . . .
>   If I didn't have a healthy dose of will power, I might very well say to hell with ambitious
> ideas and return home immediately to accompany nightingales and to enjoy the company
> of nymphs. But no! Patience, Cossack. You'll be a Hetman yet![32]

A few months later he was still writing that he wished for nothing more than to
return to Russia but feared that his serious approach to art would not satisfy
St. Petersburg's dilettantes. He continued to believe the time was not yet right
for him to attain a permanent musical post in the Russian capital.[33]

The death of Nicholas I in 1855 and the fiasco of the Crimean War
profoundly unsettled Russian life and prepared the way for greater
government tolerance of change and a more vigorous spirit in Russian society.
"The release of the brakes set in the Nicholas era," in the words of one student
of Russian culture, "led to a torrential creative outburst in which the arts
shone with particular brilliance."[34] Stimulated by the change in atmosphere,
Rubinstein's thoughts turned again to the idea of founding a music institute.
Grand Duchess Elena Pavlovna summoned him to Moscow for the festivities
surrounding the coronation of the new tsar in August 1856 and then invited
him to join her court in Nice, where she and the dowager empress spent the
following winter recuperating from the rigors of the celebration. According to
Rubinstein's memoirs, "The idea of a Russian musical society and a
conservatory was born there. I spoke with Matvei Wielhorsky [a prominent
aristocrat and amateur musician] . . . about the need to do something since the
musical situation in Russia was deplorable in all respects. Elena Pavlovna also
became interested in this." But no specific plans were laid. The grand duchess
returned to Russia, and Rubinstein resumed his career in Western Europe.[35]

By the spring of 1858, however, Anton Rubinstein was ready to return to
Russia to seek once more a permanent position in the musical life of St.
Petersburg. On 30 April 1858 he wrote his mother that he would soon be in
Moscow for a two-month visit. "What I shall do after that," he added, "I still
don't know. In any case, this coming winter in Petersburg will be decisive for
all my activities."[36]

The success of Rubinstein's project to provide the Russian capital with a
conservatory and himself with a leading place in the city's musical affairs

would depend on its public acceptance, the support of musicians, and, perhaps most important of all, backing from court circles. In 1858 Rubinstein was in a good position to command all three. Although still in his twenties, he was respected for his foreign musical training and his success abroad as a composer and concert artist. No musician in St. Petersburg could rival his European reputation.[37] As one Russian critic wrote in 1859, "no-one doubts any longer that Rubinstein belongs among the finest contemporary European pianists, that he possesses a brilliant talent as a performer."[38]

Among musicians, Rubinstein's popularity was less unanimous. His remarks on the indifferent quality of most Russian musicians, in particular his statements published in 1855 in *Blätter für Theater, Musik und Kunst,* had earned him the enmity of many;[39] others, as will be seen, considered him a foreign intruder in their musical preserve. Nevertheless, he had close friends among St. Petersburg's prominent musicians. In the early 1850s he had shared the concert platform with many of the city's leading instrumentalists,[40] and every Saturday evening he had gathered a group of musical friends at his apartment for playing, singing, and conversation about music. Regular participants in these evenings included Alexander Fitztum, the organizer of the semiprofessional University concerts, their conductor Karl Schubert, and the principal professional members of the orchestra.[41] Rubinstein could hope to find musicians in this group to aid his plans for a conservatory.

Rubinstein also had important court connections, especially through Grand Duchess Eleva Pavlovna and Count Matvei Wielhorsky. Although best known to historians for her active encouragement of the emancipation of the Russian peasantry,[42] Elena Pavlovna was also passionately interested in the arts, especially music. She was sympathetic to Rubinstein's wish to improve musical standards in Russia and, as the aunt of Alexander II, was in a position to provide both money and influence in government circles to help him achieve it. Wielhorsky, a frequent visitor to Rubinstein's musical evenings,[43] was not only a member of the high Russian aristocracy but also a frequenter of the highest court circles.[44] Richard Wagner, who met Wielhorsky in St. Petersburg in 1863, later dubbed him "Protector of Music" for the Russian court.[45]

With backing from court circles and leading musicians, his European reputation as a pianist and composer, and the freer social and political atmosphere in Russia following the death of Nicholas I and the end of the Crimean War, Rubinstein prepared to advance his plans for developing musical professionalism in Russia. Upon his return to St. Petersburg in the summer of 1858 he resumed his Saturday evenings of chamber music with Schubert, Fitztum, and other musical friends.[46] There he shared his ideas and found the whole-hearted support he needed. Later, he would give particular credit to Vasily Kologrivov, a landowner from Tula, amateur cellist, and regular participant in his Saturday soirées, as co-instigator of the project. Rubinstein usually had little regard for nonprofessional musicians, but he considered Kologrivov a fine one with an excellent knowledge of Europe and its music.[47] Together they worked out the strategy for founding a conservatory in Russia.

Although the reactionary spirit of Nicholas I's reign had begun to dissipate, conditions still discouraged the founding of an entirely new institution. To sidestep this obstacle, Kologrivov suggested that at first they revive the defunct Symphonic Society, of which he had been a memeber. Although that group's only function had been to organize occasional orchestral concerts, its renewed charter could provide a suitable organizational basis for founding a conservatory as well.[48] Count Wielhorsky invited the available former members of the Symphonic Society to his home 27 January 1859, and they resolved to revive its activities. Rubinstein, Wielhorsky, Kolgrivov, Dmitri Kanshin, and Dmitri Stasov were elected directors of the revitalized Society.[49] The first three had actively participated in the birth and development of the idea of creating a society. Dmitri Stasov was a lawyer, music-lover, and brother of the famous art and music critic Vladimir Stasov. He was a close friend of Rubinstein and an assistant in organizing the programs of both the Concert Society and the University concerts.[50] Kanshin, a wealthy landowner who did not belong to Rubinstein's circle, was himself preparing to establish some sort of musical society in St. Petersburg at the same time as Rubinstein, and he agreed to join the latter in order to avoid a wasteful division of forces.[51]

The board of directors of the new organization submitted a charter for government approval but disguised it as a request for permission to continue the work of the Symphonic Society—that is, to organize concerts. Approval was quickly granted, and the Russian Musical Society (RMS) received its official charter on 1 May 1859.[52] According to its provisions, the Society would strive for "the development of music education and the taste for music in Russia and the encouragement of native talent." To promote this, the Society proposed to perform "the best works of music as perfectly as possible" and also to provide "the opportunity for native composers to hear their own compositions in performance."[53] Although the charter made no provision for founding an educational institution, it is significant that "the development of music education" appeared first among the goals of the RMS. A conservatory remained Rubinstein's ultimate aim. In the meantime, however, the RMS could serve as a valuable organizational base for the future conservatory. As a concert-giving organization, it could also offer St. Petersburg much-needed orchestral concerts of professional quality and provide Anton Rubinstein with his first permanent and conspicuous post in St. Petersburg's musical life.

The new RMS had first to sell memberships and raise money for its inaugural concert season. Membership was open to all citizens for an annual fee of fifteen rubles, which granted admission to all concerts. A donation of one thousand rubles or agreement to contribute one hundred rubles a year earned the title "honored member."[54] The directors and their supporters solicited donations from prominent music-lovers, sold regular memberships around the city, and sometimes even collected contributions "literally a ruble at a time," according to Rubinstein's memoirs. Rubinstein gives special credit to Kologrivov for attacking this task "with all the ardor of his soul, with a fanaticism bordering on crudeness. He recruited everyone and everything for the Society; he practically seized people on the street, cajoled, harangued, enlisted, solicited funds."[55]

The campaign for donations and members met with considerable success. Grand Duchess Elena Pavlovna officially took the RMS under her protection and contributed one thousand silver rubles, as did several wealthy aristocrats. The emperor gave five hundred rubles, the empress one hundred and fifty, and several other members of the Imperial family took the title "honored member." In its first year the RMS recruited all together twenty honored members, nearly five hundred regular members, and around one hundred performer-members, who paid five rubles for the privilege of singing in the chorus. Receipts totaled more than fifteen thousand rubles.[56]

Rubinstein himself, although only one of five directors of the Society, took charge of all artistic matters and conducting duties. With Kologrivov's assistance, he selected the best instrumentalists from the Russian and Italian opera theaters for the Society's orchestra,[57] and he trained and rehearsed the amateur chorus that took part in some of its concerts.[58] To aid him in selecting repertory, especially works by Russian composers, the Society appointed an advisory committee that included Karl Schubert, conductor of the University concerts, Alexander Dargomyzhsky, St. Petersburg's most respected composer after the death of Glinka, Gavriil Lomakin, conductor of the finest Russian chorus of his day, and Prince Vladimir Odoevsky, a distinguished music critic and long-time friend of Glinka.[59] But even these prominent and imposing figures had little influence on Rubinstein, as can be inferred from a half-ironic letter from Odoevsky to the RMS directors complaining that the committee's recommendations were never heeded.[60] Rubinstein considered the RMS, not without some justification, his own creation and set about shaping the Society's concerts to match the standards of his chosen models, the great orchestral concerts of Paris, Vienna, Berlin, and especially Leipzig.[61] Rubinstein's friend Felix Mendelssohn had gained recognition as the first great virtuoso conductor with the Gewandhaus Orchestra in Leipzig during the 1830s and 1840s;[62] Rubinstein aspired to his example.

For its inaugural season in the winter of 1859-60, the RMS presented ten symphonic concerts. Considering Rubinstein's personal taste and his German models, it is not surprising that the repertory depended heavily on the German classics.[63] Beethoven was best represented, with three symphonies (including the enormous and challenging Ninth to close the season), a piano concerto, and several other compositions. Mendelssohn followed close behind. Rubinstein also included at least one major work and some smaller pieces by both Weber and Schubert. In addition, the programs included incidental pieces by a number of then well-known but now little-heard Germans, such as Spohr and Hiller.

Although these nineteenth-century German works formed the core of the repertory, the rest of the selections were unusually varied. In this also, Rubinstein followed the example of Mendelssohn, who included music from a wide range of periods and styles in his Leipzig concerts.[64] Rubinstein explained the principle behind his choices in a letter of November 1859 to Franz Liszt: ". . . we have founded a musical society, which sets as its task, among other goals, the performance of works of all masters of all schools and all times."[65] From the eighteenth century Rubinstein selected arias by Mozart and Haydn, major works by Bach and Gluck, and excerpts from Handel oratorios. Even more interesting were his excursions into the works of the advanced composers of 1860. Except for Schumann (who must be numbered in this group because he was still almost unknown in Russia), Rubinstein had little sympathy for them, but he nevertheless included two major works of Liszt and one each by Berlioz and Wagner, in addition to two symphonies by Schumann. In the letter to Liszt cited above, Rubinstein even asked help in acquiring the score for a second composition by Wagner that he wished to program.[66]

Every concert of the first RMS season also included at least one composition by a Russian composer. Most were small-scale works (songs, overtures, dances) reflecting the predominant interest of Russian composers in opera and vocal music and the resultant scarcity of works suitable for orchestral concerts. Nevertheless, Rubinstein presented two extended works by Glinka and the overtures to his two operas, plus Rubinstein's own Piano Concerto in G Major. In addition, he chose works by six other Russians, including Verstovsky, Dargomyzhsky, and two members of the embryonic "new Russian school," Modest Musorgsky and César Cui. All together, fourteen works by eight Russian composers appeared in the first ten RMS symphonic concerts.

On the whole, the Russian Musical Society's first concert season fulfilled the promise spelled out in its charter to perform "the best works," including some by Russian composers. Each program featured at least one major composition still recognized today as a classic of the first half of the nineteenth century. In addition, there were a considerable number of Russian works, more than a taste of the Baroque period, and several forays into the advanced contemporary school.

The first RMS concert took place on Monday, 23 November 1859, with the rest following on consecutive Mondays, except for the first week in January, until 1 February 1860. The Society apparently managed to circumvent the Imperial Theater Directorate's monopoly on all musical performances during the opera season through the intercession of Elena Pavlovna and other prominent court members.[67] Except for the amateur University concerts, the RMS gatherings were the only nonoperatic public musical performances in the Russian capital before the Lenten concert season. In this exceptionally favorable position and with their excellent orchestra and interesting programs, the RMS concerts attracted considerable public interest. Rubinstein and other memoirists later recalled that the auditorium of the Assembly of the Nobility, which served as the setting for the first season's concerts, was always filled.[68] In fact, the Society showed every sign of success, ending its first season with a budget surplus of more than five thousand rubles.[69]

Anton Rubinstein remained musical director of the Russian Musical Society for seven more seasons, conducting ten subscription symphonic concerts each year and holding true to the pattern of a serious and varied repertory that he had established in the first season.[70] Beethoven's music was best represented, appearing on more than fifty of the seventy programs, while Rubinstein conducted works of Mendelssohn and Schumann at about half the concerts. In addition, he regularly performed music of Mozart, Haydn, Weber, and Schubert. Each year's programs also included a few forays into the Baroque period, the now little-known German conservative school, and the advanced school of Liszt, Wagner, and Berlioz. In spite of a promise in its annual report for 1859-60 to include at least one work by a Russian composer at each concert,[71] the Society offered as few as six in some seasons. Other seasons, however, featured as many as a dozen works by Russians; Glinka's name appeared on twenty-six of the seventy programs, and nearly twenty other Russian composers were also represented. Considering the comparatively small number of talented Russians, such representation must be considered impressive even if some concerts included no native composers. The broad and varied repertory, the excellent professional orchestra, and the privilege of performing outside the Lenten season soon secured for the RMS concerts "the most prominent position in the musical life of St. Petersburg," in the words of César Cui, a critic by no means well disposed toward the Society.[72]

In addition to its regular cycle of ten concerts, the RMS also sponsored four to ten programs of chamber music each year—forty-nine in all during Rubinstein's eight years as music director. These programs could not offer such varied repertory including Russian music as the Society's symphonic concerts, because serious chamber literature was the almost exclusive province of the German classical masters. Nevertheless, the programs were distinguished by the high quality of the performers, including Rubinstein himself, one of Europe's most celebrated pianists, and leading soloists from the Imperial opera orchestras. In some seasons, visiting foreign artists, such as Clara Schumann, the widow of Robert Schumann and a famous pianist in her own right, also took part.[73] The Society's chamber concerts never approached the popularity of its orchestral programs, but they won the support of St. Petersburg's most dedicated and discerning music-lovers and enhanced the Society's reputation as the leading purveyor of serious music in the Russian capital.

Thus, the Russian Musical Society, under Anton Rubinstein's leadership, succeeded in establishing itself at the center of Petersburg musical life. It provided the capital with regular, professional symphonic and chamber concerts, comparable in quality and repertory to the best that Western Europe had to offer, and in the process it made Rubinstein a power in Russian music as he had long wanted to be. But this was still not enough for him. Since 1852 he had dreamed of founding and directing a professional conservatory of music in Russia; within months of the establishment of the RMS he had taken the first steps toward that goal, using the RMS as its foundation.

In December 1859, only a few weeks after the RMS's first concert, the directors of the Society, at Rubinstein's urging, resolved to open free music classes to be taught in the homes of the instructors and paid for by the RMS. The first classes, in singing, opened in the spring of 1860.[74] Sixty-three women and thirty-six men appeared for lessons, and enrollment had to be curtailed for lack of sufficient teachers. The RMS also gave a free class in the fundamentals of music.[75] In the fall of 1860 Elena Pavlovna offered space for teaching in her own Mikhailovsky Palace, allowing the Society to expand its program of music classes. Outstanding musicians, mainly foreigners or Russians trained abroad, joined the staff to teach not only singing but also piano, violin, cello, elementary music theory, and practical composition.[76] With such an enlarged program, the RMS could no longer pay all the expenses, but the modest fee instituted to defray part of the cost of instruction did little to discourage attendance. As Rubinstein later recalled, "The best musical forces of the time in Petersburg donated their time and energy . . . for only a silver ruble per lesson. Quite simply an incredible situation! Students of all positions, means, and ages quickly filled the classes."[77] During the 1860-61 season the RMS paid 4,622 rubles in salary to its nine music teachers while collecting 2,267 rubles in fees from students.[78]

These efforts alone, however, could never satisfy Rubinstein's dream of a real conservatory. Without official government sanction, no school of music could offer its graduates the legal status of "free artist" that he wanted to win for deserving Russian musicians—and for himself. Therefore, simultaneously with the program of informal classes, Rubinstein set about through the RMS to win government acceptance of the idea of a conservatory.

The minutes of the meeting of the RMS directors of 13 March 1860 record their resolution "to found a conservatory in the shortest possible time."[79] Acting in the name of the Society, Rubinstein promptly sent the minister of education a proposal for such an institution, to be called the Imperial Music School, whch would enjoy rights and privileges comparable to those of the Academy of Fine Arts. These would include, of course, the title "free artist" for students who passed the final examinations. The RMS would take responsibility for administering the school, but the government would appoint an inspector to oversee its work and name the examining panel for judging candidates for diplomas. The letter proposed either a government subsidy or a national subscription to support the school.[80] But the Ministry of Education rejected the proposal, terming the project a "luxury" from which nothing useful could be expected.[81]

The RMS next turned for support to the educated Russian public. In January 1861 Rubinstein penned a rare public appeal in an article entitled "About Music in Russia." He argued that Russia needed a conservatory because its musical life suffered from the dominance of amateurs: "By an unusual concurrence of circumstances, there are almost no artist-musicians in the usual sense of the word in Russia. This results, of course, from the fact that our government does not grant the art of music, at present, the same privileges enjoyed by the other arts, . . . i.e., does not grant the title 'artist' to those whose occupation is music." So long as musicians are denied this rank and the accompanying exemption from military recruitment and the poll tax, he continued, only members of the nobility or Russians with an independent profession could afford to dabble in music. "But can music really be left in the hands of such people," he asked, "who see in it only a means of killing time?" Rubinstein believed that accomplishments of substance could only come from a professional musician completely devoted to music, one who viewed it as his fundamental means of livelihood, yet he saw Russia filled with ill-trained and inadequate composers and performers who lacked the time and the dedication to master their art. "It is painful to see such an order of things in a country where music could achieve such a high level of perfection," Rubinstein continued. To remedy the situation, he proposed a conservatory empowered to grant legal rights to musicians. "Some will tell us that great geniuses rarely come out of conservatories; we agree, but who can deny that from conservatories come good musicians? And that is just what our vast fatherland needs."[82]

Instead of rallying public support for Rubinstein and his proposal, the article seems mainly to have stirred up the wrath of the "amateur" musicians who dominated Russian musical life.[83] One critic termed his demand for serious music training in Russia "German guild-hall pedantry," and another saw in his proposals only "amusing notions from those ancient tales where the hero is an artist."[84]

Having failed to attract broad public support, Rubinstein turned again to Grand Duchess Elena Pavlovna. In March 1861 he compiled a "Report on the Necessity of Opening a Music School in Petersburg" and submitted it to her in the name of the Russian Musical Society. It outlined the deficiencies in Russian musical life discussed in his public appeal and asked her assistance not just to finance a conservatory but also to secure government approval for the right to grant legal privileges to qualified musicians.[85] Elena Pavlovna, already the "most august president" and official protector of the RMS, took up the cause.[86] Instead of directing her efforts toward the Ministry of Education, which had already turned down Rubinstein's project the previous year, she used her influence where it was likely to be greatest—in the Ministry of the Imperial Court. As a result, the Court Ministry granted an annual subsidy of five thousand rubles for a music school,[87] and on 17 October 1861 the government approved a charter for Russia's first advanced school of music, which would be attached to and directed by the Russian Musical Society and under the protection of Elena Pavlovna. The Imperial Court Ministry assumed responsibility for appointing government representatives to the panel that would examine graduating students and grant diplomas.[88]

With the nucleus of a faculty for the new school already functioning in the music classes in the grand duchess's palace, the RMS now turned to fund raising for the new organization. Elena Pavlovna offered one thousand rubles a year from her own resources,[89] the Society gave two special benefit concerts in the spring of 1862, and its members solicited contributions not only in St. Petersburg but also in Moscow and other cities of the Russian Empire.[90] By the summer of 1862 these efforts had raised over twelve thousand rubles,[91] which, together with the government subsidy, provided sufficient capital to open the school. Earlier that spring the RMS directorate had rented space in a private mansion to house the new conservatory and had appointed Rubinstein director and Kologrivov inspector.[92] The first newspaper announcements for fall enrollment in the new school had appeared in March. Enrollment actually began in mid-August, and on 8 September 1862 the St. Petersburg Conservatory officially opened its doors.[93]

A number of persons, including Prince Odoevsky, Dargomyzhsky, and Dmitri Stasov, had contributed to the original charter of the Conservatory,[94] but it was essentially identical to the proposal Rubinstein had submitted to the Ministry of Education in 1860 and thus reflected his main goals: to provide a well-rounded music education and to award the official rank of "free artist" to graduates, regardless of their inherited social status. According to the charter, the Conservatory would offer a broad curriculum of music courses, including singing, performance on the piano and all orchestral instruments, composition and orchestration, music history, aesthetics, and declamation. Students could choose their own specialties, but all would have to study piano, music history, and aesthetics and participate in the chorus. In addition, the Conservatory promised courses in the Russian language and the basic principles of Russian history, geography, and literature. In all, the academic program lasted six years. Admission was open to persons "of both sexes and all estates of at least fourteen years of age" who were literate and could read music. To insure that non-noble students could attend, the charter guaranteed exemption from military service while attending the Conservatory for members of classes subject to recruitment and specified that the Russian Musical Society would provide a certain number of full scholarships, in so far as its means allowed. All students successfully completing the Conservatory's six-year course and passing a final public examination would receive the title and rank of "free artist." Even persons not studying formally in the school who passed an equivalent test administered by the Conservatory could earn the same title and rank. The charter spelled out the high standards required for such an award: "The examiners must confer the rank of free artist with the most strict scrupulousness and exclusively to those persons who have proven not only their artistry in the mechanics of performing on some instrument but also their basic understanding of music theory and orchestration."[95] The minutes of a meeting of the Committee of Ministers in October 1861 indicate that the government added the phrase "with the most strict scrupulousness" to the above passage, in keeping with its policy of limiting opportunities to gain privileged legal status,[96] but the other stipulations coincided with Rubinstein's previously stated principles. Any additional restrictions required by the government merely supported his view that only the most superior and dedicated musicians deserved the title of artist.

In practice, the new Conservatory could not always perfectly fulfill its official promises, but its lapses were generally minor, and Rubinstein, on the whole, adhered to his high artistic standards. In its very first semester the school offered a full curriculum of subjects, including fundamental musical principles and notation for students with insufficient basic knowledge, mandatory classes in piano and theory for all students, and more advanced classes in piano, organ, voice, orchestral instruments, and music theory.[97] Students of the earlier RMS music classes could receive credit for their previous work, but since these had been open only two and a half years, the Conservatory initially offered courses only for the first three terms of its six-term program. Upper-level classes, particularly counterpoint and free composition, were added as necessary until the curriculum was complete in 1865, the year of the school's first graduation.[98] In addition, from its first year the Conservatory offered classes in religion, history, geography, mathematics, and the Russian, Italian, and German languages for students deficient in any of these subjects.[99]

Besides providing this broad curriculum, Rubinstein encouraged students to pursue musical interests beyond their specialties and the mandatory subjects. For example, when Hermann Laroche, a theory student, indicated an interest in the music of Johann Sebastian Bach, Rubinstein himself paid for him to study the organ. Rubinstein also immediately established an orchestra of students to provide them with practical experience in ensemble performance and conducting. When he discovered that the Conservatory lacked sufficient wind players, he himself contributed funds to supply lessons for any student wishing to study an instrument needed for the orchestra.[100] In the Conservatory's first year Rubinstein donated seven hundred rubles to be used for scholarships for players of wind instruments, and in later years he contributed still more.[101] To expose students to a wide range of repertory and the demands of public performance, the Conservatory organized weekly student and faculty recitals beginning in the fall of 1863.[102] These programs usually featured solo literature or chamber music, but in 1865 the student orchestra began to take part as well, and in 1867 Rubinstein conducted a complete performance of Gluck's opera *Orfeo,* using student soloists and the orchestra and chorus of the Conservatory.[103] Some of the programs were open to the public, and these free recitals quickly became popular with the Petersburg musical public, which took a keen interest in the work of the Conservatory.[104]

In addition to these opportunities for practical exposure to music within the Conservatory, Rubinstein also saw to it that the students could attend the finest professional performances in the city. Vasily Kologrivov, cofounder of the RMS, was simultaneously inspector of the Conservatory and inspector of orchestras for the Imperial theaters. With his aid, the Conservatory students frequently gained free admittance to the opera. One of them later explained that Kologrivov would use any means to get them into the theater:

> Usually he dispatched us to the orchestra, for which we wore black suits or, for those who had them, white tie and tails, which gave us a deceptive resemblance to the orchestral musicians; or else he gave us passes to the balconies or the parterre (this was fully in his power when the theater was not full, which was then often the case); finally, in special cases, the Conservatory rented whole boxes, usually to the Italian opera for the voice majors and to both opera houses for the theory students to see novelties.[105]

The organizational ties between the Conservatory and the RMS also ensured the students access to the Society's concerts. In fact, the Conservatory's charter specified that students must take part in RMS concerts as needed. In practice, they were required to sing in the Society's chorus.[106] When the program did not require their service as choristers, students could still attend final rehearsals for the RMS concerts, and at performances a section of the auditorium was reserved for them.[107]

For his faculty, Rubinstein hired most of the teachers involved earlier in the RMS's music classes and sought out other experienced instructors and talented performers from St. Petersburg, be they Russian or foreign. The resulting professorate boasted several figures of European renown, including Rubinstein himself, who was one of four professors of piano, the famous pianist Theodor Leschetizky, and the violin virtuoso Henryk Wieniawski,[108] as well as a roster of professors whose very names suggest the cosmopolitan character of the faculty: Herke, Dreyschock, Schubert, Ferrero, Ciardi, Zabel, Cavallini, Nissen-Saloman, Zaremba, Deutsch, Liadov, Luft, Krankenhagen, and Metzdorf.[109] There were a few more Russians among the lower ranks of the faculty, but their number was small. Many of the professors with non-Russian names, however, were born in Russia or at least had adopted the Empire as their homeland. Karl Schubert, for example, had lived in Petersburg more than a quarter of a century.[110] Nikolai Zaremba, a Pole by birth, was known for his fanatical Russian patriotism and was reputed to have "felt not the slightest sympathy for his fellow countrymen" during the Polish insurrection of 1863.[111] Rubinstein himself, of course, was born in Russia and spent most of his life there. Still, artists of non-Russian background and training dominated the faculty of the St. Petersburg Conservatory in the 1860s.

Given Rubinstein's insistence on the highest standards of professional training, this could hardly have been otherwise. Rubinstein had frequently complained, both in private and in public, that Russia lacked fully trained native musicians; remedying this situation was one of the stated goals of the Conservatory. Rubinstein could hardly be expected to hire imperfectly educated Russian teachers to produce fully trained graduates, so he turned to foreigners of proven talent and abilities. This does not mean he was not happy to hire a qualified Russian when possible. A few months before the opening of the Conservatory, for example, he wrote Kologrivov that he thought hiring Konstantin Liadov to teach musical fundamentals for beginning students would be very beneficial because "he is both a talented man and a Russian, and we should keep the latter point in mind most of all."[112]

Rubinstein's pleasure at finding a qualified Russian raises the question of his nationalistic sentiments, for Soviet scholars contend that his satisfaction at hiring Liadov resulted from his personal patriotic feelings.[113] It seems more likely, however, that it sprang chiefly from his hopes to turn aside the criticism by Russian nationalists that the Conservatory was in the hands of foreigners. Rubinstein always considered himself a loyal Russian citizen and patriot, but he deplored the more extreme forms of nationalism rampant in Russia following the Crimean War, and, considering his own background, he could hardly count a Russian name and ancestry essential for service to Russian music. On the other hand, he is known to have tailored some of his policies as director of the Conservatory to fit the widespread nationalistic sentiment of the 1860s. In the first years of its existence, for example, the Conservatory was officially called a music college [*muzykal'noe uchilishche*] out of deference to this spirit. In his memoirs, Rubinstein explained that "there was a trend then toward jingoism. In writing the charter we had to avoid foreign words. What does conservatory mean? Music school. And so we called it a music school."[114] It was probably for similar reasons, rather than any personal feelings of nationalism, that Rubinstein was particularly pleased to have Liadov and other qualified Russians join the Conservatory staff.

It is not surprising that, with such a cosmopolitan faculty, mostly trained in Western Europe, educational methods and literature at the St. Petersburg Conservatory differed little from those in the famous conservatories in Germany and France. The charter required that all teaching "if possible" be in Russian,[115] but in other respects study at Russia's first institution of higher musical education barely acknowledged its Russian setting. The programs from student recitals indicate that in the 1860s voice and instrumental majors studied almost exclusively the classics of Western music. Very few Russian compositions were performed, and the student orchestra played no Russian works during the first decade of its existence.[116] Theoretical subjects at the St. Petersburg Conservatory were also oriented entirely toward Western European models. Nikolai Zaremba, professor of music theory and composition, was completely German in his taste and training, and, like his own teacher, the Berlin pedagogue Adolph Marx, conservative as well. One student later wrote that Zaremba "knew nothing of the newest movement in music in Germany, headed by Schumann. Likewise, he did not know Berlioz and ignored Glinka."[117] Rubinsteins's goal, however, was never to provide *Russian* music training—only music training for Russians. For him, the best possible music education was that offered in Germany and France, based on the Western classics on which he himself was trained and which he loved and respected.

Rubinstein demanded high professional standards and efficiency in operating the Conservatory. Although St. Petersburg society tended to keep late hours, with most offices not opening before ten o'clock in the morning and high officials rarely receiving visitors before noon, Rubinstein was always at work by nine o'clock and insisted his staff do likewise.[118] He even went so far as to institute a system of fines for every lesson that a professor missed. He was similarly strict with students who missed class, refusing to accept all but the most serious excuses: "If your head aches, you should be glad that it is letting you know you have one on your shoulders."[119] He also insisted on high standards of artistic seriousness in his faculty. In October 1866 he even tried to ban the teaching of popular salon and virtuoso showpieces. The Faculty

Council voted to allow each professor to teach whatever he or she chose, but Rubinstein responded with a passionate plea for the highest artistic standards:

I cannot agree with the opinion of the majority because I consider it the purpose of the Conservatory to form the students' musical taste, to acquaint them with the masterpieces of the classic composers, to open for them the exalted horizon of musical art, etc. To achieve this goal, I consider it impossible to allow a teacher to give a student compositions without artistic merit, and which are based only on more or less elegant melodies and [virtuoso] passages, that is, the so-called fashionable music.[120]

Although committed to the highest artistic standards, Rubinstein rarely tried to impose his personal aesthetic tastes on the faculty and students. As in the RMS concerts, where he conscientiously presented a wide variety of music, some of which he did not like, he tolerated a variety of viewpoints in the Conservatory. In his orchestration class, for example, he argued in favor of the small orchestra used by Beethoven and Mendelssohn, but he also taught the capabilities and techniques of the expanded ensembles used by Berlioz, Wagner, and Liszt.[121] When one of the theory students confessed that he had begun attending the weekly musical gatherings of the Conservatory's most outspoken critic, Alexander Serov, Rubinstein blandly responded that he "wished the students to have the chance to hear various opinions and become acquainted with varying trends."[122]

According to its charter, the Conservatory was open to persons of both sexes and all classes. The number of potential students applying for admission far exceeded the capacity of the new institution,[123] and Rubinstein insisted on limiting the student body to those who showed genuine talent and a serious interest in music, regardless of the school's capacity. Because most Russians had had no opportunity for theoretical study of music, he could not demand such knowledge from prospective students. More than three-fifths (110 of 179) of the first Conservatory class had to enroll in the elementary course in musical fundamentals before being allowed to take music theory.[124] Nevertheless, Rubinstein endeavored to select only those students with exceptional talent, however lacking they might be in formal music training. He personally participated in the entrance examinations for all applicants, and one voice student in the Conservatory's first class later recalled that he often dismissed singers with inferior voices in the middle of their auditions.[125] According to his memoirs, Rubinstein was also very concerned to eliminate any students who might be applying for the wrong reasons, particularly to win exemption from military service or to acquire both music training and a general education for a single modest fee.[126] He even claimed that parents often brought their children to him when they could not gain admittance to any other school: "It sometimes happened that a youngster—a real imbecile—would be brought straight to me, the director, and I would be told, in all seriousness, 'He is ill, no institution will take him, they all reject him; so I have brought him to study music.' " Rubinstein was equally wary of society ladies who hoped the Conservatory would serve as a finishing school for their daughters and who laughed when they heard that business in the Conservatory was conducted in Russian, not French.[127]

The students of the new institution had only their promise of talent and serious interest in music in common. The first class, in the words of one of its members, was "a motley crowd" gathered from "the most varied levels of society and from the most distant corners of Russia." Most were sixteen or seventeen years old, but one was only twelve and a few were thirty or older.[128] An official memorandum to the Petersburg police on the social background of all students attending the school in the calendar year 1865 provides proof that the Conservatory adhered to the promise in its charter to admit persons of all classes. Of 299 students, 129 came from the gentry class, while 150 more came from the classes subject to the poll tax. The remaining twenty were presumably children of merchants, priests, or "raznochintsy," the non-gentry intellectuals. The data on religious persuasion provide some indication of the mixed national composition of the student body. 168 students were Orthodox, 68 Roman Catholic, 55 Protestant, and 8 were practicing Jews.[129] These figures show that the conservatory did, in fact, comprise a wide variety of nationalities and classes. Only about one-third of the student body claimed hereditary nobility, while fully one-half came from the lower, unprivileged ranks of Russian society. Although the proportion of Russian Orthodox students appears unusually small (56 percent) for a school in the Russian capital, Petersburg was a cosmopolitan city, the capital of a multinational Empire, and accessible to influences from both the Protestant Baltic provinces and Catholic Poland, where musical training had long existed on a higher level than in Russia itself.

The large number of non-noble students was made possible by a combination of moderate tuition costs and scholarships. Full-time Conservatory students paid only fifty rubles a semester, which did not cover the institution's expenses. In its first year, for example, tuition payments totaled 17,700 rubles, but salaries and operating expenses came to more than 29,000 rubles.[130] Government subsidies and private contributions made up the deficit. The directorate of the RMS urged an increase in fees, however, especially after the Ministry of the Imperial Court ceased paying its annual five-thousand-ruble subsidy in 1865. Rubinstein, however, resisted any increase, paying thousands of rubles from his own pocket to reduce expenses.[131] Although he had no source of income other than concertizing and conducting, he accepted no additional money for his teaching duties or for conducting the student orchestra and chorus. More than half of his salary as the school's director (initially fifteen hundred rubles annually, later raised to three thousand) he turned over to provide scholarships and lessons on instruments needed for the student orchestra.[132] Furthermore, he gave the proceeds from many of his own concerts to the Conservatory.[133] Grand Duchess Elena Pavlovna also greatly aided Rubinstein in keeping down tuition costs by her contributions to the Conservatory while he was director. Besides her annual one-thousand-ruble gift, she also provided for extra expenses totaling up to twelve thousand rubles in some years.[134]

For students unable to pay even the modest tuition, the Conservatory's supporters provided scholarships. In 1862, the inaugural year, Elena Pavlovna sponsored five students, Rubinstein seven, the RMS two, and various other contributors one or two apiece for a total of 31 out of the class of 179.[135] By the fall of 1865 the share of sponsored students was 59 of 229, or more than one in four. Furthermore, the RMS arranged for needy students to lodge in a private boarding house for only seventy-five rubles a year.[136] Thus, the Conservatory did all it could to ensure persons of all classes, regardless of wealth, access to the musical training it offered.

In December 1865 the Conservatory conducted its first public graduation examinations. Twelve students completed the course in their specialties, and of these, seven were judged proficient in all the requirements for the title "free artist." These included such talented men as Pyotr Tchaikovsky, Gustave Kross, later a famous professor of piano at the Conservatory, and Vasily Bessel, for many years Russia's most prominent music publisher. At the next final examination the following December more than twice as many students completed the course, and fifteen won the rank of "free artist." These included several more future conservatory professors and one of Russia's most prominent music critics of the late nineteenth century, Hermann Laroche.[137] Even critics opposed to Rubinstein and his music school publicly admitted that the first graduates of the Conservatory included an impressive number of truly professional musicians.[138]

Thus, Rubinstein had accomplished the educational program outlined in his article of January 1861 and in the charter of the St. Petersburg Conservatory. He had founded a school of higher music education on the level of the great conservatories of Western Europe. He had provided Russian citizens of all classes with access to this training and the possibility of obtaining the legal rank of "free artist." Finally, after only a few years, the Conservatory had provided Russia with a group of talented and professionally trained musicians, of whom many would win popular renown throughout Russia and one, Tchaikovsky, would gain worldwide fame. Critics charged that there was virtually nothing *Russian* about the St. Petersburg Conservatory, and they were largely correct, but Rubinstein had never considered "Russianness" in itself a virtue, nor had he promised a "Russian" music school. What he had promised, he achieved.

Rubinstein and the other leaders of the RMS were not content to bring professional concerts and music education to St. Petersburg alone. While they were raising the standards of musical life in the Russian capital, they were simultaneously laying the foundatin for similar developments throughout the empire. In 1860, at Anton Rubinstein's urging, his brother Nikolai opened a branch of the RMS in Moscow. Two more branches opened in 1863, in Kiev and Kharkov, and another in Saratov two years later.[139] Like the Petersburg organization, the new branches established concert series and music classes. On 24 December 1865 the Moscow branch received permission to open a conservatory with Nikolai Rubinstein as its director, and on 1 September 1866 the Moscow Conservatory opened its doors.[140]

Thus, Anton Rubinstein's prophecy fifteen years earlier that his first plans for a Russian conservatory might have "great consequences" both for music in Russia and for himself had been fulfilled. By 1867 he had brought regular professional concerts and advanced musical training to St. Petersburg and, at least indirectly, to other major cities of the Russian Empire while simultaneously creating for himself a leading position in the musical life of the Russian capital. In the process, however, he had acquired many enemies and generated serious divisions within the RMS and the St. Petersburg Conservatory, which led in 1867 to his resignation from all duties in both organizations.

The Russian Musical Society's internal conflicts resulted in large part from the way in which the Society had been first organized. It sprang not from a single group but from the union of factions—Rubinstein's personal friends and a wider circle of persons linked to Grand Duchess Elena Pavlovna. In addition, the original directors invited several prominent musical figures who belonged to neither group to take responsible posts in the organization. These several circles and individuals represented differing aesthetic views and tastes. Furthermore, many of the figures involved were strong-willed personalities, distinctly conscious of their status and ready to defend it against all attacks. Behind the idealistic phrases and philanthropic goals of the Society stood human beings with personal needs and desires.

Relations between Rubinstein and Elena Pavlovna, official protectress of the RMS, were always somewhat strained. Each possessed a forceful, even tempestuous nature, and a clash of wills always threatened their relationship. The grand duchess was a brilliant woman, well-read and intellectually curious.[141] Her salon enjoyed a reputation for discussing all the most pressing political and social questions of the day, especially those too sensitive, controversial, or esoteric to be considered in the suite of the emperor himself.[142] In musical matters Elena Pavlovna was sufficiently well-versed to impress favorably a number of leading Western European musicians who visited St. Petersburg.[143] She was also accustomed to getting her own way.

Rubinstein once described her as a "magnificent personality. . . . a woman of caprices, willful, a tyrant."[144] Even an admitted admirer points out in his memoirs "how jealously she guarded her authority."[145]

In the early 1850s Rubinstein had been happy to join her court because she supported him financially and treated him with sympathy and friendliness.[146] As a passionate music-lover, Elena Pavlovna greatly admired his playing and enjoyed the prestige of his presence at her musical evenings. Furthermore, his formal study with a teacher of European renown, training rare among Russian musicians, won him a special authority in musical questions and earned the grand duchess's respect.[147] When he returned to St. Petersburg in 1858 after four years abroad, however, Rubinstein's attitude toward Elena Pavlovna had changed markedly. He needed her financial support and influence in court and government circles for his plans to found a conservatory in Russia, but he was also more self-assured than before and less willing to play the role of a salon musician. In the autumn of 1858 he complained to his mother, "I am living here like a real *court jester*, now for the old empress, now for the young one, and most often for my grand duchess."[148] Only two days earlier a maid of honor of Empress Maria Alexandrovna described in her diary the unfortunate conditions under which Rubinstein sometimes had to play for the Imperial family. She had just heard him perform for the empress and her court, but he had not been the sole focus of attention, for the dowager empress had suggested that the children play games at the other end of the hall. "I blushed looking at Rubinstein's face," the diarist wrote; "he did not even try to hide the impression that the noise made on him."[149] Despite such treatment, Rubinstein could not afford to break with Elena Pavlovna. His plans to raise musical standards in Russia and to become the arbiter of St. Petersburg's musical life depended on her.

Something of the carefully balanced tension created between these two strong personalities by such circumstances can be sensed in an incident that occurred at one of Elena Pavlovna's soirées early in 1860. The grand duchess, apparently dissatisfied with the music, asked Prince Odoevsky, a frequent visitor to her court, to tell Rubinstein to "play something good." Fearing that this would show disrespect to the musicians who had already performed, Odoevsky tried to dissuade her, but she insisted that he use all his diplomatic skills. "I turned to Rubinsteins," Odoevsky recorded in his diary, "but he would have nothing to do with it; the grand duchess insisted, however." Now Elena Pavlovna herself approached Rubinstein, who soon began to play. When asked how she had managed to persuade him, the grand duchess replied enigmatically that she had resorted "to extreme measures."[150] Elena Pavlovna could be a difficult and demanding patroness, but she was also a vital supporter for Rubinstein's projects; he was not about to offend her unnecessarily.

The further his work advanced, the more Rubinstein resented his role as accompanist for the grand duchess's musical evenings. By 1861 he thought of his function at the Thursday evening soirees at the Mikahilovsky Palace as "the most demeaning role in Petersburg" and seriously contemplated boycotting these occasions, which seemed to him "incompatible with the dignity" of his art.[151] But he avoided an actual break with the grand duchess. She was a valuable, even necessary, supporter of the Russian Musical Society, who not only contributed money but offered space in her own palace for chorus rehearsals as well and provided funds to invite foreign artists to take part in RMS concerts.[152] In exchange for such wholehearted support, however, she expected to have a say in even the smallest details of the Society's operations.[153] Rubinstein, in turn, resented her constant interference. Surely he had not only other patrons but Elena Pavlovna herself in mind when he wrote:

> What I cannot bear is *the hypocrisy of the patronizing magnates.* Interference in the name of sponsorship and trampling underfoot wherever the occasion arises—that is what revolts me. I always say: you do not love art, you do not understand it—leave it in peace: "König, bleib bei deiner Krone." Or else just dabble in it from time to time to make the people believe in it or in order to have a clear conscience in the knowledge that you have fulfilled, so to speak, the duties of a magnate—and nothing more![154]

Rubinstein's alliance with Elena Pavlovna did not, as he had hoped, attract significant support from the high aristocratic and court circles of the Russian capital. Prince Odoevsky wrote in his diary after the first RMS concert that "high society was conspicuous by its absence, as in all patriotic undertakings. Of all the aristocratic names, mine alone stands out at all these occasions."[155] Alexei Lvov, director of the choir of the Imperial Chapel and of the Concert Society, which was patronized mainly by aristocratic circles, even ordered his singers to have nothing to do with the Musical Society.[156] He was reputedly offended because he had not been chosen a member of the organization's board of directors.[157] The membership rolls of the RMS showed a sprinkling of princesses, counts, and the like,[158] but for the most part fashionable society continued to attend the Italian Opera for its musical entertainment. Thus, Rubinstein's linkage with Elena Pavlovna's court, although probably necessary for the achievement of his plans, introduced conflict into the direction of the Society and did not assure wider aristocratic patronage.

Personality conflicts and rivalries also infected the directorate and repertory committee of the RMS. Odoevsky's charges that Rubinstein never followed the recommendations of the committee on repertory have already been mentioned. Within the committee itself, Dargomyzhsky constantly threatened to resign, complaining that his opinions were being slighted.[159] In private letters he admitted that he was little interested in the Society, preferring operatic to symphonic music. He agreed to be a member of the repertory committee, he wrote, "only to prove that I was not offended, as was Alexei Lvov, that neither he nor I was originally chosen for the directorate of the society."[160] In spite of such disclaimers, Dargomyzhsky apparently thought he should have been named a director, and his behavior on the repertory committee indicated his resentment.

Trouble also developed within the board of directors. A somewhat enigmatic entry in Prince Odoevsky's diary for 20 December 1860 suggests an attempt by several of the assistant directors, apparently rivals of Rubinstein, to influence policy by assuming the authority of directors in the temporary absence of Kologrivov and Kanshin. The attempt failed, however. Odoevsky wrote that "Stasov announced that Kologrivov had returned; thus both Shustov and Shchelkov remain without director's prerogatives, and therefore with tied hands."[161] Personal conflicts developed even among the five original directors, all personally selected by Rubinstein and, except for Kanshin, his close friends. In 1865 Dmitri Stasov actually resigned from the directorate after such a conflict, telling his friends that he did so because he could not get along with Rubinstein.[162] The previous year Rubinstein had even recommended to Kologrivov that the number of directors be reduced to two or at most three to avoid arguments: "Believe me, this is very important for simplifying matters. Just you and me, and one more!"[163] Apparently he wanted a directorate in which he and Kologrivov, his most trusted colleague, would always constitute a majority.

In fact, Rubinstein himself was a major source of tension and conflict within the Russian Musical Society. He treated the entire organization as his personal domain and tenaciously fought off any encroachments on his prerogatives, whether from Elena Pavlovna, Dmitri Stasov, or the musicians. An incident that occurred in December 1860 illustrates his capricious reaction to any threat to his authority and sense of dignity as an artist. The amateur chorus of the RMS was rehearsing under Rubinstein's direction when he heard a mistake from one of the sopranos. He eventually isolated the problem in a group of three women and asked them to sing the line individually. The women refused, so he dismissed them from the chorus.[164] He may very well have accompanied the episode with verbal abuse of the offenders.[165] "Then," according to Prince Odoevsky, "a *scandale* erupted; two score men began to shout that Rubinstein should beg the women's pardon; the women, sensing support, fell into hysterics, swoons, etc." Rubinstein walked out.[166] The next day he wrote to the RMS board of directors:

> The unpleasantnesses that are cropping up more and more often every day and have as their subject only myself and my direction of the Society's musical affairs—plus yesterday's very deplorable scene at the [Choral] Academy, where I had to despotically

expel three women and thereby offend, I am assured, the entire chorus—force me to think that I am an obstacle to the healthy functioning of the Society. . . . Therefore, I consider it my duty to resign from all the responsibilities I have borne as a director and conductor of the Society.[167]

He agreed to return to his duties only after Odoevsky organized a petition signed by the entire chorus requesting him to stay.[168]

The internal clashes and squabbling that plagued the Russian Musical Society appeared even more strongly in the St. Petersburg Conservatory during Rubinstein's tenure as director. As in the RMS itself, the most basic conflict lay between the director and Elena Pavlovna. As the official patroness and a generous benefactor of the school, she virtually considered its faculty and students members of her own court. Rubinstein and other famous virtuosos from the Conservatory frequently played at her soirées, and when she moved to her summer palace at Oranienbaum, a prominent figure from the Conservatory would frequently accompany her court to entertain in the evenings.[169] The grand duchess even pressed students into service at her musical gatherings. "Not very grand duchess-like" was the description Pyotr Tchaikovsky applied to the twenty rubles he received for playing at one of her soirées in the spring of 1863.[170]

The grand duchess's treatment of the Conservatory staff as private retainers galled Rubinstein, but her actual power over the functioning of the school bothered him still more. According to its charter, all actions and regulations by the RMS board of directors on the financial and scholastic operations of the school required her approval, as did the appointment of the director.[171] These privileges were not mere formalities, for Elena Pavlovna insisted on taking an active part in the operation of the Conservatory; moreover, it was even more dependent on her support than was the RMS. For the Musical Society she was essentially a source of money, but for the Conservatory she served as a vital link to the government. Legally, the Conservatory was a private educational institution, but it depended on government approval and participation to fulfill its most important purpose. Without the approval of an examining committee that included government delegates, selected by the Imperial Court Ministry, the Conservatory could not grant a diploma or the legal rank of "free artist."[172] This tied Rubinstein's hands in his conflicts with the grand duchess; without her, he might lose the all-important government participation in his work.

Still, Rubinstein tried to strengthen his own authority as director of the Conservatory and limit opportunities for outside interference. On 28 September 1863 he sent the RMS directorate a proposal for new charters for the Society and Conservatory. He recommended making the Conservatory's director solely responsible for all artistic matters, subject only to the majority opinion of the Faculty Council. "During his term of office," according to

Rubinstein's proposal, the director should be "in complete charge of the Conservatory; no one has the right to give any orders without his approval."[173] By the following summer his proposal had neither been adopted nor rejected, so on 15 June 1864 Rubinstein wrote Kologrivov that he would not return to his duties in the fall if his proposed charters were not accepted. Concerning Elena Pavlovna's obstruction of the project he added:

> She will intrigue against us and all because of me. Well, isn't she the old lady? Who is right? But what is most important is to try to become an Imperial institution, to be assigned to the Ministry of the Court or of Education—then when there is trouble, you don't have to cope with women.[174]

Such a change was far in the future, however, and Rubinstein continued to have to deal with Elena Pavlovna.

Although his proposed charters were not adopted by the beginning of the 1864-65 academic year, Rubinstein postponed his threatened resignation from the leading position in Russian musical life that he had created for himself. Instead he reached a compromise agreement with Elena Pavlovna: he would stay on for another year on condition that the RMS and Conservatory would be fundamentally reformed. He would be free to leave without reservations in the spring if he were not satisfied.[175] By the summer of 1865, however, the RMS had been changed only by the creation of a new Chief Directorate to oversee its several branches. Soon after its founding in 1860 the Moscow branch of the RMS had begun to petition for independence from the St. Petersburg Society. Early in 1865 Elena Pavlovna decided to grant all branches of the Russian Musical Society equal rights and to create a Chief Directorate in St. Petersburg that would have authority over all the organizations, including the original Society in the Russian capital.[176] Clearly this was not the kind of reform that Rubinstein had had in mind, for it would reduce rather than increase his own control. During the debate among the directors of the St. Petersburg RMS over the new Chief Directorate, Rubinstein even demanded that its charter mandate the inclusion of the entire board of directors of the Petersburg branch plus his brother Nikolai from the Moscow RMS. Elena Pavlovna's representative is reported to have asked in disbelief, " 'What? Are we to introduce Nikolai Rubinstein into the charter?' 'So introduce him,' replied Anton."[177] Not surprisingly, Rubinstein's proposal was rejected. Instead, the new Chief Directorate consisted mainly of figures from outside Rubinstein's circle. The grand duchess herself took the presidency, and her trusted friend, Prince Dmitri Obolensky, became vice-president.[178] Nevertheless, Rubinstein still did not resign at the end of the 1864-64 academic year. Instead he sent Elena Pavlovna an ultimatum, promising to quit as of 1 January 1866 unless his proposed charters for the RMS and Conservatory were approved unconditionally and Matvei Wielhorsky and Kologrivov appointed vice-president of the Chief Directorate and its delegate from the Petersburg branch, respectively.[179]

His demands were still not met by the end of 1865, but Rubinstein once again hesitated to carry out his threats. The Conservatory had just held its first graduation examinations, and he was not entirely satisfied with them. On 20 December 1865 Rubinstein's wife confided to her mother that although everyone else was happy with the results, Anton believed that they had not proved that he had achieved his artistic goals for the Conservatory and that he therefore had to stay until the next graduation.[180] There is no doubt that Rubinstein had a strong sense of responsibility, especially to his role as a serious musician, but it does not seem too presumptuous to assume that he again hesitated to resign, as he had several times before, at least in part because he did not want to give up the important musical career he had created for himself in St. Petersburg.

During the next year Rubinstein's relations with Elena Pavlovna remained severely strained, and his defense of his prerogatives as conservatory director led to serious conflicts with his faculty as well. In the spring of 1866, for example, when Rubinstein discovered that Andrei Markovich, a member of the RMS directorate, had privately asked Elena Pavlovna not to confirm Rubinstein's candidate for inspector of the Conservatory, he wrote Markovich:

> I recognize her formal right to confirm my orders for the Conservatory, but I do not recognize her formal right not to confirm them. Therefore, I propose to you the following end to this affair—either I resign, or you resign, or the inspector I have appointed will be confirmed in his post, at your request, by 1 June of this year.[181]

The formation in the same year of a Select Council of five elected professors to sit in place of the full Faculty Council when the entire body could not meet led to further annoyance for Rubinstein. As long as all professors had to attend meetings of the Faculty Council, it met very rarely, and he had a reasonably free hand in running the Conservatory. The Select Council, however, kept a much closer watch on his activities.[182]

In December 1866 Rubinstein disagreed with the examining committee for graduating students (characteristically demanding higher standards for a diploma than they), but the Faculty Council and Grand Duchess Elena Pavlovna upheld the committee. This was the last straw for Rubinstein. According to the minutes of the meeting of the directors of the St. Petersburg RMS of 6 June 1867,

> A. G. Rubinstein announced to the Directorate that, as a result of disagreements that have arisen between himself and the Council of Professors of the Conservatory over the granting of diplomas to several students of the Conservatory whose graduation he deemed premature, and [as a result] of generally being hampered by resolutions of the Council of Professors, whose decisions he must obey, very often against his own convictions, he, Rubinstein, gives up his post as Director of the Conservatory.[183]

As so often before, he still drew back from a final break with the RMS and the St. Petersburg Conservatory, agreeing to stay on until the end of the academic year, but on 16 July 1867 he wrote Prince Obolensky to announce that he would not return to his duties or even to St. Petersburg in the autumn of 1867.[184]

In his memoirs, Rubinstein blames his departure on his disagreement in December 1866 with the Conservatory professors on standards for graduation,[185] but this was only the last in a long series of disputes with his faculty, fellow RMS directors, and Elena Pavlovna. He simply could not continue to tolerate interference in his musical work. As early as 1864 he had seriously threatened to resign because the grand duchess would not confirm the new charters he had drawn up for the RMS and Conservatory. At the end of 1865 he had told his wife he would stay on only until the second Conservatory graduation examination in December 1866. The coincidence of his dispute over standards for diplomas with that occasion suggests that the dispute may well have been a pretext for carrying out a decision he had already made. In any case, after years of fighting to defend his authority and prerogatives as director of the RMS and its first conservatory, he finally gave up the battle.

With his departure from St. Petersburg, Anton Rubinstein concluded nearly a decade of work for the Russian Musical Society and the St. Petersburg Conservatory. Although it ended in frustration and premature retirement, he had achieved nearly all the goals he had originally set for the benefit of music in Russia. He had created the most active and professional concert society in the Russian capital and a conservatory providing advanced musical training of high quality to talented students of all classes. He had even won legal recognition of the music profession, as signified by the granting of the legal rank of "free artist" to musicians for the first time ever in Russia. He was less successful, however, in achieving his personal goals. Through his work for the RMS and the Conservatory he secured for himself a central position in the musical life of St. Petersburg as something more than simply a virtuoso pianist, and he achieved sufficient financial reward (although certainly less than he might have had as a touring recitalist) to feel able to donate a large share of his salary to the Conservatory. He also gained the legal rank of "free artist" for himself a few months after the opening of the Conservatory.[186] But his position did not satisfy more subtle and personal needs. He had founded the Russian Musical Society partly because he considered his role as a traveling virtuoso degrading, but he still had to serve Elena Pavlovna as a court entertainer after becoming the Society's director. He had hoped to earn the sort of serious reputation and widespread admiration as a composer-conductor that his friend Felix Mendelssohn had enjoyed in Germany, but instead he became (as will be seen in later chapters) a controversial and often bitterly maligned figure. Finally, his exalted and idealized view of the true musician as a pure servant of art made him strive to achieve higher artistic standards than were possible. His belief in the almost sacred righteousness of his cause made it nearly impossible for him to compromise on any of his fundamental principles, so he tried to control all musical matters and vigorously fended off any diminution of his real or imagined prerogatives, whether by Elena Pavlovna, the RMS directors, or the Conservatory's faculty. Naturally, compromises had to be made, but Rubinstein viewed each one as a betrayal of his role as a true musician-artist. His constant struggle for dominance and the inevitable accommodations with standards lower than his own, along with the sharp public criticism of his work and the necessity of remaining a salon musician for Elena Pavlovna, corrupted whatever satisfaction he might have enjoyed at the striking success of his work. Thus, when he finally left his posts as director of the RMS and the St. Petersburg Conservatory in 1867, he left Russia as well, determined to seek some other position or role that would better fit his view of himself as a servant of art.

Notes to Chapter II

1. Barenboim, *A. G. Rubinshtein*, 1:13-18.

2. Rubinshtein, "Avtobiograficheskie rasskazy," 1:400.

3. Barenboim, *A. G. Rubinshtein*, 1:42-43, 46-48.

4. N. M. Lisovskii, "Letopis' sobytii v zhizni i deiatel'nosti A. G. Rubinshteina: S ukazaniem na otzyvy i stat'i o nem i ego proizvedeniiakh v russkoi pechati, 1829-1889" [A chronicle of events in the life and work of A. G. Rubinstein: with references to reviews and articles about him and his compositions in the Russian press, 1829-1889], *Russkaia starina* 64 (1889):607.

5. Barenboim, *A. G. Rubinshtein*, 1:68-69.

6. L. Korabel'nikova, "Stroitel' muzykal'noi Moskvy" [The builder of musical Moscow], *Sovetskaia muzyka,* June 1960, p. 81.

7. Bessel', "Moi vospominaniia," 372-73; Alfred J. Swan, *Russian Music and Its Sources in Chant and Folk-Song* (London: John Baker, 1973), p. 74.

8. A. Rubinstein to K. M. Fredro, 15 July 1854, in Anton Grigor'evich Rubinshtein, *Izbrannye pis'ma* [Selected letters], ed. Lev Aronovich Barenboim (Moscow: Gosudarstvennoe muzykal'noe izdatel'stvo, 1954), pp. 33-34.

9. Bessel', "Moi vospominaniia," pp. 371-72.

10. "Avtobiograficheskie rasskazy," 2:454.

11. Reprinted in Boris Vladimirovich Asaf'ev [Igor' Glebov], *Anton Grigor'evich Rubinshtein v ego muzykal'noi deiatel'nosti i otzyvakh sovremennikov* [Anton Grigorievich Rubinstein in his musical activity and reviews of his contemporaries] (Moscow: Gosudarstvennoe izdatel'stvo, muzykal'nyi sektor, 1929), pp. 57-58.

12. Bessel', "Moi vospominaniia," p. 373.

13. Boborykin, *Vospominaniia*, 2:461.

14. Larosh, *Izbrannye stat'i*, 2:284.

15. Boborykin, *Vospominaniia*, 2:455.

16. "Avtobiograficheskie rasskazy," 1:417.

17. The complete article appears in Asaf'ev, *A. G. Rubinshtein*, pp. 56-61.

18. "Avtobiograficheskie rasskazy," 1:417.

19. Leningrad Conservatory, *100 let*, p. 8.

20. Letter of 15 October 1852 in Rubinshtein, *Izbrannye pis'ma*, p. 29.

21. Arthur Loesser, *Men, Women and Pianos: A Social History* (New York: Simon and Schuster, 1954), p. 413.

22. Rubinshtein, "Avtobiograficheskie rasskazy," 1:410.

23. Letter of 28 December 1850 in Rubinshtein, *Izbrannye pis'ma*, p. 19.

24. Barenboim, *A. G. Rubinshtein*, 1:113.

25. A. Rubinstein to his mother, 4 June 1852, in Rubinshtein, *Izbrannye pis'ma*, p. 24.

26. Rubinshtein, "Avtobiograficheskie rasskazy," 1:410.

27. A. Rubinstein to his mother, 4 June 1852, in Rubinshtein, *Izbrannye pis'ma*, p. 24.

28. Letter of 19 August 1852, *ibid.*, p. 28.

29. See W. Bruce Lincoln, *Nicholas I, Emperor and Autocrat of All the Russias* (Bloomington: Indiana University Press, 1978), pp. 293-324.

30. Excerpt of an unpublished letter of 3 February 1853 quoted in an editor's note in Rubinshtein, *Izbrannye pis'ma*, p. 29.

31. Barenboim, *A. G. Rubinshtein*, 1:119-20.

32.   Letter to K. M. Fredro of 7 November 1854 in Rubinshtein, *Izbrannye pis'ma*, pp. 40-41.

33.   Letter to his mother of 27 June 1855, *ibid.*, pp. 43-44.

34.   Swan, *Russian Music*, p. 73.

35.   "Avtobiograficheskie rasskazy," 1:415.

36.   Rubinshtein, *Izbrannye pis'ma*, p. 52.

37.   M. B. R[ozenberg], "Anton Grigor'evich Rubinshtein: Zametki k ego biografii, doktora M. B. R—ga" [Anton Grigorievich Rubinstein: notes on his biography by Doctor M.B.R.—g], *Russkaia starina* 64 (1889):584.

38.   "Peterburgskaia zhizn'," *Sovremennik* (Sovremennoe obozrenie) 74 (March 1859):190.

39.   Rubinshtein, "Avtobiograficheskie rasskazy," 1:414.

40.   Barenboim, *A. G. Rubinshtein*, 1:146-47.

41.   Rozenberg, "A. G. Rubinshtein," p. 584.

42.   See W. Bruce Lincoln, "The Circle of the Grand Duchess Yelena Pavlovna, 1847-1861," *Slavonic and East European Review* 48 (July 1970):373-87.

43.   Rozenberg, "A. G. Rubinshtein," p. 584.

44.   Anna Fedorovna Tiutcheva, *Pri dvore dvukh imperatorov: Dnevnik 1855-1882* [At the court of two emperors: a diary 1855-1882], trans. E. V. Ger'e, ed. S. V. Bakhrushin (Moscow: Izdanie M. i S. Sabashnikovykh, 1929), pp. 85-86, 144.

45.   *Mein Leben*, ed. Martin Gregor-Dellin, 2 vols. (Munich: Paul List Verlag, 1969), p. 730.

46.   Bessel', "Moi vospominaniia," p. 353.

47.   Rubinshtein, "Avtobiograficheskie rasskazy," 1:416-17.

48.   *Ibid.*, 1:416.

49.   Memoirs of Dmitri Stasov, quoted in Asaf'ev, *A. G. Rubinshtein*, p. 75; Findeizen, *Ocherk RMO*, pp. 11-12.

50.   Komarova, Varvara Dmitrievna [Vladimir Karenin], *Vladimir Stasov: Ocherk ego zhizni i deiatel'nosti* [Vladimir Stasov: a survey of his life and work], 2 vols. (Leningrad: Mysl', 1927), 1:344-45.

51.   Rubinshtein, "Avtobiograficheskie rasskazy," 1:418.

52.   *Ibid.*, 1:416; "Peterburgskaia zhizn'," *Sovremennik* (Sovremennoe obozrenie) 76 (July 1859):136.

53. Quoted in Findeizen, *Ocherk RMO*, p. 14.

54. "Peterburgskaia zhizn'," *Sovremennik* (Sovremennoe obozrenie) 76 (July 1859):136.

55. "Avtobiograficheskie rasskazy," 1:415-16, 418.

56. "Peterburgskaia zhizn'," *Sovremennik* (Sovremennoe obozrenie) 81 (June 1860):297, 299; Findeizen, *Ocherk RMO*, pp. 16-17.

57. Memoirs of Dmitri Stasov, quoted in Asaf'ev, *A. G. Rubinshtein*, p. 79; Larosh, *Izbrannye stat'i*, 2:289.

58. Bessel', "Moi vospominaniia," 354.

59. "Peterburgskaia zhizn'," *Sovremennik* (Sovremennoe obozrenie) 81 (June 1860):297.

60. Letter of 18 January 1860 in Odoevskii, *Muzykal'no-literaturnoe nasledie*, pp. 508-9.

61. Auer, *My Long Life*, p. 134.

62. Young, *Concert Tradition*, pp. 157, 163.

63. Complete programs appear in Findeizen, *Ocherk RMO*, appendix, pp. 1-2.

64. Young, *Concert Tradition*, pp. 200-201.

65. Letter of 15 November 1859, quoted in Asaf'ev, *A. G. Rubinshtein*, p. 83.

66. *Ibid.*

67. Thirteen years later Hermann Laroche ascribed it to "especially fortunate circumstances and the patronage of highly placed persons" *(Sobranie muzykal'no-kriticheskikh statei* [Collected musico-critical articles], 2 vols. [Moscow: Muzykal'no-Teoreticheskaia Biblioteka v Moskve and Gosudarstvennoe muzykal'noe izdatel'stvo, 1913-1922], 1:308-9.

68. Rubinshtein, "Avtobiograficheskie rasskazy," 1:419; Rubets, "Vospominaniia," 7 May 1912, p. 4.

69. "Peterburgskaia zhizn'," *Sovremennik* (Sovremennoe obozrenie) 81 (June 1860):299.

70. Complete programs appear in Findeizen, *Ocherk RMO*, appendix, pp. 2-8.

71. *Ibid.*, p. 18.

72. *Izbrannye stat'i*, p. 66.

73. Programs appear in Findeizen, *Ocherk RMO*, appendix, pp. 76-79.

74.   Barenboim, *A. G. Rubinshtein*, 1:260. Some sources claim these classes only began in the fall of 1860 (see Leningrad Conservatory, *100 let*, p. 11), but Odoevsky's diary proves that entrance examinations were conducted in February 1860 ("Dnevnik V. F. Odoevskogo, 1859-69 gg." [The diary of V. F. Odoevsky, 1859-69], *Literaturnoe nasledstvo* [Literary legacy] 22/24 [1935]:105-6).

75.   "Peterburgskaia zhizn'," *Sovremennik* (Sovremennoe obozrenie) 81 (June 1860):298.

76.   B. M—ch, "Russkoe muzykal'noe obshchestvo (K izdateliu Severnoi Pchely)" [The Russian Musical Society (to the editor of Severnaia pchela)], *Severnaia pchela*, 19 May 1861, p. 454.

77.   "Avtobiograficheskie rasskazy," 1:418.

78.   Findeizen, *Ocherk RMO*, p. 24.

79.   Leningrad Conservatory, *100 let*, p. 10.

80.   The complete letter appears in Asaf'ev, *A. G. Rubinshtein*, pp. 80-83. It is undated, and some authors, including Asafiev, attribute it to 1859, but internal evidence indicates it followed the meeting of the RMS directors on 13 March 1860. See Barenboim, *A. G. Rubinshtein*, note 112 to chapter 14, p. 386.

81.   Leningrad Conservatory, *100 let*, p. 11.

82.   The complete article appears in Asaf'ev, *A. G. Rubinshtein*, pp. 87-92.

83.   Rubinshtein, "Avtobiograficheskie rasskazy," 1:416.

84.   Quoted in Findeizen, *Ocherk RMO*, p. 28.

85.   Barenboim, *A. G. Rubinshtein*, 1:261.

86.   Leningrad Conservatory, *100 let*, p. 12.

87.   Iulii Anatol'evich Kremlev, *Leningradskaia gosudarstvennaia konservatoriia, 1862-1937* [Leningrad State Conservatory, 1862-1937] (Moscow: Gosudarstvennoe muzykal'noe izdatel'stvo, 1938), p. 14.

88.   Pavel Aleksandrovich Vul'fius, ed., *Iz istorii Leningradskoi konservatorii: Materialy i dokumenty, 1862-1917* [From the history of the Leningrad Conservatory: materials and documents, 1862-1917] (Leningrad: Muzyka, 1964), pp. 11, 14.

89.   Kremlev, *Leningradskaia konservatoriia*, p. 14.

90.   Findeizen, *Ocherk RMO*, p. 29; "Zametka na pis'mo po povodu odnogo byvshego kontserta (K izdateliu Severnoi Pchely)" [A note on a letter about a certain past concert (to the editor of Severnaia pchela)], *Severnaia pchela*, 6 April 1862, p. 2.

91.   *Otchet Russkogo muzykal'nogo obshchestva za 1862-1863 god* [The annual report of the Russian Musical Society for the year 1862-1863] (St. Petersburg, 1864), p. 3.

92. Leningrad Conservatory, *100 let*, p. 16.

93. Kremlev, *Leningradskaia konservatoriia*, pp. 14-15. For reasons to be discussed below, the Conservatory was officially called a *muzykal'noe uchilishche* or music college, but from the beginning it was always referred to as a conservatory in the press and even in the RMS's annual reports.

94. Findeizen, *Ocherk RMO*, pp. 28-29.

95. See Vul'fius, *Iz istorii konservatorii*, pp. 11-15, for the entire text of the charter.

96. Excerpt quoted in Kremlev, *Leningradskaia konservatoriia*, p. 20.

97. *Otchet RMO za 1862-63*, pp. 33-42.

98. German Avgustovich Larosh, "Anton Grigor'evich Rubinshtein: V vospominaniiakh byv. uchenika Spb. konservatorii" [Anton Grigorievich Rubinstein: in the memoirs of a former student of the St. Petersburg Conservatory], *Russkaia starina* 64 (1889):591.

99. Findeizen, *Ocherk RMO*, p. 31.

100. Larosh, "A. G. Rubinshtein," p. 592.

101. *Otchet RMO za 1862-63*, p. 2; Larosh, *Izbrannye stat'i*, 2:287.

102. Vul'fius, *Iz istorii konservatorii*, p. 158.

103. *Ibid.*, p. 182; Barenboim, *A. G. Rubinshtein*, 1:273.

104. Rubets, "Vospominaniia," 17 June 1912, p. 4.

105. Larosh, *Izbrannye stat'i*, 2:292.

106. Vul'fius, *Iz istorii konservatorii*, p. 14; Leningrad Conservatory, *100 let*, p. 21.

107. Larosh, *Izbrannye stat'i*, 2:289.

108. Rubets, "Vospominaniia," 21 May 1912, p. 3, and 4 June 1912, p. 4.

109. *Otchet RMO za 1862-63*, pp. 33-41.

110. Leningrad Conservatory, *100 let*, p. 18.

111. Larosh, *Izbrannye stat'i*, 2:278.

112. Letter of 22 June 1862 in Rubinshtein, *Izbrannye pis'ma*, p. 60.

113. See, for example, Barenboim, *A. G. Rubinshtein*, 1:263-64.

114.   "Avtobiograficheskie rasskazy," 1:420.

115.   Vul'fius, *Iz istorii konservatorii*, p. 11.

116.   *Ibid.*, pp. 175, 182-83.

117.   Larosh, *Izbrannye stat'i*, 2:280.

118.   Auer, *My Long Life*, pp. 127-28.

119.   Rubets, "Vospominaniia," 21 May 1912, p. 3.

120.   Letter to the Faculty Council of the Conservatory, 21 October 1866, in Rubinshtein, *Izbrannye pis'ma*, p. 69.

121.   Larosh, *Izbrannye stat'i*, 2:285-86.

122.   *Ibid.*, 2:294.

123.   Leningrad Conservatory, *100 let*, p. 22.

124.   *Otchet RMO za 1862-63*, pp. 31, 40-42.

125.   Rubets, "Vospominaniia," 7 May 1912, p. 4.

126.   "Avtobiograficheskie rasskazy," 2:458.

127.   *Ibid.*, 1:420.

128.   Larosh, "A. G. Rubinshtein," p. 590.

129.   Cited in Kremlev, *Leningradskaia konservatoriia*, p. 16.

130.   *Otchet RMO za 1862-63*, pp. 14-15.

131.   Kremlev, *Leningradskaia konservatoriia*, pp. 21-22.

132.   Barenboim, *A. G. Rubinshtein*, 1:266, 270.

133.   Kremlev, *Leningradskaia konservatoriia*, p. 23.

134.   Dmitrii Aleksandrovich Obolenskii, "Moi vospominaniia o velike kniagine Elene Pavlovne" [My memoirs about Grand Duchess Elena Pavlovna], *Russkaia starina* 138 (1909):270-72.

135.   *Otchet RMO za 1862-63*, p. 2.

136.   Findeizen, *Ocherk RMO*, pp. 31, 35.

137.   Lisovskii, "Letopis' Rubinshteina," pp. 612-13.

138.   Kiui, *Izbrannye stat'i*, p. 83.

139. Barenboim, *A. G. Rubinshtein*, 1:250.

140. N. V. Tumanina, ed., *Vospominaniia o Moskovskoi konservatorii* [Memoirs about the Moscow Conservatory] (Moscow: Muzyka, 1966), p. 20; M. Chaikovskii, *Zhizn' Chaikovskogo*, 1:252.

141. Lincoln, "Circle of Yelena Pavlovna," p. 375.

142. Tiutcheva, *Pri dvore*, p. 38.

143. Wagner, *Mein Leben*, pp. 729-30; Joseph Joachim to his wife, 8 January 1872, in Johannes Joachim and Andreas Moser, comps., *Briefe von und an Joseph Joachim*, 3 vols. (Berlin: Julius Bard, 1911-1913), 3:82; Ferdinand Hiller, *Erinnerungsblätter* (Cologne: M. Dumont-Schauberg'schen Buchhandlung, 1884), pp. 29-31.

144. "Avtobiograficheskie rasskazy," 1:411.

145. Obolenskii, "Moi vospominaniia," 138:275.

146. Rubinshtein, "Avtobiograficheskie rasskazy," 1:410.

147. Rozenberg, "Moi vospominaniia," p. 584.

148. Unpublished letter of 13 October 1858 quoted in Barenboim, *A. G. Rubinshtein*, 1:226.

149. Tiutcheva, *Pri dvore*, p. 166.

150. Odoevskii, "Dnevnik," p. 106.

151. Letters to Edith Rahden of 14 February 1861 and 21 March 1861 quoted in Barenboim, *A. G. Rubinshtein*, 1:227.

152. Bessel', "Moi vospominaniia," 354; Obolenskii, "Moi vospominaniia," 138:273; Varvara Dmitrievna Komarova [Vladimir Karenin], "Klara Shuman v Rossii: Vospominaniia D. V. Stasova i pis'ma k nemu Klary Shuman" [Clara Schumann in Russia: memoirs of D. V. Stasov and Clara Schumann's letters to him], in A. N. Rimskii-Korsakov, ed., *Muzykal'naia letopis': Stat'i i materialy* [Musical chronicle: articles and materials], 3 vols. (Petrograd: Mysl', 1922-1925), 1:92.

153. Obolenskii, "Moi vospominaniia," 138:275; Kremlev, *Leningradskaia konservatoriia*, p. 20.

154. Letter to Edith Rahden of 23 February 1862, quoted in Barenboim, *A. G. Rubinshtein*, 1:227-28.

155. "Dnevnik," p. 100.

156. *Ibid.*, p. 108.

157. Alexander Dargomyzhsky to L. I. Karmalina, 1860, in Dargomyzhskii, "Materialy dlia ego biografii," 13:432.

158.   See, for example, the list in *Otchet RMO za 1862-63,* pp. 19-27.

159.   Odoevskii, "Dnevnik," pp. 114, 119.

160.   Letters to L. I. Karmalina of 20 November 1859 and 1860 in Dargomyzhskii, "Materialy dlia ego biografii," 13:426, 432.

161.   "Dnevnik," p. 121.

162.   Mily Balakirev to V. M. Zhemchuzhnikov, December 1865, in Balakirev, *Vospominaniia,* p. 97.

163.   Letter of 15 June 1864 in Rubinshtein, *Izbrannye pis'ma,* p. 66.

164.   Odoevskii, "Dnevnik," p. 120.

165.   For an account of such behavior at other rehearsals see Larosh, "A. G. Rubinshtein," p. 593.

166.   "Dnevnik," p. 120.

167.   Letter of 14 December 1860 in Rubinshtein, *Izbrannye pis'ma,* p. 58.

168.   Odoevskii, "Dnevnik," pp. 121-23.

169.   Auer, *My Long Life,* p. 143; Mar'ia Grigor'evna Nazimova, "Dvor velikoi kniagini Eleny Pavlovny (1865-1867)" [The court of Grand Duchess Elena Pavlovna (1865-1867)], *Russkii arkhiv* 37, pt. 3 (1899):315.

170.   Letter to his sister of 15 April 1863 in P. Chaikovskii, *Polnoe sobranie,* 5:78.

171.   Vul'fius, *Iz istorii konservatorii,* pp. 11-12.

172.   *Ibid.,* p. 14.

173.   Editor's note 1 to letter 24 in Rubinshtein, *Izbrannye pis'ma,* p. 67.

174.   Rubinshtein, *Izbrannye pis'ma,* pp. 64-65.

175.   Excerpt from a letter from Rubinstein to Kologrivov of 3 August 1864, quoted in Barenboim, *A. G. Rubinshtein,* 1:343.

176.   Obolenskii, "Moi vospominaniia," 138:262; Leningrad Conservatory, *100 let,* p. 15.

177.   Odoevskii, "Dnevnik," p. 192.

178.   Barenboim, *A. G. Rubinshtein,* 1:343.

179.   Letter of 28 May 1865, quoted in Barenboim, *A. G Rubinshtein,* 1:344.

180.   *Ibid.,* 1:344.

181. Undated letter, probably from the spring of 1866, in Rubinshtein, *Izbrannye pis'ma*, pp. 68-69.

182. Findeizen, *Ocherk RMO*, p. 36.

183. Quoted *ibid.*, p. 38.

184. Rubinshtein, *Izbrannye pis'ma*, pp. 70-71.

185. "Avtobiograficheskie rasskazy," 1:421.

186. Barenboim, *A. G. Rubinshtein*, 1:263.

Chapter III

The Opponents of the Russian Musical Society

For all the success of the Russian Musical Society and the St. Petersburg Conservatory, Anton Rubinstein's efforts met with constant and active opposition from certain segments of St. Petersburg's musical community. Although the public continued to idolize him as a virtuoso pianist, he became the object of attacks and disdain from many of the Russian capital's leading musicians. Some harbored continuing resentment because of his contempt for Russia's musical amateurism or simply "could not forgive him for not being enraptured with their pet composers."[1] Others envied his success in accomplishing what they themselves could not even attempt.[2] A few had more specific grievances against Rubinstein. Prince Pyotr Oldenburgsky and the composer Adolf Henselt had planned to establish an advanced school to train music teachers for the country's academies for women, but their project was thwarted by the opening of the Conservatory.[3] Of all Rubinstein's opponents, however, the most formidable were the composer and critic Alexander Serov and the circle of young composers headed by Mily Balakirev, for they possessed sufficient talent and prestige to pose a serious threat to the Russian Musical Society and its work.

Balakirev's musical circle, the so-called *Moguchaia kuchka* or Mighty Handful, took form between 1856 and 1862. In late 1855 the not yet nineteen-year-old Mily Balakirev moved to St. Petersburg from his native Nizhny Novgorod. Although he had little training in composition and analysis, he had shown considerable gifts as a pianist and had a burning passion to compose. He was soon introduced into St. Petersburg's musical gatherings and began meeting the like-minded young men who would comprise his circle. Glinka, the dean of Russian composers, was still living in the Russian capital, and Balakirev attended his musical evenings. There, early in 1856, he met the Stasov brothers, Dmitri and Vladimir.[4] At first his acquaintance with them remained casual, but in two or three years Vladimir became an intimate friend.[5] Although Stasov himself had no interest in composing, he was a passionate music-lover and became the aesthetic adviser to Balakirev and all his musical comrades.

About the same time that he met the Stasovs, Balakirev happened to attend an evening of chamber music at the home of Alexander Fitztum, the inspector of the University and a well-known amateur musician. There Balakirev met a young army officer, César Cui, who shared his interest in music. They immediately struck up a conversation about their favorite composers and soon became inseparable friends.[6] In the latter half of 1857 a new member joined the group when Cui met Modest Musorgsky, a young guards officer with musical leanings, at the home of Alexander Dargomyzhsky. Soon Cui introduced his new acquaintance to Balakirev.[7] The next important recruit for the circle was a young cadet at the Naval Academy, Nikolai Rimsky-Korsakov. Rimsky's piano teacher took him to Balakirev in November 1861 to arrange lessons in music theory and composition. There the seventeen-year-old midshipman also met Cui and Musorgsky, and he was soon accepted as a member of their group.[8] The last major member, Alexander Borodin, entered the circle in the autumn of 1862. At twenty-eight, he was older than the rest of the group and already a promising chemist, but his interest in music drew him to these younger musicians. He had already met Musorgsky by chance in the late 1850s, but only in 1862 did he meet Balakirev and fall under his spell.[9] Other young musical amateurs occasionally enjoyed Balakirev's friendship in the late 1850s and early 1860s (some, such as Apollon Gussakovsky, were even considered part of his "working company"),[10] but none of these stayed for long. By 1862 the Balakirev circle had reached its full complement of five amateur composers—Balakirev, Cui, Musorgsky, Rimsky-Korsakov, and Borodin— with critic Vladimir Stasov associated as friend and aesthetic adviser.

The five young musicians of the Balakirev circle shared not only a passion for music but also a nearly total lack of theoretical music training. Balakirev alone could be considered a genuine musician at the time of the group's formation, but he had acquired his training largely on his own through practical experience and studying scores, not from professors and courses in the traditional disciplines. He was born in Nizhny Novgorod on 21 December 1836 to an impoverished noble family.[11] His mother was his first piano teacher, and he showed sufficient musical talent to be sent to Moscow at the age of ten for a summer of piano lessons from the famous pedagogue Alexander Dubuc. Balakirev then began studying with Karl Eisrich, conductor of Nizhny Novgorod's theater orchestra,[12] through whom he acquired a patron in the person of Alexander Ulybyshev, a wealthy landowner. Ulybyshev was the author of a massive biography of Mozart and a great music-lover, who regularly arranged evenings of chamber music and occasionally even hired the local theater orchestra to perform major symphonic works for himself and his friends. Recognizing Balakirev's precocious talent, he invited him to take part in his frequent musical soirées and even to conduct the orchestra.[13]

At Ulybyshev's Balakirev came to know first-hand an enormous quantity of Western European music, especially Mozart and Beethoven, and enjoyed the experience of rehearsing an orchestra, all while he was still in his early teens.[14] Despite his piano lessons and extensive exposure to the classics of European music, however, Balakirev never formally studied music theory or composition. There was no one in Nizhny Novgorod to help him with these subjects. Nevertheless, he wanted to write music, so he began composing without any systematic theoretical training. A fellow student and friend at Kazan University, where Balakirev studied in the department of mathematics and physics from September 1853 to June 1855, writes in his memoirs of Balakirev's early compositional efforts:

> I even remember the two compositions he wrote at Kazan: a fantasia on themes from some opera (in the then fashionable style of such transcriptions) and an attempt at a quartet, which he began to write without any guidance at all. I do not remember his having any textbook on music theory, orchestration, or harmony. There were no Russian textbooks, and he did not know German very well.[15]

Thanks to his natural talent and aptitude, Balakirev's haphazard musical training bore surprisingly mature fruit. When Ulybyshev took the nineteen-year-old youth to visit Glinka in St. Petersburg, Balakirev greatly impressed the older musician with his skill as both a composer and pianist, performing his own piano fantasy on themes from his host's opera *A Life for the Tsar*.[16] In his first six months in St. Petersburg Balakirev appeared before the musical public three times—as soloist in a piano concerto of his own composition at a University concert, in a solo piano recital, and in a chamber music concert. Although not yet twenty, he won public recognition as both a pianist and a composer of great promise.[17] The combination of natural aptitude, a passion for music, and the advantage of extensive practical experience hearing, playing, and even conducting the classics of Western music had made him a practicing musician of considerable attainment even without formal training. In this respect he far exceeded the other young composers of his circle. When they joined the group, they were all strictly musical amateurs with outside professions and little musical experience.

César Cui was a newly commissioned officer in the Engineering Corps of the Russian army and only twenty-one years of age when he met Balakirev in 1856. He was born on 6 January 1835 in the Polish-Lithuanian city of Vilna, the son of a Lithuanian mother and a French father who had taken part in Napoleon's Moscow campaign and remained in Russia after the Grand Army's retreat.[18] He learned to play the piano at home and, while still a child, performed piano arrangements of fashionable Italian operas for his father. At the age of fifteen he began to study music theory and composition with the Polish composer Stanislaw Moniuszko, but the lessons ended after only seven months when Cui was sent off to St. Petersburg to the academy of military engineering.[19] This, along with frequent visits to St. Petersburg's opera houses and some amateurish attempts at composing an opera, constituted the extent of Cui's musical education before meeting Balakirev.

Musorgsky was two years younger than Balakirev and four years younger than Cui. Born into an ancient family of landowners in a village in the Pskov province on 9 March 1839, he studied the piano as a child with his mother and then with a local German woman. At age ten he moved with his family to St. Petersburg, where he continued his piano study with the well-known pedagogue Anton Herke.[20] Musorgsky became an accomplished pianist, surpassed in Balakirev's group only by Balakirev himself, but he learned nothing of music theory or composition. His brother reported: "Herke gave my brother Modest lessons only in piano playing and nothing else."[21] In 1856 Musorgsky entered the prestigious Preobrazhensky Guards. He frequently attended the Italian Opera with his fellow officers and entertained them at the piano with excerpts from the fashionable Verdi and Bellini works of the day.[22] Borodin has left a vivid description of Musorgsky, the musician, in 1856:

> Modest was then still very boyish, extremely elegant, the very picture of a young officer. . . . Ladies all made a fuss over him. He would sit down at the piano, and smartly lifting his hands in the air, play excerpts from *Trovatore, Traviata,* etc., very sweetly and gracefully, while all around him murmured together, "charmant, delicieux," and so forth.[23]

Until he met Balakirev, Musorgsky showed no especially serious interest in music. His talent at the piano amounted to little more than an amusing and even fashionable avocation, which facilitated his access to society.

Rimsky-Korsakov was only seventeen when he joined Balakirev's group in 1861, making him the youngest—a full seven years younger than Balakirev. Born in the town of Tikhvin in Novgorod province on 6 March 1844 into an aristocratic family long distinguished for its government service, he was prepared as a child for a career in the navy and entered the Corps of Naval Cadets in St. Petersburg at the age of twelve. Except for piano lessons with a local teacher, his parents gave little support to his early interest in music. Not until he took up residence in the Russian capital did he first hear adequate performances of great music.[24] Rimsky describes in his memoirs the deep impression left on him by his visits to Petersburg's Italian and Russian Operas, the University concerts, and the symphonic programs given during Lent by the Imperial Theater Directorate. These encouraged his musical leanings, and in the fall of 1859 he began piano lessons with Fedor Kanille, a teacher of no great distinction.[25] Two years later Kanille introduced him to Balakirev. Although by then Rimsky had already attempted his first compositions, he did not even know, by his own admission, the names of all the chords and intervals.[26]

Alexander Borodin was the oldest of the five composers in Balakirev's circle; he was born in St. Petersburg on 31 October 1833, over a year before Cui, more than three years before Balakirev, five before Musorgsky, and more than a decade before Rimsky-Korsakov. The last to join the group, he had already earned the degree of Doctor of Medicine in 1858, had spent nearly three years studying abroad, and was well on the way to becoming a chemist of international reputation.[27] As a musician, however, he was no better off than his companions. As a youth he had studied the flute, piano, and cello, but he never became truly proficient at any of them. He also began writing music while still in his early teens but without any instruction in composition. He did know a great deal of music when he met Balakirev, for he had attended many concerts and private evenings of chamber music in St. Petersburg.[28] He had also spent several years in Germany, where he heard complete Wagner operas years before any were staged in Russia and came to know other new German music as well.[29] Nevertheless, until he joined the Balakirev circle Borodin considered himself a scientist whose musical interests had only peripheral significance.[30]

The members of the Balakirev circle exemplified perfectly Anton Rubinstein's diagnosis of the weaknesses of musical life in mid-nineteenth-century Russia. None of the five had substantial formal training in music beyond instruction on an instrument. Only Balakirev and Borodin were acquainted with a broad range of Western music; the others mainly knew the fashionable Italian operas of the day. Finally, only Balakirev had devoted himself entirely to music—composing and giving piano lessons. The rest pursued nonmusical careers, which limited the time they could devote to their musical avocation. Their attempts to overcome their deficiencies did not follow, however, in the direction that Rubinstein pointed. Instead of imitating Western European models of musical education, they relied on their own communal, practical studies under the guidance of Balakirev, their most experienced musician.

Balakirev dominated the circle by the sheer force of his personality and talent. He inspired the others to take up music seriously and molded their musical opinions. Cui declared later, "Balakirev was a full head taller than the rest of us in everything. He busied himself with us like a broodhen with her chicks."[31] A born leader, Balakirev craved followers on whom he could exercise his will. Throughout his life, he sought out younger or less experienced friends who would submit to his direction. If his instructions and criticism were defied or ignored, he soon rejected the pupils and moved on to new ones.[32] In the early years of the circle, however, Balakirev had little trouble commanding obedience. Rimsky-Korsakov describes in his memoirs the power Balakirev exercised over his musically inexperienced associates in the early 1860s:

Young, with marvellously alert fiery eyes, with a handsome beard; unhesitating, authoritative, and straightforward in speech; ready at any moment for beautiful piano improvisation, remembering every music bar familiar to him, instantly learning by heart the compositions played for him, he was bound to exercise that spell as none else could. . . . His influence over those around him was boundless, and resembled some magnetic or mesmeric force.[33]

Balakirev had gained his own musical expertise by two methods: study of the musical classics and trial-and-error composition. These were also the means he applied in training the members of his circle. Meeting with them either individually or as a group, now at his own apartment, now at Cui's, Vladimir Stasov's, or later Borodin's, Balakirev undertook to turn them into composers.[34]

Although neither the place nor the composition of the gatherings was constant, the correspondence among the circle's members and Rimsky's memoirs indicate that the sessions were frequent and always centered on playing and discussing music. In the early years, before Rimsky and Borodin joined the company, these evenings of music amounted to nothing less than a critical survey of the major musical compositions of the preceding hundred years. As Balakirev himself admitted, he was no theoretician and could not teach the rules of harmony or counterpoint, but he used the classics of Western music and the works of Glinka to explain what he termed "the form of composition." Of his early work with Musorgsky Balakirev later wrote: "we played in four-hand piano arrangements (he was a splendid pianist) all the repertory of classical music, old and new, that existed then, namely, Bach, Handel, Mozart, Haydn, Beethoven, Schubert, Schumann, Berlioz, and Liszt. He already knew well—not without some assistance from me—the music of Glinka and Dargomyzhsky."[35] Along the way, Balakirev would analyze and criticize each work as best he could with no systematic knowledge of harmony or counterpoint. In this way he imparted to his pupils his own aesthetic views on music and a rudimentary knowledge of its structure while simultaneously broadening their knowledge of musical repertory as well as his own. Both Cui and Musorgsky claim in memoirs that under Balakirev's guidance they became acquainted with all the great works of the masters of music.[36] This is undoubtedly an exaggeration, for they apparently studied mainly the instrumental works of the major Austro-Germanic composers of the eighteenth and early nineteenth centuries, but it is true that Balakirev greatly expanded their musical horizons and made them aware of an enormous quantity of music previously unknown to them.

By the time Rimsky-Korsakov joined the group the circle already had three regular members with a considerable knowledge of the musical classics and several completed compositions of their own. As a result, Balakirev's perusal of musical literature with his associates shifted its emphasis from the works of the past to the latest compositions from abroad or from the circle itself. In the early 1860s the music of Berlioz, which was just beginning to be known in Russia, was played especially often, along with works by Balakirev, Cui, and Musorgsky.[37] Still, the object of the gatherings was the same—to impart Balakirev's musical opinions and an understanding of basic musical structure and form. In his memoirs, Rimsky describes how Balakirev would introduce a new work in fragments, a few bars at a time, not even always in order, for the sake of explaining and judging each part. Instead of considering a composition as a whole, Balakirev would criticize each element separately: "The first four bars were said to be excellent, the next eight weak, the melody immediately following good for nothing, the transition from it to the next phrase fine, and so forth."[38]

Balakirev considered the study and criticism of scores by other composers sufficient training in composition for his circle. Since he himself had begun composing with no preparatory schooling, he could see no need of it for others. Knowledge would come through practice.[39] Therefore, he did not hesitate to encourage his pupils to tackle even advanced musical compositional forms from the very beginning of their training. For example, almost immediately after he met Musorgsky, whose familiarity with music literature was notably limited, Balakirev assigned his new pupil a symphonic movement. Musorgsky apparently found the work very difficult and soon wrote Balakirev to report that he was sick to death of his Allegro, yet it remained unfinished. "I have not despaired, however," he added, "and hope to see you next week to try out my apprentice work on your piano."[40] As the student pieces progressed, Balakirev considered each new phrase, actively criticizing and often revising each bar. He would play the new works for the others in the circle, following the same analytic techniques that he used on other compositions. In his memoirs, Rimsky describes the process this way:

> A pupil like myself had to submit to Balakirev a proposed composition in its embryo, say, even the first four or eight bars. Balakirev would immediately make corrections, indicating how to recast such an embryo; he would criticize it, praise and extol the first two bars, but would censure the next two, ridicule them, and try hard to make the author disgusted with them.[41]

Balakirev did not limit such supervision only to the early years of his pupils' training but continued it throughout his association with them. Nearly a decade after Cui attached himself to Balakirev, for example, his compositions were still subject to Balakirev's inspection and retouching.[42]

The composition of Rimsky-Korsakov's First Symphony illustrates Balakirev's role in his companions' works. At their first meeting in 1861, the seventeen-year-old naval cadet showed Balakirev the fragments of a symphony he had started, and Balakirev immediately insisted that the lad begin composing the work in earnest. It made no difference that his new pupil knew practically nothing of music theory. The first movement went well, and Balakirev approved it with few corrections, but he had to orchestrate the first page to provide Rimsky with a model for the rest of the movement.[43] A few months later found Rimsky writing Balakirev for approval and advice about a good key setting of a theme he had worked out for the symphony's finale.[44]

Shortly afterwards, in the autumn of 1862, Rimsky's assignment to the clipper *Almaz* and the beginning of a three-year cruise interrupted his work on the symphony, but he later resumed composing aboard ship. His correspondence shows Balakirev's continued direction of the work. On 22 April 1863 Cui wrote Rimsky that Balakirev had received the slow movement of his symphony and was planning to write an extensive critique of it. Balakirev had played Cui the movement but, characteristically, "in excerpts (not all together)."[45] On 1 May Balakirev himself wrote Rimsky, pointing out the flaws he found in the composition and orchestration of the movement. Two weeks later Rimsky replied, ". . . indeed the ending is awful and trivial, I must change it. The pedal point in F sharp with the Schumannesque sentimentality and the triplet should be written and orchestrated as you wrote it." Rimsky dragged his feet about other changes: "As for the A Major fortissimo passage, I agree it must be changed. You don't like it [and] I believe you when you say it's weak; but the fact of the matter is, that . . . to rewrite it means to rewrite the entire andante because the whole thing leads to this fortissimo."[46] Ten days later Rimsky wrote Cui about his work on the score for the rest of the symphony:

> I am now making a clean copy of the first movement, correcting the orchestration as well as I know how and rewriting the places Balakirev corrected. I will do the same with the finale and scherzo; although they do not have Balakirev's written corrections I will correct them from memory of what he told me and from my own judgment.[47]

In June Balakirev wrote Rimsky that he was reorchestrating the symphony's slow movement and promised a full exposition of the secrets of scoring upon Rimsky's return to St. Petersburg.[48] If Balakirev exercised such strict supervision over the work of a pupil hundreds of miles away, one can easily imagine how thoroughly he controlled those he saw regularly in person.

Balakirev did not treat all the members of his circle alike, however. Cui, the first member of the group, always enjoyed a special status. From the start he impressed Balakirev with his knowledge of opera, and from then on Balakirev, who was little interested in vocal music, relied on his opinion in such matters.[49] As a result, according to Rimsky, Balakirev allowed Cui greater freedom than the rest of the group, "treating with indulgence many an element that did not meet his own tastes." Even the similarity of Cui's work to certain French comic operas that Balakirev ordinarily despised "was justified by his half-French origin and was kindly winked at."[50] Such special treatment cannot be explained by Cui's abilities as a composer, for he was, without a doubt, the least talented member of the circle. Balakirev must simply have been influenced by their long-time personal relationship. Cui had shared Balakirev's earliest Petersburg successes and watched the entire development of the group. Their correspondence reveals an intimacy and an element of equality that never appears in Balakirev's correspondence with any of his other pupils.[51] As a result, Balakirev shrugged off the flaws in Cui's compositions.

Balakirev treated the rest of the group more as students than colleagues; the degree of cordiality in the relationship was proportionate to their compliance with Balakirev's ideas. At first he was very friendly with Musorgsky, serving not only as his music teacher but also as his confidant.[52] After a few years, however, Balakirev grew impatient both with Musorgsky's way of life and his music. Early in 1861 they quarreled bitterly; Balakirev accused Musorgsky of dissipating his talent in dissolute living, and Musorgsky replied that it was time for Balakirev to stop viewing him "as a child who needs to be led so he will not fall."[53] About the same time, Musorgsky's compositions began to diverge from his teacher's ideals. When Balakirev's efforts to bring his unruly pupil back to the prescribed path failed, he gave him up as a lost cause.[54] Rimsky later recalled that Balakirev and Cui, though "sincerely fond" of Musorgsky, "treated him like a lesser light, and of little promise at that, in spite of his undoubted talent." Balakirev frequently said he had " 'no head' or that his 'brains were weak.' "[55] In the summer of 1863, for example, Balakirev wrote that he considered Musorgsky "almost an idiot."[56] Although he remained in the group and shared its basic aesthetic principles, Musorgsky was considered something of an *enfant terrible* for the eccentricities in both his personal life and his music.[57]

Whatever hopes Balakirev had had for Musorgsky he quickly transferred to Rimsky-Korsakov when the latter joined the circle. Here, at least at first, Balakirev found the obedient and respectful pupil Musorgsky could not be. Balakirev liked both Rimsky's music and his obvious devotion. In October 1862 Balakirev wrote Vladimir Stasov, "Korsinka [his affectionate nickname for Rimsky] has made me terribly happy not just by his own compositions but also by the following: I played my concerto for him and he exclaimed, striking the table with his fist, that it is better than 'Lear' [Balakirev's incidental music to *King Lear,* which was much admired within the circle]."[58] For a long time Rimsky continued to follow Balakirev's directions.[59] The result was a close friendship but not an equal one. "If Balakirev loved me as a son and pupil," Rimsky recalled, "I, for my part, was literally in love with him. In my eyes his talent surpassed all bounds of possibility, and every word and opinion of his were absolute truth to me."[60] In

1862, shortly after Rimsky's ship left Petersburg on its lengthy cruise, Balakirev wrote, "I miss you very much, . . .the more so now since I no longer expect anything to come of anyone [here] except Cui. . . . I expect great things from you and set my hopes on you like an old woman on her young lawyer nephew."[61]

Balakirev's relationship with Borodin was friendly but a bit formal—neither as close as with Rimsky nor as stormy as with Musorgsky. Borodin had two qualities much appreciated by Balakirev: talent and a willingness to accept Balakirev's direction. Within a month of his joining the circle, Borodin's fiancée noticed that he had been "definitively reborn" as a musician.[62] Balakirev himself later wrote of Borodin's early studies with him:

> He set about enthusiastically composing his symphony in E flat. Every bar passed my scrutiny, and this process helped develop in him the critical artistic sense that ultimately defined his musical tastes and sympathies. . . . As for my work with him, it consisted of friendly discussions and took place not only at the piano but also over the tea table. Borodin (like all of our band then) would play his new composition and I would comment on its form, orchestration, etc.[63]

Their relationship was friendly but not as personal as Rimsky's ties with Balakirev. The manuscript score of Borodin's First Symphony, which is filled with corrections in Balakirev's hand,[64] testifies that Borodin deferred to Balakirev's judgment in musical questions, but he was not an impressionable adolescent like Rimsky. He was Balakirev's senior by three years, a doctor, and, beginning in 1864, a professor of chemistry at the Academy of Medicine. Furthermore, his scientific work so severely limited his musical activity (he worked on his First Symphony for over five years) that Balakirev had little hope of a great musical future for him.

Although Vladimir Stasov was not a composer member of the Balakirev circle, he was so closely associated with the group from its inception that a word must be said about his relationship with Balakirev. Already thirty-two years old and a man of broad experience and interests, he met Balakirev in 1856. Educated in the School of Jurisprudence in St. Petersburg, he had lived in Western Europe for several years, had written articles on music, art, and literature, and was employed doing research for the St. Petersburg Public Library.[65] His acquaintance with Balakirev flowered into close friendship that has been documented in nearly two hundred extant letters, many very lengthy and personal, for the years from 1858 to 1867.[66] The letters chronicle a sometimes stormy relationship marked by violent quarrels, usually over politics,[67] but they also show that each considered the other his most intimate friend and relied on his support in times of emotional stress.[68] Balakirev and Stasov frequently visited one another, attended operas and concerts together, and Stasov often took part in gatherings of Balakirev's circle of young composers. As a practicing critic of the arts and avowed disciple of Vissarion Belinsky, nineteenth-century Russia's most influential literary commentator, Stasov provided a theoretical basis for the artistic principles and musical tastes of Balakirev and his followers.

As indicated earlier, Balakirev thoroughly dominated his circle, at least through the mid-1860s, imposing his musical standards and aesthetic position on the rest of the group. One can, therefore, speak legitimately of the circle's common musical views in this period. Even so, these views are surprisingly difficult to define precisely. It is an accepted commonplace in the historical literature on nineteenth-century Russian culture that the group stood for Russian nationalism in music,[69] but like most such generalizations, this statement, while not incorrect, is so over-simplified that it does more to confuse the issue than to clarify it. Nationalism, although part of its platform, was not the sole basis of the group's ideas, nor did it mean simply support of Russian composers or music based on Russian subjects or folk melodies, as is usually assumed.

Balakirev certainly advocated a Russian national school of composition, following Glinka's lead. According to a friend of Balakirev at Kazan University, he worked out his musical platform only after moving to St. Petersburg in 1855,[70] but by then, as we have seen, he had already been sufficiently attracted to the music of Glinka to compose a piano fantasia on themes from *A Life for the Tsar*. His patron, Alexander Ulybyshev, was a friend and admirer of Glinka,[71] and he promptly introduced the not yet nineteen-year-old Balakirev to the famous composer in December 1855. Balakirev's contacts with the great man, although lasting for only four months, profoundly shaped his aesthetic views.[72] After their initial meeting Balakirev frequently returned to Glinka's home to play his own early compositions and to discuss music.[73] Glinka was so impressed by his young colleague that when he left St. Petersburg for Berlin in April 1856, he made his sister promise to entrust the musical training of his beloved niece Olga to no one else should he himself die. According to his sister's memoir, Glinka told her, "Balakirev is the first person in whom I have found views so similar to my own in all things concerning music. You can entrust little Olga to him completely and be assured that she will follow in the footsteps of your brother, and I tell you that in time Balakirev will be a second Glinka."[74]

Glinka's most important legacy for Balakirev was the idea of a distinctly and self-consciously nationalist Russian music. According to his memoirs, Glinka had decided to try "composing like a Russian" after becoming dissatisfied with the Italianate works he was writing while living in Milan in the early 1830s.[75] To do this, he turned to Russian folk songs, the popular musical language of Russia, as the basis for a new style of art music. Russian composers had incorporated folk tunes in their works long before Glinka but in an essentially superficial manner, grafting the tunes on the established forms of Western music. Glinka, however, attempted to create an original musical language from authentic folk music or, more often, invented themes that mimicked the melodic, harmonic, and rhythmic idiosyncrasies of Russian popular song.[76] In doing so, he pushed beyond the conventional boundaries of harmony and form that the most advanced Western composers of his day were just beginning to expand and created a personal style marked by daring harmonies, dynamic and flexible rhythms, and bright, pure orchestral colors.[77] This was the innovative style Balakirev accepted as the hallmark of authentic Russian national music.

Balakirev modeled his own compositions after Glinka's example[78] and fostered the same approach among his students as the only legitimately "Russian" way to write music. For a composer to be Russian or to use Slavic folk material was not enough to satisfy him. He condemned such popular Russian song composers as Gurilyov and Aliabiev as "gypsy authors who successfully produce their pieces in that center of all that is slavish, indecent and unartistic—in Moscow," and he dismissed Anton Rubinstein's *Sons of the Steppe* as "a German opera in 4 acts," despite its Russian setting and "a dash of Little Russian [i.e., Ukrainian] themes, which give a certain amount of color" to its "commonplace" music.[79] In fact, the use of actual or imitation Russian folk themes had little importance for Balakirev's judgment of the "Russian" character of a work. Glinka had applied his personal style to folk tunes of many nations—Poland, Spain, and Persia, among others—and Balakirev accepted this as part of the Russian national style. He himself frequently used non-Russian folk material, as in his incidental music to Shakespeare's *King Lear,* his most important work during the early years of the circle, which he based on old English folk tunes supplied by Vladimir Stasov.[80] Balakirev, as Glinka before him, became particularly enthralled by melodies from the Caucasus Mountains and used them as the basis of two more of his important works, the piano fantasia *Islamey* and his symphonic poem *Tamara.*[81] Balakirev's acceptance of Cui as an exponent of his circle's principles[82] further demonstrates the essential irrelevance of Russian folk music to Balakirev's definition of a Russian national style, for Cui's music rarely resorts to folk themes of any kind and has "not a trace of anything Russian," as even Stasov admitted.[83]

Thus, the "Russian national style" advocated by Balakirev did not imply, as one might suppose, simply music written by Russians or employing Russian folk themes. Instead, it implied music composed in the innovative harmonies, rhythms, and compositional methods pioneered by Glinka. These derived originally from the idiosyncrasies of Russian folk music, but they could be applied to other material, whether of folk origin or not, and still produce music that Balakirev considered Russian. The so-called Russian style exemplified in the works of Balakirev and his circle was not linked directly to the tradition of Russia's native folk music but to Glinka's personal methods of composing. Most of the traits we now associate with the Russian musical style are Russian only because they were first used widely by Russian composers following Glinka's example.[84] Balakirev's advocacy of Russian music was not so much a matter of nationalism as of taste; he liked the kind of music Glinka wrote, he composed in the same style, and he taught his friends to do the same.

That Balakirev's musical stance was not essentially national becomes more obvious when one examines his views of Western music. As already discussed, he trained his pupils by analyzing the works not only of Glinka but also of all the great Western composers from Bach and Handel to his own day. It is true that some of this music, especially that of the eighteenth-century composers or such nineteenth-century classicists as Mendelssohn, interested Balakirev only as a pedagogic exercise,[85] and he could complain that an "ancient" symphony of Mozart always reminded him of the elaborate and outdated "coiffure of Maria Theresa."[86] But if Balakirev found little of interest in the classically oriented composers, he deeply loved many of the European Romantics. He liked the music of Schubert and Weber[87] and especially admired the powerful later works of Beethoven, such as his last string quartets and the *Missa Solemnis.*[88] He was even more impressed by advanced Romantic composers of his own day. As already mentioned, he played the music of Berlioz particularly often in the early 1860s. He was less consistently impressed by Liszt but admired some of his music. He once wrote Stasov that he knew the world was degenerating if only because "the Beethoven of our time is Liszt,"[89] but in the mid-1860s he frequently played the latter's *Mephisto Waltz* and *Todtentanz* for his circle and ridiculed Anton Rubinstein for his supposed low opinion of the second work.[90] Balakirev also loved the music of Robert Schumann. He once even had a dream in which the German musician appeared to him. As he described it to Stasov, he addressed Schumann in French, saying something like: "You see before you a Russian musician who is your great admirer." Then he tried to question Schumann about the form of the finale of his C Major Symphony and asked for his autograph![91] Of all the advanced Romantic composers of the day, only Wagner received little admiration in the Balakirev circle. Balakirev professed to find little of interest in his music,[92] and the writer Pyotr Boborykin, who knew Balakirev well both before and after he moved to St. Petersburg, claimed that he never heard any discussion about Wagner at his friend's.[93]

Dedication to the cause of "nationalism" in Russian music cannot alone explain Balakirev's tastes and aesthetic judgments about the music of Russian and Western composers. If his views have consistency, it must lie in some principle other than nationalism. The single thread that runs through all these opinions appears to be an admiration for what he judged to be innovative, original, free of hidebound tradition, and "expressive" in a truly contemporary way that rejected the canons of musical orthodoxy, especially as embodied in academic composition. He did not dislike Western music, only what he found to be the formalist, emotionally restrained, "traditional" music of Bach, Haydn, or Mendelssohn, and he equally disliked such music when it was the work of Russians. Even Glinka earned Balakirev's criticism for some conventional chromatic counterpoint and for adhering to traditional forms in his operas.[94] Balakirev liked not only Glinka's highly emotional, rhythmically vital, harmonically daring music; he also liked such music by Liszt, Berlioz, and Schumann. He admired not only Russian folk materials but also the freshness of all folk song—whether Russian, English, or Caucasian—which he recognized as a source for musical sonorities unbounded by the conventions of conservative European musical thought.

That a revolt against musical conservatism was the essence of Balakirev's musical position becomes clearer from an examination of the aesthetic discussions recorded in his correspondence with Vladimir Stasov, his philosophical mentor. Stasov followed the radical critics of his day, especially Belinsky and Chernyshevsky.[95] His understanding of their principles and his own ideas on art were sometimes vague, but he accepted their demand for realism or "truth" and social utility in art and their condemnation of the old classical standards of symmetry and formal beauty as the ultimate ideals in art. In the 1860s Stasov "violently berated the Academy of Fine Arts for its classicism and routine . . . his voice roared with new, national thunder, the living power of realism resounded in his arguments."[96] He applied the same principles to music and urged them on Balakirev. "The whole younger generation of Russia was brought up on Belinsky," Stasov wrote Balakirev in 1859, "and so I want you to get to know his marvelous, direct, clear, and powerful nature. I love him *very* much."[97] The correspondence of the two friends is sprinkled with discussions of the radical critics and appointments to read and debate the writings of Chernyshevsky or Dobroliubov.[98] How much influence such radical thought had on the circle is open to question. Its members certainly discussed the need for truth in music and were known to acquaintances as "realist-popularists,"[99] but realism applies with notorious difficulty to such an abstract art form as music. Of the five, only Musorgsky eventually developed a workable concept of musical realism, based on matching in music the general contour and rhythmic cadences of specific examples of human speech.[100] The important point, however, is not the direct influence of Chernyshevsky or Dobroliubov on Balakirev and Stasov but the fact that the latter considered themselves adherents of the most advanced aesthetic school, which rejected the traditional academic concepts of art.

Likewise, in their discussions of specific questions of musical aesthetics,

Balakirev and Stasov consistently took the most radical position. Their very belief in a national school of composition and the use of folk music in art music was still considered shocking by some traditionalists in their day. On the contemporary issue of program music versus absolute music (that is, music based on some specific poetic or pictorial subject versus music devoid of extramusical implications) they clearly sided with the then still controversial program music. "Any good musical composition carries within itself a program," wrote Balakirev, "about which the author may not even be conscious."[101] Likewise, they agreed that the traditional formal schemes— sonata, rondo, and so forth—were no longer mandatory. "The symphony must cease to be composed of four movements as Haydn and Mozart thought it up one hundred years ago," wrote Stasov. "The future form of music is formlessness."[102] In his encouragement of the concept of Russian national music, Stasov emphasized that such music would have to be not only Russian but *new*. In the letter just quoted he speaks of his belief that Balakirev is creating "Russian music—new, great, undiscovered, never before imagined, even *newer* in form (and especially content) than that which Glinka undertook, to the scandal of all."[103]

Balakirev's views on music education further support the thesis that revolt against musical conservatism and academism lay at the heart of his aesthetic position. Having never systematically studied harmony and counterpoint, Balakirev thought them unnecessary or even harmful, because they stifled imagination.[104] As the corollary to this principle, he always denied the validity of any authority beyond personal judgment. Although in practice he attempted to impose his own tastes on his colleagues, he denied in theory even his own right, much less that of any other teacher or critic, to dictate their views. For example, he wrote Rimsky in 1862: "Once and for all I advise you not to adhere blindly to any authorities; believe more in yourself than in anyone else." He offered his personal opinions as an experienced musician but cautioned his pupil not to accept them unquestioningly.[105] He rejected on principle the idea that any chord, any form, any orchestral combination was wrong simply because it violated a traditional rule or because some teacher or critic said so. Balakirev acknowledged no judge as superior to his own ear and personal taste.

The fundamental theme of Balakirev's musical creed was not so much nationalism as musical modernism and rejection of established authorities. His advocacy of the innovative Russian style pioneered by Glinka represented but one aspect of a larger campaign for "advanced" music in a country where foreigners and those he considered conservatives dominated musical life. This is not to say that Balakirev was not personally nationalistic. His letters indicate a strong pride in the Russian nation,[106] and at times his patriotism took on strong overtones of Slavophilism (the movement of ultranationalists who rejected the West as a model for Russian development) as it did when he wrote Stasov in 1863 that he preferred "Orthodoxy in all its crudity to civilized, petty Protestantism," the despotism of Tsar Nicholas to the "vapid constitution" advocated by some of the Russian liberals.[107] But Balakirev's national pride, although it added fervor to his advocacy of the music of Glinka and his circle, did not override his more basic aesthetic principles. However strong his nationalism, Balakirev never accepted a work of music just because it was composed by a Russian or was based on a Russian subject or Russian folk melodies. It also had to meet his criteria of modernness. This remained the touchstone of his musical judgments, the basis for all the musical views he inculcated in his circle.

Given such an aesthetic stance, it is not at all surprising that Balakirev and his circle opposed the work of Anton Rubinstein, the musical conservative and supporter of academic training. As early as 1856, before Balakirev had even met Rubinstein but after the latter's attack on Russian musical amateurism was published in Vienna, Balakirev and Cui already considered themselves his ideological opponents. The idea that they might ever sympathize with Rubinstein's position seemed laughable.[108] In the summer of 1858 Stasov wrote Balakirev, "when you return [to St. Petersburg] Rubinstein will be here, and you will have to take part in skirmishes of one kind or another with him"[109] The ideological basis of Balakirev's opposition to Rubinstein was not, however, essentially a matter of Russian nationalism versus Westernism but of modernism versus conservatism.

Balakirev disliked both Rubinstein's musical taste and his ideas on music education. In conversations with his friends, Balakirev railed against Rubinstein's music, which he termed "antimusic" or "nonmusic."[110] Disparaging comments about Rubinstein's compositions appear in a number of Balakirev's letters.[111] As Balakirev's friend Boborykin put it, Balakirev's circle "of course recognized Rubinstein as the 'first pianist'; but they did not get along with him especially well, apparently because he kept aloof from them, was not attracted by their 'Russian' orientation, and adhered to the traditions of classical German music."[112] Balakirev occasionally expressed interest in some of Rubinstein's works but only in certain technical aspects or, as in the case of the "Ocean" Symphony, in their programmatic content.[113] Balakirev and Rubinstein shared an appreciation for the music of Beethoven, Schumann, and even Glinka, but beyond this their tastes diverged sharply. Balakirev could not accept Rubinstein's fondness for the eighteenth-century composers or for Mendelssohn, and he frequently ridiculed Rubinstein's distaste for the supposed excesses and harmonic daring of Liszt or Berlioz. Similarly, he deplored Rubinstein's rufusal to accept the idea of nationalism in music and denied, on this basis, that the latter could properly appreciate Glinka, despite his claims. Balakirev and his friends saw particular danger in

Rubinstein's plans for a conservatory because they felt it would perpetuate its founder's false musical tastes and ideals. Musorgsky once summed up the circle's view of the new music school in a colorful depiction of it as a place where Rubinstein (whom he dubbed "Stupidstein" [*Tupinshtein*]) and Zaremba, "in professorial, antimusical togas, first pollute their students' minds, then seal them with various abominations."[114]

Differences in principles and taste certainly set Balakirev and his circle apart from Rubinstein, but they do not alone fully explain the antipathy that the circle felt for the founder of the Russian Musical Society. More personal factors were at work as well. Balakirev and his friends, like Rubinstein, were young musicians facing the very limited opportunities offered by St. Petersburg for a successful musical career. Cui, Borodin, Musorgsky, and Rimsky-Korsakov all had nonmusical professions when they met Balakirev, but only the first two found their primary careers satisfying and followed them throughout their lives. Musorgsky left the Preobrazhensky Guards in 1858 to devote all his time to music and went into government service in 1863 only because financial reverses at the family estate following the emancipation of the serfs in 1861 forced him to earn a living.[115] Rimsky quickly grew disillusioned with naval life, which, as he says in his memoirs, hardly suited his rather shy, refined character;[116] music had been his first love, and he wanted to make a career of it. Even Cui and Borodin, although devoted to their respective professions, took their musical work seriously and wanted public recognition of it.

Success in music was even more important for Balakirev, for he had neither the desire not the qualifications for any other career, and he had no other source of income. His father, an impoverished landowner, could never hold a job, even as a menial bureaucrat. He not only could not support his son but actually had to ask Mily for help in supporting himself and his unmarried daughters.[117] Ulybyshev had sponsored the young Balakirev and even paid for his trip to St. Petersburg, but Ulybyshev soon returned to Nizhny Novgorod, where he died in 1858, leaving Balakirev to rely on his own resources while trying to make a career for himself in music.[118] Balakirev faced essentially the same difficulties that Anton Rubinstein had met a few years before when he first tried to make a place for himself in St. Petersburg's musical life. There were simply very few opportunities for a young Russian to become a successful musician. He tried giving piano lessons and playing in fashionable salons, but this barely supported him: "I eat, I sleep, I go calling, I give lessons, I play at soirées of the aristocracy," he wrote a Moscow friend, "yet I never have any money."[119] Furthermore, like Rubinstein he was too serious a musician to be happy as a piano virtuoso. In 1857 he wrote, "All virtuosos are the most antimusical people. They think first of all of money, not of art. . . . Of all virtuosos only Liszt became a musician, because he stopped being a virtuoso."[120] Like Rubinstein, Balakirev tried composing as, in his eyes, a more honorable way of earning a livelihood as a musician. 1859 witnessed the first public performances of Balakirev's orchestral works. This brought him some recognition from the Petersburg musical world but no money. That same year he sold fourteen songs to a publisher but received only fifteen rubles for each.[121] Glinka had usually been paid fifty rubles for a song.[122]

Under such circumstances, Balakirev and his friends could not help but envy Anton Rubinstein's success at creating for himself a permanent post as a leading professional musician in St. Petersburg. Although he rejected for himself the role of virtuoso pianist, Balakirev still envied the adulation Rubinstein received as a pianist in high society. An unmistakable aroma of sour grapes pervades his account of a concert he gave in Yaroslavl, a distinctly provincial Russian town: "The ladies were so electrified by Beethoven's 'Appassionata' sonata, which I played quite well for them, that at supper when I reached for a chop, they fell all over each other rushing to pass me the platter, just exactly like Petersburg's fine ladies with Rubinstein."[123] Balakirev quickly added that he found such adulation very offensive, but his assertion does not quite ring true, for the very mention of this display of attention shows that he was proud of it and quite aware that Rubinstein regularly enjoyed such demonstrations of admiration.

Balakirev and his friends particularly resented Rubinstein's success as music director of the Russian Musical Society, because it not only gave him a permanent musical post that one of them might have occupied, but it also made him master of the most prestigious public forum in St. Petersburg for new instrumental compositions. Of course they craved performances of their works, but they knew very well that Rubinstein preferred music more traditional than theirs. Moreover, they considered him anti-Russian. Thus they felt defensive about submitting their music to the judgment of the Russian Musical Society and resented the necessity of depending on the Society in trying to establish their own musical reputations. In November 1860, for example, when the RMS decided to audition formally a composition Musorgsky had submitted for performance, Musorgsky took it as an insult, made some excuse, and withdrew the work. He explained to Balakirev, "That disreputable company just wanted [an excuse] to lecture me. I will get my chorus back, and I'm sincerely glad that I avoided a run-in with Rubinstein."[124] In the first years of the RMS's existence Balakirev and his friends submitted several compositions, and a number of them, especially by Cui, were accepted for performance.[125] But they soon began looking for a more dependable and tractable public outlet for their works, one that would not require them to submit themselves to Rubinstein's judgment.

To the reasons already given for the Balakirev circle's antipathy toward Anton Rubinstein—namely, professional jealousy and divergent aesthetic principles and musical tastes—must be added simple personal dislike. Balakirev seems to have inherited from Glinka not only his style of composition but his aversion for Rubinstein as well. Glinka was a sick and unhappy man when Balakirev met him, embittered by what he deemed the insufficient recognition he had received in his homeland.[126] Rubinstein's 1855 article criticising Russian music especially angered him. On 29 November 1855, only a few weeks before he met Balakirev, Glinka vented his anger at Rubinstein in an anti-Semitic tirade:

> The yid Rubinstein has taken it on himself to tell Germany about our music and has written an article in which he does us all dirty and handles my old woman—*A Life for the Tsar*—rather insolently.
>
> As a result, a few days later a column to defend my old woman and to deride the impudent yid Rubinstein appeared in the St. Petersburg German newspaper. The column . . . was written coolly and sensibly, but the yid got what he deserved.[127]

According to Vladimir Stasov, Glinka repeated his complaint about Rubinstein's article dozens of times to all those around him.[128] Although we have no definite evidence, it is probable that Glinka shared his opinion with Balakirev also and that some of the latter's antipathy for Rubinstein stemmed from his sympathy for his offended idol.[129]

Certainly simple prejudice and national chauvinism inflamed the antipathy of Balakirev and his followers for Anton Rubinstein and his work. Rubinstein and many of his associates, especially the teachers in the RMS's music classes and then the St. Petersburg Conservatory, were not of Russian descent. This aroused the resentment of many nationalistic Russians. During the second RMS concert season Prince Odoevsky wrote Count Wielhorsky that "enemies of the Society are spreading rumors that the whole Society was founded just to give Germans money and advancement."[130] The following May an anonymous defender of Rubinstein and the RMS described this problem in a prominent Petersburg newspaper:

> We still have here, you see, such fiery patriots, such ardent zealots of Russianness, who deny the right of being a great Russian artist to anyone whose name does not have the good fortune to end in "ov" or "in". On such grounds these fiery patriots, "hating the alien sound" in Mr. Rubinstein's name, not only do not allow him to call himself their compatriot but even make the most out-of-date allusions to his foreign origin.[131]

Balakirev and the members of his circle were among those who considered Rubinstein a foreigner and the RMS a German club. In their correspondence they referred to the Society as the "German Musical Ministry" or the *"Russian*!!! Musical Society."[132]

In fact, as will be seen, Balakirev's nationalism at times verged dangerously close to paranoid xenophobia directed particularly against what he rather vaguely termed "the Germans" or "the German party." While he never defined the terms clearly, they apparently referred to all non-Russians who tried to impose their ideas and customs on Russia. He associated the terms specifically with court circles, the St. Petersburg bureaucracy, and the leading cultural institutions of the country, in all of which non-Russians, especially Germans from abroad or the Baltic provinces of the Empire, played prominent roles.[133] Although his xenophobia only reached its height in the late 1860s, Balakirev linked the RMS and Rubinstein with the "German" threat to Russian society much earlier. In 1862, for example, he wrote Rimsky that the new conservatory's goal was to train "musical functionaries who would subject all Russian music to the yoke of the German (Baltic) musical generals, and then woe to those who oppose them. The Germans have a great advantage over us; having a base talent for organizing themselves, they easily subject unorganized Russians to their influence." In case there was any doubt about the identity of the "German generals" he feared, Balakirev added a note explaining that he meant "not Beethoven or Schumann, but Rubinstein himself, Karl Schubert, these conservatives incarnate."[134]

Even though Rubinstein was a Russian citizen, baptized in the Russian Orthodox Church, Balakirev and his friends generally referred to him as a German or a foreigner, presumably referring to his German musical tastes and training. The term "foreigner" was probably also a thinly veiled reference to his Jewish birth. Glinka's anti-Semitic attack on Rubinstein for his 1855 article on Russian music has already been cited, and anti-Semitism was a common prejudice among nationalistic Russians. Musorgsky frequently made overtly anti-Semitic comments about Rubinstein, such as a reference in a letter of June 1863 to "Petersburg's leading yids, Leschetizky, Jacob [i.e., Anton] Rubinstein and company."[135] While the rest of the group apparently restricted its epithets for Rubinstein to "German" or "foreigner,"[136] they occasionally used the common derogatory terms for Jews in other contexts.[137] Therefore, it seems reasonable to assume that anti-Semitism, either latent or overt, contributed to the Balakirev circle's hostility toward Rubinstein.

That the antipathy of the Balakirev circle toward the Russian Musical Society and its founder derived at least partly from personal aversion for Rubinstein and some of his associates is demonstrated by the circle's friendly ties with other leaders of the Society. The best example is Dmitri Stasov, who was one of the five directors of the RMS from 1859 to 1865 and Vladimir Stasov's brother. The brothers were very close,[138] and on occasion Vladimir even assisted Dmitri in the administrative work of the RMS.[139] During Balakirev's serious illness in 1858 Dmitri Stasov helped nurse him back to health, and the two remained on friendly terms thereafter.[140] Dmitri was also closely linked with Liudmila Ivanovna Shestakova, the sister of Glinka and a close friend of both Balakirev and Vladimir Stasov. After the death of her brother in 1857 Shestakova devoted her life to propagating his music in Russia and abroad. Dmitri Stasov, a practicing lawyer, helped her with the legal matters surrounding the ownership of Glinka's scores[141] and, on a more personal note, had a long love affair with her before his marriage in 1861; he was the father of her daughter Olga.[142]

Balakirev was also a friend of Vasily Kologrivov, another of the original directors of the RMS. Shortly after his arrival in Petersburg in 1855 Balakirev even lived for a time in Kologrivov's home. Kologrivov's wife Alexandra took piano lessons from Balakirev, and he dedicated one of his early piano works to her.[143] The good relations were maintained in the 1860s in spite of Kologrivov's friendship with Rubinstein and his work for the Russian Musical Society.[144] Likewise, Balakirev's circle maintained more-or-less close ties with Dargomyzhsky although he served on the RMS's Repertory Committee and the later became an "honored member" of the Society.[145] Musorgsky and Cui first met while attending one of Dargomyzhsky's musical gatherings. In the late 1850s Cui, Balakirev, and Musorgsky frequently visited the older composer—at first at his regular soirées, later privately—and the latter became something of an adviser to the group on vocal music, one field where Balakirev did not claim full competence or authority.[146] In the early 1860s the contacts grew less frequent, but, as will be seen, the last flowering of Dargomyzhsky's compositional efforts took place in the late 1860s in the closest association with the Balakirev circle and with their active support.

Obviously the differences in taste and aesthetic principles that separated Balakirev and his pupils from Anton Rubinstein and the Russian Musical Society were not strong enough to rule out friendly or even intimate relations between some members of the two supposedly antagonistic groups. The figures involved in the disputes and rivalries that are the subject of this study were, after all, human beings with personal needs and feelings that could outweigh ideological judgments. This does not mean that aesthetic principles counted for nothing; Rubinstein and the members of the Balakirev circle were all sincerely dedicated to their own views of the proper development of music in Russia and adhered to them even to the detriment of their reputations and financial security. But membership in ideologically opposed camps did not necessarily require personal enmity. It is not alone sufficient to explain Balakirev's hostility toward Rubinstein. The other causes described above—professional jealousy, personal dislike, and simple prejudice against foreigners and Jews—played a major, even commanding role.

Although the rivalry between Anton Rubinstein's Russian Musical Society and the Balakirev circle is the most famous feud in St. Petersburg's musical life in the 1860s, Rubinstein and the Society had another opponent, Alexander

Serov, who seemed at the time even more formidable. He has been virtually
forgotten until recently[147] because his music has not survived the test of time,
and his music criticism remains almost entirely untranslated from the
Russian, but in the 1860s both enjoyed immense influence and made him an
antagonist not to be ignored.

    Serov was considerably older than all the other principal figures (except
for Vladimir Stasov) in the musical rivalries of the 1860s. Born in 1820, he was
Rubinstein's senior by nearly a decade and Balakirev's by more than fifteen
years. Well educated and a graduate of the School of Jurisprudence,[148] Serov
was entirely self-taught in music, as he often proudly proclaimed, except for
piano lessons as a child.[149] Nevertheless, even one of his most bitter enemies
had to admit that he had "acquired a solid technical knowledge [of music]
through his own initiative and perseverance."[150] In 1851 he began writing
music criticism in various St. Petersburg periodical journals. From the
beginning of his career as a critic, Serov exhibited a particular knack for
attracting public notice through a combination of impressive erudition and
controversial opinions expressed with the utmost self-assurance. This was
especially true after he became the chief assistant in 1855 for the newly
founded weekly newspaper *Muzykal'nyi i teatral'nyi vestnik* [Music and
Theater Herald].[151] As a rival critic later recalled,

> Not three months passed before our whole musical world began to talk about Serov's
> articles. His titanic pride and self-assurance, awareness of his own power, and denial of all
> Russian critics before him appeared in every line written by A.N. Serov. This gave him
> from his very first articles great authority in the eyes of the contemporary public.[152]

The publisher of a journal in which Serov's work occasionally appeared in the
late 1850s even asserted that his reviews, despite their specialized nature,
attracted the interest of the general reading public by their controversial,
polemical style.[153]

    Serov doubtless angered as many readers as he pleased, but he earned
the grudging respect of even those who disagreed with him.[154] In 1856, for
example, Cui wrote Balakirev about a musical soirée he had attended at
Alexander Fitztum's: Serov's name came up in conversation, and soon the
entire gathering began to abuse him, "while admitting, nevertheless, that he is
the best critic in St. Petersburg."[155] Thus, when Rubinstein founded the
Russian Musical Society, Serov had already established himself as a
recognized authority on music even though he had yet to write a single
composition for public performance. At a time when the musical public of St.
Petersburg barely knew Balakirev, much less the members of his circle, Serov
had already won it genuine, if grudging respect.

    Serov adhered in his aesthetic position to decidedly "advanced" ideas for
his day. Much like the members of Balakirev's circle, he accepted in principle

the ideal of realism advocated by the radical literary critics; although he never defined clearly what he meant, he claimed to stand for "truth in music."[156] Serov, like Balakirev, also consistently denied the value of any musical authority beyond one's own judgment. "In our time," he declared, "in everything relating to the cognitive faculty—the role of authorities is 'zero.' "[157] Serov acknowledged no rules of form or harmony beyond his personal judgment.

In more concrete terms, Serov's taste in music reflected much the same sort of rejection of classicism and adherence to the most modern developments as did Balakirev's. He idolized Glinka and advocated the advancement of Russian music while at the same time admiring Beethoven and the vanguard among Western composers—Liszt, Berlioz, and Wagner.

In the 1850s Serov vied with Stasov in championing the music of Glinka in the press, and his praise knew no bounds. In one article, for example, he compared the Russian composer with Beethoven and lamented that he was not generally recognized as the equal of the German master. He concluded the article with a call to all Russians "who already understand and value this high order of genius" to work for the ever-wider dissemination of Glinka's music.[158] Serov himself accepted this obligation and even worked to propagandize Glinka's music abroad. In the summer of 1859, for example, he visited Franz Liszt in Weimar and pleaded Glinka's case before him. "I am enlightening him and his circle about *A Life for the Tsar* and *Ruslan,* "Serov wrote to a Russian friend. "Liszt thinks very highly indeed of much in Glinka's music."[159]

The claim that Serov lost his taste for Glinka during the 1860s—an idea advanced in some modern studies of Russian musical life in the late nineteenth century[160]—cannot be substantiated by documentary evidence. Once Serov himself began to compose operas, it is true, a hint of envy did occasionally creep into his attitude toward his idol,[161] but until his death Serov continued to preach the cause of Glinka's music, writing of it in the most glowing terms. The belief that Serov lost interest in Glinka in the 1860s probably derives from uncritical acceptance of Vladimir Stasov's authority. In a debate over the future of Russian music,[162] Stasov made unquestioned admiration of particular works of Glinka a shibboleth and then branded Serov a heretic for his supposedly incorrect appreciation of them. Because of Stasov's greater present-day fame and the relative accessibility of his writings, his view of Serov's opinion of Glinka, although inaccurate, has generally prevailed.

Serov did not confine his efforts in behalf of Russian music only to promoting Glinka's music. In his articles he frequently spoke out for the development of Russian music in general and chided the Petersburg public for its servile reverence toward the music of foreigners. In his enthusiastic review of the premiere in 1859 of Balakirev's *Overture on Three Russian Themes,* for example, he lauded Balakirev as a potential leader of Russian national music and denounced the audience's cool reception of the work—no fault of the composition, he noted sarcastically, but only of the composer's name being "Balakirev and not Balakirini or Balakirstein."[163]

Like Balakirev, however, Serov was selective in his advocacy of Russian music. The mere fact that a composer was Russian or that his composition was based on a Russian subject or Russian folk song was not sufficient to win his favor. Only scores adhering to the advanced idiom originated by Glinka satisfied him. Serov subjected Baron Boris Fitingof's opera *Mazeppa*, for example, to a withering assault for its old-fashioned forms and lack of dramatic realism, despite its Russian text, setting, and story, and its author's status as a respected Petersburg composer.[164]

Serov's devotion to Russian music did not preclude his appreciation of Western music. Like Balakirev, he believed that a musician must develop his critical faculties by studying "*all* the major works of *various* artists, with their *various* ideals, depending on their century, nationality, and individual character."[165] He did not, however, like all the music he studied. Again like Balakirev, Serov definitely preferred Beethoven and the modern, advanced composers of his day to the earlier classical masters. Although he confessed admiration for Mozart, he claimed he was no more than an extremely skillful musical craftsman;[166] Mendelssohn's music, except for a few works, he simply rejected out of hand on the grounds that it failed to meet the standards set by modern artistic ideals.[167] Beethoven, on the other hand, he loved. According to a close friend, Serov kept a portrait of Beethoven, "his idol," on his wall and, when he discussed music, spoke "mainly of Beethoven and Glinka."[168]

Serov also developed a passion for the modern composers who were hardly known yet in Russia: Berlioz, Liszt, and especially Wagner. In the summer of 1858 he traveled to Germany where he was able, as he wrote in his brief autobiography, "to become good friends with one of his chief musical heroes," Franz Liszt, in whose home he stayed almost the entire summer.[169] There he heard a good deal of Berlioz's music that was unknown to him and which he praised effusively in a letter to his sister Sofia.[170] Serov's most important experience that summer, however, was his acquaintance with the music of Wagner in performance. As early as 1856 Serov had been attracted by Wagner's early works, though he knew them only from scores or piano reductions;[171] experiencing them on the stage turned him into a passionate and life-long Wagnerite. During the summer of 1858 Serov wrote the first of many reviews and articles about his new idol. Dubbing opposition to Wagner "musical cretinism," he proclaimed that in fact "one must be an 'idiot' in the realm of art in order not to feel the breath of life and beauty that flows so fully in this music."[172] The next spring Serov wrote a friend that he was proud to consider himself Wagner's "apostle in Russia."[173] During the summer of 1859

Serov again visited Western Europe, this time to become personally acquainted with his hero. He succeeded in meeting Wagner and, as a result, became even more enthralled with his music, which he declared to be superior to all other music for the stage.[174]

Serov's Wagnerism set him apart from the Balakirev circle, where Wagner was little appreciated, but in other respects his aesthetic standards closely resembled those of Balakirev. He advocated realism in music, opposed all old standards of form or harmony, supported "advanced" Russian music, especially Glinka's, and preferred Beethoven, Berlioz, and Liszt to Mozart and Mendelssohn. Serov also agreed with Balakirev in his views on music education. He prided himself on being entirely self-taught as a musician and denied the value of all musical rules and authorities. Therefore, it is not surprising that he opposed formal conservatory training for musicians. In the summer of 1858 he wrote that he had always opposed conservatories because it seemed to him that "the 'artisan' element, which has nothing in common with art, always predominates in them."[175] Like Balakirev and his followers, Serov considered the discipline of conservatory training a threat to creative imagination and originality.

Considering Serov's musical tastes and objections to conservatory training, it comes as no surprise that he opposed Anton Rubinstein and the work of the Russian Musical Society. Like the Balakirev circle, Serov considered Rubinstein a "backward classicist with German training."[176] Even before Rubinstein founded the RMS and the St. Petersburg Conservatory, Serov had publicly denounced the very idea of a conservatory and condemned Rubinstein's music. The following passage from Serov's review of Rubinstein's piano quintet typifies the tone of his comments on the latter's music in the late 1850s:

> One's impression after the notorious and very long quintet is just the same as after his famous symphony.
> If the symphony is called "Ocean," why wasn't "Desert" placed on the title page of the quintet?—at least we would have known what to expect.
> How unfortunate that our era still cannot free itself from the influence of tedious Mendelssohnism and that precisely those aspects of that great talent which are weak and harmful for art . . . have found such a zealous and prolific disciple in Rubinstein![177]

In essence, Serov was publicly on record as opposed to all of Rubinstein's principles before the latter ever undertook to foster them through the RMS. Serov's battle against that organization and its work was a natural outgrowth of his long-held musical views.

Serov's antagonism toward Rubinstein, however, although consistent with his aesthetic position, did not spring exclusively from principle. As with the Balakirev group, Serov also had purely personal reasons for opposing

Rubinstein. He too was a Russian musician facing the limited opportunities offered by St. Petersburg for a successful career in music; he also found most of these opportunities blocked by Anton Rubinstein.

By the end of the 1850s Serov had won himself the leading position among St. Petersburg's music critics, but he was not satisfied. He wanted a more active role in the city's musical life. He complained to friends that he was nearing forty and had only "some transcriptions and little articles in journals" to show for it.[178] He undoubtedly also hoped to supplement the income from his journalistic career, for despite his steady employment by *Muzykal'nyi i teatral'nyi vestnik* from 1855 to 1860, he had been forced to resort to the uncongenial post of a part-time censor of foreign magazines in order to support himself.[179] Even the most prominent music critic in Russia could not live on the earnings of his pen alone.

Therefore, in the winter of 1858-59 Serov prepared a series of public lectures on music.[180] The project was a failure. On 20 February 1859 he wrote Prince Odoevsky for help in publicizing them because attendance was poor. "It is painful," he added, "that I have so long had to fight for my cause without success (either moral or pecuniary)."[181] A few weeks later his complaints, especially about lack of pecuniary success, were more bitter. On 7 April 1859 he wrote a close friend:

> My circumstances are abominable! Since the middle of the series (since the ninth lecture) there are only about forty listeners! Not a half-kopek profit; I am paying for the lights at the lectures with articles! There's Petersburg for you!
>
> For literally weeks at a time I don't have three kopeks. Sometimes I have to borrow to take a cab![182]

Serov foresaw even greater difficulties for his work in the future when Anton Rubinstein initiated his ventures in the Russian capital. On 2 April 1859 he wrote Franz Liszt that it appeared that Rubinstein would soon monopolize all music in St. Petersburg.[183] For a while Serov even considered leaving Russia entirely and settling in Germany, where he would have more opportunities for a successful career in music.[184]

In the fall of 1859, when the Russian Musical Society actually began its work, Serov wrote his sister that it was obviously impossible for him to have anything to do with an organization led by such people as Rubinstein and company. He succinctly defined his relationship to the RMS: "Ma position c'est l'opposition," adding that he did not think this was necessarily bad.[185] Nevertheless, he obviously envied Rubinstein's success in carving out for himself a central niche in St. Petersburg's musical life. Shortly after the opening of the St. Petersburg Conservatory Serov wrote a friend: "Had I not shown the public that I understand a bit about music, I would be one of the directors of the Musical Society, co-director of the Conservatory, and also something in the Theater Directorate. But now—it's impossible!!!—I'm a dangerous man!"[186] He later complained bitterly to the director of the Imperial theaters that although he had never been able to secure a post commensurate with his knowledge, "Russian, 'music-lovers (!)' fanatically sacrifice tens of thousands of rubles on the ventures of a stupid German pianist."[187]

Serov's hostility toward Rubinstein and the RMS was inflamed by his resentment of what he saw as the Society's snubs. Although he admitted that he could never get along with Rubinstein and company, he was nevertheless proud enough of his musical knowledge and sufficiently concerned for his status as an important musical figure in St. Petersburg to take offense when the RMS leaders offered him no role whatsoever in the Society nor even a complimentary membership so that he could attend its concerts as a critic. On 23 November 1859, the day of the RMS's first concert, Serov wrote Dmitri Stasov, a former friend, to complain that the Society had passed over someone like himself, who had done so much for music in Russia. "Either you *did not understand* your obligation," wrote Serov "or you wanted to worm your way into the favor of Rubinstein and Kologrivov, while ignoring the absurdity of your Society's role in relation to a man whom you cannot hide from the public!"[188] As if to prove his final point, he aired his grievances in his review of the RMS's first concerts, accusing the Society's leadership of being "bureaucratic" and "monopolistic" for not inviting the opinions of a variety of musical figures (presumably including himself) on the goals and organization of the Society. He also objected to his exclusion, despite his long years of musical work, from the list of honored guests invited free to the concerts. "I was not surprised at this," he added, "having noted among the Society's directors persons not especially well disposed to me personally; but I imagined that . . . the Society should place itself infinitely far above such petty vanities and personal considerations."[189] Even ten years later when he wrote his brief autobiography, Serov still complained bitterly that he was *"left aside completely, passed by* without even an observance of the formal proprieties by the founders of the Russian Musical Society."[190]

Serov also felt slighted by the RMS's treatment of a short choral piece he submitted to its Repertory Committee in the winter of 1859-60. He had begun composing twenty years earlier, while still a student, but had never completed a major work or released any composition for public performance.[191] Apparently encouraged by the RMS's promise to give native composers an opportunity to have their works performed and his own desire to find a more active and creative role in St. Petersburg's musical life, he finished a Christmas hymn for chorus and soloists and sent it to the Society. He anticipated, however, that he was submitting his work to an unsympathetic jury, so he accompanied it with a letter accusing the panel of partisanship, requiring the exclusion of one of the jury and demanding as well an explanation if the piece were turned down.[192] The Society accepted the work and scheduled it for the last concert of the first season, but it was not performed because the soloists found it too difficult to sing.[193] Serov considered this an affront to his competence as a composer and decided the RMS would never provide a platform for his music. Like the Balakirev group, he sought other outlets for his compositions in order to avoid offering them to the judgment of Rubinstein and his supporters.

Although Serov publicly condemned conservatory training for musicians, he privately resented not being invited to join the faculty of the St. Petersburg Conservatory. According to his wife, he interpreted this as an insult to his expertise as a musician.[194] Although he liked to deny that formal, academic music education conferred any special status on a musician, he realized only too well that others did not share this opinion. After his lecture series in the winter of 1858-59 failed to attract public support, he bitterly suggested to a friend that perhaps if he should go off to Berlin to "study fugues and such" and then try his lectures again, he might have more success.[195] He remained touchy throughout his life about his technical knowledge of music history and theory and constantly sought public recognition that he was, in fact, a fully qualified musician.

Finally, Serov's hostility toward Rubinstein and the Russian Musical Society was fed by chauvinism and anti-Semitism. Like Balakirev and his friends, Serov disliked Rubinstein not only because he was an ideological opponent and a more successful rival for leadership of St. Petersburg musical life, but also because he considered him a foreign intruder on an already severely restricted field of action. In his public writings about Rubinstein and the RMS, Serov frequently accused them of being "foreign" or "German";[196] in his private correspondence he was less reticent and vented his anti-Semitic feelings, dubbing the RMS a "Yid *Musikverein*"and calling the St. Petersburg Conservatory "some kind of piano synagogue" headed by a man "who babbles and writes in three or four languages, but equally ungrammatically in all (since all these languages are alien to him)."[197] Although detailed speculation about the psychological roots of Serov's anti-Semitism is out of the question here, it is not, perhaps, irrelevant to note that his mother was the daughter of a German Jew.[198] His anti-Semitism may have been a subconscious defense against the fear of being stigmatized as a Jew himself. In any case, his anti-Semitism added fervor to his antagonism toward Rubinstein.

Although Serov avowed his opposition to the Russian Musical Society, like Balakirev and his friends he did not and could not isolate himself from the organization's active members. Like the Balakirev circle, he was an occasional visitor at Alexander Dargomyzhsky's musical evenings in the 1850s,[199] and he did not sever his ties after Dargomyzhsky accepted appointment to the RMS's

Repertory Committee. In fact, in the early 1860s, when Serov was composing the opera *Judith,* he submitted parts of it for Dargomyzhsky's opinion.[200] Serov also maintained friendly relations with another member of the RMS Repertory Committee, Prince Vladimir Odoevsky.[201] Early in the 1860s Odoevsky retired to Moscow, but he continued to work for the RMS there. Serov not only continued to cultivate Odoevsky's friendship but also apparently enjoyed cordial relations with the entire Moscow leadership of the RMS, who, elected him an honorary member of the Society in 1865.[202] That same year the Moscow RMS invited Serov to join the faculty of the new Moscow Conservatory, which would open the following year—an offer Serov accepted.[203] Only the conviction that Moscow would be less hospitable to his compositions than St. Petersburg eventually persuaded him to change his mind.[204] Nevertheless, he came close to abandoning his long-standing condemnation of conservatory training when tempted by a permanent musical post and its concomitant public recognition of his musical erudition.

Financial need also occasionally forced Serov to kowtow before leaders of the St. Petersburg RMS. In December 1864, for example, he wrote the treasurer of the Society, who was also the wife of one of the wealthiest men in St. Petersburg, asking her help with present "difficulties and humiliations," evidently economic. A few weeks later he politely thanked her for her willingness to aid him, especially since he belonged to "an enemy camp!"[205] Such contacts with leading figures of the Russian Musical Society show that Serov, like Rubinstein and the members of the Balakirev circle, did not respond only to questions of aesthetic principle. Personal friendships, financial need, or ambition for a successful career and public recognition could outweigh ideological considerations.

It might seem that Serov and the Balakirev circle, given their similar aesthetic principles and tastes, should have been natural allies against Rubinstein and the Russian Musical Society. But this was not to be. Although Serov was a close friend of Balakirev, Vladimir Stasov, and company in the 1850s, toward the end of the decade they had a falling out, and in the 1860s they were to wage independent campaigns against Rubinstein while sniping simultaneously at one another.

Balakirev first met Serov at Glinka's home late in 1855. The young man from Nizhny Novgorod immediately impressed Serov with his talent. In February 1856, before Balakirev's first public appearance in St. Petersburg as a pianist and composer, Serov wrote a notice of the event in *Muzykal'nyi i teatral'nyi vestnik,* accompanying it with a favorable comment on Balakirev. Following the concert Serov wrote in the *Vestnik:* "On the occasion of the announcement of this concert I gave my opinion of the talent of this young musician, who is an excellent virtuoso and, still more important, a remarkable composer. And I do not retract a single word of my recommendation."[206] The two quickly became close friends. After Balakirev met Cui, he introduced him to Serov, and the three began to meet regularly to discuss music. Serov's letters to Balakirev from 1856 and 1857 reveal a genuine intimacy between them and a sharing of ideas and ideals.[207] Their common adoration for Glinka and advocacy of "modernism" in music especially bound them together. Vladimir Stasov also frequently joined Balakirev, Cui, and Serov for their musical discussions. He was not only a friend of Balakirev and Cui but had been an intimate associate of Serov as well since they were schoolmates at the School of Jurisprudence in the early 1840s.[208] Thus, in 1856 and 1857 Serov was as much a member of the Balakirev's circle as was Cui.

In the last years of the decade, however, Serov and the members of Balakirev's group parted company. He ceased attending their gatherings, and in the 1860s he and Balakirev's supporters frequently exchanged brutal journalistic blows. Stasov always claimed that Serov's estrangement from the circle resulted from his espousal of Wagner at the expense of Glinka,[209] but this explanation is only accurate in part. Balakirev and company certainly had little appreciation of Wagner, and the earliest public attack on Serov by Balakirev's group was an article by Stasov, published in Germany in 1859, criticizing Serov precisely for his espousal of Wagnerian principles.[210] Furthermore, Serov's version of the break, according to his wife, credited it to Stasov's unwillingness to tolerate Serov's intellectual independence,[211] which would certainly be consistent with Stasov's ascription of the breach to differences of taste and musical opinion. Nevertheless, Stasov's charge that Serov lost all respect for Glinka is simply not true. Moreover, the first signs of the split appeared at the end of 1857, well before Serov's first trip to Germany in the summer of 1858 triggered his fanatical Wagnerism.[212] Serov's love of Wagner doubtless aggravated the existing rupture, but its origin lay elsewhere.

Although the evidence is circumstantial, certain information strongly suggests that the falling out originated in a personal conflict between Serov and Stasov involving Serov's sister. In his memoirs, Rimsky records that when he joined the Balakirev circle in 1861 the attitude toward Serov was already "most hostile" but that no one would discuss the reason. He only heard "snatches of reminiscences . . . , chiefly ironical" and "a scandalous story of unprintable nature" about the group's former intimate friend.[213] Boborykin claims that Balakirev told him something about a "personal score" Stasov had to settle with Serov, a score that "involved the female sex."[214] Vladimir Stasov's letters to Balakirev refer obliquely to some sort of personal conflict between himself and Serov that also involved his brother Dmitri and Serov's sister Sofia. In May 1858 Stasov wrote that Serov had done something that caused Dmitri "to break definitively with him and, it seems, with his other relations [probably Sofia] who also took part."[215] A year and a half later, writing about Serov's enmity toward himself and his brother, Stasov explained that "the chief cause of all this viciousness and dirty tricks is Sofia." He then continued, "without her everything might have been different, and the time might even have been postponed for Alexander Nikolaevich [Serov] to become a complete scoundrel."[216] Of course, Stasov's own earlier love affair with Sofia may well have played a part in the rift. (Vladimir was the father of Sofia's daughter Nadezhda.)[217] In any case, Dmitri Stasov's daughter attributed the quarrel between her uncle and Serov partly to the former's breaking off relations with Serov's sister.[218] Whatever the real reasons the foregoing evidence should be sufficient to show that the falling out between Vladimir Stasov and Serov originated in more than mere musical differences.

Serov's break with Stasov quickly involved Balakirev as well. Three letters from Serov to Balakirev in the winter of 1857-58 indicate that the latter was avoiding all contacts. On 1 March 1859 Serov wrote to ask Balakirev to return the music he had borrowed and to renew their friendship. "How can I convince you," Serov concluded, "that it is pointless and wrong to have as an enemy someone who could be affectionately disposed toward you."[219] But Balakirev was not to be moved. Stasov was his closest friend, and he naturally sided with him against Serov in their feud.

Despite Balakirev's indifference or even hostility toward him, Serov continued to write favorable comments about Balakirev in the press.[220] In 1861, while he was working on his opera *Judith,* he even sent the score of the first act to Balakirev for his opinion.[221] Balakirev responded that while he could not really judge an entire opera by one act he found "many artistic pretensions" in the orchestration and that "most of them do not turn out well." He noted further that "the author has a poor command of massed instruments" yet still acknowledged, perhaps a trifle superciliously, that the "ending is very pretty."[222] This produced the final break between Serov and Balakirev. Serov was furious, both at the criticism and at Balakirev's casual treatment of the matter. From this time on he relegated Balakirev to the ranks of musical pedants who could not appreciate true music because of their myopic concentration on technique and rules. He wrote an acquaintance:

> I confess I had until now a much higher opinion of Mily Alexeevich [Balakirev], but I am now convinced that he also belongs entirely to the detachment of hack musicians *ex professo,* who are equally ready, given the chance, to make music for the fables of Krylov or the handbook of Kaidanov's World History, so long as they have notes and chords.[223]

After this, instead of reviewing Balakirev's music favorably, Serov consistently attacked him in the press. This reversal obviously resulted from Serov's pique over Balakirev's criticism of his opera.

Balakirev's harsh criticism of *Judith* and his continued aspersions on Serov's music for the rest of the decade also probably resulted, at least in part, from personal rancor. His judgment of Serov's talent seems to have been vindicated by time, for Serov's music proved to have only a short-lived interest for the public. But if this proves that he was, in fact, an untalented composer, then it also proves the same thing of Cui, who nevertheless always enjoyed Balakirev's high praise. Furthermore, as Stasov himself admitted in a letter to Balakirev, Serov's *Judith* followed the latest principles of operatic music, the very principles the Balakirev circle espoused for the operatic stage.[224] Serov may not have upheld these principles with exceptional brilliance, but apparently neither did Cui, and Serov at least showed enough skill and talent to win enormous, if temporary public success—something Cui's operas never achieved. Nevertheless, Balakirev praised Cui and castigated Serov. Presumably the difference in Balakirev's opinion resulted from the difference in his relations with the two men. Cui was a friend and a pupil, while Serov was no longer part of his group. At an even more fundamental level, Balakirev possibly treated Serov's work with particular harshness because he resented his former friend's independence, even though he himself was partly responsible for it. Balakirev tolerated little deviation from his own views within his circle. He only remained happy with his disciples so long as they agreed with his opinions and followed his judgments. To the day of his death, according to Cui, Balakirev insisted that only the music composed by his followers while still under his supervision was any good.[225] As the first of Balakirev's friends to write music without his help and advice, Serov was also the first to suffer rejection of his works by Balakirev. A Soviet musicologist has suggested that both Serov and Balakirev were too strongly individualistic to have gotten along well indefinitely, that a split was inevitable because neither could long tolerate being less than the predominant figure among his colleagues.[226] The argument is certainly persuasive, considering the vigor with which both men lashed out at any deviation from their own views.

In any case, as a result of personal feuding, aggravated and embittered by aesthetic differences, the close ties between Serov and the members of the Balakirev circle in the 1850s turned into sharply enmity in the 1860s. On several occasions Serov tried to patch up his relations with Stasov but to no avail.[227] The hostility was too great and the enmity continued. As a result, Serov and the Balakirev circle were unable to wage a common struggle against Anton Rubinstein and the Russian Musical Society. Although they shared an adherence to advanced musical principles and the tradition of Russian national music created by Glinka, a taste for Beethoven and the avant-garde Western composers, and an antipathy for academism and conservatory training, they could not form a united front against a man who represented quite a different aesthetic position. Although they envied Rubinstein's success, chafed at his control of the best public platform for their own compositions, and personally disliked him as a "foreigner" and a Jew, they could not reconcile their mutual differences. Therefore, in the 1860s the Balakirev circle and Serov mounted separate campaigns against Rubinstein, often from different directions and with different weapons, while skirmishing simultaneously with each other.

Notes to Chapter III

1. Boborykin, *Vospominaniia,* 2:452.

2. M——ch, "Russkoe muzykal'noe obshchestvo," pp. 453-54.

3. Rubets, "Vospominaniia," 21 May 1912, p. 3.

4. Anastasiia Sergeevna Liapunova and E.E. Iazovitskaia, comps., *Milii Alekseevich Balakirev: Letopis' zhizni i tvorchestva* [Mily Alexeevich Balakirev: a chronicle of his life and work] (Leningrad: Muzyka, 1967), pp. 24, 27.

5. Sergei Mikhailovich Liapunov and Anastasiia Sergeevna Liapunova, "Molodye gody Balakireva" [Balakirev's young years], in Balakirev, *Vospominaniia,* p. 49.

6. Kiui, *Izbrannye stat'i,* p. 544; Liapunova, *Balakirev: Letopis',* pp. 26, 28.

7. Stasov, *Izbrannye sochineniia,* 2:165-66.

8. Nikolay Andreyevich Rimsky-Korsakov, *My Musical Life,* trans. Judah A. Joffe, ed. Carl Van Vechten, 3rd rev. English ed. (New York: Alfred A. Knopf, 1942), pp. 18-19.

9. Aleksandr Porfir'evich Borodin, *Pis'ma A.P. Borodina* [Letters of A.P. Borodin], ed. Sergei Dianin, 4 vols. (Moscow: Gosudarstvennoe izdatel'stvo, Muzykal'nyi sektor, 1927/28-1950), 4:297-99.

10. Balakirev to V. Stasov 27 September 1859, in Milii Alekseevich Balakirev and Vladimir Vasil'evich Stasov, *Perepiska* [Correspondence], ed. Anastasiia Sergeevna Liapunova, 2 vols. (Moscow: Muzyka, 1970-71), 1:91. This source will hereafter be cited as simply *Perepiska,* without authors.

11. Liapunova, *Balakirev: Letopis',* p. 13.

12. Milii Alekseevich Balakirev, "Avtobiograficheskie zametki M.A. Balakireva (Iz pisem ego k N. Findeizenu 1903 i 1907 g.)" [Autobiographical notes of M.A. Balakirev (from his letters to N. Findeizen of 1903 and 1907)], *Russkaia muzykal'naia gazeta* [Russian musical gazette] 17, no. 41 (1910):861.

13. A.S. Gatsiskii, "Aleksandr Dmitrievich Ulybyshev," *Russkii arkhiv* 24, no. 1 (January 1886):59, 66; Anna Shteinberg, "U istokov russkoi mysli o muzyke" [At the sources of Russian thought about music], *Sovetskaia muzyka,* October 1967, p. 78.

14. Boborykin, *Vospominaniia,* 1:101-2; Grigorii Timofeev, "M.A. Balakirev: Na osnovanii novykh materialov" [M.A. Balakirev: on the basis of new materials], *Russkaia mysl'* [Russian thought] 33, no. 6 (1912):41-42.

15. Boborykin, *Vospominaniia,* 1:103.

16. Liudmila Ivanovna Shestakova, "Iz neizdannykh vospominanii o novoi russkoi shkole" [From unpublished memoirs about the new Russian school], *Russkaia muzykal'naia gazeta* 20, nos. 51-52 (1913):1180-81.

17. Liapunov, "Molodye gody Balakireva," pp. 51-53.

18. Marie Clotilde de Mercy-Argenteau, *César Cui: Esquisse critique* (Paris: Librairie Fischbacher, 1888), pp. 5-7.

19. Kiui, *Izbrannye stat'i,* pp. 542-43.

20. Georgii Khubov, *Musorgskii* (Moscow: Muzyka, 1969), pp. 7, 14, 19, 21.

21. Quoted in Stasov, *Izbrannye sochineniia,* 2:167.

22. *Ibid.,* 2:163-64.

23. Borodin, *Pis'ma,* 4:297.

24. Anatolii Aleksandrovich Solovtsov, *Zhizn' i tvorchestvo N.A. Rimskogo-Korsakova* [The life and work of N.A. Rimsky-Korsakov] (Moscow: Muzyka, 1964), pp. 5, 13-20.

25. *My Musical Life,* pp. 11-15.

26. *Ibid.,* p. 34.

27. Sergei Dianin, *Borodin,* trans. Robert Lord (London: Oxford University Press, 1963), pp. 7, 19, 23, 40.

28. *Ibid.,* pp. 10-15, 22.

29. Kruglikov, "Vospominaniia o Borodine," pp. 247-48.

30. Stasov, *Izbrannye sochineniia,* 3:346.

31. *Izbrannye stat'i,* p. 549.

32. Swan, *Russian Music,* p. 77.

33. *My Musical Life,* pp. 27-28.

34. Komarova, *Vladimir Stasov,* 1:361; Rimsky-Korsakov, *My Musical Life,* p. 58.

35. Letter to Michel Calvocoressi of 22 July 1906 in Milii Alekseevich Balakirev, "Iz perepiski M.A. Balakireva" [From the correspondence of M.A. Balakirev], *Russkaia muzykal'naia gazeta* 18, no. 38 (1911):752.

36. Kiui, *Izbrannye stat'i,* p. 544; Modest Petrovich Musorgskii, *Literaturnoe nasledie* [Literary legacy], ed. M.S. Pekelis, 2 vols. (Moscow: Muzyka, 1971-72), 1:268.

37. Rimsky-Korsakov, *My Musical Life,* p. 35.

38. *Ibid.,* pp. 28-29.

39. *Ibid.,* p. 32.

40. Letter of 25 January 1858 in Musorgskii, *Literaturnoe nasledie,* 1:37.

41. *My Musical Life,* p. 29.

42. Balakirev to Cui, 15 July 1864, in Tsezar' Kiui, *Izbrannye pis'ma* [Selected letters], ed. I.L. Gusin (Leningrad: Gosudarstvennoe muzykal'noe izdatel'stvo, 1955), p. 496.

43. Rimsky-Korsakov, *My Musical Life,* pp. 19, 22.

44. Letter of 24 April 1862 in Nikolai Andreevich Rimskii-Korsakov, *Polnoe sobranie sochinenii* [Complete writings] (Moscow: Gosudarstvennoe muzykal'noe izdatel'stvo, 1955-), 5:17.

45. Kiui, *Izbrannye pis'ma,* p. 57.

46. Rimskii-Korsakov, *Polnoe sobranie,* 5:55, 57.

47. *Ibid.,* 5:249.

48. Letter of 4 June 1863 *ibid.,* 5:61.

49. Swan, *Russian Music,* p. 78.

50. *My Musical Life,* p. 30.

51. See, for example, Cui to Balakirev, 17 July 1856, in Kiui, *Izbrannye pis'ma,* p. 33.

52. Z. Savelova, "Musorgskii v krugo ego lichnykh znakomstv: Materialy k biografii" [Musorgsky in the circle of his personal acquaintances: materials for his biography], in Iurii Vsevolodovich Kel'dysh and Vasilii Iakovlev, eds., *M.P. Musorgskii: K piatidesiatiletiiu so dnia smerti, 1881-1931: Stat'i i materialy* [M.P. Musorgsky: on the fiftieth anniversary of the day of his death, 1881-1931: articles and materials] (Moscow: Gosudarstvennoe muzykal'noe izdatel'stvo, 1932), p. 169.

53. Musorgsky to Balakirev, 19 January 1861, in Musorgskii, *Literaturnoe nasledie,* 1:56-57.

54. Swan, *Russian Music*, p. 85.

55. *My Musical Life*, p. 60.

56. Letter to V. Stasov of 3 June 1863 in *Perepiska*, 1:212.

57. Al. Borodina, "Moe vospominanie ob A.S. Dargomyzhskom" [My memoirs about A.S. Dargomyzhsky], *Russkaia starina* 165 (1916):33.

58. Letter of 11 October 1862 in *Perepiska*, 1:192.

59. Rimsky-Korsakov, *My Musical Life*, p. 30.

60. *Ibid.*, pp. 21-22.

61. Letter of 7 November 1862 in Rimskii-Korsakov, *Polnoe sobranie*, 5:27.

62. Kruglikov, "Vospominanie o Borodine," p. 250.

63. Letters to V. Stasov of 22 February 1887 and 8 December 1888 in *Perepiska*, 2:102, 140-41.

64. Arnol'd Naumovich Sokhor, "Stranitsy tvorcheskoi druzhby" [Pages of creative friendship], *Sovetskaia muzyka,* May 1960, p. 64.

65. George Andrew Olkhovsky, "Vladimir Stasov and His Quest for Russian National Music" (unpublished Ph.D. dissertation, Georgetown University, 1968), pp. 6-56, *passim.*

66. *Perepiska,* 1.

67. See Stasov to Balakirev, 12 August 1861 and 4 January 1862, and Balakirev to Stasov, 4 January 1862 and 20 March 1864, in *Perepiska,* 1:169, 180, 226.

68. See Balakirev to Stasov, 14 November 1859 and 3 June 1863, and Stasov to Balakirev, 17 May 1863, *ibid.,* 1:93, 212, 203.

69. See, for example, Pavel Nikolaevich Miliukov, *Ocherk po istorii russkoi kul'tury* [A survey of the history of Russian culture], 3 vols., Jubilee ed. (Paris: Izdatel'stvo "Sovremennyia Zapiski," 1931), 2:624; Victor I. Seroff, *The Mighty Five: The Cradle of Russian National Music* (New York: Allen, Towne and Heath, 1948), p. 98.

70. Boborykin, *Vospominaniia,* 1:304.

71. Shteinberg, "U istokov," p. 81.

72. Anastasiia Sergeevna Liapunova, "Glinka i Balakirev" [Glinka and Balakirev], *Sovetskaia muzyka,* February 1953, pp. 75-81.

73. Balakirev to V. Stasov, 27 January 1906, in *Perepiska,* 2:242.

74.   Shestakova, "Iz vospominanii o russkoi shkole," p. 1181.

75.   *Memoirs,* trans. Richard B. Mudge (Norman, Okla.: University of Oklahoma Press, 1963), pp. 82-83.

76.   Gerald Abraham, *Studies in Russian Music* (London: William Reeves, 1935), pp. 30-36; Swan, *Russian Music,* p. 65.

77.   Gerald Abraham in Calvocoressi, *Masters of Russian Music,* pp. 62-63; Calvocoressi, *Russian Music,* pp. 28-35.

78.   Abraham, *Studies,* pp. 53-54; Calvocoressi, *Russian Music,* p. 39.

79.   Letter to Rimsky-Korsakov, 11 January 1863, in Rimskii-Korsakov, *Polnoe sobranie,* 5:38.

80.   V. Stasov to Balakirev, 19 June 1858, in *Perepiska,* 1:64-65.

81.   Rimsky-Korsakov, *My Musical Life,* p. 65.

82.   Balakirev to Rimsky-Korsakov, 26 December 1863, in Rimskii-Korsakov, *Polnoe sobranie,* 5:36; Borodina, "Moi vospominaniia," p. 34.

83.   *Selected Essays,* p. 97.

84.   See, for example, Gerald Abraham's characterization of the Russian style in *Studies,* pp. 3-19.

85.   Rimsky-Korsakov, *My Musical Life,* p. 20.

86.   Letter to Rimsky-Korsakov of 7 November 1862 in Rimskii-Korsakov, *Polnoe sobranie,* 5:27.

87.   Balakirev to V. Stasov, 26 February 1859 and 11 December 1862, in *Perepiska,* 1:86, 194.

88.   Balakirev to V. Stasov, 20 June 1861, in *Perepiska,* 1:139; Rimsky-Korsakov, *My Musical Life,* p. 20.

89.   Letter of 24 July 1864 in *Perepiska,* 1:231.

90.   Rimsky-Korsakov, *My Musical Life,* p. 66.

91.   Letter of 16 January 1861 in *Perepiska,* 1:116-17.

92.   Letter to Rimsky-Korsakov of 8-15 March 1863 in Rimskii-Korsakov, *Polnoe sobranie,* 5:46.

93.   *Vospominaniia,* 1:306.

94.   Balakirev to V. Stasov, 14-15 July 1861, in *Perepiska,* 1:148-50; Balakirev to Rimsky-Korsakov, 14 December 1863, in Rimskii-Korsakov, *Polnoe sobranie,* 5:74.

95.   Olkhovsky, "Vladimir Stasov," pp. 66-71; for a brief summary of the relationship of the philosophy of the radical critics to music, see Richard Taruskin, "Realism as Preached and Practiced: The Russian Opera Dialogue," *The Musical Quarterly* 56 (July 1970):432-38.

96.   Il'ia Repin, *Dalekoe blizkoe* [Remote nearness], ed. Kornei Ivanovich Chukovskii (Moscow: Izdatel'stvo Akademii khudozhestv SSSR, 1960), pp. 192-93.

97.   Letter of 12 February 1859 in *Perepiska*, 1:85.

98.   See, for example, Stasov in Balakirev, 12 January 1862, and Balakirev to Stasov, 20 April 1863 and 27 April 1863, in *Perepiska*, 1:182, 198-99.

99.   Boborykin, *Vospominaniia*, 1:308.

100.   Calvocoressi, *Russian Music*, pp. 47-51.

101.   Letter to V. Stasov of 25 July 1858 in *Perepiska*, 1:72.

102.   Letter to Balakirev of 13 February 1861 in *Perepiska*, 1:124.

103.   *Ibid.*, 1:122.

104.   Rimsky-Korsakov, *My Musical Life*, p. 27.

105.   Letter of 24 April 1862 in Rimskii-Korsakov, *Polnoe sobranie*, 5:18.

106.   See, for example, Balakirev to Stasov, 5 July 1858, in *Perepiska*, 1:62-63.

107.   Letter of 3 June 1863 in *Perepiska*, 1:210.

108.   Cui to Balakirev, 3 September 1856, in Kiui, *Izbrannye pis'ma*, p. 38.

109.   Letter of 11 August 1858 in *Perepiska*, 1:78.

110.   Letter of 20 March 1856 in Aleksandr Nikolaevich Serov, "Pis'ma k M.Balakirevu"[Letters to M. Balakirev], *Sovetskaia muzyka*, May 1953, p. 69.

111.   See, for example, his letters to Rimsky-Korsakov of 7 November 1862 and 11 January 1863 in Rimskii-Korsakov, *Polnoe sobranie*, 5:27, 38.

112.   *Vospominaniia*, 2:450-51.

113.   Balakirev to V. Stasov, 14-15 July 1861, and Stasov to Balakirev, 13 February 1861, in *Perepiska*, 1:148, 121-22.

114.   Letter to Balakirev of 28 April 1862 in Musorgskii, *Literaturnoe nasledie*, 1:62.

115.   Khubov, *Musorgskii*, pp. 64, 176.

116.   *My Musical Life*, p. 48.

117. Evgeniia Mikhailovna Gordeeva, *Moguchaia kuchka* [The mighty handful], 2nd ed., enl. (Moscow: Muzyka, 1966), pp. 111-12.

118. Liapunov, "Molodye gody Balakireva," pp. 58-59.

119. Undated letter to N. Zatkevich, probably of 1858, quoted in Emiliia Lazarevna Frid, "Milii Alekseevich Balakirev (1837-1910)," in Emiliia Lazarevna Frid, ed., *Milii Alekseevich Balakirev: Issledovaniia i stat'i* [Mily Alexeevich Balakirev: research and articles] (Leningrad: Gosudarstvennoe muzykal'noe izdatel'stvo, 1961), p. 14.

120. Letter to N. Zatkevich of 19 February 1857 quoted *ibid.*, p. 15.

121. Timofeev, "M.A. Balakirev," 33, no. 6, pp. 51-53.

122. Glinka to K.A. Bulgakov, 24 April 1856, in Mikhail Ivanovich Glinka, *Literaturnoe nasledie* [Literary legacy], ed. V.M. Bogdanov-Berezovskii, 2 vols. (Leningrad: Gosudarstvennoe muzykal'noe izdatel'stvo, 1952-1953), 2:584.

123. Letter to V. Stasov of 3 June 1861 in *Perepiska*, 1:137.

124. Letter of 11 November 1860 in Musorgskii, *Literaturnoe nasledie*, 1:51.

125. Findeizen, *Ocherk RMO*, appendix, pp. 1-8.

126. Glinka to V. Engelhardt, 29 November 1855 and 11 April 1856, in Glinka, *Literaturnoe nasledie*, 2:560, 579-80; Shestakova, "Poslednye gody Glinki," pp. 421-22.

127. Letter to V. Engelhardt in Glinka, *Literaturnoe nasledie*, 2:560. This source omits the term "yid" *(zhid)*, replacing it by three dots enclosed in brackets, but Boris Asaf'ev published this passage of the letter intact in *A.G. Rubinshtein*, p. 61.

128. "Mikhail Ivanovich Glinka: Novye materialy dlia ego biografii" [Mikhail Ivanovich Glinka: new materials for his biography], *Russkaia starina* 61 (1889):393.

129. Nikolai Dmitrievich Kashkin, who knew Balakirev in the late 1860s, suggested this possibility in his memoirs about Balakirev in his *Stat'i o russkoi muzyke i muzykantakh* [Articles about Russian music and musicians], ed. S.I. Shlifshtein (Moscow: Gosudarstvennoe muzykal'noe izdatel'stvo, 1953), p. 14.

130. Letter of 20 December 1861 in Odoevskii, *Muzykal'no-literaturnoe nasledie*, p. 516.

131. M——ch, "Russkoe muzykal'noe obshchestvo," p. 454.

132. Musorgsky to Balakirev, 16 January 1861, in Musorgskii, *Literaturnoe nasledie*, 1:54; Letter of 29 October 1862 in Milii Alekseevich Balakirev, "Pis'ma M.A. Balakireva k A.P. Arsen'evu" [M.A. Balakirev's letters to A.P. Arseniev], *Russkaia muzykal'naia gazeta* 17, no. 42 (1910):901.

133. According to Walter M. Pintner, "The Social Characteristics of the Early Nineteenth-Century Russian Bureaucracy," *Slavic Review* 29, no. 3 (September 1971):437-38, in the

mid-nineteenth century 15 percent of high-ranking officials in St. Petersburg were Lutherans, and the figure was as high as 40 percent in some small agencies.

134.   Letter of 14 November 1862 in Rimskii-Korsakov, *Polnoe sobranie,* 5:31.

135.   Letter to Balakirev of 10 June 1863 in Musorgskii, *Literaturnoe nasledie,* 1:69. In its published version the letter says "leading Jews," but the word "Jews" is in brackets, indicating that the editors have replaced a more derogatory term, probably *zhid,* by the acceptable *evrei.*

136.   We have no way of knowing, of course, if unflattering colloquialisms have been purged from the published texts of their letters.

137.   See, for example, Balakirev to P. Tchaikovsky, 19 April 1868, in Balakirev, *Vospominaniia,* p. 122, and Borodin to his wife, 24 September 1870, in Borodin, *Pis'ma,* 1:236.

138.   V. Stasov to Balakirev, 24-25 July 1861, in *Perepiska,* 1:153-54.

139.   V. Stasov to D. Stasov, 9 July 1859, in Vladimir Vasil'evich Stasov, *Pis'ma k rodnym* [Letters to relations], ed. Iurii Vsevolodovich Kel'dysh *et al.,* 3 vols. (Moscow: Gosudarstvennoe muzykal'noe izdatel'stvo, 1953—1962), 1, pt. 1: 274-75; V. Stasov to Balakirev, 10 June 1862, in *Perepiska,* 1:187.

140.   Timofeev, "M.A. Balakirev," 33, no. 6, p. 51; Balakirev to V. Stasov, 23 October 1861, in *Perepiska,* 1:177; Balakirev to V.M. Zhemchuzhnikov, December 1865, in Balakirev, *Vospominaniia,* p. 97.

141.   Liudmila Ivanovna Shestakova, "Mikhail Ivanovich Glinka: V vospominaniiakh ego sestry L.I. Shestakovoi" [Mikhail Ivanovich Glinka: in the memoirs of his sister L.I. Shestakova], *Russkaia starina* 44 (1884):602.

142.   V. Stasov to Balakirev, 24-25 July 1861, in *Perepiska,* 1:154, and editor's note 4 to this letter, p. 401.

143.   Liapunov, "Molodye gody Balakireva," pp. 58-59; Editor's note 1 to letter 45 in *Perepiska,* 1:383.

144.   Rimsky-Korsakov to Balakirev, 18 May 1863, in Rimskii-Korsakov, *Polnoe sobranie,* 5:59.

145.   *Otchet RMO za 1862-63,* p. 17.

146.   Vladimir Timofeevich Sokolov, "Aleksandr Sergeevich Dargomyzhskii v 1856-1869 gg." [Alexander Sergeevich Dargomyzhsky in 1856-1869], *Russkaia starina* 46 (1885):342; Stasov, *Izbrannye sochineniia,* 3:393.

147.   Richard Taruskin has begun to remedy this situation in his "Opera and Drama in Russia: The Preachment and Practice of Operatic Esthetics in the Eighteen Sixties" (unpublished Ph.D. dissertation, Columbia University, 1975) and "Glinka's Ambiguous Legacy and the Birth Pangs of Russian Opera," *Nineteenth Century Music* 1 (November 1977): 142-62.

148. Georgii Khubov, *Zhizn' A. Serova* [The life of A. Serov] (Moscow: Gosudarstvennoe muzykal'noe izdatel'stvo, 1950), pp. 3-5.

149. Letter to S.A. Gedeonov, 4 September 1867, in Aleksandr Nikolaevich Serov, "Pis'mo A.N. Serova" [A letter of A.N. Serov], *Russkii arkhiv* 52, pt. 1 (1914):450.

150. Stasov, *Selected Essays,* p. 85.

151. Feofil Matveevich Tolstoi, "Aleksandr Nikolaevich Serov, 1820-1871 gg.: Vospominaniia Feofila Matveevicha Tolstogo" [Alexander Nikolaevich Serov, 1820-1871: memoirs of Feofil Matveevich Tolstoy], *Russkaia starina* 9 (1874):340-41.

152. *Ibid.,* pp. 341-42.

153. Al'bert Vikent'evich Starchevskii, "Kompozitor A.N. Serov (Iz vospominanii)" [The composer A.N. Serov (from my memoirs)], *Nabliudatel'* [The observer] 7, no. 3 (March 1888):151.

154. Larosh, "A.G. Rubinshtein," p. 595.

155. Letter of 13 June 1856 in Kiui, *Izbrannye pis'ma,* pp. 31-32.

156. See, for example, Serov to F. Tolstoy, 7 June 1863, in Tolstoi, "A.N. Serov," p. 357.

157. *Izbrannye stat'i,* 2:161-62. See also Serov's letter of 7 June 1863 to F. Tolstoy in Tolstoi, "A.N. Serov," p. 364.

158. *Izbrannye stat'i,* 1:179.

159. Letter to M.P. Anastasieva, 27 June 1859, in Serov, "Materialy dlia ego biografii," 21:153.

160. See, for example, Swan, *Russian Music,* p. 89.

161. See Serov to M.P. Anastasieva, 10 September 1861, in Serov, "Materialy dlia ego biografii," 21:153.

162. For a detailed discussion of the debate, see Taruskin, "Opera and Drama," pp. 16-60.

163. *Izbrannye stat'i,* 2:586.

164. *Ibid.,* 2:66-71.

165. *Ibid.,* 2:163.

166. Serov to K.I. Zvantsov, 31 January 1859, in Konstantin Ivanovich Zvantsov, "Aleksandr Nikolaevich Serov v 1857-1871 gg.: Vospominaniia o nem i ego pis'ma" [Alexander Nikolaevich Serov, 1857-1871: memoirs about him and his letters], *Russkaia starina* 59 (1888):358.

167. Serov, *Izbrannye stat'i,* 2:576.

168. Zvantsov, "A.N. Serov," pp. 344-45.

169. *Izbrannye stat'i*, 1:70.

170. Letter of 25 August 1858 in Aleksandr Nikolaevich Serov, *Pis'ma Aleksandra Nikolaevicha Serova k ego sestre S.N. Diu-Tur (1845-1861 gg.)* [Alexander Nikolaevich Serov's letters to his sister S.N. DuTour (1854-1861)] (St. Petersburg: Tipografiia N. Findeizena, 1896), pp. 214-18.

171. Dargomyzhsky to Serov, summer of 1856, in Aleksandr Sergeevich Dargomyzhskii, *Izbrannye pis'ma* [Selected letters], ed. M.S. Pekelis (Moscow: Gosudarstvennoe muzykal'noe izdatel'stvo, 1952), p. 42.

172. *Izbrannye stat'i*, 1:522.

173. Letter to M.P. Anastasieva, 7 April 1859, in Serov, "Materialy dlia ego biografii," 20:534.

174. Serov to V. Odoevsky, 28 August 1859, in I.A. Bychkov, comp., "Iz perepiski kniazia V.F. Odoevskogo" [From the correspondence of Prince V.F. Odoevsky], *Russkaia starina* 159 (1904):432.

175. *Izbrannye stat'i*, 1:523.

176. Boborykin, *Vospominaniia*, 2:451.

177. *Izbrannye stat'i*, 2:584.

178. Letter to V. Stasov, February 1857, in Serov, "Materialy dlia ego biografii," 20:532.

179. Serov, *Izbrannye stat'i*, 1:71.

180. Khubov, *Zhizn' Serova*, p. 42.

181. Aleksandr Nikolaevich Serov, "Pis'ma A.N. Serova k kniaziu Odoevskomu" [A.N. Serov's letters to Prince Odoevsky], in *Muzykal'naia starina: Sbornik statei i materialov dlia istorii muzyki v Rossii* [Musical antiquity: a collection of articles and materials on the history of music in Russia] 4 (1907):118-20.

182. Letter to M.P. Anastasieva in Serov, "Materialy dlia ego biografii," 20:533.

183. Quoted in Asaf'ev, *A.G. Rubinshtein*, p. 78.

184. Serov to M.P. Anastasieva, 7 April 1859, in Serov, "Materialy dlia ego biografii," 20:533.

185. Letter of 5 November 1859 in Serov, *Pis'ma k ego sestre*, pp. 228, 232-33.

186. Letter of 18 November 1862 in Aleksandr Nikolaevich Serov, "Pis'ma k V. Zhukovoi" [Letters to V. Zhukova], *Sovetskaia muzyka*, August [1954], p. 75.

187. Letter to S.A. Gedeonov, 4 September 1867, in Serov, "Pis'ma," p. 452.

188. Aleksandr Nikolaevich Serov, "Pis'ma k V.V. i D.V. Stasovym" [Letters to V.V. and D.V. Stasov], *Muzykal'noe nasledstvo*, 3:187-88.

189. *Izbrannye stat'i*, 2:602-3.

190. *Ibid.*, 1:72.

191. Khubov, *Zhizn' Serova*, pp. 8-29, *passim*.

192. V. Odoevsky to Serov, 30 December 1860, in Odoevskii, *Muzykal'no-literaturnoe nasledie*, pp. 505-6.

193. Odoevsky to Serov, 12 January 1860, *ibid.*, p. 507; Odoevskii, "Dnevnik," p. 103.

194. Valentina Serova, *Serovy Aleksandr Niklaevich i Valentin Aleksandrovich: Vospominaniia* [The Serovs, Alexander Nikolaevich and Valentin Alexandrovich: memoirs] (St. Petersburg: Izdatel'stvo "Shipovnik," 1914), p. 10.

195. Letter to M.P. Anastasieva, 7 April 1859, in Serov, "Materialy dlia ego biografii," 20:533.

196. See, for example, *Izbrannye stat'i*, 1:189; 2:604, 613.

197. Letter to M.P. Anastasieva, 19 March 1860, in Serov, "Materialy dlia ego biografii," 21:154; Letter to F. Tolstoy, 7 June 1863, in Tolstoi, "A.N. Serov," pp. 357, 563-64.

198. Zvantsov, "A.N. Serov," p. 347.

199. Sokolov, "A.S. Dargomyzhskii," p. 342.

200. Zvantsov, "A.N. Serov," p. 654.

201. See Serov's letters to Odoevsky in Bychkov, "Iz perepiski Odoevskogo," 119:428-38.

202. Serov to M.P. Anastasieva, 11 January-1 February 1866, in Serov, "Materialy dlia ego biografii," 21:175.

203. Serov to M.E. Slavinsky, 19 April 1865, in "Iz zabytykh pisem i vospominanii" [From forgotten letters and memoirs], *Sovetskaia muzyka*, December 1966, p. 103.

204. Letter of 6 January 1867 in Serov, "Pis'ma k Odoevskomu," pp. 138-39.

205. Letters of 22 December 1864 and 15 January 1865 in Aleksandr Nikolaevich Serov, "Pis'ma A.N. Serova k Iu. F. Abaze" [A.N. Serov's letters to Iu. F. Abaza], *Biriuch petrogradskikh gosudarstvennykh akademicheskikh teatrov: Sbornik statei* [The herald of the Petrograd state academic theaters: a collection of articles], 2 (1920):245, 250.

206. Quoted in Liapunov, "Molodye gody Balakireva," p. 51.

207. Serov, "Pis'ma k Balakirevu," pp. 68-75.

208.   Stasov, *Izbrannye sochineniia,* 3:396.

209.   *Ibid.*

210.   *Ibid.,* 1:40-43.

211.   Serova, *Serovy,* p. 22.

212.   Letter of 26 December 1857 in Serov, "Pis'ma k Balakirevu," p. 75.

213.   *My Musical Life,* p. 70.

214.   *Vospominaniia,* 1:306.

215.   Letter of 3 May 1858 in *Perepiska,* 1:57.

216.   Letter of 16 January 1860 in *Perepiska,* 1:101; see also his letter of 18 July 1860 *ibid.,* 1:108.

217.   Andrei Konstantinovich Lebedev and Aleksandr Vasil'evich Solodovnikov, *Vladimir Vasil'evich Stasov: Zhizn' i tvorchestvo* [Vladimir Vasilievich Stasov: life and work] (Moscow: Iskusstvo, 1976), p. 86.

218.   Komarova, *Vladimir Stasov,* 1:351.

219.   Serov, "Pis'ma k Balakirevu," p. 75.

220.   See, for example, *Izbrannye stat'i,* 1:339-42; 2:585-86.

221.   Tolstoi, "A.N. Serov," p. 351.

222.   Undated letter, probably of late 1861, in Tolstoi, "A.N. Serov," p. 351.

223.   Letter to M.P.M., presumably Modest Musorgsky, *ibid.,* p. 352.

224.   Letter of 17 May 1863 in *Perepiska,* 1:206.

225.   *Izbrannye stat'i,* p. 549.

226.   Gozenpud, *Russkii opernyi teatr,* 2:63.

227.   See V. Stasov to Balakirev, 20 January 1862, in *Perepiska,* 1:182; Serov to M.P. Anastasieva, 11 January 1866, in Serov, "Materialy dlia ego biografii," 21:174-75.

Chapter IV

The Challenge to the Russian Musical Society, 1859-1867

From its inception in 1859 until Anton Rubinstein's resignation in 1867, both the Russian Musical Society and its founder faced a steadily increasing challenge to their authority in Russian musical life from Alexander Serov and the Balakirev circle. The Society's opponents mounted press campaigns to denigrate its work and defame its leader. These attacks became particularly serious when the antagonists of the RMS began their own public musical careers, for their successes bolstered the force of their criticism and offered the St. Petersburg musical world an alternative to the work of Rubinstein and his colleagues.

The weapon most readily available for wielding against Rubinstein was the critic's pen, and Alexander Serov was well situated to wield it. He was already an established and widely respected, if little-loved, critic when the RMS launched its inaugural season. As chief assistant for Petersburg's only weekly music journal, *Teatral'nyi i muzykal'nyi vestnik*,[1] he had a regular outlet for extensive and detailed reviews. He lost this particular platform in 1860 when the journal closed, but this did not end his career as a critic. Although he frequently complained to friends about the difficulty of finding a suitable forum for his writings and threatened to give up journalism altogether,[2] he managed from 1861 to 1867 to publish nearly two dozen articles, including several lengthy historical and analytical studies, in eight Petersburg newspapers and journals.[3] He resumed full-time activity as a critic in 1867, when he and his wife founded their own journal, *Muzyka i teatr*, a biweekly paper devoted exclusively to music and theater criticism.[4] Despite his limited output of music criticism during much of Anton Rubinstein's tenure as director of the Russian Musical Society, the polemical character of his articles and his great success in other public musical endeavors assured Serov of an interested audience for his critical opinions.

Serov's press campaign against the RMS began during the Society's first year with lengthy reviews of all ten symphonic concerts of its 1859-60 season. He began his series of articles by accusing the Society's directors of cliquishness for not inviting him to take part in the organization's work. After such an introduction, it is not surprising that the reviews that followed were generally captious in tone. Serov made some bow toward objectivity, finding the Society's stated goals "excellent" and the first concert, "at least in some parts, satisfactory,"[5] but for the most part his reviews criticized sharply every aspect of the Society's work.

To start, Serov attacked the concerts for their repertory. His most serious and often-repeated charge was that it was not Russian:

> The stamp of the *Russian* Musical Society is not merely letters to be imprinted on tickets; it should also be imprinted from the very beginning on the Society's musical *actions.*
>
> Except for the overture to *Ruslan,* that single piece tossed into the jaws of the Cerberus of patriotism, the *entire* program of the first concert of the *Russian* Musical Society, in the *Russian* capital, might have belonged to any mediocre German "Musikverein" anywhere in Halle or Marburg. There would not be the slightest difference.[6]

In addition to Glinka's overture, the program also included Rubinstein's own Piano Concerto in G Major, but Serov refused to recognize this as a Russian composition because it was not written in the national style created by Glinka and because its composer had been born a Jew. Throughout the first season, Serov's reviews echoed the charge that the programs were not Russian, and he dubbed the Society "Rubinstein's *Musikverein.*"[7] That Rubinstein programmed fourteen works by eight Russian composers in the first ten concerts failed to satisfy Serov.

Serov also criticized the selection of non-Russian works for being conservative and old-fashioned. He objected to most of the Classical and Baroque works, finding them dull, tasteless, or remnants of the "epoch of routine virtuosity that has sunk irretrievably into the past." He doubted whether the music of Mendelssohn and his followers could possibly elevate the musical taste of the Russian public.[8] He even caviled at the inclusion of those Western works that he did like because he considered them beyond the capabilities of the Society's performing forces.[9]

Serov aimed his second major complaint about the RMS concerts at Rubinstein's conducting, which he found wholly inadequate:

> Every concert of the Russian Musical Society has served as clear proof of Mr. Rubinstein's limited talent and complete inexperience as a conductor.
>
> Perhaps these very concerts were deliberately thought up by the patrons and well-wishers of this pianist as a splendid opportunity for Mr. Rubinstein to *learn* little by little to conduct. But if this is the idea, what is the *role of the public,* who, having paid fifteen rubles for a member's ticket, . . . have the full right to demand in these concerts the very best orchestral forces in Petersburg, entrusted to the direction not of a beginner but of one of the heroes of conducting, such as Berlioz, Liszt, or Wagner?[10]

The legitimacy of Serov's complaint in this case is difficult to judge. He was certainly right about Rubinstein's lack of experience, but the continued success of the Society's concerts, both during and after the first season, suggests audience satisfaction with Rubinstein's work. Furthermore, the idea that someone like Berlioz, Wagner, or Liszt should conduct the RMS concerts contradicts Serov's position that the concerts were insufficiently Russian. Would any of these three men have contributed to the "Russianness" of the programs or performances?

In any case, even if Serov were justified in his negative view of Rubinstein's talents as a conductor, his sarcastic tone and the gratuitous slurs he heaped on Rubinstein's compositions indicate that he was hardly an impartial judge. He intended not to evaluate Rubinstein fairly but to blacken his musical reputation. Thus, he characterized Rubinstein's performance of Beethoven's Ninth Symphony as "the most inadmissible caricature" and a "filthy stain" on the work. He then impugned Rubinstein's fidelity to Liszt's performance instructions: "Perhaps Mr. Rubinstein, himself the composer of symphonies (!), considers himself above these indications and composer's instructions; perhaps he thinks that he is doing Liszt's compositions a great favor if he conducts them just as imprecisely, off-handedly, in a word, just as badly as [he conducts] the works of Beethoven, Wagner, and Glinka." As for Rubinstein's own compositions, Serov denied that they were music![11]

Serov responded to the announcement that the RMS would open a conservatory in Petersburg with an article in *Severnaia pchela* [The Northern Bee] even sharper in tone than his criticism of the Society's concerts. Before this, he had been approached for suggestions on the proposed charter of the school—probably an attempt by the RMS directors to deflect further charges that the Society ignored the opinions of leading musical figures outside its own leadership—and he had indeed submitted a detailed examination of the subject.[12] But the ploy failed to avert an attack. In his article, Serov challenged the very idea of a conservatory, claiming it would produce a "musical officialdom for the propagation of mediocrities" because no true talent would "subject itself to the judgment of privileged pedants, ignoramuses, and the envious." But Serov went beyond this restatement of his opposition to conservatories in general to indulge in a crude personal attack on Rubinstein, particularly playing on his audience's nationalistic sentiments. Serov began his remarks with the claim that in the field of art, Russians are all too ready to "stretch out their necks beneath the yoke that any foreign charlatan thinks to lay on them." Continuing in the same vein, he soon made it clear precisely whom he considered to be the "foreign charlatan":

> We should see clearly that if a foreign virtuoso pianist who, on the strength of the
> support and protection of our Maecenases (!) has seized for himself a certain influence,
> founds a musical institution and places in charge, *besides himself* (a novice conductor and

ignoramus in musical pedagogy), persons unknown musically not only to the public but
even to himself, then the result of such an institution may turn out to be beneficial for the
superficial reputation of this pianist and . . . for the pockets of certain of his unmusical
associates, but for Russia it is impossible to expect anything from this institution except
actual harm, as from everything based on falsehood, fraud, ignorance, shortsightedness,
and self-seeking.[13]

In addition to his articles and reviews devoted specifically to Rubinstein and
the Russian Musical Society, Serov also used other public occasions to
denigrate them. His writings on subjects unrelated to the RMS and its work
often contained oblique attacks, usually harping on the same themes. He
called the RMS "the party of German musical reactionaries (with A.
Rubinstein at the head)"[14] and referred to the "so-called concerts of the so-
called 'Russian' (!) Musical Society."[15] He scoffed at the very idea "that
anyone *in Russia*" would consider Rubinstein " 'a symphonic composer' (!)."
He asserted that Rubinstein had "profaned" the music of Beethoven with his
"soporific conducting." He continually and flatly denied the value of
academic music training.[16]

In public and private talk, Serov hectored Rubinstein and the
Conservatory just as consistently. In the spring of 1864 he delivered a series of
ten lectures in which, according to a Conservatory student who attended
them, he made "desperate efforts . . . to undermine the Conservatory's
authority."[17] The following passage from an article based on these lectures
gives an idea of their tone:

> Familiarity with precedents must claim first priority for anyone who wishes to work in
> the arts. Certainly the Conservatory courses affirm this, but there they *put off the living*
> study of art by obtuse, pedantic formalism in order to exhaust the student with simple-
> minded rules that stupefy the spirit—a practice more *tedious* and *repressive* for the student
> than monastic scholasticism.[18]

In private, Serov's diatribes were likely to be especially sharp and vigorous.
The novelist Pyotr Boborykin recalls seeing Serov in action in the winter of
1861-62 at a gathering to hear writer Alexei Pisemsky read from his latest
novel. Boborykin was shocked to hear Serov abusing Anton Rubinstein "in an
extremely malicious tone, calling him a 'dance-hall pianist.' "[19]

Serov's public attacks on Rubinstein, the RMS, and the St. Petersburg
Conservatory clearly lead to the conclusion that they were motivated only in
part by differences of opinion. There is no reason to doubt that he sincerely
disagreed with Rubinstein's taste in music and his views on music education,
for in his private correspondence and in reviews written before the founding of
the RMS he took the same position on these subjects as in his later public
attacks on the Society and its founder. But their hectoring tone indicates that
these public writings were inspired at least in part by Serov's anti-Semitism

and envy of the success of a man he considered a foreign interloper in his own domain. Serov's libelous charges that Rubinstein was a charlatan, an ignoramus, and a fraud go far beyond the limits of an impersonal, intellectual argument. Furthermore, Serov carried his constant assertion that the RMS and its leader were not "Russian" to absurd lengths. He criticized the Society's first ten concerts for having nothing Russian about them in spite of the inclusion of fourteen works by eight different composers of Russian birth. At the same time, he turned around and suggested that these concerts should be conducted by some foreigner, such as Liszt, Berlioz, or Wagner. He regularly castigated Rubinstein for trying to subjugate Russia to Europe, but he saw nothing paradoxical in his own self-professed role as Wagner's apostle to Russia. These inconsistencies and excesses make sense only when Serov's abortive efforts as a music educator, the supposed snub he received from the RMS in its first season, and his anti-Semitism are taken into consideration. Then it becomes clear that his antipathy for Rubinstein was less a matter of principle or a patriot's reaction to foreign domination than the irrational hatred and envy of a bigot for someone he sees as an outsider who has managed to take over what he regards as his own rightful place. When Richard Wagner, during his visit to St. Petersburg in 1863, begged Serov to avoid antagonizing Rubinstein, he reputedly replied, "I hate him and can make no concessions."[20]

At the founding of the RMS in 1859 the Balakirev circle had only started to form. Thus it was in no position to challenge Rubinstein and his supporters. Rimsky and Borodin were not yet members, and the others were very young and almost unknown. Vladimir Stasov, their older friend and aesthetic adviser, already an author and critic, had so many interests that he only occasionally published articles on music. Not until the appearance in January 1861 of Rubinstein's article on the deficiencies of Russian musical life and the need for a conservatory did the Balakirev group respond publicly. Their reaction was an article written by Stasov and published anonymously in *Severnaia pchlela*. Compared with Serov, the tone was a model of restraint. In measured but pointed phrases, Stasov refuted each of Rubinstein's arguments. He denied that dilettante-musicians held a monopoly on bad compositions or that their influence in Russia was so great. He claimed that Rubinstein exaggerated the faults of Russian amateur musicians, that none of them would assert "the surprising things" in Rubinstein's article. The rank of "free artist," he said, would only attract talentless people to take up music for the sake of privileges. And finally, he charged that a conservatory would harm rather than help music in Russia because such institutions destroyed originality. "Perhaps Mr. Rubinstein does not know of the view, which has taken root in most of Europe, that academies and conservatories serve only as a breeding ground for the talentless and facilitate the consolidation of pernicious notions and tastes in art."

Stasov skirted a personal attack on Rubinstein by his suggestion that some of Rubinstein's errors in judging Russian musical life might be excused or at least explained because he was not a Russian. "Mr. Rubinstein is a foreigner among us, having nothing in common with our nationality or our art . . . , a foreigner with no understanding of either the needs of the former or the historical development of the latter." This sounds similar to Serov's claims but without the excesses or hysteria. Likewise, Stasov's concluding appeal to reject Rubinstein's proposal was moderate and reasoned:

> [Rubinstein] offers only measures for transplanting to us what now exists elsewhere. But what is the use of such a proposal. We all know how many foreign products have been transplanted here and how few of them have flourished. It is time, it seems, to cease these unconsidered transplantations and to think about what is actually useful and appropriate specifically for our own soil and our own nationality.

He ended with a rhetorical question: would Russia ignore the lesson to be drawn from Europe's experience that conservatories are harmful to art?[21]

Stasov's moderate tone and the close correspondence of these publicly expressed views with those shared privately in the Balakirev circle suggest that matters of principle prompted Stasov to write the article. Such a conclusion is supported by Stasov's own remarks in a letter to Balakirev:

> From jealousy of Russia and sheer folly, Anton is taking on something that, in my judgment, must come to a bad end. I hope—if there's still a chance—to stop it or at least to delay those who bustle about like industrious ants trying to drag off the log pointed to by the brilliant maestro's finger. I've got to see to it that the whole Rubinstein regiment of Odoevskies, Elena Pavlovnas, *et al.*, at least knows what's going on.[22]

Here the tone sharpens a bit, but the emphasis remains on Stasov's disagreement in principle with Rubinstein's remedy for Russia's musical ills.

The Balakirev circle acquired a permanent journalistic platform in the spring of 1864 when the editor of *Sankt-Peterburgskie vedomosti* [St. Petersburg Gazette] hired César Cui as a regular music critic. Not only was this the oldest newspaper in Russia and distinguished for its staff of leading literary figures, but for over a decade it had led all other Russian daily papers in its musical coverage as well. Thus, it provided the Balakirev circle with a conspicuous and prestigious forum for its views on music.[23] For the next decade, under the sigla of three asterisks, Cui wrote frequent columns and reviews for this paper—nearly two hundred in all.[24] As he explained many years later, his goal was "the popularization of the ideas" of Balakirev's circle and "support for the composers of the New Russian School," that is, for himself and his friends.[25] Although his tone never became as vitriolic as Serov's, Cui did not hide his partisanship, unceasingly praising his friends and condemning his enemies. Because of Cui's controversial and sharply expressed views, the editor of the paper felt obliged to publish a notice in

December 1864 disclaiming responsibility for the critic's opinions and offering "to provide space for any reasonable objection to the opinions of the associate for music criticism, which can seem . . . too extreme and harsh."[26]

Anton Rubinstein was one of Cui's favorite targets. In the first three months of his journalistic career Cui discussed the RMS concerts and reviewed Rubinstein's work as a conductor, composer, and pianist. Only Rubinstein's pianism escaped censure. Cui found the programs of the RMS concerts too conservative and filled with works by mediocre German composers: "It is a lot if we hear two or three new, interesting pieces during an entire season; still worse, among the remainder there are often pieces that cannot withstand the slightest scrutiny." As examples, he mentioned several composers of the contemporary German school, including Johannes Brahms. He complained that a Bach passacaglia, a Mozart motet, or choruses by Lully or Rameau, all performed by the RMS in its 1863-64 season, could interest only musical archaeologists. "This is rudimentary music," he added, "which produces absolutely nothing but boredom."[27] In later seasons Cui repeated the same charges, objecting to the "influx of works by second-rate German composers," and claiming that the RMS concerts had become "almost exclusive champions of bad German music" by second-rate composers.[28]

Cui dismissed Rubinstein as a serious conductor in one of his very first newspaper columns, complaining that St. Petersburg needed "an outstanding conductor-musician." A few weeks later he lamented the loss of "all traditions of good conducting" in the city since Berlioz's visit in 1847.[29] Cui also attacked Rubinstein the composer in one of his early reviews, claiming that "on the whole, his compositions are long, boring, soulless; throughout one sees an instinctive attachment to prescribed musical forms and a desire to be profound and erudite. To be sure, in such an enormous mass of compositions there are rather nice spots, but they vanish amidst the general tedium and bad taste."[30] As long as Rubinstein remained musical director of the RMS, Cui continued to criticize his work as both conductor and composer.[31]

Nor did Cui fail to attack the St. Petersburg Conservatory. His reviews are sprinkled with slighting references to the school and to conservatories in general, which he blamed for perpetuating sterile formalism.[32] Cui's criticism of Rubinstein's educational work reached its culmination in a discussion of Russia's two new conservatories published early in 1867. The Balakirev circle planned this article as the ultimate blow against musical academism in Russia. Both Stasov and Musorgsky contributed material and suggestions "in order to abuse both conservatories in a proper manner."[33] Musorgsky dubbed the piece "the *coup de grace* for the Conservatory."[34] Besides disputing specific practices of the Moscow and St. Petersburg schools, Cui challenged in no uncertain terms the whole concept of a conservatory, using arguments similar to those in Stasov's major article on the subject six years earlier. He claimed that musical development required only talent, elementary training, and study of the great works of the masters. If conservatories would limit their activity to assisting in such study, he insisted, they could be useful, but instead

> they want to create composers and therefore they make of music, that language of emotion, some kind of scholastic science, they introduce the teaching of musical rhetoric, they create rules with no basis, they correct Beethoven.
>   Such a view of music is very attractive to the talentless. It is actually possible, without inspiration or inner fire, just by keeping to all the rules of harmony and counterpoint that one has been taught and satisfying the conventional musical forms, to become a composer and even, perhaps, thanks to the assiduous clique of conservatory associates, a famous one.

Any talented student, Cui charged, would soon lose all his creative imagination in a conservatory because he would constantly be punished for violating the rules and worn down by having to write canons and fugues. Cui characterized all conservatories as bastions of pedantry:

> Conservatories ignore what is important and universal; they love what is petty and second-rate. In our conservatory, they have taught music history, but it was taken only up to Mendelssohn. This means that they talked about various Netherlanders and Italians, about various Ockeghems, Orlandos, Lassos, when music did not yet even exist, but they did not talk about the present state of music. It stands to reason that in a Russian conservatory, it is not worth speaking of Russian music—of Glinka, of Dargomyzhsky.[35]

Cui clearly resorted to many of the same arguments advanced by Serov against Rubinstein. Like Serov, Cui complained that Rubinstein was a poor conductor and a worse composer, that his concert programs were conservative and uninteresting, and that the Conservatory was a haven for mediocrity. But he moderated the tone of his criticism. On occasion, he even had kind words for Rubinstein and the RMS. In one review he included the Society's concerts among the city's most notable musical events and even praised them for their seriousness. In another article he thanked the Society for programming the first scene of Glinka's *Ruslan and Liudmila* without the cuts usually made in stage performances, for introducing some major works of Schumann and Berlioz, and for regularly performing Beethoven's Ninth Symphony, albeit imperfectly. Elsewhere, he even admitted that Rubinstein conducted some works adequately.[36] Balakirev actually chided Cui, perhaps ironically, for not making his sympathies and antipathies sufficiently obvious, asserting that his "manner of unclear expression" might leave the impression that he "liked . . . Rubinstein."[37]

Although Balakirev certainly exaggerated Cui's moderation, his reviews were nevertheless much more restrained in tone than Serov's writings. For the most part, Cui confined himself to musical questions and avoided personal invective. He argued against Rubinstein and his Society on the basis of aesthetic principles and, for the most part, kept his group's personal antipathies out of his writing. This is particularly noticeable in his avoidance of the issue of Rubinstein's nationality. While Serov publicly excoriated Rubinstein as a foreign charlatan, and the Balakirev circle privately referred to him as a foreigner, a German, or even a "yid," Cui's reviews made no great issue of his background. He complained that the RMS concerts included fewer Russian works every year but did not specifically lay the blame for this on the foreignness of the conductor, as did Serov.[38] Perhaps Cui, as the son of a French father and a Lithuanian mother, realized that an attack on someone else for not being a true Russian would be inappropriate. But he may have emphasized Rubinstein's conservatism and academism, rather than his foreignness, simply because he considered modernism, not nationalism, the basic aesthetic issue. In any case, Cui's attacks on Rubinstein never skirted the libelous as did Serov's, but he nonetheless joined Serov in his efforts to denigrate Rubinstein's musical authority and to undermine the prestige of the Conservatory.

Despite the public criticism he and his work received from Serov, Stasov, Cui, and other critics,[39] Anton Rubinstein never replied publicly. In fact, he forbade his associates and students to write for the newspapers. As one student later explained, Rubinstein "did not like polemics generally, and . . . seemed, at least on the surface, to pay them no attention, constantly advising everyone to take care of his own work as he ought to and thus to avoid the possibility of reproaches."[40] In the spring of 1864 Hermann Laroche, a Conservatory student, wrote a polemical response to Serov's attacks on the Conservatory and had it published in *Severnaia pchela,* signed "a conservatory student." When his identity was discovered over a year later, he was almost expelled for having violated the ban on press appearances by students.[41] As a result of Rubinstein's policy, the battle in the press clearly went to his opponents. During his years as director, no regular music critic of stature consistently defended Rubinstein, the Russian Musical Society, or the St. Petersburg Conservatory against their enemies in the press.

The press foes of the RMS were powerful, but they dissipated some of their force by lack of unity. Serov and the Balakirev circle, despite their general agreement on most musical questions, failed to coordinate their writings against Rubinstein and instead exchanged critical blows with one another. Their opinions of Rubinstein and his work were nearly identical, and in their reviews Serov and Cui shared many other causes, such as denigration of Italian opera (and its large Petersburg audience) and promotion of the works of Beethoven, Schumann, Liszt, and Berlioz,[42] but the differences of opinion and personal animosity described earlier kept Serov and the Balakirev circle from working together.

As early as 1859 Stasov published an attack on Serov for his espousal of

Wagnerian principles, and in 1862 the two exchanged polemics over the authenticity of several published Glinka songs.[43] Cui's work as a music reviewer elicited Serov's criticism from the very beginning. In March 1864, immediately after the appearance of Cui's first three columns, all anonymous, Serov published a critique of Russian music critics obviously aimed at Cui. It read, in part:

> The responsibility of a critic appearing in the press is first of all: justice, impartiality. . . . Here in Petersburg, [however], a remarkable absence of control reigns in musical matters. Anyone writes, and writes absolutely whatever comes into his head about composers, conductors, performers, and very often does not even consider it necessary to inform the public of his name, however renowned or completely unknown.[44]

Cui promptly responded with his own sarcastic review of Serov's articles:

> We have such little music criticism and so few critics that it is sad to see one of the best of earlier days begin to decline and grow weak. Firm musical convictions, it is true, Serov never had. . . . But he nevertheless had important merits. Now and then there were fresh ideas ardently expressed, adroit polemics, and fierce battles against authorities. . . . But what now? Blind and servile worship of anything contemporary, even if ungifted, fiery outbursts without merit or force, attacks that miss the point, battles *for* "authorities" (Serov now probably considers himself among their number), and even the language itself now serves him poorly.[45]

In 1865 and 1866 Cui and Stasov reviewed Serov's music several times, always negatively, but he did not respond until 1867 when he founded his journal *Muzyka i teatr*. He saw this publication primarily as a platform for attacks on his opponents, privately dubbing it "a specialized critical (merciless) journal,"[46] and wasted no time directing his new weapon against the Balakirev circle. His introductory article in the first issue assailed the weaknesses of his competitors in Russian music criticism. Although he never mentioned Cui directly, Serov obviously had him in mind when he condemned critics like "the ardent pen-pusher who glibly and insolently 'advertises' for the benefit of his own circle and the detriment of others" and "flaunts views and convictions of the wildest and absurdest nature" just to attract public attention.[47] Cui retorted with an evaluation of the first issue of *Muzyka i teatr*, claiming the goal of this new journal to be not musical enlightenment but "glorification of Mr. Serov's musical works" at the expense of any other work that might "throw the slightest shadow" upon them.[48]

Serov's major attack against Stasov and Cui in 1867 focused on their supposedly false evaluation of Glinka and in particular his opera *Ruslan and Liudmila*. Prompted by their recent articles lauding *Ruslan* as an unsurpassed masterpiece, Serov included in his first ten issues of *Muzyka i teatr* a series of seven articles analyzing Glinka's second opera. Entitled *"Ruslan* and the Ruslanists," the series was clearly directed against Stasov and Cui for their allegedly uncritical admiration of the work. Serov himself was a declared partisan of Glinka and had written extensively on his life and music,[49] but he argued that *Ruslan*'s undramatic plot compromised its immense musical beauties and that as a work for the stage it was inferior to Glinka's first opera, *A Life for the Tsar*. While praising the musical glories of *Ruslan*, Serov skillfully exposed the dramatic flaws in the work that have, in fact, precluded genuine popularity for it even to the present day.[50] Along the way, he denounced Stasov and Cui for exaggerating the importance of the work and for having insinuated that he, Serov, neither understood nor appreciated it. He diagnosed them as suffering from "Ruslanomania, a disease that has now developed in Mr. Stasov and his 'echo' [i.e., Cui] to monstrous proportions." Serov refuted Stasov's claim that Glinka was the greatest of all opera composers:

> Glinka's primacy among Russian opera composers is already decided, subject neither to new proof nor dispute.
>
> But the place Glinka occupies in music generally is still not determined; the panegyrics and publicity of V. Stasov and Co. in this case do not help but only hurt the cause by perpetrating on the public confused, untrue, and even absurd notions.[51]

This series of articles led to several more exchanges of journalistic abuse, with Cui charging Serov with "bombast, insipidness, frequent repetitions, and a mania for beginning everything he talks about with Adam and Eve,"[52] and Serov accusing Cui of deliberately twisting and distorting his arguments.[53] Polemics such as this continued for several more years,[54] preventing any easing of the antagonism between Serov and the Balakirev circle.

The bitter tone and personal insults of Serov's articles about Cui and Stasov are not surprising since they were also typical of his reviews of Rubinstein and the Russian Musical Society. Cui's indulgence in personal attacks against Serov, however, is noteworthy. In dealing with the RMS he generally confined himself to aesthetic and musical questions. In the conflict with Serov there were few differences in musical principles or taste; therefore, Cui fell back on invective. The extra harshness in his dealing with Serov undoubtedly also resulted in part from the direct rivalry with a fellow critic and the heat of a two-sided exchange, a development absent in Cui's press relations with Rubinstein because of the latter's refusal to reply publicly to his critics. Another factor must have been that Balakirev and his followers felt greater personal animosity toward Serov than toward Rubinstein. Serov had once been a friend and supporter of the circle, but he had withdrawn from the group. The intensity of Cui's criticism and the central position in the debate of seemingly fine distinctions over the significance of Glinka's works suggest that the Balakirev circle saw Serov not merely as an opponent, like Rubinstein, but as a renegade, a heretic who was all the more dangerous for his closeness to the true faith. Therefore, their press campaign against him was more heated and intense than that against Rubinstein, and they could not ally with Serov against the man whose musical views were directly opposed to both Serov's and their own.

Had the Russian Musical Society's opponents confined their musical activities to the press criticism of the Society and one another just described, they could have been dismissed as petty complainers, bickering among themselves and impotently carping at a successful organization from a combination of legitimate disagreement on aesthetic principles, personal antipathy, and bigotry. But their challenge to the RMS had a positive as well as a negative side. Serov and the members of the Balakirev circle were creative musicians in their own right. Their press attacks on Rubinstein and the RMS served not only to denigrate an opponent but also to publicize and promote their own budding musical careers, to offer themselves as preferable alternatives to Rubinstein as leaders of musical life in St. Petersburg. Furthermore, as they became successful as practicing musicians, their press attacks on the RMS attracted more attention and acquired greater authority among the music-lovers of St. Petersburg. It was this that made Serov and the Balakirev circle truly formidable opponents of Rubinstein and the Russian Musical Society.

Other than criticism, Serov's chief musical activity in the 1860's was composing operas. After the RMS failed to perform the work he submitted in its first season, Serov gave up any hope of becoming famous at home as a composer of symphonic and choral music and turned instead to a potentially much more promising arena—the opera.[55] Not only was opera far more popular in St. Petersburg than serious orchestral concerts, but Serov had begun to establish friendly contacts with the management of the Imperial theaters.[56] This boded well for Serov's chances to have an opera of his own produced by the Imperial theaters, and he was not one to pass up such an opportunity.

Serov chose the Biblical story of Judith and Holofernes as a subject after seeing the celebrated Italian actress Adelaida Ristori in a spectacularly successful stage version of it in St. Petersburg late in 1860.[57] He ordered a libretto prepared from the play and, with an eye clearly fixed on the taste of the Petersburg public, began setting *Judith* to music.[58] Despite his publicly expressed disdain for Meyerbeer's operas,[59] Serov tailored his own first effort in the field to the popular Meyerbeerian model, with plenty of processions and choral scenes, an orgy for stage spectacle, and even the obligatory third-act ballet. In an even more obvious bid for popularity he originally began setting *Judith* to an Italian text in the hope of having it premiered by the Imperial Italian Opera.[60] Considering Serov's advocacy of Russian music and his criticism of foreign domination of Russian musical life, one can only assume that this violation of his principles sprang from his desire for the great public success that only the Italian Opera seemed to offer. In any case, the plan came to nothing, because the prima donna of the Italian company refused to perform it. Therefore, Serov decided to rewrite his libretto in Russian, "having taken leave," as he wrote in his autobiography, "of the fantasy of coming to terms with Italian routine for his debut."[61]

Although he had to give up his dream of beginning his career as a composer with the kind of spectacular triumph that only the Italian Opera could produce in St. Petersburg, Serov was very successful in the rest of his plans for *Judith*. He submitted the work to the Russian Opera in the fall of 1862, having first assured its acceptance by acquiring a highly placed patron.[62] The Theater Directorate promptly agreed to stage *Judith*[63] and permitted Serov to supervise much of the preparation for its premiere in May 1863.[64]

Serov was just as adept at interesting the Petersburg public in his opera as he was at pursuading the Russian Opera to mount the work as he wished it performed. His music criticism was as controversial as ever,[65] and in the spring of 1861 he found an even more effective way to increase his notoriety by breaking up a public concert led by Alexander Lazarev, a Russian composer who claimed superiority to Beethoven.[66] Before Lazarev could begin a Beethoven overture for comparison with his own compositions Serov, according to an official report of the incident, stood up on his seat and addressed the audience: "Ladies and gentlemen! After the rubbish we have just heard, not a single note of Beethoven should be allowed, and I am sure that the public will not permit it. Lazarev has swindled several rubles from each of us, and for this impudence he should be showered with rotten potatoes." Despite Lazarev's efforts to continue, the concert turned into a riot, with the audience shouting, whistling, and even throwing placards and programs—presumably for want of the suggested potatoes—until the orchestra and Lazarev fled the stage.[67] The police arrested Serov and confined him to the Admiralty guardhouse for one week.[68] This was a small price to pay for the publicity the incident brought him. A few weeks after his release Serov wrote a friend that at least "the silly event compelled the public to pay a little more attention" to him.[69] According to a contemporary, Serov's real popularity began with the publicity he received for breaking up Lazarev's concert: "One only had to pronounce Serov's name and everyone would laughingly add: 'Is that the one who pelted maestro Lazarev with rotten apples?' "[70]

In the spring of 1862, a year after this incident, the performance of an orchestral fragment from *Judith* at a Lenten concert notified the public that the controversial critic was at work on an opera,[71] and soon rumors about his new work were spreading among Petersburg's musical circles.[72] In April 1863 official notices and increasingly detailed reports about the approaching

premiere of the opera began to appear in Petersburg newspapers.[73] By the time
of its first performance in May 1863, there could hardly have been a music-
lover in St. Petersburg who did not know of Serov's new opera.

The success of *Judith* was all that Serov could have desired. Vladimir
Stasov attended the premiere on 16 May 1863, and the next day he wrote
Balakirev that "from the very first note Serov became the idol of Petersburg. . . .
You can have no conception of what happened yesterday. Everyone is crazy,
everyone is enraptured as never before, they all say that nothing like this has
ever happened to us before, that he is our first composer since the creation of
the world."[74] From the rest of Stasov's very long letter it is clear that he
exaggerated Serov's triumph somewhat because he was shocked and
dismayed to see the victory of a personal enemy, but nevertheless all the
evidence indicates a considerable success for Serov's first opera. Not only was
the theater full for the premiere, despite the unfashionable time of year and
increased ticket prices,[75] but *Judith* continued to fill the theater thereafter.
The following January Prince Odoevsky attended the eighteenth performance
and noted in his diary that "the auditorium was packed" in spite of the Italian
Opera's performance on the same night of its latest sensation, Gounod's
Faust.[76] Most of the critics rated the new work the best Russian opera since
Glinka's *Ruslan and Liudmila,* and some even ranked Serov above Glinka.[77]
Even Feofil Tolstoy, a long-time rival of Serov, reluctantly admitted that
Judith "had a great and *fully deserved* success."[78]

Serov realized full well that such a success would not only advance his
musical career but also aid his campaign against Rubinstein. More than a year
before *Judith's* premiere Serov had described to a close friend what he hoped
to achieve with his opera:

> *My opera on the stage,* even if with only a small "succès d'estime," will give me a
> completely different position in the eyes of *everyone.* Then I may hope for subscribers for a
> journal. Then they will surmise that I do not only "chat" about music but am in fact a
> *musician* (even if they don't like my music at all). Then it will be difficult for even the
> Russian Musical Society to ignore me. In order to clear themselves before the public, they
> will have to change their attitude toward me. In general, the battle will take on a *different*
> character.[79]

In fact, the premiere of *Judith* brought Serov the recognition he craved.
Grand Duchess Elena Pavlovna, patroness of the Russian Musical Society,
sent him congratulations and a gift of one thousand rubles.[80]

Emboldened by his critical and popular triumph and encouraged by the
one hundred rubles he received for each performance of *Judith,*[81] Serov
promptly began writing a new opera, *Rogneda,* based on a legend about pre-
Christian Russia. As he told Feofil Tolstoy, he had chosen a non-Russian
subject for his first opera to avoid competing with Glinka, but with *Rogneda*

he planned a work beyond comparison with any "Ruslans" or "Rusalkas."[82] He had probably also noticed that the wave of nationalistic fervor that swept Russia following the Polish rebellion of 1863 had made operas on patriotic subjects, such as Glinka's *A Life for the Tsar,* more popular than every before, producing enthusiastic public demonstrations whenever they were performed.[83] Taking his cue from the success of *Judith,* Serov filled *Rogneda* with hunts and revels, religious processions, miraculous visions, minstrels, sorcerers, and even dancing bears[84]—in short, all the tricks so dear to the hearts of audiences who considered Meyerbeer one of the greatest of all composers.

It is not surprising then that the eagerly awaited premiere of Serov's second opera in the fall of 1865 was an even more spectacular triumph than *Judith* had been. According to Rimsky-Korsakov, it "created a furor. Serov grew a full foot in artistic stature."[85] By 3 February 1866, little more than three months after its premiere, *Rogneda* had achieved twenty-two performances, all to full houses.[86] Critical opinion about *Rogneda* was more divided than on *Judith,* but Serov's supporters were still more extreme in their praise of his second opera than of his first.[87] *Rogneda* even won Serov a life pension of one thousand rubles a year from the tsar "in consideration of his excellent talent and remarkable musical compositions."[88] Thus, Serov's work in opera brought him fame and financial reward. He achieved the successful career as a creative musician that he had long desired, and the triumph of his operas also increased the weight of his critical pronouncements against the RMS and Anton Rubinstein.

Despite the great success of Serov's two operas, the Balakirev circle refused to recognize in him any more than a mediocre talent for writing popular music. They acknowledged that he took his task seriously and attempted to write operas according to the advanced principles of the day, avoiding the old-fashioned operatic conventions they despised. Still Balakirev, Stasov, and Musorgsky all included detailed and unfavorable critiques of *Judith* in their private correspondence; Cui dismissed it in two patronizing sentences: "There are, after all, interesting things in *Judith.* There are beauties, although of the most shallow kind, and it is written seriously but without sufficient talent."[89] *Rogneda* elicited still harsher criticism. Rimsky later recalled that the group frequently made fun of it, finding only one or two sections adequate. Although Rimsky himself "liked a good deal of it" and could play parts of it at the piano from memory, he did not dare praise it before Balakirev and his friends.[90] Borodin even wrote a full-length operetta, *Bogatyri* [The Valiant Knights], satirizing the plot and parodying the music of Serov's opera.[91]

Predictably, Cui and Stasov carried the Balakirev circle's private criticism of Serov's music into their public press campaign against him. In

April 1864, only six weeks after beginning his journalistic work, Cui reviewed a chorus and duet from Serov's unfinished *Rogneda* performed at a symphonic concert. He judged the chorus boring and uninspired, the recitatives "not very good musically," the melodies of "routine Italian construction," and the orchestration "very ordinary."[92] Nine months later Cui devoted the bulk of one article to *Judith,* praising it for its seriousness and reflection of modern operatic concepts but finding it fatiguing and monotonous because of Serov's "lack of creative ability."[93] In his review of *Rogneda*'s premiere Cui criticized Serov's talent even more sharply, claiming he had proven "his incapacity for dramatic music" and presented "an ordinary opera with a commonplace but showy text, without contemporary tendencies, without characterization of persons or nationalities." Most of the music, charged Cui, "is mediocre and . . . more often than not leads to mortal weariness and boredom."[94]

Harsher still was Stasov's criticism of *Rogneda.* He declared that public acclaim derived from the work's cheap effects:

> Just look at all that is in Mr. Serov's new opera: requiems, hymns, and the Christianizing of Russia for the pious; hunts and revels for the gay *bons vivants;* popular assemblies and resolutions for the Slavophiles and "men of the soil"; cheap Verdi-isms for the "music-lovers"; counterpoint and thematic combination for the schoolboys and teachers. Each gets a special treat so all are happy, and thankful, and touched, and all applaud.

Stasov dubbed Serov "the Russian Meyerbeer" for his alleged triviality, shallowness, and concern with superficial stage effects, but he claimed that Serov lacked the musical skill and imagination of his foreign counterpart.[95]

The success of Serov's two operas in the 1860's proved ephemeral,[96] as it was based at least partly on Serov's manipulation of the public's taste for spectacle. Nevertheless, recent studies suggest that these works had considerable artistic merit.[97] As for the Balakirev circle's ridicule, it appears clearly to have been prompted by other than musical judgments, particularly in the case of Stasov's article, which turned into a personal attack on Serov's motives as well as his talent.

The Balakirev circle's musical activity from 1859 to 1867, aside from criticism, was more diverse and complex than Serov's for it encompassed not only composition but educational work and public concerts as well. Balakirev himself, as the only experienced, full-time musician in the group, led the way. As early as 1859 he succeeded in having his first compositions (a collection of songs) published in St. Petersburg, to be followed in the 1860s by a series of original piano pieces, piano transcriptions of orchestral works by Glinka, Beethoven, and Berlioz, and songs suitable for home performance. In 1866 he published a popular collection of Russian folk songs in his own arrangements for voice and piano.[98] Although he did not much care for the role of a concert pianist, Balakirev also occasionally resorted to personal benefit recitals to earn money and public attention. He gave such a concert, consisting of solo piano literature and chamber music, each spring from 1863 through 1865.[99]

Balakirev and his circle also succeeded in having a number of their compositions performed publicly in St. Petersburg. Balakirev's first public performances of his orchestral music came in 1859, and the Russian Musical Society played pieces by Cui and Musorgsky during its first season. In later seasons Rubinstein occasionally programmed other compositions by circle members, especially Cui.[100] The Imperial Theater Directorate also now and then performed music by Balakirev and his followers at its symphonic concerts. In April 1861, for example, the Theater Directorate presented a symphonic concert entirely of Russian works, including compositions by Balakirev, Cui, Musorgsky, and Apollon Gussakovsky, at the time a member of Balakirev's group.[101] Vasily Kologrivov, who was both a close friend of Balakirev and the inspector of orchestras for the Theater Directorate, possibly used his official position to achieve the inclusion of so much music by the circle at this concert.[102] Works by the Balakirev circle also appeared occasionally at benefit or commemorative concerts such as a literary-musical evening in honor of the three-hundredth anniversary of Shakespeare's birth given by the Society for the Aid of Needy Writers and Scholars in the spring of 1864. Balakirev conducted the musical selections, including his own incidental music to *King Lear*.[103] He probably owed this opportunity to appear publicly as both composer and conductor to Dmitri Stasov, who was a member of the sponsoring organization and in charge of arranging its benefit concerts.[104]

Until Cui began writing music reviews in 1864, Vladimir Stasov was the Balakirev circle's only press spokesman, but he did not very often write articles on music and disliked the job of publicizing the works of his friends. He left unheeded Balakirev's pleas to review his overture for *King Lear* when it was premiered at one of the University concerts in the winter of 1859-60,[105] for example, and turned down a similar appeal a year later, explaining that he was disgusted by "the vulgar role of a gushing friend who is ready to write to order or on request."[106] Nevertheless, for important occasions Stasov took up his pen to advertise the musical work of the Balakirev circle. He reviewed Balakirev's personal benefit recital in the spring of 1863, for example, applauding his friend for "a performance that one does not encounter among the common piano virtuosos, those musical plagues and pestilences, but only among true musicians who are able to reproduce the creations of others because they are gifted with a genuine understanding of music." Stasov called the concert "one of only three *Russian* concerts" of the season, one of only three concerts that proved the existence of "a *Russian* school of music and *Russian* musicians."[107]

Once Cui became a regular music critic, the Balakirev circle no longer had to contend with Stasov's reticence. Cui apparently had no qualms about publicizing the activity of his friends. He frequently wrote about their music and public appearances, almost always in terms of the highest praise. He reviewed the literary-musical evening in honor of Shakespeare mentioned earlier, for example, applauding both Balakirev's conducting and his music for *King Lear*.[108] Balakirev's collection of Russian folk songs, published in 1866, elicited Cui's recommendation as the best of all such collections, which "should become a handbook" for anyone claiming to be a musician.[109]

Publication of piano pieces and folk songs, occasional public appearances as a conductor or pianist, and performances now and then of his own music and that of his friends at various concerts brought Balakirev public attention, but they could hardly satisfy his desire to propagate what he considered Russian national music or to become the leader of St. Petersburg's musical life. Balakirev needed a permanent position in a prominent musical organization, preferably one that could also serve as a public platform for his own music and that of his friends. Balakirev found such a position in the Free Music School, which he helped to organize in 1862 and turned into a rival to both the St. Petersburg Conservatory and the concerts of the Russian Musical Society.

The original director of the Free Music School was Gavriil Lomakin, the most distinguished choral conductor in mid-nineteenth-century Russia. Not only was he the chorus director for several Petersburg educational institutes, but he also led Count Dmitri Sheremetev's private chorus, the most famous in Russia. Several members of the royal family, including Grand Duchess Elena Pavlovna, attended services in the count's church just to hear Lomakin's choir, and all the famous Western musicians who visited Russia were taken to admire the quality of this ensemble.[110] According to Lomakin, his idea of founding a music school developed from discussions he had in the early 1860s with such musical friends as Balakirev, Vladimir Stasov, and Serov, who urged him to broaden his musical work and make it accessible to the masses.[111] The Sunday school movement, a program to teach basic literacy to illiterate adults, was then at its height in St. Petersburg, with volunteer teachers establishing dozens of free schools throughout the city.[112] Lomakin decided to establish a similar school to teach the fundamentals of music to the musically illiterate. He "was convinced that choral singing was all that was needed for the musical enlightment of Russia,"[113] and this conviction lay at the heart of his pedagogic approach.

Lomakin invited Mily Balakirev to join the enterprise. Little interested in choral singing, Balakirev nevertheless volunteered to help Lomakin by directing a small amateur orchestra attached to the school. Lomakin says that Balakirev envisioned this as an opportunity for young Russian composers— presumably himself and his friends—to try out their newest works before submitting them to public scrutiny, but the circle of amateur instrumentalists on which Balakirev had counted for his orchestra proved inadequate for the job.[114]

On 4 January 1862 Balakirev wrote Vladimir Stasov that the mayor of St. Petersburg had successfully petitioned for government permission to open a free school of singing.[115] By the end of January newspapers had published reports of the impending opening of "a free music school, the chief goal of which is the spread of music education. . . . The founders accept as their charge the teaching of music and singing to persons of all estates."[116] Two benefit concerts by Count Sheremetev's chorus in March and April 1862 raised enough money to permit the school to open.[117]

The Free Music School (FMS) officially opened on 18 March 1862. Ten days later Balakirev wrote a friend that two hundred pupils appeared the first Sunday and that more were expected in the future when the school added an earlier class, which would not coincide with the classes of the Sunday schools teaching basic literacy. "There are many good voices and everything is going successfully,"[118] he added. The summer holidays soon interrupted the school's activities, but they resumed the following September.[119] The program drawn up for the FMS by Balakirev and Lomakin specified classes in reading music, vocal training, solo singing, choral singing, and elementary music theory. To accommodate the schedules of his amateur students, Lomakin arranged to hold classes three evenings a week plus Sunday afternoon in the auditorium of the city hall. For ladies who found evening classes inconvenient, he also held daytime sessions in Count Sheremetev's palace.[120] By March 1863, after only one year in existence, the FMS boasted seven hundred students.[121]

Although most of the school's first students knew nothing of music and had to begin in the elementary class to read notes, Lomakin and Balakirev decided to schedule a public concert for early 1863. In spite of the students' handicaps, particularly their irregular attendance, the chorus managed to learn eight pieces in four months, and the Free Music School's first public concert took place with great success on 25 February 1863,[122] to be followed shortly by a second successful performance. This established a pattern that the FMS followed for a number of years, giving two annual public concerts, usually during the Lenten concert season.[123] Apparently Lomakin was an extraordinarily talented choral director who produced excellent results from his amateur students. Vladimir Sokolov, himself a singer, composer, and voice teacher in St. Petersburg for several decades, called Lomakin "the finest teacher of choral singing" he had ever known and described his FMS concerts as "models of ideally perfect performance."[124] In the first six years of the school's existence more than one thousand students passed through the FMS classes. Former FMS students formed two new church choirs, and several of them went on to become famous opera singers.[125]

By rights, no rivalry should have developed between Lomakin's Free Music School and Rubinstein's Conservatory, which opened the same year. The two institutions had entirely different purposes—the former to provide rudimentary musical skills to the masses, the latter to train professional musicians. Furthermore, Lomakin was on friendly terms with Rubinstein. He served on the RMS Repertory Committee and earlier had taught choral singing for the Society's music classes in the Mikhailovsky Palace.[126] Rubinstein attended the first FMS concert and praised Lomakin for his great success.[127] In addition, Grand Duchess Elena Pavlovna, official protectress of the RMS and the St. Petersburg Conservatory, had taken an active interest in the fortunes of the FMS and succeeded in 1863 in winning for the school the patronage of her nephew Nikolai, the heir to the throne.[128] Nevertheless, the Balakirev circle saw in the FMS a potential rival to the St. Petersburg Conservatory and used articles and reviews to turn the school into a weapon in its campaign to undermine the authority of the RMS. Even Serov used it to censure Rubinstein until it became obvious that to continue would aid Balakirev.

As early as May 1862 Serov published an article comparing the FMS with Rubinstein's recently announced plans to open a conservatory. He viciously excoriated the projected conservatory as a haven of mediocrities, sponsored by foreign quacks, but he wished the FMS and its *Russian* director the full support of the Petersburg public for its "salutary undertakings, which stand above the tawdry gloss of charlatanism and lead so truly to a sensible, elevated and sacred goal!" He found the educational program of a conservatory destructive for Russian art but praised the FMS's limited course of instruction: "Let all for whom the musical education of Russians, beginning with the first elements of that education, for whom the dissemination among us of musical literacy, not high-flown titles and splendid honorifics, . . . is dear pay due attention to the *free music school,* founded by Gavriil Lomakin."[129]

Once Balakirev's role in the school became obvious, Serov dropped his support, but then Stasov and Cui took over. In a lengthy review of the Free Music School's two concerts of early 1863, Stasov flatly declared that the FMS was the only "truly Russian music school" in Russia, implicitly dismissing the Conservatory as an alien institution. He particularly praised the FMS's efforts to provide basic music education for the masses, seeing in this, rather than the training of professional musicians, the proper goal of music education. He complained only that at the choral concerts

it would be a hundred times better if the dense ranks of hoopskirts and tailcoats would move aside and the long-skirted frock coats and high-collared tunics hiding behind them would step forward; if more and more of these . . . would attend the school and if to them were added those who have not yet appeared there—the seamstresses from the shop, the dressmaker, the chambermaid, the milliner, in a word, all those of the laboring class who only a short while ago were flocking so eagerly to the Sunday schools.[130]

Cui also devoted an article to a comparison of the FMS with the St. Petersburg Conservatory, much to the detriment of the latter. He admitted that the Conservatory's program was fuller and its fees moderate, but he complained that even a modest fee excluded many students, as did the requirement of being able to read music. The FMS, on the other hand, while limiting itself to teaching singing, was open to all, even "factory workers, shop assistants, [and] clerks from Gostinny Dvor." Then he compared the results of the two schools in the one area where this was possible, their choruses, claiming that the choir of the FMS had been brought "to a perfection of which we in Petersburg had previously not even had a notion."[131] Thus, despite the different goals of the Free Music School, Stasov, Cui, and even Serov for a short time publicized it as an *alternative* to the Conservatory and exploited its successes to denigrate the RMS's educational work.

Similarly, Balakirev and his friends turned the concerts of the Free Music School into a weapon against the Russian Musical Society. Lomakin originally intended the FMS concerts only as a means of raising money for the school and as a public showcase for fine choral singing. Balakirev, however, succeeded in turning them into "a center for new Russian music," meaning, in effect, for himself and his friends.[132]

The earliest FMS concerts were devoted almost entirely to choral music, and the influence of Balakirev, who cared little for most vocal music, was barely in evidence. The two benefit concerts in 1862 required a small, hired orchestra, but only to accompany the chorus and for the obligatory orchestral overture without which a concert was considered incomplete. Lomakin himself conducted all the choral pieces, and Karl Schubert, the veteran leader of the University concerts and friend of Rubinstein, conducted the overture at each concert.[133] The programs also fully reflected Lomakin's tastes and included works by Mendelssohn, Mozart, Haydn, and earlier Western composers ranging all the way back to the fifteenth century. The only evident concession to Balakirev's aesthetic viewpoint was the programming of his *Overture on Three Russian Themes,* which was not finally performed due to unexplained technicalities.[134]

With the concerts of 1863, all this began to change. Balakirev now took charge of the orchestra and pursuaded Lomakin to give it a larger role.[135] He had announced his intentions earlier in a letter to Rimsky-Korsakov of November 1862: "Our music school is doing splendidly; by the time you return to Petersburg, you will surely find well-organized concerts in which you will conduct your own symphonies."[136] In 1864 Balakirev made his continued association with the school contingent on keeping its concerts "a center for our Russian talent."[137]

The FMS concerts quickly showed the effects of Balakirev's influence. The two programs given in the spring of 1863 each presented not one but two works for orchestra, and they were all by Russian composers—Glinka, Cui, and Balakirev. Even the vocal works, which Lomakin conducted, now included music of Weber, Glinka, and Schumann in addition to Mendelssohn and the Classical and Baroque masters. The following season Balakirev conducted seven orchestral works—two by Glinka and the rest by Cui, Dargomyzhsky, Balakirev himself, Schumann, and Liszt. All together, over the five seasons from 1863 through 1867, Balakirev shared the podium with Lomakin at ten FMS concerts, conducting twenty-eight orchestral works. Of these, eighteen were by members of the Balakirev circle or by other Russian composers they admired. The remaining ten works were by Liszt, Schumann, or Berlioz, the "advanced" Western composers. Glinka's music appeared seven times, Balakirev's and Liszt's five times each, and Cui's and Rimsky's twice each. In addition, the vocal portions of the FMS concerts, under Lomakin's direction, presented music of Glinka, Dargomyzhsky, Cui, Musorgsky, Berlioz, and Schumann, as well as Lomakin's more usual repertory of Palestrina, Handel, Mozart, and Mendelssohn. As long as Lomakin remained in charge of the FMS chorus, Baroque and Classical works remained on the programs, and orchestral literature was not allowed to take over completely. Still, Balakirev managed to win parity for the orchestra and, ignoring any pretense of choosing orchestral repertory from all schools and periods as the RMS did, presented a large number of works by his own circle and its preferred Russian and Western colleagues.[138]

Just as Stasov and Cui used the educational work of the FMS to denigrate the St. Petersburg Conservatory, so they also publicized the FMS concerts as a positive alternative to the RMS concerts. On 30 April 1863 Stasov published a lengthy review of the Free Music School's first two concerts. He praised Lomakin and the chorus very highly, finding them fully capable of performing all choral music of every epoch, but he called on them to concentrate on their most important task, the performance of contemporary music by the vanguard of Western and Russian composers. He then singled out Balakirev for special attention:

> Those who listen intently to a musical performance, disregarding fashion and acknowledged reputations, were convinced from the first notes of the second concert of the Free Music School that before them, with the conductor's baton in his hand, stood a man with an important future, who will turn out to be a most wonderful Russian conductor. In this concert Glinka's "Jota [Aragonesa]," one of the most brilliant creations of Russian music, was performed as never before since the day it was written. Other performances that we have heard were pale and insignificant by comparison.[139]

The fact that Rubinstein had conducted Glinka's "Jota" during the previous RMS season suggests that Stasov meant to compare Balakirev to Rubinstein—to the latter's detriment.

Cui also took on the task of publicizing the FMS concerts from the time of his first regular employment as a critic in 1864. Although he often quibbled with Lomakin's choral selections, he found the orchestral repertory excellent and frequently compared the FMS concerts favorably to those of the RMS.[140] Writing in March 1865, Cui reported that the Free Music School concerts, in only two years, had attracted public attention by their high standards of performance and generally excellent choice of repertory: "Their popularity at once surpassed the popularity even of the concerts of the Russian Musical Society: an extremely varied, mixed, and numerous audience attends the former; the public for the latter consists of a much more limited, uniform, and unchanging stratum of lovers of serious music."[141]

Cui also publicized the FMS concerts as a distinctly Russian phenomenon, unlike the concerts of the RMS. In March 1866, for example, he appealed to his readers' national loyalties by lauding the Free Music School's concerts as "proof that even without the help of Germans, excellent music can be excellently performed" in Russia, explaining,

> Two Russians are in charge of them, and that is why there is no one-sidedness in the composition of the programs, and it is possible to hear works of *Russian* composers (Dargomyzhsky, Balakirev, Rimsky-Korsakov), for whom, evidently, the *Russian* Musical Society is quite inaccessible.[142]

The performances of the circle's music at the FMS concerts generated no such public or critical furor as did Serov's operas, but Cui did his best as critic for St. Petersburg's leading newspaper to promote the music of his friends. Over and over again he wrote about the latest works by the group and their potential for laying the foundation of a new Russian school of composition. After hearing Balakirev's *Second Overture on Russian Themes* he announced that its originality showed that Balakirev "and those like him" could be the source of a new national school.[143] He greeted Rimsky-Korsakov's Symphony in E Minor as "the first Russian symphony," dismissing Rubinstein's works in this form as "purely German compositions like Mendelssohn's symphonies."[144]

Thus, Balakirev and his circle gradually turned the Free Music School into an agency for their own work and a rival to Anton Rubinstein and the Russian Musical Society. During his tenure as director, Lomakin placed some restraints on Balakirev's use of the school, but with his retirement on 28 January 1868 direction of the institution fell solely to Balakirev as its cofounder.[145] Lomakin may well have withdrawn because he realized that he was losing control to Balakirev, whose purpose differed fundamentally from his own.[146] Certainly he and Balakirev disagreed in their taste in music, and the latter's views more and more dominated the FMS's concert repertory. Lomakin's memoirs tactfully contrast the different goals of the two leaders:

"[I] had in mind and hoped to organize . . . something like a nursery for teachers of religious and secular choral singing; Balakirev also had good intentions—to make of the school a center for talented Russians and others."[147]

Balakirev's work with the Free Music School advanced his own reputation and that of his friends, but it was not yet the musical career he wanted. The FMS gave only two public concerts each year, while the RMS gave ten, and it could not pay salaries to its staff. But Balakirev hoped to use his post in the FMS as a springboard to a more prominent and lucrative position. As early as 1863 the circle's press spokesmen had hinted that Balakirev deserved a more prominent and regular platform for his conducting talent.[148] An opportunity to push Balakirev forward as a candidate for a more prominent conducting post arose in December 1866, when the newspaper *Nedelia* [The Week] printed a suggestion that the Imperial Theater Directorate engage Balakirev to conduct its Lenten concerts. On 1 January 1867 Cui wrote Balakirev, who was then in Prague, about the article: "This . . . makes me unspeakably happy, and for my part it will not go unanswered. I am full of the best possible hopes, believe me, that we are advancing our cause slowly but surely. In two or three years, the Symphonic concerts will be in your hands."[149] Balakirev was obviously interested in the idea, for he promptly wrote Liudmila Shestakova, asking that a copy of the *Nedelia* article be sent to him.[150] True to his promise, Cui quoted the *Nedelia* article in his column of 31 January 1867 and heartily seconded its suggestion that the Theater Directorate could only gain by hiring Balakirev.[151]

Balakirev's conducting activities in the first half of 1867 strengthened his claim to such recognition of his talent. Early in the year he considerably advanced his reputation when he led performances of Glinka's two operas in Prague. Early the previous year Liudmila Shestakova, Glinka's sister, found out the Czechs were planning to produce *A Life for the Tsar* as a sign of their appreciation of the musical accomplishments of a fellow Slav. She decided to try to have *Ruslan* also performed in Prague and asked Balakirev, who had been assisting her for several years in preparing her brother's scores for publication, to arrange it.[152] Balakirev traveled to Prague in the summer of 1866 but stayed only two days before the advance of Prussian troops fighting the Seven Weeks' War forced him to withdraw to Vienna and then return home.[153] In September, after the quick Prussian victory, Shestakova herself went to Prague and arranged with the directors of the local opera theater to mount *Ruslan* with Balakirev in charge.[154] After arriving in Prague in December 1866 Balakirev prepared *Ruslan* for performance and conducted its premiere outside Russia in February 1867. He also took over the conducting of *A Life for the Tsar,* which had already been premiered in Prague before his arrival.[155] Balakirev himself considered his appearances in

Prague his coming of age as a conductor. He wrote Cui, "I have acquired enormous experience as a conductor, having produced *Ruslan* myself. I am now fully a conductor."[156]

To make sure that Balakirev's achievements in Prague did not pass unnoticed in St. Petersburg, Stasov published three separate articles about them in *Sankt-Peterburgskie vedomosti*—one in the preceding November, a second on the day of the foreign premiere of *Ruslan*, and a third one, including laudatory reviews from the Bohemian press, a month later.[157] He ended the final article with the hope that Balakirev would at last assume in Russia "the place he deserves both by his outstanding abilities and the profoundly beautiful character of his artistic activity."[158] Cui, in his review of the Free Musical School's concert of 6 March 1867, specifically cited Balakirev's success in Prague in justifying his call for Balakirev's expanded conducting activity: "Not only does he serve here as a spokesman for Russian music; not only does all of young musically talented Russia gather at his concerts, but it is he who contributed principally to the unprecedented success of *Ruslan* in Prague."[159]

Balakirev further advanced his reputation as a conductor in May 1867, when he led a special Slavic concert organized by the Free Music School for the foreign delegates to the Slavic Ethnographic Congress in Moscow. Balakirev had always had an interest in Slavic history and culture and a strong streak of nationalism in his character. When he discovered that the delegates to the Pan-Slavic Congress would visit St. Petersburg, he decided to give a concert of Slavic music in their honor.[160] It resulted in a great personal success for Balakirev and his circle. The program consisted mainly of music by Glinka, Dargomyzhsky, Rimsky-Korsakov, and Balakirev himself, including the premieres of a fantasia on Serbian themes and an overture on Czech themes written especially for the occasion by Rimsky and Balakirev, respectively.[161] Cui and Stasov praised the concert extravagantly.[162] In his review Stasov unwittingly coined the nickname that would be attached forever to the Balakirev circle—a nickname at first repeated sarcastically by the group's opponents but finally accepted as an appropriate designation for them:

> May God grant that our Slavic guests never forget today's concert, may He grant that they preserve forever the memory of how much poetry, feeling, talent, and ability there is in the *small but already mighty handful* [*moguchaia kuchka*—literally, mighty little heap] of Russian musicians.[163]

Serov's personal grudge against the circle incited him to challenge the growing musical stature of Balakirev and his friends. In 1859 and 1860 he had commented favorably about the early compositional efforts of the group, finding Cui's Scherzo in F major "extraordinarily remarkable," judging

Musorgsky's first publicly performed composition "very fine but unfortunately too short," and speaking of Balakirev's "most brilliant future."[164] But after Balakirev's unkind comments on the first act of *Judith* in 1861 Serov's attitude changed. Commenting in 1864 on Balakirev's incidental music to *King Lear,* he patronizingly suggested that "Mr. Balakirev needs to study much, much more in order to understand how far he must still grow to achieve the great aims in art."[165] For the most part, however, Serov simply ignored the Balakirev circle in his occasional articles between 1861 and 1867, when he founded *Muzyka i teatr.* But once possessed of a regular forum he used it not only to attack the critical opinions of Cui and Stasov but also to assail Balakirev's growing reputation as a conductor and his circle in general. About Balakirev's Slavic concert, he complained that no excerpts from his own operas were included on the program. He accused Cui of insincerity for deploring that the Slavic guests "did not succeed in becoming acquainted with a single excerpt from Serov's operas"[166] since Balakirev might well have presented such excerpts had he wished. Serov concluded with the comment that since his music was recognized by neither "the camp of German pianist-concertmasters" nor "the 'handful' of musical Slavophiles," then it would be better for him to deal directly with the appreciative public.[167]

In perspective, the musical activities of both Serov and the Balakirev circle during the period of Anton Rubinstein's leadership of the Russian Musical Society can be seen to reflect not only abstract aesthetic principles, as is so often claimed, but also concrete personal prejudices and self-interest. Their press campaigns against Rubinstein and his work certainly revolved around the fundamental issue in their aesthetic position—"modernism" versus "traditionalism" or "academicism" in the cause of Russian music—but this was hardly the only factor at work. Serov's vitriolic excesses against Rubinstein's "foreignness" and "charlatanism" must be ascribed to his anti-Semitism and jealousy. Similarly, the about-face in his evaluation of Balakirev's talent stems all too clearly from Balakirev's criticism of *Judith.* Cui was more careful to keep his group's personal antipathy for Rubinstein out of his reviews, but his bitter attacks on Serov, a fellow Russian who supported and composed music that reflected the principles of Romantic "modernism," certainly prove that his criticism could be tinctured by personal feelings. Balakirev's repertory as a conductor similarly reflected both his artistic views and his personal antipathies; he programmed the advanced Western music favored by his circle, as well as their own and other works by Russian composers, but he excluded Serov, even though the latter was admittedly "progressive" in his techniques and at least as talented a composer as Cui.

In addition to questions of aesthetic disagreement and personal antagonisms, simple self-interest played a most important role in Serov's and the Balakirev circle's campaign against the RMS and one another. Their public attacks were intimately tied to the question of their own advancement in public favor. The press campaigns against Rubinstein for ignoring Russian music and for his conservatism and academicism, while consistent with their personal aesthetic views and prejudices, cannot be separated from the fact that they themselves were Russians who lacked formal music training yet were seeking recognition for their own music. Serov claimed to stand for the cause of contemporary Russian music, but from his condemnation of both the "camp of German pianist-concertmasters" and the "handful of musical Slavophiles" it seems clear that he stood mainly for his own music. Similarly, the Balakirev circle spoke in private and in the press about the advancement of "new Russian music," but both from its attacks on Serov and from Balakirev's selective programming for the FMS concerts it is just as clear that this actually meant the advancement of its own music, not all "new Russian music." Most likely they could not distinguish in their own minds between devotion to the selfless cause of Russian musical development and the selfish cause of personal advancement. When Serov wrote to a friend that he hoped *Judith* would have a huge success so he could finally defeat the "wantons" in the RMS,[168] or when Stasov recommended to Balakirev that he seek a permanent conductor's position because he wanted "many good things,"[169] or when Cui wrote Balakirev that he was cheered that the group was advancing its cause through Balakirev's successful conducting,[170] each doubtless consciously thought his cause a noble one. But, in each case, victory for the cause would also mean personal success.

By 1867 Serov and the Balakirev circle had achieved considerable success both in their own musical careers and in their campaign against the RMS. Serov was no longer just a famous critic but also the most popular living Russian composer. Balakirev and his friends, although they lagged behind Serov in popularity, had emerged as significant though controversial composers. Balakirev was also codirector and soon to be sole leader of the Free Music School and its concerts. His personal reputation as a conductor was rising rapidly. At the same time, the Russian Musical Society, the chief enemy of Serov and Balakirev's circle, was torn by the internal dissension that resulted in Anton Rubinstein's resignation from his duties as conductor of the Society's concerts and as director of the St. Petersburg Conservatory. Although Rubinstein left mainly because of conflicts with other leaders of the RMS and the Conservatory faculty, his departure appeared to be a victory for Serov and the Balakirev circle. It left them in a position to dominate St. Petersburg's musical life.

Notes to Chapter IV

1. Entitled *Muzykal'nyi i teatral'nyi vestnik* when founded in 1856, the journal changed its title to *Teatral'nyi i muzykal'nyi vestnik* with issue No. 36, 1857. See *Spisok russkikh povremennykh izdanii s 1703 po 1899 god s svedeniiami ob ekzempliarakh, prinadlezhashchikh biblioteke imperatorskoi akademii nauk* [A list of Russian periodical publications from 1703 to 1899 with information about copies belonging to the library of the Imperial Academy of Sciences] (St. Petersburg: Tipografiia imperatorskoi akademii nauk, 1901), p. 592.

2. Serov to V.K. Anastasiev, 5 February 1861, in Serov, "Materialy dlia ego biografii," 21:160; Serov to K.I. Zvantsov, 9 August 1862, in Zvantsov, "A.N. Serov," p. 655.

3. Tamara Nikolaevna Livanova and O.A. Vinogradova, comps., *Muzykal'naia bibliografiia russkoi periodicheskoi pechati XIX veka* [A musical bibliography of the Russian periodical press in the nineteenth century] (Moscow: Sovetskii kompozitor, 1960-   ), 5, pts. 1 and 2, *passim*.

4. Serov to S.A. Gedeonov, 4 September 1867, in Serov, "Pis'ma," p. 452.

5. *Izbrannye stat'i*, 2:602, 605.

6. *Ibid.*, 2:604. Italics in this and other quotations from Serov's writings, unless otherwise noted, are in the originals.

7. *Ibid.*, 2:613.

8. *Ibid.*, 2:611, 613, 606.

9. *Ibid.*, 1:574; 2:613.

10. *Ibid.*, 1:573.

11. *Ibid.*, 1:573, 575, 568; 2:604.

12. Vul'fius, *Iz istorii konservatorii*, pp. 265-71.

13. *Izbrannye stat'i*, 2:167-69.

14. Quoted in Iulii Anatol'evich Kremlev, *Russkaia mysl' o muzyke* [Russian thought on music], 3 vols. (Leningrad: Gosudarstvennoe muzykal'noe izdatel'stvo, 1954-60), 2:70.

15. *Izbrannye stat'i*, 2:168.

16. *Ibid.*, 1:581, 558, 125; 2:596.

17. Larosh, *Izbrannye stat'i*, 2:293.

18. Serov, *Izbrannye stat'i*, 2:203.

19. Boborykin, *Vospominaniia*, 1:207.

20. Wagner, *Mein Leben*, p. 728.

21. "Zamechaniia na stat'iu g. Rubinshteina" [Remarks on Mr. Rubinstein's article], *Severnaia pchela*, 24 February 1861, pp. 181-82.

22. Stasov to Balakirev, 1 March 1861, in *Perepiska*, 1:126.

23. Livanova, *Muzykal'naia bibliografiia*, 5, pt. 1, p. 9; A.G. Dement'ev, A.V. Zapadov, and M.S. Cherepakhov, eds., *Russkaia periodicheskaia pechat' (1702-1894): Spravochnik* [The Russian periodical press (1702-1894): a guide] (Moscow: Gosudarstvennoe izdatel'stvo politicheskoi literatury, 1959), pp. 19-20.

24. See Kiui, *Izbrannye stat'i*, pp. 624-35, for a complete list of his articles for this period.

25. *Ibid.*, p. 547.

26. Quoted in an editor's note, *ibid.*, p. 567.

27. *Izbrannye stat'i*, pp. 14-15.

28. "Muzykal'nye zametki" [Musical notices], *Sankt-Petersburgskie vedomosti*, 24 March 1866, p. 1, and 23 February 1867, p. 1. The title of this newspaper will hereafter be abbreviated as *St.P. ved.*

29. *Izbrannye stat'i*, pp. 12, 31.

30. *Ibid.*, p. 20.

31. See, for example, *ibid.*, pp. 49, 56, 57.

32. See, for example, *ibid.*, p. 51.

33. Cui to Balakirev, 6 January 1867, in Kiui, *Izbrannye pis'ma*, p. 71; Musorgsky to Balakirev, 26 January 1867, in Musorgskii, *Literaturnoe nasledie*, 1:83.

34. Musorgsky to Balakirev, 26 January 1867, in Musorgskii, *Literaturnoe nasledie*, 1:83.

35. *Izbrannye stat'i*, pp. 85-87.

36. *Ibid.*, pp. 63, 15-16, 54.

37. Balakirev to Cui, 20 July 1864, in Kiui, *Izbrannye pis'ma*, p. 499.

38. *Izbrannye stat'i*, p. 15.

39. See, for example, M.R[appaport], "Teatral'naia i muzykal'naia khronika," *Syn otechestva*, 3 July 1860, p. 860; 2 October 1860, p. 1218; Findeizen, *Ocherk RMO*, p. 20.

40. Rubets, "Vospominaniia," 4 June 1912, p. 4.

41. Larosh, "A.G. Rubinshtein," pp. 595-98.

42. See Serov, *Izbrannye stat'i*, 1:344, 565, 581, 588; 2:507, 515, 610 and Kiui, *Izbrannye stat'i*, pp. 3-4, 19, 29, 46-47, 53, 59, 87.

43. Stasov, *Izbrannye sochineniia*, 1:40-43; Stasov to Balakirev, 10 June 1862, in *Perepiska*, 1:187.

44. Quoted in Vasilii Iakovlev, "K istorii 'Raika' i 'Klassika' " [On the history of "The Peepshow" and "The Classicist"], *Sovetskaia muzyka*, June 1967, p. 106.

45. Quoted *ibid.*

46. Serov to K.I. Zvantsov, 28 January 1867, in Zvantsov, "A.N. Serov," p. 669.

47. *Izbrannye stat'i*, 2:217.

48. "Muzykal'nye zametki," *St. P. ved.*, 30 March 1867, p. 1.

49. See, for example, Serov, *Izbrannye stat'i*, 1:129-92, 343-53.

50. *Ibid.*, 1:218, 220-21, 241.

51. *Ibid.*, 1:245-46, 252.

52. *Izbrannye stat'i*, pp. 111-18.

53. *Izbrannye stat'i*, 2:228-34.

54. Editor's note in Kiui, *Izbrannye stat'i*, pp. 579-80.

55. Zvantsov, "A.N. Serov," p. 371.

56. Letter of 30 January 1860 in Serov, *Pis'ma k sestre*, pp. 235-36; Serov to M.P. Anastasieva, 19 March 1860, in Serov, "Materialy dlia ego biografii," 21:154-55.

57. Abram Akimovich Gozenpud, "Opernoe tvorchestvo A.N. Serova" [The operatic creations of A.N. Serov], *Sovetskaia muzyka*, July 1971, pp. 92-93.

58. Serov to V.K. Anastasiev, 5 February 1861, in Serov, "Materialy dlia ego biografii," 21:159.

59. See, for example, Serov, *Izbrannye stat'i*, 2:372-95.

60. Serov to V.K. Anastasiev, 5 February 1861, in Serov, "Materialy dlia ego biografii," 21:159.

61. *Izbrannye stat'i*, 1:73.

62. Serov to M.P. Anastasieva, 29 August 1862, in Serov, "Materialy dlia ego biografii," 21:170.

63. Letter of 18 October 1862 in Serov, "Pis'ma k V. Zhukovoi," p. 73.

64. Serov to K.I. Zvantsov, 23 May 1863, in Zvantsov, "A.N. Serov," 657-58.

65. See, for example, his nearly libelous attack on Anton Rubinstein in *Izbrannye stat'i,* 2:167-71.

66. "Peterburgskaia zhizn'," *Sovremennik* (Sovremennoe obozrenie) 86 (March 1861) :171.

67. Adjutant General Patkul', Report on the arrest of A.N. Serov at Alexander Lazarev's concert of 26 March 1861, in *Russkii arkhiv* 21, pt. 3 (1833) :202.

68. Serov to M.P. Anastasieva, 10 September 1861, in Serov, "Materialy dlia ego biografii," 21:163-64.

69. Letter of 8 May 1861 in Serov, "Pis'ma k V. Zhukovoi," p. 61.

70. Starchevskii, "Kompozitor Serov," p. 150.

71. Letter of 14 March 1862 in Serov, "Pis'ma k Zhukovoi," p. 64.

72. Vol'f, *Khronika teatrov s 1855,* p. 118.

73. Feofil Matveevich Tolstoi [Rostislav], "Zapadnaia reklama, perenesennaia na russkuiu pochvu" [Western publicity transferred to Russian soil], *Severnaia pchela,* 14 May 1863, p. 506.

74. *Perepiska,* 1:199-200.

75. Serov to K.I. Zvantsov, 23 May 1863, in Zvantsov, "A.N. Serov," p. 659; Vol'f, *Khronika teatrov s 1855,* p. 118.

76. "Dnevnik," p. 178.

77. Gozenpud, *Russkii opernyi teatr,* 2:62.

78. [Rostislav], "Neskol'ko slov o pervom predstavlenii opery 'Iudif'" [A few words about the first performance of *Judith*], *Severnaia pchela,* 19 May 1863, p. 525.

79. Letter of 14 March 1862 in Serov, "Pis'ma k Zhukovoi," pp. 63-64.

80. Obolenskii, "Moi vospominaniia," 138:274.

81. Serova, *Serovy,* p. 25.

82. Tolstoi, "A.N. Serov," 368-69.

83. Nikitenko, *Dnevnik,* 2:326-27.

84. Khubov, *Zhizn' Serova,* pp. 102-4.

85. *My Musical Life*, p. 69.

86. Vol'f, *Khronika teatrov s 1855*, p. 121.

87. Gozenpud, *Russkii opernyi teatr*, 2:84.

88. Serov to M.P. Anastasieva, 11 January and 1 February 1863, in Serov, "Materialy dlia ego biografii," 21:174.

89. Balakirev to Stasov, 3 June 1863, in *Perepiska*, 1:208-10; Stasov to Balakirev, 17 May 1863, *ibid.*, 1:199-207; Musorgsky to Balakirev, 10 June 1863, in Musorgskii, *Literaturnoe nasledie*, 1:64-69; Cui to Rimsky-Korsakov, 27 December 1864, in Kiui, *Izbrannye pis'ma*, p. 61.

90. *My Musical Life*, pp. 69-70.

91. Boris Vladimirovich Asaf'ev [Igor' Glebov], "Iz zabytkh stranits russkoi muzyki"[From the forgotten pages of Russian music], in A.N. Rimskii-Korsakov, *Muzykal'naia letopis'*, 1:61-78.

92. *Izbrannye stat'i*, p. 17.

93. "Muzykal'nye zametki," *St.P. ved.*, 26 January 1865, p. 2.

94. " 'Rogneda,' opera g. Serova" ["Rogneda," Mr. Serov's opera], *St.P. ved.*, 6 November 1865, pp. 1-2.

95. *Izbrannye sochineniia*, 1:150-51.

96. Gozenpud, "Opernoe tvorchestvo Serova," pp. 91-92.

97. Taruskin, "Opera and Drama," p. 155; G. Abramovskii, "Opera Serova 'Rogneda' " [Serov's opera *Rogneda*], *Sovetskaia muzyka*, December 1976, p. 101.

98. Liapunova, *Balakirev: letopis'*, pp. 57, 75, 96, 106, 110, 119.

99. *Ibid.*, pp. 88, 99, 108.

100. Findeizen, *Ocherk RMO*, appendix, pp. 1-8.

101. "Peterburgskoe obozrenie," *Severnaia pchela*, 10 April 1861, p. 317.

102. Rimsky suggests that Kologrivov played such a role in propagating the music of the Balakirev circle on other occasions. See *My Musical Life*, pp. 61-62.

103. Liapunova, *Balakirev: letopis'*, p. 100.

104. V. Stasov to Balakirev, 23 December 1860, in *Perepiska*, 1:97.

105. Balakirev to V. Stasov, 23 December 1860, *ibid.* and editor's note, 1:385.

106. V. Stasov to Balakirev, 26 January 1861, *ibid.*, 1:119.

107. *Izbrannye sochineniia*, 1:63.

108. *Izbrannye stat'i*, p. 30.

109. *Ibid.*, pp. 77, 82-83.

110. Gavriil Iakimovich Lomakin, "Avtobiograficheskie zapiski, s primechaniiami V.V. Stasova" [Autobiographical notes, with annotations by V.V. Stasov], *Russkaia starina* 49 (1886):655-56.

111. *Ibid.*, 50:311.

112. Patrick L. Alston, *Education and the State in Tsarist Russia* (Stanford, Cal.: Stanford University Press, 1969), pp. 57-59.

113. Rubets, "Vospominaniia," 25 June 1912, p. 4.

114. "Avtobiograficheskie zapiski," 50:314-15.

115. *Perepiska*, 1:181; Liapunova, *Balakirev: letopis'*, p. 76.

116. "Peterburgskoe obozrenie," *Severnaia pchela*, 24 January 1862, p. 90.

117. Lomakin, "Avtobiograficheskie zapiski," 50:313; Liapunova, *Balakirev: letopis'*, p. 78.

118. Letter of 28 March 1862 in Balakirev, "Pis'ma k A.P. Arsen'evu," 17, no.41, p. 869.

119. Lomakin, "Avtobiograficheskie zapiski," 50:313-14.

120. *Ibid.*, 50:315.

121. Feofil Matveevich Tolstoi [Rostislav], "Zamechatel'nye iavleniia v russkom muzykal'nom mire" [Remarkable events in the Russian musical world], *Severnaia pchela*, 13 March 1863, p. 273.

122. Lomakin, "Avtobiograficheskie zapiski," 50:315-16.

123. Liapunova, *Balakirev: letopis'*, pp. 87-155, *passim*.

124. "Iz moikh vospominanii" [From my memoirs], *Istoricheskii vestnik* [Historical herald] 37 (1889):539.

125. Rubets, "Vospominaniia," 25 June 1912, p. 4.

126. M—ch, "Russkoe muzykal'noe obshchestvo," p. 454.

127. Lomakin, "Avtobiograficheskie zapiski," 50:318.

128.   *Ibid.,* 50:319; Stasov, *Izbrannye sochineniia,* 3:79.

129.   *Izbrannye stat'i,* 2:171, 169.

130.   *Izbrannye sochineniia,* 1:62.

131.   *Izbrannye stat'i,* pp. 9-10.

132.   Quoted in Liapunova, *Balakirev: letopis',* p. 77.

133.   Stasov, *Izbrannye sochineniia,* 3:80.

134.   Complete programs appear in Liapunova, *Balakirev: letopis',* pp. 77-79.

135.   Lomakin, "Avtobiograficheskie zapiski," 50:319; Rubets, "Vospominaniia," 25 June 1912, p. 4.

136.   Letter of 7 November 1862 in Rimskii-Korsakov, *Polnoe sobranie,* 5:27.

137.   Lomakin to Balakirev, 18 December 1864, quoted in Liapunova, *Balakirev: letopis',* p. 106.

138.   Complete programs for these FMS concerts appear in Liapunova, *Balakirev: letopis',* pp. 87, 89, 98, 99, 107, 110, 112-13, 117, 124.

139.   *Izbrannye sochineniia,* 1:62-63.

140.   See, for example, *Izbrannye stat'i,* pp. 10-11, 20.

141.   *Ibid.,* p. 52.

142.   "Muzykal'nye zametki," *St. P. ved.,* 1 March 1866, p. 1.

143.   *Izbrannye stat'i,* pp. 18-19.

144.   *Ibid.,* pp. 66, 68.

145.   Stasov, *Izbrannye sochineniia,* 3:83.

146.   Rubets, "Vospominaniia," 25 June 1912, p. 4; Frid, "M.A. Balakirev," pp. 32-33.

147.   "Avtobiograficheskie zapiski," 50:321.

148.   Stasov, "Izbrannye sochineniia," 1:63-64.

149.   Kiui, *Izbrannye pis'ma,* p. 70.

150.   Letter of 9 January 1867 in Grigorii Timofeev, "M.A. Balakirev v Prage: Iz ego perepiski" [M.A. Balakirev in Prague: from his correspondence], *Sovremennyi mir* [Contemporary world], June 1911, pp. 160-61.

151. *Izbrannye stat'i*, pp. 87-88.

152. Shestakova, "M.I. Glinka," p. 601.

153. Balakirev to Cui, July 1866, in Kiui, *Izbrannye pis'ma*, p. 500.

154. Shestakova, "M.I. Glinka," pp. 601-2.

155. See Timofeev, "Balakirev v Prage," pp. 151-86.

156. Letter of 7 February 1867, in Kiui, *Izbrannye pis'ma*, p. 502.

157. *Izbrannye sochineniia*, 1:152-70.

158. *Ibid.*, 1:170.

159. *Izbrannye stat'i*, p. 92.

160. Rimsky-Korsakov, *My Musical Life*, p. 70.

161. Liapunova, *Balakirev: letopis'*, p. 126.

162. Kiui, *Izbrannye stat'i*, pp. 93-98; Stasov, *Izbrannye sochineniia*, 1:171-73.

163. *Izbrannye sochineniia*, 1:173. The italics have been added.

164. *Izbrannye stat'i*, 2:612, 616; 1:339.

165. Quoted in Kremlev, *Russkaia mysl' o muzyke*, 2:69.

166. Kiui, *Izbrannye stat'i*, p. 93.

167. Editor's note *ibid.*, pp. 578-79.

168. Serov to K.I. Zvantsov, 19 May 1862, in Zvantsov, "A.N. Serov," p. 653.

169. Stasov to Balakirev, 27 July 1863, in *Perepiska*, 1:214.

170. Cui to Balakirev, 1 January 1867, in Kiui, *Izbrannye pis'ma*, p. 70.

Chapter V

Realignment of Forces, 1867-1869

Anton Rubinstein's resignation from the Russian Musical Society and withdrawal from St. Petersburg in 1867 left an enormous vacuum in the city's musical life. Suddenly the leading positions he had held were vacant; a major shift in the balance of musical forces was inevitable.

Rubinstein's retirement left the RMS in difficult straits. He had been its sole musical director and conductor since its founding, as well as director of the St. Petersburg Conservatory. Finding a suitable replacement was no easy task. Furthermore, he resigned officially only in the middle of the summer, giving the RMS little time to find a substitute. True, he had informed the Society's directors in January 1867 of his intention to leave, but they did not take him seriously; he had announced his imminent resignation too many times before. Still, in the spring of 1867 the students and professors of the Conservatory, as well as Elena Pavlovna herself, begged him to remain,[1] and the grand duchess was apparently satisfied that these entreaties had succeeded, for she left Russia for her usual summer at the German spas without making any preparations to choose a new Conservatory director or conductor for the Society. At the close of the spring term Rubinstein went abroad as usual, but on 16 July 1867 he sent Prince Dmitri Obolensky, the vice-president of the Chief Directorate of the RMS, a letter announcing that he would not be returning in the fall.[2] Obolensky forwarded the note to Elena Pavlovna, who replied that her "surprise and indignation" equaled his own.[3]

As a solution to the problem of replacing Rubinstein, Elena Pavlovna suggested appointing Nikolai Zaremba, a professor of music theory, as interim director of the Conservatory and engaging "some artist of renown" from Western Europe to conduct the RMS concerts for one season. "In this way," she wrote, "we would satisfy the public's eagerness for novelty and make it easier to forget Rubinstein's absence."[4] Obolensky replied that the choice of Zaremba would be acceptable to all parties but that the board of directors of the St. Petersburg RMS favored inviting Balakirev to conduct the Society's concerts for the coming season and to take over as well Rubinstein's conducting duties in the Conservatory. He himself supported this decision, arguing that Balakirev would be less expensive than a foreigner and would have less trouble dealing with the Society's orchestra and chorus. As if to counter expected objections from the grand duchess, Obolensky offered an extended justification for such a choice:

> I do not know Monsieur Balakirev personally, but his talent as an orchestral conductor is much appreciated here and very recently it has been proven in the mounting of two Russian operas in Prague. His co-operation in the work of our conservatory would attract the sympathy of the public and the press. I know that your Imperial Highness mistrusts, with reason, the party that exaggerates national feeling in the realm of art; but I am convinced that in this situation your Imperial Highness's influence will prevent any sort of exaggeration.

He concluded with a plea to give Balakirev a one-year trial "in order not to complicate the matter" and "to prevent any new occasion of conflict."[5]

Since Obolensky did not know Balakirev personally, his strong support of the latter's candidacy presumably resulted from pressure by the directors of the St. Petersburg RMS and his desire to avoid a conflict between the board and the grand duchess. According to Vladimir Stasov, Rimsky-Korsakov, and Balakirev himself, the instigator of the directors' proposal to engage him was Vasily Kologrivov, who had remained a good friend of Balakirev for over a decade, notwithstanding his close association with the RMS.[6] Indeed, Kologrivov was the one who visited Elena Pavlovna during August to discuss Rubinstein's replacement and to inform her of the board's desire to hire Balakirev.[7] There is even evidence that Anton Rubinstein himself recommended to Kologrivov that Balakirev be hired to take over his conducting duties.[8] Alexander Dargomyzhsky very likely also supported Balakirev's candidacy. He and Balakirev had long been on friendly terms, and by 1867 he was entering into a close association with the Balakirev circle. Dargomyzhsky's position as president of the board of directors of the St. Petersburg Russian Musical Society would certainly have given weight to his recommendation.[9]

Elena Pavlovna reluctantly acceded to part of the proposal. She would not agree to Balakirev as the sole conductor of the RMS symphonic concerts because she felt he had not proven himself. Besides, she had once heard him conduct poorly at one of Lomakin's concerts. "That he is an intimate friend of Kologrivov is not sufficient proof for me," she continued, "but I am still impartial enough to concede to him the direction of some of our concerts, of four for example." For the rest, she proposed to engage some famous artist from abroad. She was also willing to hire Balakirev to organize the Society's public chamber music concerts and to conduct the Conservatory choir, which served mainly as the chorus for the RMS symphonic concerts. She flatly refused, however, to allow him to direct the Conservatory's instrumental ensembles. To do so, she wrote, would be

> in complete opposition to my desire to maintain the musical classics as the basis of our music education . . . To introduce Balakirev into this sanctuary of art only perhaps to remove him soon after would elicit attacks from the press rather than avoid them; certainly I am not one to praise Rubinstein, but I am far from wishing to replace him with his antithesis and his personal enemy.[10]

Elena Pavlovna sent an official letter incorporating these proposals to the directors of the St. Petersburg branch of the RMS, who met to discuss them on 28 August 1867.[11] In accordance with the wishes of the Society's august patron, the directors instructed Kologrivov "to invite Mr. Balakirev for several concerts, offering him 125 rubles for each, with the obligation to conduct the orchestra, prepare the chorus, and manage the chamber music programs."[12] On 10 September, at a meeting of the board of directors, Balakirev agreed to conduct several concerts for the RMS on the condition that he himself be allowed to select the works for each.[13] At the same meeting the board decided to invite Hector Berlioz to share the conducting duties with Balakirev.[14] According to Rimsky-Korsakov's memoirs, this choice was made at Balakirev's insistence.[15] Elena Pavlovna, of course, had already decided to invite some foreigner of renown to conduct several concerts, and she herself visited Berlioz in Paris to ask him to Russia. In exchange for conducting six concerts, he would receive fifteen thousand francs. All traveling expenses would be paid, and Elena Pavlovna would provide him with rooms in her own palace and use of a carriage. Berlioz accepted.[16]

Thus, the Russian Musical Society had temporarily solved the problem of replacing Rubinstein by dividing his duties for the 1867-68 season among three men: Zaremba, Berlioz, and Balakirev. Balakirev's selection must have surprised the musical public of St. Petersburg since his aesthetic position was well known as diametrically opposed to that of the Society's former musical director. The Society needed a new conductor immediately, however, and Balakirev had friends on the board of directors.

Balakirev's acceptance of the invitation was also somewhat surprising. He had little patience with the previous leadership and program of the Society. Rubinstein's retirement, however, had removed the most conspicuous representative of the conservative, nonnationalist trend Balakirev despised, and evidently his own supporters had achieved predominance in the directorate of the St. Petersburg branch of the RMS. Doubtless he foresaw the possibility of moderating the Society's traditional conservatism. He had insisted, of course, on selecting his own concert programs. Finally, he was ambitious. For several years Cui and Stasov had been suggesting in their published articles that he deserved a more extensive arena for his conducting activities. The RMS concerts would provide just such a platform. Balakirev was also in difficult financial straits at the time. His Slavic concert "was, in the material sense, a disaster," and his trip to Prague had left him with a debt of four hundred rubles.[17] Although he was of the gentry class, he had no outside source of income. His father was poor and died penniless in 1869.[18] Thus, the offer of 125 rubles for each RMS concert undoubtedly encouraged his acceptance. Assuming his duties, he took another step closer to a permanent and financially secure position as a leading figure in the musical life of St. Petersburg.

During the 1867-68 season Balakirev conducted only four of the RMS concerts, but he clearly stamped them with his personal tastes, programming the same sort of Russian and advanced Western works he had been conducting at the Free Music School concerts. Of the twenty-two works performed at these four concerts, nine were by Russians—Glinka, Dargomyzhsky, Balakirev, and Rimsky-Korsakov—seven by "modern" Western composers—Schumann, Liszt, and Wagner—and two more by Beethoven. No music written before the nineteenth century or by Mendelssohn and his school appeared on the programs.[19] The inclusion of a composition by Wagner would seem unusual, considering Balakirev's distaste for the music of Serov's idol, but the work in question was the early *Faust Overture,* the one Wagnerian piece respected in the circle.[20] Balakirev's RMS programs varied much less than Rubinstein's had, but the concerts conducted by Berlioz in the 1867-68 RMS season helped balance Balakirev's inclination toward "new" music. Berlioz had originally agreed to conduct five programs of his own choosing, plus one entirely of his own music.[21] He was later persuaded to include some of his own works on the other five programs as well, but these remained devoted mainly to Beethoven symphonies and music of the eighteenth century, particularly excerpts from the operas of Gluck, a special favorite of Berlioz.[22] When Berlioz's programs were added to Balakirev's, the resulting repertory differed little from Rubinstein's, except for the large number of compositions by Berlioz.

Berlioz had a tremendous success in St. Petersburg. He himself was enormously pleased with his concerts and their public reception:

> Both the public and press are most eulogistic. At the second concert I was recalled six times after the *Symphonie fantastique,* which was performed with tremendous spirit. What an orchestra! what ensemble! what precision! ... Yesterday we did the second act of *Orfeo* ... The Russians, who knew Gluck only from the mutilations committed by incompetent people, could hardly stop applauding.[23]

But if Berlioz seemed to please everyone, Balakirev's work for the Society was much more controversial. Whatever the audience's response may have been, he elicited extremely sharp press reaction. While he was conducting only the Free Music School concerts he was largely ignored by the Petersburg musical press except for the articles of Cui and Stasov. Even Serov had only occasionally bothered to attack him in the press before 1867. As a conductor of the Russian Musical Society concerts, however, he was too conspicuous to be ignored.

Cui naturally devoted much favorable attention to Balakirev's appearances, praising them lavishly for the quality of both their repertory and the performances.[24] In February 1868 he reviewed the impact of the Society's first ten programs without Rubinstein:

> The current season of concerts by the Russian Musical Society has been very brilliant and in its significance no less important than the very first season, which laid the foundation for the Russian Musical Society . . . In several concerts, four in all, Balakirev superbly performed many excellent pieces; and finally, compositions by young Russian composers are beginning to penetrate into these programs.[25]

But as one might expect, Serov wrote in entirely different terms. Reviewing the Society's first performance under Balakirev, he welcomed the possibility of "Russifying" the RMS concerts but doubted that Balakirev's conducting of only a few performances would bring any significant change in the policies of the organization. "Balakirev's appointment does not signify . . . a victory for the Russian contingent" over "the German party," he wrote, because Balakirev lacked the "inner strength necessary for the struggle and victory."[26] Serov claimed that Balakirev's previous musical activity had been limited to "unremarkable conducting of a few concerts, the composition of two overture-potpourris on Russian songs and very weak music for Shakespeare's *Lear,* and . . . publication of a not entirely successful collection of Russian songs." His conducting of the first RMS concert Serov found "limp, characterless, bad. There was no fire or enthusiasm in anyone or anything."[27] His later reviews of the RMS season were equally derogatory of Balakirev's talent.[28]

Serov's attacks all appeared in his own journal *Muzyka i teatr* and thus reached only a very small audience, but Balakirev also faced new and formidable public opposition from a press organ with a much larger readership. In the fall of 1867 Alexander Famintsyn, professor of music history and aesthetics at the St. Petersburg Conservatory, became a regular music critic for the daily newspaper *Golos* [The Voice]. Founded in 1863, this paper had a large circulation and provided especially extensive coverage of musical life. In fact, it even surpassed *Sankt-Peterburgskie vedomosti* in this respect.[29] The paper's chief music critic at the time, Feofil Tolstoy, had already publicly attacked Balakirev in the spring of 1867 as "an example of almost wholly unjustified fetishism" because Cui's reviews had so exaggerated his allegedly modest accomplishments,[30] but Tolstoy's criticism was neither sufficiently profound nor consistent enough to threaten seriously Balakirev's reputation. Famintsyn, however, was another matter. He was a graduate of the famous Leipzig Conservatory and member of the faculty of the St. Petersburg Conservatory. Anton Rubinstein, during his tenure as director of the Conservatory, had forbidden his professors to enter into public polemics over music. With his departure, however, the restriction was removed. Now the conservative, academic, nonnationalist musical views represented by Rubinstein himself and much of his staff finally acquired a public spokesman in the person of Famintsyn.

At first Famintsyn did not appear to be ill disposed toward Balakirev and his circle. In his announcement of Rubinstein's replacement as conductor of the RMS concerts he even called Balakirev "a young and very talented composer and conductor."[31] Such kind words lasted only until his review of Balakirev's first RMS concert, when Famintsyn criticized "the negligence with which the Beethoven symphony was performed."[32] Reviewing a program that included both Balakirev's *Overture on Czech Themes* and the premiere of Rimsky's tone poem *Sadko,* Famintsyn attacked the whole aesthetic position of Balakirev's circle. He criticized in particular its efforts to create new Russian music based on folk themes:

> Many people seem to think that we already have Russian instrumental music and even call it "national." But is music national just because it uses as themes for composition trivial dance tunes that automatically remind one of disgusting scenes in front of a saloon? . . . If that is "nationalism," then we can indeed boast of Russian national instrumental music, since we have quite a few *trepak* dances of various kinds in this form . . . This only shows that our composers have completely failed to distinguish between national music and rustic folk music . . . If the kernel from which an entire composition grows is not refined, then the work itself cannot be refined . . . In no case can it serve as a model or ideal of instrumental music in general. But then today most of our composers scarcely seek the higher ideals.

The so-called nationalist works, Famintsyn continued, "either fall into the formlessness of medleys of folk tunes" or copy Liszt's free rhapsodic forms, "turning their attention chiefly to the trimmings and not to what is being trimmed."[33] He admitted that Rimsky's *Sadko* revealed a composer of "notable talent" but complained that "unfortunately, he is too contaminated and saturated with rustic folksy-ness." He suggested that Rimsky should study the musical classics in order to "rid himself of the dilettantism visible everywhere in his compositions." Famintsyn found that Balakirev's overture left "a much more satisfactory impression," but he pointed out that it also "ends with a *trepak* dance (Czech this time)."[34] Famintsyn clearly represented that very "German party," conservative and nonnationalist, that Serov and the Balakirev circle had always claimed was in control of the Russian Musical Society.

Cui tried to dispose of Famintsyn as a serious challenger by characterizing him as a musical reactionary who, "with an air of wisdom, fulminates against triviality and nationalism and nonobservance of conventional musical forms and prints in *Golos* reminiscences from old textbooks on aesthetics."[35] But Famintsyn could not be dismissed so easily. Not only was he a serious critic for a major paper, he was also a professor from the conservatory with influence within the RMS—all the more important since the Society's president and chief patron, Grand Duchess Elena Pavlovna, shared his doubts about Balakirev's competence as a conductor and about the entire aim of his musical activity.

Balakirev apparently made little attempt to allay the doubts and suspicions of his opponents in the RMS. As we have seen, he selected repertory for his four concerts of the 1867-68 season almost exclusively from the modern Russian and Western composers, ignoring the classical masters so much appreciated by Elena Pavlovna, Famintsyn, and the more conservative faction in the Society. Only the balancing weight of Berlioz's more traditional programming kept Balakirev from completely overturning the familiar format of the RMS concerts. Moreover, in his personal dealings with the Society, Balakirev was often, in Rimsky-Korsakov's words, "intolerant, tactless, and unrestrained."[36] On one occasion he devoted virtually an entire rehearsal to Borodin's First Symphony, making corrections in the newly copied orchestra parts instead of moving on to other works scheduled for hearing.[37] Another time he affronted Famintsyn when the latter announced that he had composed incidental music to Schiller's *Wilhelm Tell*, and Balakirev, "without a moment's thought," sang the famous galloping theme from the overture to Rossini's opera and asked if it had also been included. "Famintsyn was exceedingly offended and never could forgive Balakirev this sally."[38] Balakirev also irritated the orchestra by speaking only Russian at rehearsals, even though most of the musicians were foreigners, mainly Germans, who either did not understand Russian or did not wish to.[39]

Balakirev had always been prejudiced against foreigners living in Russia. In 1865, for example, he wrote Stasov in disgust that Russia was probably the only place in the world where "foreigners can exist and live splendidly" without speaking a word of the native language.[40] During his tenure as conductor of the RMS concerts he even adopted a special derogatory term for all foreigners in Russia—"*Hasenfuss*" (literally "rabbit foot," i.e., a coward, though Balakirev simply used it as a general term of derision)[41]—and began to call St. Petersburg by such names as "the foul, German Palmyra of the North."[42] Such intolerance deserves note since Elena Pavlovna herself was German by birth. Undiplomatic Balakirev must have found it very difficult to conceal his feelings in personal contacts with the grand duchess.

Despite Balakirev's abrasiveness, the scepticism of the conservative members of the RMS, and the harsh criticism of his work in the press, he remained on superficially good terms with Elena Pavlovna through the spring of 1868. In April he wrote a Czech acquaintance that she had offered to send him abroad to observe the latest musical developments in Western Europe.[43] The next month he wrote his father that Elena Pavlovna had asked him to explore the possibility of opening a branch of the RMS in Tiflis. If the directorate of the Society approved the plan, his impending vacation in the Caucasus would be at the expense of the RMS.[44]

But no sooner had Balakirev left St. Petersburg than the grand duchess attempted to deprive him of his conducting duties. In June 1868 she proposed to the directorate that the St. Petersburg Society engage a German conductor, Max Seifriz, to direct its concerts for the coming season. The board of directors refused, however, recommending that Balakirev be rehired as the full-time conductor. Although she acquiesced, agreeing to "a trial period of one year,"[45] Elena Pavlovna did not give up the idea of replacing Balakirev with Seifriz. In August 1868 Berlioz, Liszt, and Wagner each received a request from the RMS for a recommendation of Seifriz.[46] In addition, Berlioz, who knew Balakirev's work first-hand, was asked to denigrate the Russian conductor—a request that angered him:

> They ask me to do impossible things. They want me to say something favourable about a German musician, which indeed I think deserves to be said, but only on condition that I say something unfavourable about a Russian one, whom they want the German to supplant, though the Russian too is very deserving. I will not do it. What the devil of a world is that?[47]

Obviously Balakirev's opponents had not abandoned their plans to remove him—at the end of his trial year if not sooner. Berlioz did not name the author of the letter to him, but Famintsyn seems a likely candidate. Stasov and Balakirev believed him to be the culprit,[48] and he eventually published excerpts from Wagner's and Liszt's recommendations of Seifriz.[49]

Such intrigues only increased Balakirev's intolerance of his antagonists and served to strengthen his prejudices. Hearing the story from Kologrivov and Stasov even before he returned to Petersburg in the fall of 1868, Balakirev concluded that it must be Zaremba who was behind the affair, and he vented his fury in a xenophobic tirade:

> In all this it is noteworthy that Zaremba is acting exceedingly adroitly, dumping everything on the Germanized padre Famintsyn, putting him up for show while he himself hides behind his priests. He could be the clever Jesuit confessor of some stupid medieval king, and his aptitude is such that he would not defame his celebrated Polish-gentry lineage. From the day I entered the Society he has been terrified at the thought that musical affairs might fall into my hands and that then Russian barbarism, in a wild, unbridled torrent, might submerge those good seeds of German musical civilization that certain virtuous fellows here, much to their own benefit, have managed to implant. That

nitwit Famintsyn (son of a bitch), over a tankard of *Bier*, has sworn fidelity to [Zaremba] because he was offended that I would not recognize his stupid compositions.[50]

Even before Balakirev learned of the intrigues against him during the summer of 1868, tensions between him and the conservative faction in the Society had endangered his friendship with his staunchest supporter in the RMS—Kologrivov.[51] In September Balakirev wrote Stasov that he still considered Kologrivov "a good and honorable fellow," but he was driven mad by the latter's "night blindness, which allows any scoundrel to dupe him." He particularly resented Kologrivov's attempts to mediate between himself and his opponents in the RMS:

> With his limited understanding of people he even imagines that it is possible to mix oil and water, myself and Zaremba, for example. But then the habit of pandering is strongly developed in him, as, for example, when he used to wish to get me together with his precious Anton [i.e., Rubinstein]. Fortunately, he is now just beginning to see clearly . . . that there really is a German party, which calls Russia a barbaric country not because of any actual barbarism but for whatever is new, independent, Russian.[52]

Balakirev conducted all but one of the RMS's usual ten concerts during the 1868-69 season. The repertory for these was more varied than for any earlier concerts under Balakirev's control but still far from the classical models favored by Anton Rubinstein and the conservative faction in the RMS.[53] Besides the predictable large doses of Liszt, Schumann, Berlioz, Beethoven, and Glinka, Balakirev programmed such unexpected pieces as Wagner's overture to *Die Meistersinger*, two Mendelssohn overtures, several works by second-rank nineteenth-century German composers, and even Anton Rubinstein's "Ocean" Symphony. Other works by Russians outside the circle were included as well. Only four compositions by members of the circle appeared, probably because there were simply few major works by Balakirev's friends that he had not already conducted. Despite the apparent variety of schools and styles, however, the ten concerts included only four works by pre-nineteenth-century composers and no music at all by Bach, Handel, Gluck, or Haydn—all figures regularly represented in earlier seasons. Furthermore, Balakirev had not selected many of the compositions outside the limits of his personal taste. Some were performed by soloists, who ordinarily had the right to choose their own music.[54] Others, including Wagner's overture, were evidently forced on Balakirev by the leaders of the RMS.[55] Thus, what little recognition these concerts gave to schools of composition beyond Balakirev's personal interest came in spite of him, not because of him.

Public attendance at the RMS concerts under Balakirev seems to have been less predictable than before. Leopold Auer, a professor at the Conservatory and occasional violin soloist with the RMS orchestra, writes that the large audiences at these programs under Rubinstein gradually fell away after Balakirev took over.[56] Balakirev remarked in a letter following the last concert of the 1868-69 season that "this time there were many more people than usual,"[57] clearly implying that his concerts that year did not always fill the auditorium. Unpredictable attendance may have been due, however, not to any general dissatisfaction with Balakirev's choice of repertory or conducting but to erratic scheduling of RMS concerts. Since the RMS hired its orchestra from the Imperial Theater Directorate, its concert schedule had to be coordinated with performances by the two opera companies. With Vasily Kologrivov's resignation as inspector of orchestras for the Imperial theaters in October 1868, problems immediately cropped up.[58] Some concerts had to be postponed at the last minute,[59] others had to be arranged on very short notice.[60] This no doubt reduced attendance, but there were signs of public support for Balakirev's work. At the final concert of the season, for example, the audience was not only large but enthusiastic. Balakirev received a silver watch from a representative of the RMS membership and hearty applause from the public. "I was called back so many times and so fiercely," he wrote Nikolai Rubinstein, "that it seemed to me that they must have taken me for Patti [Adelina Patti, the most recent sensation of the Italian Opera]. This concert was simply my triumph."[61]

Nevertheless, the empty seats in the auditorium provided ammunition for Balakirev's opponents within the Society, as did the press polemics that continued to surround his public career. Serov, Famintsyn, and Tolstoy criticized both his choice of repertory and his interpretations. This resulted in "constant wrangling, caustic remarks, bantering—in a word, party polemics in full swing."[62]

While Balakirev's concert work was eliciting such controversy in the press, it was also increasing the tension between himself and the conservative elements within the Russian Musical Society. In January 1869 Balakirev wrote a colleague that by programming Borodin's First Symphony, despite its success with the public, he had aroused "implacable hatred 'upstairs' "—that is, presumably, in Elena Pavlovna.[63] Opposition from the grand duchess was nothing new for Balakirev, but earlier he had enjoyed the support of the board of directors of the Society's Petersburg branch. On 22 March 1869, however, the directors voted down a proposal to elect Balakirev to the board and gave no response to his request to know if his services would be required in the following season.[64] The answer was already clear to Balakirev. Four days earlier he had written an acquaintance that Elena Pavlovna had engaged Max Seifriz, the same conductor with whom she had tried to replace him the preceding summer, to direct a benefit concert in St. Petersburg "probably in order to have a pretext to engage him for next year."[65]

Not only was Seifriz's appearance indeed part of a plan to oust Balakirev, but the perpetrators of the scheme included Alexander Serov as well as the conservative element in the RMS. In a letter to Famintsyn written on 25 April 1869, four days after Seifriz's concert, Serov promised to write an article in defense of Seifriz should Cui mount a campaign against him, and he requested that Elena Pavlovna be informed of his intentions.[66] This apparent cooperation of Serov with Famintsyn and the conservative faction in the Russian Musical Society against Balakirev represented a radical change in Serov's position. Although he had been criticizing Balakirev in the press for several years, his attacks on the "German party" in the RMS had been going on still longer. Furthermore, he and Famintsyn had attacked Balakirev on different grounds. Although both charged that Balakirev was an inadequate conductor, Serov's evaluation of the aesthetic stance of the Balakirev school was diametrically opposed to Famintsyn's. To see this, one needs only to look at their reviews of Rimsky's *Sadko,* premiered at an RMS concert in December 1867. Famintsyn's review of this concert was a lengthy condemnation of the basic principles of the Balakirev circle, criticizing the use of folk themes and the apparent formlessness of the music of the new school of Russian composers and recommending that Rimsky study the musical classics to overcome his dilettantism.[67] Serov, on the other hand, found Rimsky's weakness not in formlessness but in insufficient care for his work's programmatic content, and he enthusiastically welcomed the use of folk song. He declared approvingly that Rimsky's tone poem contained "a great deal that is not only Slavic generally but truly *Russian.*"[68] But in the spring of 1869 Serov and Famintsyn joined forces in their common opposition to Balakirev.

Serov may well have hoped that such an alliance would advance his faltering career by winning him recognition from the Russian Musical Society and perhaps even much-needed financial reward from Elena Pavlovna, his one-time benefactor. Since the triumph of his opera *Rogneda* in the fall of 1865 he had had few successes. He had not yet finished his next opera,[69] and the specialized music and theater journal that he and his wife had founded in 1867 had closed for lack of subscribers after only a year, depriving him of a press forum.[70] In addition, the failure of the St. Petersburg premiere of Wagner's *Lohengrin* in October 1868 had reflected directly on Serov since he had been Wagner's apostle in Russia for a decade and had been in charge of the production.[71] Finally, Serov was once more in financial need. According to his wife's memoirs, the Serovs suddenly "found themselves in a completely helpless situation" due to the closing of their journal and a temporary withdrawal of *Rogneda* from the repertory of the Russian Opera.[72] In such circumstances, Serov apparently decided to abandon his isolated position as the opponent of both the RMS and the Balakirev circle and to ally himself with one of the sides. In view of his aesthetic and musical tastes, the Balakirev circle would have seemed the obvious choice, but the RMS leadership offered greater potential benefits. The Society could give him the status of a director or at least an honored member, and Elena Pavlovna might even offer him a subsidy as she had following the premiere of his *Judith* in 1863.[73]

If Serov needed any further prodding to choose the side of Famintsyn and the grand duchess, the role of the Balakirev circle in the failure of *Lohengrin* had provided it. Not only had they openly ridiculed the work at its premiere,[74] but Cui had directed one of his more exaggerated press attacks at it. He praised Wagner for his serious approach but declared "for all that, he is an artist completely without talent and lacking any creative ability; furthermore, there is a leavening of crude bad taste in Wagner's nature, from which he cannot escape."[75] Serov objected in his own review of *Lohengrin,* terming Cui's comments "the barking of mangy mongrels that inevitably accompanies an exalted and spectacular procession until the indefatigable pups are driven out of the gate with brooms or until they themselves become hoarse with fury."[76] The reviewers from the RMS camp, on the other hand, had earned Serov's guarded gratitude as being among the "moderate extollers of Wagner" (Feofil Tolstoy) and as showing "boundless respect for Wagner" (Famintsyn).[77] Common appreciation of Wagner, coupled with distaste for Balakirev, provided, then, tenuous ground for an alliance. Thus, in the spring of 1869 Serov joined forces with the representatives of the "conservative German party" in the RMS that had for so long been the object of his disdain, and together they worked to discredit Balakirev and ensure his removal from the RMS conducting post.

Serov's proffered press defense of Seifriz, however, turned out to be unnecessary because the latter's concert was so unsuccessful that Elena Pavlovna herself abandoned the idea of engaging him for the following season. Instead, she decided to hire Eduard Napravnik, who in May would replace Konstantin Liadov as chief conductor of the Russian opera troupe. On 27 April 1869 she sent Balakirev notification of her decision.[78] Thus ended Balakirev's association with the Russian Musical Society.

Balakirev's dismissal precipitated a flurry of press polemics that reached new heights of invective. Stasov blamed Balakirev's discharge on persons belonging to "the German, pseudo-classical musical party" who think of nothing but their own "petty interests":

> And thus the German party here is celebrating; the Russian party, headed by Balakirev, is humbled and repudiated. What a celebration! Is it really true that the *Russian* Musical Society was founded here in fact for this? Is the name there only for show after all? . . . Balakirev fell victim to German routinism and ignorance. What mediocrities have come forth against him, either to replace him or to declaim against him in the press! Neither talent, nor rank, nor the most wonderful, fervent aspirations—nothing helps. But perhaps some day the German party will receive its just deserts.[79]

Four days later a letter to the editor of *Golos,* signed "one of the members of the Russian Musical Society,"[80] acknowledged Balakirev's musical talent but claimed that he belonged to a group bent on "razing to the ground all hitherto existing ideas of the beautiful and artistic in the realm of music," that he had ignored the works of the classical masters, and that he "served up as masterpieces the immature works of very talented but still extremely inexperienced composers":

> Mr. Balakirev was not ruined by a hostile German party, as Mr. V. S. [Stasov] maintains; rather he was ruined and completely compromised by that very circle that exalted him excessively and, trying to place him on an inaccessible pedestal, prevented him from submitting to the legitimate requirements of the Russian Musical Society.[81]

Serov also publicly denied Stasov's charge that Balakirev's dismissal was the work of a hostile cabal: "There is neither a Russian party nor a German party among us," he wrote, "but there is a nest of self-advertising plotters who wish to run musical affairs for their own personal purposes, shoving aside the higher aims of art."[82]

The apogee of these polemics was reached in Stasov's response to his critics in *Sankt-Peterburgskie vedomosti* on 6 June 1869. He attacked Serov, Famintsyn, and Tolstoy as anti-Russian reactionaries and liars. "In music, as in any other pursuit," wrote Stasov, "there are retrograde persons. Their current arena is the newspaper *Golos*. There they swarm and wriggle." He claimed that they opposed Balakirev and his circle because they sensed in the young Russian musicians "a new, rising force that will squash them all," along with "all the roulades of Rossini, all the banalities of *Lohengrin,* all the pedantic stupidities of ancient textbooks." Stasov even charged the *Golos* critics with lying about Balakirev.[83] Famintsyn objected to Stasov's charges, but Stasov promptly repeated them in yet another aggressive diatribe.[84] Famintsyn then brought suit for libel. The court did not rule the attacks libelous but found Stasov guilty of "abuse" in print, fined him twenty-five rubles, and sentenced him to house arrest for one week. Stasov turned even this into a victory by making his enforced stay at home the occasion for a ceremonial reception for his many friends and supporters.[85]

Thus, Balakirev's two years of work for the Russian Musical Society produced not a reconciliation of his circle with the Society but an even stronger hostility than before. The blame for this must be laid on both sides. Elena Pavlovna's reluctance to engage Balakirev in the first place and her attempts to replace him during the summer of 1868 indicate that she was never happy with the association and only accepted it under pressure from the board of directors. A strong-willed and stubborn woman, she had determined to rid the RMS of this iconoclast and finally succeeded in doing so through a combination of pressure on the Society's directorate and an organized press campaign against him. Balakirev, on the other hand, had never reconciled himself to the reasonable expectations of his new position. He had been intolerant of what he considered the "conservative German party" that dominated the RMS and had accepted the conductor's post in order to advance his own career and to promote the works of his own circle and their favorite composers, not to carry forward the work Anton Rubinstein had begun. Thus, Balakirev's two-year association with the Russian Musical Society ended in hostility, intensified and complicated by personal antagonisms on both sides.

Given Balakirev's difficult character and the strength of his convictions about music, it might have been expected that his association with the Society would end badly, but it certainly could not have been anticipated that the association would precipitate Serov's reconciliation with the Society. His alliance with Tolstoy and Famintsyn and his public defense of the Society's dismissal of Balakirev marked a reversal of long-held positions. For years Serov had criticized the RMS for its failure to recognize Russian artists, and for years he had attacked the conservatism of its leadership. Yet in the spring of 1869 he conspired with a conservative professor to oust an "advanced" Russian musician from the direction of the Society's concerts. The explanation for this surprising development lies in a combination of Serov's personal antipathy for Balakirev and his own desire for public recognition. His alliance with Famintsyn and Elena Pavlovna provided not only the opportunity for a great victory over Balakirev and his circle but also offered a chance finally to gain the Society's acknowledgment of his stature in Russian music.

Balakirev's two years with the RMS also brought the first signs of his eventual estrangement from the members of his circle. In earlier years Balakirev had totally dominated the tastes and aesthetic views of his inexperienced pupils, but by 1867 they were becoming sufficiently mature to challenge his judgment and seek other advisers. Faced with this questioning of his authority and busy with the work of the Free Music School and the Russian Musical Society, Balakirev began to lose interest in his original circle and seek out new musical followers.

Musorgsky was the first in the circle to rebel openly against Balakirev. When Balakirev demanded major revisions of his tone poem *Night on Bald Mountain* in September 1867 Musorgsky flatly refused:

> I used to consider, now consider, and will not stop considering this piece rather good . . .
> Whether or not you, my friend, agree to perform my "witches," I will change nothing in the general plan and treatment, nothing intimately connected with the substance of the scene, nothing carried out sincerely, without sham or imitation . . . I have fulfilled my task as best I could.[86]

Musorgsky's new challenge to Balakirev's authority was symptomatic of a general and growing discontent among the others at Balakirev's insistence on obedience even in petty details.[87] This was particularly conspicuous in Rimsky, the youngest member of the circle and the one in whom Balakirev had placed his greatest hopes in the early 1860s. Rimsky's independence began to assert itself openly by the spring of 1868. According to his memoirs, it was then that his devotion to Balakirev first began to cool: "It was pleasant to come together and spend an evening with Balakirev, but possibly it was still more pleasant to spend the evening without him. It seems to me I was not alone in this feeling, that the other members of our circle shared it."[88] Rimsky was then composing his symphonic suite *Antar*, about which Balakirev had reservations, but Rimsky would not succumb to his teacher's pressure. In August 1868 he wrote Musorgsky that he knew Balakirev would hate at least one movement and be dissatisfied with another, but he added: "I will not alter anything, for I have expressed the idea, and well at that."[89]

By 1867 even Balakirev's relations with his closest friend of the early 1860s, Vladimir Stasov, had become clouded by disagreement. From 1865 their mutual correspondence declined in both quantity and intimacy. This was certainly due in part to Balakirev's expanding musical activity, which occupied much of his time, but it also reflected a cleavage in their political views.[90] For all his Russian nationalism, Stasov was always basically a Westernizer. He did not reject Western Europe as a model for Russian development but instead hoped his nation would learn from the lessons of the West. As Balakirev's Slavophilism grew and blossomed into xenophobic chauvinism, it could not help but put a strain on his friendship with Stasov because the whole question of the proper path for Russian national development was central to the political and artistic beliefs of both men. The effect of this growing disagreement can be seen in a letter Balakirev wrote Stasov from Prague in February 1867. He described his own hatred and fear of the anti-Russian forces he believed to be growing in Western Europe and accused his friend of blindness for not sharing his feelings: "Your naive, childish outlook on these issues does not allow you to see things as they actually are and that is why you look at everything through cosmopolitan pince-nez."[91] A year and a half later Balakirev agreed to Stasov's suggestion that they try to see one another more frequently but admitted that there were sides of Stasov to which he could never reconcile himself.[92] Thus Balakirev was not only losing his unquestioned authority over his pupils but was also becoming estranged from his closest friend and his circle's aesthetic adviser.

Balakirev's declining dominance over his circle in the late 1860s was reflected in its very organizational structure. In the early years of its existence the group usually met at the home of one of its members, and the sessions amounted chiefly to lessons in composition and discussions of aesthetics attended only by the young composers themselves and, often, Vladimir Stasov. In the latter half of the 1860s, however, the group began to gather occasionally at the homes of friends and associates from outside the circle itself. At these sessions, music-making rather than instruction took the predominant place. Beginning in 1866 Liudmila Shestakova, Glinka's sister, opened her home to Balakirev and his friends for regular gatherings.[93] In the spring of 1868 the circle began to meet frequently at Alexander Dargomyzhsky's apartment as well. There they became acquainted with Alexandra and Nadezhda Purgold, two young pupils of Dargomyzhsky, and soon they were frequent guests at the home of Vladimir Purgold, the young women's uncle.[94]

The Balakirev circle's association with Dargomyzhsky was particularly significant, because the older composer soon became a second teacher to Balakirev's pupils. Although Balakirev treated him with more than a touch of condescension, in 1868 Dargomyzhsky began to seek the companionship and support of the Balakirev circle. He was then composing the most advanced and unusual work of his career, a work that may very well have been conceived in response to criticism of his opera *Rusalka* by the circle.[95] The work in question was an opera based on Pushkin's version of the Don Juan story, *The Stone Guest,* and its novelty lay in the composer's effort to set the prose text of the play, unaltered in any way, directly to music that would follow the natural inflections of speech. Dargomyzhsky's experiment made a profound impression on his young colleagues. They thought it the realistic music of the future that they had been espousing all along. A decade later Cui would write that *The Stone Guest* was "the most mature, outstanding, and characteristic work" of the entire school of operatic composition fostered by the Balakirev circle. [96] Dargomyzhsky thus became an authority to rival Balakirev in the eyes of Rimsky, Borodin, Cui, and especially Musorgsky. Moreover, all were then working on operas of their own, a genre in which Balakirev could offer little assistance.

It is easy to imagine Balakirev's resentment of his pupils' challenge to his authority in the circle and their enthusiasm for another senior composer and teacher. He had always jealously guarded his own primacy in musical questions and insisted that the members of his group agree with him even on small details. When the entire group began to resist his advice and suggestions, Balakirev started to lose interest in all his pupils and was frequently absent from their gatherings. Although the circle often met at Dargomyzhsky's during 1868, Balakirev attended infrequently[97]—a situation duly noted by his friends. Borodin found Balakirev's behavior disturbing enough to comment about his "cooling of interest in the music of our circle and the fact that he does not show his face anywhere."[98]

Just as Balakirev had transferred his intense interest to Rimsky when Musorgsky first challenged his authority in the early 1860s, so too, did he seek out new followers when his entire circle began to draw away from his exclusive control in the late 1860s. This time he directed his attention toward an unlikely candidate—Pyotr Tchaikovsky, one of the first graduates of the St. Petersburg Conservatory and then a professor at the Moscow Conservatory. Although trained in the opposition camp, he was still in his twenties and sufficiently young and impressionable to be seen by Balakirev as a potential new pupil. The two met for the first time early in January 1868 in Moscow.[99] Until then Balakirev and his circle had known Tchaikovsky only through a few compositions performed in St. Petersburg, and they had been little impressed. Cui had reviewed Tchaikovsky's conservatory graduation piece quite harshly and had passed over in silence the two movements of his First Symphony performed at one of Anton Rubinstein's last RMS concerts.[100] "As a product of the Conservatory," Rimsky writes in his memoirs, "Tchaikovsky was viewed [by the circle] rather negligently if not haughtily."[101] For his part, Tchaikovsky had good reasons to be suspicious of Balakirev and his friends. They were opponents of the St. Petersburg Conservatory, from which he had graduated, and severe critics of Anton Rubinstein, whom he almost idolized.[102] Furthermore, Cui's review of his graduation piece had wounded him very deeply. He told a friend that after reading it he had wandered the streets of St. Petersburg in a daze, repeating over and over, "I am barren, I am insignificant, I will never produce anything, I am a mediocrity."[103] He must have resented the Balakirev circle and much of what it stood for.

All this apparently changed with the beginning of Balakirev's personal acquaintance with Tchaikovsky. The older composer was sufficiently impressed by the younger man's work to volunteer to program one of his pieces at an RMS concert in St. Petersburg, and the latter realized the value of Balakirev's musical advice and his connections. On 21 January 1868 Tchaikovsky sent Balakirev the music for an entr'acte and set of peasant dances from his opera *The Voyevoda* with the following formal note:

> In accordance with our agreement I am sending you the score of my "Dances"; if it is possible to perform them at some concert under your direction, I would be extremely obliged to you. But if it is impossible, then please return them at your convenience; and in any case, send me if possible a word of encouragement. To receive it from you would be pleasant in the highest degree for me.[104]

A month later Balakirev replied that he had been unable to program Tchaikovsky's dances for the RMS because his season had already ended, but he reported that he had submitted them to the Directorate of Imperial Theaters and that they had been accepted for one of the Directorate's symphonic concerts. As for the word of encouragement Tchaikovsky had requested, Balakirev declared it "neither appropriate nor honest." He explained, "Encouragement is used only for young children in art, but from your score I see in you, both in the orchestration and the writing, a completely finished artist, to whom only *strict criticism* and not encouragement is applicable. When I see you in person I will be happy to tell you my opinion."[105] Here we see the same combination of respect and condescension that marked Balakirev's relations with the young members of his own circle. Presumably he already saw in Tchaikovsky a potential follower of great promise.

Tchaikovsky gave every sign of his respect and interest in Balakirev and his group. "He readily took on the role of a sort of 'legate' in Moscow" for Balakirev's circle, according to his brother Modest, serving as their liaison with the Moscow RMS and the local music publisher, Peter Jurgenson.[106] In March 1868 Tchaikovsky even published a defense of Rimsky-Korsakov's *Serbian Fantasy* against the attack of an anonymous Moscow critic. He had never before written for the press, but he had come to appreciate the *Serbian Fantasy* while attending the rehearsals for the benefit concert at which it received its Moscow premiere (his own dances from *The Voyevoda* were also on the program); moreover, he was already a friend of Balakirev.[107] Although he found Rimsky still clearly under the influence of Glinka and Balakirev, Tchaikovsky concluded that "there is no doubt that this remarkably gifted man is fated to become one of the finest adornments of our art."[108]

This article came to the attention of Balakirev and his circle, and when Tchaikovsky traveled to St. Petersburg in the spring of 1868 to visit his father for Easter, they gave him a friendly welcome.[109] In his memoirs, Rimsky recalls the occasion:

> I don't know how it happened, but during one of his visits to St. Petersburg Tchaikovsky made his appearance at Balakirev's soirée, and our acquaintance began. He proved a pleasing and sympathetic man to talk with, one who knew how to be simple of manner and always speak with evident sincerity and heartiness. The evening of our first meeting he played for us, at Balakirev's request, the first movement of his Symphony in G Minor; it proved quite to our liking; and our former opinion of him changed and gave way to a more sympathetic one, although Tchaikovsky's Conservatory training still constituted a considerable barrier between him and us.[110]

A more tangible barrier was the distance between Moscow and St. Petersburg.

Balakirev himself, however, corresponded frequently with Tchaikovsky, and their friendship gradually assumed something of the character of Balakirev's earlier relationship with the members of his circle. His blunt critique of Tchaikovsky's tone poem *Fate* illustrates the point:

> The piece itself I don't like. It's not fully formed, as if it were written off-handedly. All the seams and basting threads are visible. The form once and for all is not successful; nothing fits together. Laroche ascribes this to the fact that you apply yourself too little to the classics. In my opinion, it results from just the opposite; you are little acquainted with new music. The classics will not teach you free form. In them you will find nothing new, nothing unknown to you. Everything that you will find there you have already long known since the days when you sat at a desk and reverently followed Zaremba's wise treatises

about the connection between Rondo form and the fall of Adam and Eve. At the same concert [at which *Fate* received its St. Petersburg premiere] we performed Liszt's *Les Preludes*. Look at what miraculous form it has. How everything flows naturally one from another.[111]

Tchaikovsky waited more than a month to reply to this criticism, but his ultimate response rang with the humility and submissiveness once shown by Balakirev's original group of colleague-students. He wrote that he was "completely in agreement" with Balakirev's comments and was not offended by Balakirev's "sincere directness."[112] Five days later Balakirev replied that he was extremely happy with Tchaikovsky's response to his criticism and respected him more than ever. "Now I am sure that we will never drift apart since all our relations will be based on the most sincere truthfulness and not on the usual European courtesies."[113]

As if to prove the sincerity of his devotion, Tchaikovsky even wrote an article defending Balakirev on his dismissal by the St. Petersburg RMS. He praised Balakirev for his great talent and his "pure and selfless love for national art," enumerated his services to Russian music, and compared his dismissal to the fate of a hypothetical young man of talent who is just beginning to make a career for himself when "suddenly the whim of his superior destroys in a stroke his patiently and honestly won position" and he becomes "the outraged victim of overbearing tyranny."[114] Stasov was sufficiently pleased with Tchaikovsky's article that he reprinted it in its entirety in his own public defense of Balakirev in *Sankt-Peterburgskie vedomosti*.[115] Balakirev thanked Tchaikovsky and promised that he could still program Tchaikovsky's works in St. Petersburg, either at the Free Music School concerts or at his own annual benefit appearance.[116] Thus, it appeared that Balakirev had won Tchaikovsky as a surrogate for his once-submissive followers who had begun to reject his leadership.

As a result of the events just described, the rivalry among the chief factions in St. Petersburg's musical life differed profoundly in the summer of 1869 from what it had been two years earlier. The conservative faction in the Russian Musical Society had clearly taken charge once more after two years in eclipse. Furthermore, it had acquired a formidable public spokesman in Alexander Famintsyn and was further bolstered by an alliance with the Society's former enemy Alexander Serov. By contrast, the Balakirev circle was losing its cohesion. Balakirev's interest in his original students had begun to decline as they outgrew their need for his instruction, and Balakirev himself had begun to direct his interest elsewhere. He had not, however, abandoned his rivalry with the Russian Musical Society's conservative leadership. His two years of work for the Society and his unceremonious dismissal had only increased his antipathy. Now he was ready to renew the struggle with greater intensity than before.

Notes to Chapter V

1. Lisovskii, "Letopis' Rubinshteina," p. 614; Rozenberg, "A.G. Rubinshtein," p. 585.

2. Rubinshtein, *Izbrannye pis'ma*, pp. 70-71.

3. Obolenskii, "Moi vospominaniia," 138:264.

4. Elena Pavlovna to Obolenskii, summer of 1867, *ibid.*, 138:265.

5. Obolenskii to Elena Pavlovna, summer of 1867, *ibid.*, 138:267.

6. Stasov, *Izbrannye sochineniia*, 3:85; Rimsky-Korsakov, *My Musical Life*, p. 81; Balakirev to V. Stasov, 8 December 1888, in *Perepiska*, 2:141.

7. Liapunova, *Balakirev: letopis'*, p. 128; Findeizen, *Ocherk RMO*, p. 45.

8. Nikolai Dmitrievich Kashkin, *Vospominaniia o P.I. Chaikovskom* [Memoirs about P.I. Tchaikovsky] (Moscow: P. Iurgenson, 1896), p. 62; Barenboim, *A.G. Rubinshtein*, 1:350-51.

9. Barenboim, *A.G. Rubinshtein*, 1:350.

10. Elena Pavlovna to Obolensky, 14 August 1867, in Obolenskii, "Moi vospominanii," 138:268.

11. Findeizen, *Ocherk RMO*, pp. 45-46.

12. Liapunova, *Balakirev: letopis'*, p. 129.

13. *Ibid.*, p. 130; Stasov, *Izbrannye sochineniia*, 3:351.

14. Liapunova, *Balakirev: letopis'*, p. 130.

15. *My Musical Life*, p. 81.

16. Berlioz to M. and Mme. Massart, 4 October 1867 (N.S.), in Hector Berlioz, *A Selection from his Letters*, ed. Humphrey Searle (New York: Harcourt, Brace & World, 1966), p. 208.

17. Balakirev to V.M. Zhemchuzhnikov, 19 June 1867, in Balakirev, *Vospominaniia*, pp. 99-100.

18. Liapunova, *Balakirev: letopis'*, p. 160.

19. For complete programs, see Findeizen, *Ocherk RMO*, appendix, pp. 8-9.

20. Rimsky-Korsakov, *My Musical Life*, pp. 81-82.

21. Berlioz to M. and Mme. Massart, 4 October 1867 (N.S.), in Berlioz, *A Selection*, p. 208; Jacques Barzun, *Berlioz and the Romantic Century*, 2 vols. (Boston: Little, Brown and Co., 1950), 2:279.

22. For complete programs, see Findeizen, *Ocherk RMO,* appendix, p. 9.

23. Berlioz to E. Alexandre, 15 December 1867 (N.S.), in Berlioz, *A Selection,* p. 210.

24. See, for example, "Muzykal'nye zametki," *St. P. ved.,* 1 November 1867, p. 2; and 16 November 1867, p. 1.

25. *Izbrannye stat'i,* p. 140.

26. Quoted in Kremlev, *Russkaia mysl' o muzyke,* 2:70.

27. Quoted in Liapunova, *Balakirev: letopis',* p. 132.

28. See, for example, Serov, *Izbrannye stat'i,* 2:618.

29. Livanova, *Muzykal'naia bibliografiia,* 5, pt. 1, p. 12.

30. Kremlev, *Russkaia mysl' o muzyke,* 2:481.

31. *Ibid.,* 2:537.

32. Liapunova, *Balakirev: letopis',* p. 131.

33. Iakovlev, "K istorii 'Raika,' " p. 105.

34. Kremlev, *Russkaia mysl' o muzyke,* 2:539.

35. *Izbrannye stat'i,* p. 129.

36. *My Musical Life,* p. 106.

37. Letter of 8 December 1888 in *Perepiska,* 2:141.

38. Rimsky-Korsakov, *My Musical Life,* pp. 83-84.

39. Kashkin, *Stat'i o russkoi muzyke,* p. 27.

40. Letter of 7 or 14 February 1865 in *Perepiska,* 1:238.

41. See for example, Balakirev to P. Tchaikovsky, 19 April 1868, in Balakirev, *Vospominaniia,* p. 122.

42. Balakirev to V. Stasov, 14 September 1868, in *Perepiska,* 1:256.

43. Liapunova, *Balakirev: letopis',* p. 141.

44. Letter of 19 May 1868 in Balakirev, *Vospominaniia,* p. 84.

45. Liapunova, *Balakirev: letopis',* p. 144.

46.   Stasov, *Selected Essays,* p. 169.

47.   Berlioz to V. Stasov, 21 August 1868 (N.S.), in Berlioz, *A Selection,* p. 215.

48.   Balakirev to V. Stasov, 14 September 1868, in *Perepiska,* 1:258.

49.   Liapunova, *Balakirev: letopis',* p. 158.

50.   Letter of 14 September 1868 in *Perepiska,* 1:257.

51.   Musorgsky to L. Shestakova, 30 June 1868, in Musorgskii, *Literaturnoe nasledie,* 1:99.

52.   Letter of 14 September 1868 in *Perepiska,* 1:258.

53.   For complete programs, see Findeizen, *Ocherk RMO,* appendix, pp. 9-10.

54.   See, for example, Balakirev's letters to N. Rubinstein about the program for the latter's concert in Milii Alekseevich Balakirev, *Perepiska s N.G. Rubinshteinom is M.P. Beliaevym* [Correspondence with N.G. Rubinstein and M.P. Belyaev], ed. V.A. Kiselev (Moscow: Gosudarstvennoe muzykal'noe izdatel'stvo, 1956), pp. 15, 20-23.

55.   Rimsky-Korsakov, *My Musical Life,* p. 102.

56.   *My Long Life,* p. 172.

57.   Balakirev to N. Rubinstein, 29 April 1869, in Balakirev, *Perepiska s N. Rubinshteinom,* p. 27.

58.   Editor's note 3 to letter 204, *Perepiska,* 1:442.

59.   Balakirev to N. Rubinstein, 12 November 1868, in Balakirev, *Perepiska s N. Rubinshteinom,* p. 20.

60.   Balakirev to P. Tchaikovsky, 11 March 1869, in Balakirev, *Vospominaniia,* p. 125.

61.   Balakirev to N. Rubinstein, 29 April 1869, in Balakirev, *Perepiska s N. Rubinshteinom,* p. 27. See also Balakirev's letter to his father of 30 April 1869 in Balakirev, *Vospominaniia,* p. 90.

62.   Rimsky-Korsakov, *My Musical Life,* p. 103.

63.   Balakirev to N. Rubinstein, 15 January 1869, in Balakirev, *Perepiska s N. Rubinshteinom,* p. 24.

64.   Liapunova, *Balakirev: letopis',* p. 155.

65.   Balakirev to P. Tchaikovsky, 18 March 1869, in Balakirev, *Vospominaniia,* p. 130.

66.   Liapunova, *Balakirev: letopis',* p. 156.

67. Iakovlev, "K istorii 'Raika,' " p. 105: Kremlev, *Russkaia mysl' o muzyke,* 2:539.

68. *Izbrannye stat'i,* 2:618-20.

69. Khubov, *Zhizn' Serova,* p. 113.

70. Livanova, *Muzykal'naia bibliografiia,* 5, pt. 1, p. 27.

71. Zvantsov, "A.N. Serov," pp. 665-66.

72. Serova, *Serovy,* p. 91.

73. Balakirev believed in May 1869 that Serov had joined the cabal against him in order to win for himself the post of director of the Conservatory. Balakirev further claimed that Elena Pavlovna gave Serov one thousand rubles for his articles supporting her position. (See Balakirev to Tchaikovsky, 8 May and 25 May 1869, in Balakirev, *Vospominaniia,* pp. 133-35.)

74. Rimsky-Korsakov, *My Musical Life,* p. 101.

75. "Muzykal'nye zametki," *St. P. ved.,* 11 October 1868, p. 1.

76. *Izbrannye stat'i,* 1:449.

77. *Ibid.*

78. Balakirev to N. Rubinstein, 29 April 1869, in Balakirev, *Perepiska s N. Rubinshteinom,* pp. 27-28; Balakirev to Tchaikovsky, 8 May 1869, in Balakirev, *Vospominaniia,* p. 134. Some sources, notably Rimsky's memoirs, state that it was Balakirev who broke off his conducting work for the Society, but these letters and Balakirev's request in March to be notified whether his services would be needed for the next year prove that the initiative for his departure came from Elena Pavlovna.

79. *Izbrannye sochineniia,* 1:195-96.

80. Stasov claimed it was by Feofil Tolstoy (see *Izbrannye sochineniia,* 3:86-87) as does Kremlev, *Russkaia mysl' o muzyke,* 2:484. Livanova, *Muzykal'naia bibliografiia,* 5, pt. 2, p. 498, however, does not identify the author.

81. Quoted in Kremlev, *Russkaia mysl' o muzyke,* 2:484-85.

82. Quoted in Stasov, *Izbrannye sochineniia,* 3:86.

83. "Muzykal'nye lguny" [Musical liars], *St. P. ved.,* 6 June 1869, pp. 1-2.

84. "Pis'mo v redaktsiiu i ob'iasnenie" [A letter to the editor and an explanation], *St. P. ved.,* 18 June 1869, p. 3.

85. Kremlev, *Russkaia mysl' o muzyke,* 2:118; Komarova, *V. Stasov,* 1:373.

86. Musorgsky to Balakirev, 24 September 1867, in Musorgskii, *Literaturnoe nasledie,* 1:94-95.

87. Swan, *Russian Music,* p. 93.

88. *My Musical Life,* p. 90.

89. Letter of 7 August 1868 in Rimskii-Korsakov, *Polnoe sobranie,* 5:308.

90. Editor's introduction to Balakirev and Stasov, *Perepiska,* 1:11.

91. Letter of 10 February 1867 in *Perepiska,* 1:247-50.

92. Balakirev to V. Stasov, 14 September 1868, *ibid.,* 1:156.

93. Liudmila Ivanovna Shestakova, "Moi vechera" [My soirees], *Ezhegodnik imperatorskikh teatrov,* 1893-94, appendix 2, pp. 119-20.

94. Rimsky-Korsakov, *My Musical Life,* pp. 86-88; Akademiia nauk SSSR, *Istoriia Leningrada,* 2:531-32.

95. Taruskin, "Opera and Drama," pp. 412-13.

96. *La Musique en Russie,* p. 53.

97. Borodina, "Moe vospominanie," p. 36.

98. Letter to his wife of 16 October 1868 in Borodin, *Pis'ma,* 1:121.

99. Liapunova, *Balakirev: letopis',* p. 136.

100. M. Chaikovskii, *Zhizn' Chaikovskogo,* 1:204, 262.

101. *My Musical Life,* p. 75.

102. Larosh, *Izbrannye stat'i,* 2:285; Kashkin, *Vospominaniia o Chaikovskom,* p. 15.

103. Vasilii Iakovlev, ed., *Dni i gody P.I. Chaikovskogo: Letopis' zhizni i tvorchestva* [The days and years of P.I. Tchaikovsky; a chronicle of his life and work] (Moscow: Gosudarstvennoe muzykal'noe izdatel'stvo, 1940), p. 600.

104. P. Chaikovskii, *Polnoe sobranie,* 5:131.

105. Letter of 21 February 1868 in Balakirev, *Vospominaniia.* p. 118.

106. M. Chaikovskii, *Zhizn' Chaikovskogo,* 1:289. See Tchaikovsky's letters to Balakirev of 25 February and 3 March 1868 and 13 March and 3 May 1869 in P. Chaikovskii, *Polnoe sobranie,* 5:134, 135, 159, 163.

107. M. Chaikovskii, *Zhizn' Chaikovskogo,* 1:287.

108. Petr Il'ich Chaikovskii, *Muzykal'no-kriticheskie stat'i* [Musico-critical articles], ed. Vasilii Iakovlev, 2nd ed. (Moscow: Gosudarstvennoe muzykal'noe izdatel'stvo, 1953), p. 27.

109. M. Chaikovskii, *Zhizn' Chaikovskogo*, 1:288.

110. *My Musical Life*, p. 75.

111. Balakirev to P. Tchaikovsky, 31 March 1869, in Balakirev, *Vospominaniia*, p. 131.

112. Letter of 3 May 1868 in P. Chaikovskii, *Polnoe sobranie*, 5:162-63.

113. Letter of 8 May 1868 in Balakirev, *Vospominaniia*, p. 133.

114. P. Chaikovskii, *Muzykal'no-kriticheskie stat'i*, pp. 28-30.

115. Stasov, *Izbrannye sochineniia*, 1:194-96.

116. Letter of 8 May 1869 in Balakirev, *Vospominaniia*, p. 133.

Chapter VI

Renewal of the Rivalry, 1869-1873

Although Balakirev's dismissal from the post of music director for the concerts of the Russian Musical Society in the spring of 1869 was a great blow to his efforts to establish himself and his circle as the leading musical authorities in St. Petersburg, it by no means ended his campaign. He had lost the most conspicuous conductor's platform in the concert life of the Russian capital, but he retained the position of director and chief conductor of the Free Music School, which he had acquired upon Gavriil Lomakin's retirement early in 1868. Furthermore, he still had the press support of Cui and Vladimir Stasov. With these means, Balakirev renewed his competition with the RMS, which had been temporarily suspended during his two seasons as the Society's chief conductor. In the fall of 1869 he began once more his campaign to win public recognition for the music and tastes of his circle by turning the Free Music School's concerts into a successful rival of the RMS concerts as the most prestigious center for orchestral music in Russia.

During Balakirev's tenure as chief conductor for the Russian Musical Society his work for the Free Music School had definitely taken second place to his demanding duties for the RMS. He employed his influence in the RMS to win the FMS permission to use the premises of the Conservatory for some of its classes, and the FMS chorus took part in a number of the Russian Musical Society's concerts,[1] but Balakirev had little time for the Free Music School's independent work. According to one of the school's teachers, "little or no attention was paid to choral classes. If choral pieces appeared then on the concert programs, it was only the repetition of pieces learned and performed under Lomakin."[2] In the 1867-68 and 1868-69 seasons the school gave three concerts, all led by Balakirev. Each included a single large choral work along with some orchestral pieces. At the first concert the chorus performed Mozart's *Requiem*, which Lomakin had conducted two seasons earlier, and at both the second and third concerts the choral selection was the same—Berlioz's *Te Deum*. Except for one chorus from the work, which had been performed in 1864, the Berlioz was new at the FMS concerts and a very demanding piece at that, but its inclusion as the sole choral composition at two successive concerts indicates that Balakirev did not give the attention Lomakin had to training the FMS's chorus and preparing its concerts. In fact, while he was simultaneously conductor of both the RMS and FMS concerts, Balakirev apparently could not even find time to study and prepare new scores for the purely orchestral portions of the FMS performances, even though the participation of a hired professional orchestra eliminated the lengthy rehearsals required to teach the amateur chorus a new composition. Of the four orchestral works on the three FMS programs, Balakirev had already conducted all but one at earlier concerts.[3] It is obvious that he was devoting much more time and effort to the Russian Musical Society than to the Free Music School.

Following Balakirev's dismissal by the RMS his half-hearted interest in the Free Music School gave way to feverish activity in its behalf. Now he felt a burning desire to use it to surpass the musical prestige and authority of the RMS, which had just publicly humiliated him. "Rivalry between the concerts of the Russian Musical Society and those of the Free Music School became the main object of Balakirev's activity as conductor," Rimsky tells us.[4] Barely a month after Grand Duchess Elena Pavlovna notified him that the RMS would not re-engage him for the 1869-70 season, Balakirev was already planning a competitive series of FMS concerts.[5] On 1 September 1869 he proposed to the FMS council that in the coming season the school present not one or two public performances as in the past but an integral series of five concerts sold by subscription.[6] Cui's music column in *Sankt-Peterburgskie vedomosti* for 25 September closed with a brief announcement of the planned FMS concert series "for lovers of excellent music and choice performance."[7] Balakirev wrote Nikolai Rubinstein the same day that his programs were almost entirely worked out and that he had already arranged for the participation of all but one of the soloists on whom he had counted.[8] Borodin observed in late October that Balakirev was "bustling about and working with such energy and passion as never before."[9] Obviously, he had taken up the gauntlet in his renewed rivalry with the RMS.

The programs for the Free Music School's subscription concerts were carefully chosen to be as interesting as possible without compromising Balakirev's basic aesthetic principles. They contained the usual heavy quota of Liszt, Schumann, and Beethoven, several major works by Dargomyzhsky, Glinka, and members of Balakirev's own circle, and virtually nothing written before the nineteenth century or in the conservative line of contemporary nineteenth-century music. Whatever these programs may have lacked in variety of styles they made up in novelty, however, for they included the St. Petersburg premieres of five works, including major compositions by Liszt,

Schumann, and even Anton Rubinstein.[10] The latter work, a tone poem entitled *Ivan the Terrible,* would appear to have been programmed in an attempt to attract some of the supporters of Balakirev's former rival and perhaps even to conciliate Rubinstein himself. Nevertheless, even in this Balakirev apparently remained faithful to his own aesthetic principles since the work turned out to be one of the very few of Rubinstein's compositions to win praise from Balakirev's circle. Borodin wrote his wife that it contained, "surprisingly, much that is good; it is simply impossible to recognize that it is A. Rubinstein,"[11] and Cui also reviewed it favorably.[12]

In addition to interesting and even provocative repertory, the 1869-70 FMS concert series also featured some of the most popular St. Petersburg soloists. These included not only stars of the Russian opera company but also leading instrumentalists from the faculty of the St. Petersburg Conservatory. The most noteworthy soloist of all was Nikolai Rubinstein, the brother of Anton and director of the Moscow RMS and the Moscow Conservatory. Not only was he reputed to be as fine a pianist as his brother, but the infrequency of his concerts outside Moscow also made his St. Petersburg appearance a special occasion. Balakirev had begun cultivating Nikolai Rubinstein's friendship during his directorship of the St. Petersburg RMS concerts,[13] and even afterwards he was careful to preserve his contacts with the director of the Moscow branch of the Society. Nikolai Rubinstein's appearance at the FMS concert on 30 November 1869 represented a significant victory for Balakirev against his St. Petersburg rivals. Not only did Rubinstein perform for the Free Music School and not for the St. Petersburg RMS, but he also demonstrated his support for Balakirev's cause by performing the premiere of *Islamey*, a virtuosic piano fantasy on Caucasian themes that Balakirev had composed for him during the preceding summer.[14] Borodin wrote his wife that the Russian Musical Society was "thunderstruck" by Nikolai Rubinstein's appearance at an FMS concert and that Grand Duchess Elena Pavlovna was so angry that she refused to receive the director of the Moscow RMS when he attempted to make his required appearance before her as patron of the Society.[15]

Top ticket prices for the FMS concerts were hardly inexpensive (ten rubles for five concerts as compared to the RMS fee of fifteen rubles for ten concerts), but most seats sold for a competitive price of seven rubles for the series or slightly less than the RMS's rate of one-and-a-half rubles per concert.[16] To further attract subscribers, the Free Music School offered season tickets to the galleries for only three rubles. As Cui pointed out to his readers, this was an excellent bargain for serious symphonic concerts in St. Petersburg.[17]

While Balakirev was doing all in his power to make the subscription concert series of the Free Music School an artistic and popular success, the Russian Musical Society was not standing idly by. Its leadership was also making extraordinary efforts to meet the challenge from Balakirev. To replace Balakirev as chief conductor of its concerts, the RMS engaged Eduard Napravnik, a young musician who was quickly earning an excellent reputation in the Russian capital. Although a Czech by birth, Napravnik had come to Russia in 1861, at the age of twenty-two, to conduct the private orchestra of Prince Nikolai Yusupov and would spend the rest of his life in Russia.[18] In 1863 he was hired as an assistant to the conductor of the Russian opera, in 1867 he was named second conductor and in 1869, principal conductor.[19] Napravnik was not, however, to enjoy sole leadership of the RMS concerts. Just as the Society had engaged Berlioz to conduct some of its performances during Balakirev's first season, so now it hired a foreign artist, Ferdinand Hiller, a respectable German composer, pianist, and conductor, to lead four concerts during the 1869-70 season.[20] Presumably Elena Pavlovna hoped in this way to add prestige and novelty to the Society's series.

For repertory the RMS returned to the pattern of Anton Rubinstein's years as music director, which resulted in a selection less novel than Balakirev's but also much more varied. Beethoven was by far the most frequently performed composer, and the nineteenth-century German conservatives were also well represented. In addition, the programs included major works by Haydn and Mozart and a taste of earlier music, with compositions by Palestrina, Handel and Bach. The modern school was represented primarily by Schumann, but there were also works by both Liszt and Wagner. Russian music was represented by three works by Glinka and two by Anton Rubinstein, whose style was, however, more German than Russian.[21] A new composition by Serov, an unofficial associate of the RMS since the spring of 1869, was also announced for performance but was omitted due to the illness of the vocal soloist.[22] No music by members of Balakirev's circle appeared on the programs. This return to more classically oriented programs after Balakirev's emphasis on the contemporary school reflected a policy apparently set by Elena Pavlovna herself. Hiller had been advised to draw up programs for his four concerts that would give preference to the classics and avoid Balakirev's unsatisfactory predilection for modern composers.[23] Both Balakirev and Borodin claimed privately that a guest soloist's request to perform a Liszt piano concerto at one of the RMS concerts was turned down by Napravnik on the grounds that Elena Pavlovna had ordered him "to tear out the previous trend by the roots."[24]

The RMS concerts also presented their own list of popular or interesting soloists. In addition to featuring such well-known figures as Leopold Auer, solo violinist at two RMS concerts the previous season, the Society opened its season with a controversial soloist—Désirée Artôt, the latest sensation of the Italian opera troupe in Moscow. Opera singers were not infrequent soloists at previous RMS concerts, but they were usually native artists from the Russian

Opera performing scenes from Gluck, songs by Schumann, or other serious literature. Artôt, on the other hand, was an expensive foreign singer, and she performed such light virtuoso showpieces as a vocal arrangement of a Chopin mazurka. Another young soloist, a German pianist with the familiar surname Rubinstein, though unrelated to Anton and Nikolai, was guaranteed to arouse curiosity in musical circles of the Russian capital.

To further enhance the attractiveness of the RMS concerts for St. Petersburg's high society, Elena Pavlovna herself attended them with her entire court, thus giving them a heightened social prestige.[25] Hoping to appeal to the less well-to-do music lovers, the RMS also altered its traditional policy on single tickets. In the past the Society had discouraged the purchase of single tickets by charging five rubles for them, while admission to all ten symphonic concerts and several chamber music programs cost only the fifteen-ruble price for RMS membership. For the 1869-70 season the Society maintained its charge of fifteen rubles for membership but reduced the fee for a single admission to two rubles for the main floor (little more than the price per concert of a season ticket) and a mere half ruble for the galleries[26]—even less than the price per concert for the least expensive Free Music School ticket.

The rivalry between the FMS and RMS inherent in their competing concert series was articulated in the musical press, which each side used to publicize its own concerts and to denigrate those of its opponent. As in earlier years, Balakirev's regular press spokesman was César Cui, who was occasionally joined by Vladimir Stasov. Cui reviewed all the FMS concerts, praising them in the most glowing terms for both their progressive, modern repertory and the quality of Balakirev's conducting.[27] He particularly praised the compositions of his own friends performed at the FMS concerts, even suggesting that the author of "the foolish tale" *Rogneda* (i.e., Serov) should study Balakirev's tone poem *1,000 Years* to learn how "a true artist" develops his carefully chosen themes while avoiding "even the slightest tinge of banality."[28]

Cui also reviewed all the RMS concerts of the 1869-70 season and, not surprisingly, found them decidedly inferior to those of the FMS. Although he had high praise for Napravnik, terming him "a splendid conductor . . . who yields in this respect to Mr. Balakirev but who far surpasses A. Rubinstein,"[29] he announced that Hiller, both as conductor and pianist, had treated his audiences to "nine or ten hours of tedium" in his four concerts.[30] But Cui's major complaint was aimed not at the performance standards of the RMS concerts but at their repertory. This he found "quite poor and colorless."[31] Artot's vocal showpieces he found unworthy of any concert with pretensions to seriousness.[32] The eighteenth-century classics sprinkled throughout the season prompted him to scoff at efforts "to revive artificially the long-dead corpse of pre-Beethovenian music."[33] Most of all, he resented the absence of works by modern Russian composers. After only four RMS concerts he declared that the Society

> has renounced the two-year trend set by Balakirev; it did not like the fact that Balakirev performed only good music, rich in vitality and content, no matter when or by whom it was written, even if by our contemporaries, or even by Russians; it has dragged out dry and outdated pieces from every quarter; it has tried to present worthless formalism and cold playing-with-sounds as models of human genius.[34]

Meanwhile, Famintsyn, Feofil Tolstoy, and Serov, the chief participants in the press campaign against Balakirev's direction of the RMS concerts in the two preceding seasons, continued to challenge the authority of Balakirev and his circle. In October 1869, in the first issue of his new specialized music journal *Muzykal'nyi sezon* [*The Music Season*], for example, Famintsyn charged Cui with nihilistic attacks on the classics of music and "monstrous one-sidedness" in his partisanship for Russian music. He proposed historical objectivity and unbiased study of both the past and the present as the ideal aesthetic position for a critic.[35] This implicitly challenged the entire direction of Balakirev's FMS concerts and his claims to leadership in musical taste, because Balakirev clearly gave overwhelming predominance to the modern school. The RMS concerts, whatever their faults, offered a greater variety of music and far surpassed Balakirev in exploring all schools and periods of music. In the second issue of his journal Famintsyn had some kind words for the Free Music School's concerts, finding the performances "quite successful" and even praising the programs as "very interesting,"[36] but he then proceeded to undermine Balakirev's musical stature by sharply criticizing his compositions.[37]

Serov criticized Balakirev and his FMS concerts more harshly than Famintsyn. In the spring of 1868 he became a regular contributor to the *Journal de St.-Petersbourg*, a French-language daily newspaper widely read by members of Petersburg high society.[38] He used this forum in the fall of 1869 to charge that Balakirev's choice of repertory suffered from "an important failing: party spirit," to claim that anyone who could produce such a work as Balakirev's *1,000 Years* would "never fall into the category of musician," and to blame a poor performance of Beethoven's Fifth Symphony on "the inability of an uneducated Russian musician [Balakirev] to grasp the ideas of the great German composer."[39] All this does not mean, however, that Serov had adopted the aesthetic position of Balakirev's conservative opponents in the RMS. Although he had co-operated with them in ousting Balakirev from the directorship of the Society's concerts and, from the spring of 1869, began to publish occasional articles in Famintsyn's *Muzykal'nyi sezon,* he still maintained a certain independence in his critical outlook. In his column of 9 November 1869 in the *Journal de St.-Petersbourg* Serov made it clear that he did not oppose Balakirev out of any condemnation of Glinka or the contemporary school of Western composers, for he asserted once again his love of Liszt, Wagner, and Glinka.[40] He even went so far as to criticize some of the repertory of the RMS concerts on the same grounds as Cui, finding one particular program, for example, lacking in "high aesthetic considerations" precisely because it could be from "a German classical concert of 1820."[41] It thus appears that Serov's attacks on Balakirev, as before, were motivated more by personal animosity and envy than by sharp differences of taste or aesthetic opinion. Nevertheless, his opposition tacitly aligned him with the RMS in the rivalry of concert series and contributed to the campaign of Famintsyn and company against Balakirev's claims to leadership of enlightened musical opinion in Russia.

The competitive efforts of the Free Music School and the Russian Musical Society each to make its own concerts attractive and to denigrate the rival series resulted in a stalemate harmful to both. The RMS found that its membership at the beginning of the 1869-70 season numbered only a little over two hundred. This was less than half of the previous season's figure of approximately five hundred.[42] It compared even less well with the nearly nine hundred members boasted by the Moscow RMS in the same season.[43] It must be admitted that the competition there for the musical audience was less, but the city was also much smaller than St. Petersburg.

The small number of RMS season subscribers made little difference for its first concert. The participation of Désirée Artôt, the presence of Elena Pavlovna and her court, and the reduced price for single tickets made the opening of the RMS season "notable for the large audience," as Cui publicly admitted.[44] But attendance declined sharply in the middle of the season. Borodin attended the seventh concert and reported afterward that guest conductor and pianist Ferdinand Hiller "had produced no effect at all," that the auditorium was "more than half empty," and that even the box directly in front of Elena Pavlovna's was completely vacant except for Serov and Feofil Tolstoy.[45] The last RMS concert was the most poorly attended of all. Napravnik was not even called out for a bow, in sharp contrast to the presentation of gifts to Anton Rubinstein and Balakirev at the concluding performances of previous RMS seasons.[46]

The decline in RMS membership, the falling attendance at its concerts, and the public criticism of its programs were sufficiently serious to force the Society in December 1869 to reform its administration by establishing a committee to select the repertory for future concerts,[47] presumably in the hope that a committee could select programs with a broader appeal. A further indication of the seriousness of the Russian Musical Society's crisis was its decision to reduce the number of its concerts for the following season. In the fall of 1870 the RMS announced that it would present only six symphonic concerts (and two chamber music evenings), while the price of a season subscription remained fifteen rubles. This was, as Cui was quick to point out, the best evidence of how unprofitable the Society's previous season had been.[48] It eventually turned out that the RMS was able to give eight orchestral concerts that season,[49] but this still represented a notable effort to reduce expenditures.

Although the Free Music School's rivalry brought declining atttendance and rising deficits to the Russian Musical Society, the results for the FMS itself were little better. The most favorable aspect of the FMS season was audience response. Although not all of its concerts attracted full houses, its attendance in general appears to have been better than for the RMS programs. At the first FMS concert, Cui admitted, there were seven or eight rows of empty seats,[50] but as the season advanced the attendance steadily improved.[51] Furthermore, the audiences for the FMS concerts were very enthusiastic and demonstrative, calling Balakirev back for bows over and over again.[52]

The Free Music School's apparent triumph over the Russian Musical Society in attracting public interest and support was, however, a Pyrrhic victory at best. From the beginning of the season the FMS concerts were in financial trouble. Although Borodin wrote his wife the day after the first concert that advance ticket sales had already covered expenditures,[53] shortly afterward Balakirev complained to Tchaikovsky that the concerts were barely covering their expenses and that he was beginning to suffer from "inflammation of the brain" due to worry.[54] The final accounting of all income and expenses from all five concerts showed a deficit of over four hundred rubles.[55] This figure does not seem very large until it is recalled that in previous years the School's annual pair of concerts was a major source of its income. One concert in 1868, for example, produced a profit of more than fourteen hundred rubles.[56] Since attendance at its five 1869-70 concerts was quite good, the deficit for that season presumably resulted from the greater expenses resulting from engaging popular soloists and the extra rehearsals needed to present the many new and difficult works that Balakirev had programmed. Balakirev had proved that concerts planned according to his own aesthetic principles could successfully compete with the RMS in attracting sizable audiences, but he had won this moral victory at the financial expense of the Free Music School, which depended heavily for its continued existence on a substantial profit from its concerts.

So serious was this crisis for the school that Balakirev attempted to organize a special benefit concert featuring stars of St. Petersburg's Italian opera company, including Adelina Patti.[57] This plan met with the violent opposition of Cui and Vladimir Stasov, who considered it a betrayal of the high artistic principles advocated by Balakirev and his circle.[58] Cui was so incensed that he threatened to print a denunciation of the School should Balakirev carry out the plan, and Stasov wrote Balakirev that he would be "*very* glad" if Cui would "rebuke the Free School in print as strongly as possible for this shameful act" if the concert took place.[59] Despite this opposition from his closest musical associates, Balakirev persisted in his attempts to reach agreement with Patti,[60] failing only, as he wrote Tchaikovsky, "because that macaroni [i.e., Patti], if you please, went bad ahead of time—that is, fell ill."[61] Balakirev's frantic efforts to save the situation first with a huge popular concert timed to coincide with an artistic-industrial exposition to be held in St. Petersburg at the end of May 1869, and then with a benefit concert by Nikolai Rubinstein also proved fruitless.[62] Thus, the Free Music School ended its 1869-70 concert season with a deficit rather than the substantial profit typical of earlier seasons. Despite its artistic successes, Balakirev's concert series had been a financial failure for the school.

For Balakirev himself, the 1869-70 season had been not merely a financial failure but an economic catastrophe as well. He received no pay from the Free Music School,[63] yet his efforts there ate into the time he needed to teach. Borodin summarized his friend's plight:

> For the sake of the concerts, he had to run about, petition, seek out and maintain various connections needed for the struggle with Elena and company. This, along with rehearsals and chorus practices, devoured all of Mily's time, all his strength and energy. Regular, punctual occupation, teaching by the hour, became impossible.[64]

Balakirev was therefore in severe financial need by the summer of 1870. In June, he had to borrow five hundred rubles from Liudmila Shestakova. To repay her and raise some money for himself, he returned in August to his native city, Nizhny Novgorod, to give a piano recital.[65] The concert was a disaster. Instead of the one thousand rubles he expected, and without which, he had told his friends, he would "have to throw himself into the river Neva," he cleared only eleven rubles![66] Nevertheless, he was still planning FMS concerts for the new season, 1870-71, early in September.[67] By mid-October, however, the hopelessness of this project had become obvious.[68] Balakirev could not afford to devote all his time to an unpaid job. In addition, the Free Music School had no money on hand to invest in a new series of concerts. As Rimsky writes in his memoirs, "a temporary lull in the battle with the Directors of the Russian Musical Society was unavoidable." But Balakirev had not given up the rivalry. He intended to husband his resources for a year in order to resume the contest with renewed vigor the following year.[69]

With Free Music School concerts ruled out, Balakirev's public musical appearances for the 1870-71 season were limited to conducting or accompanying for benefit concerts by several prominent soloists during the Lenten concert season, and to leading an all-Glinka concert sponsored by the St. Petersburg Assembly of Artists to raise money for a monument to

Glinka.[70] Thus, the Russian Musical Society once again enjoyed undisputed leadership of serious concert activity in the Russian capital. Its position was not entirely enviable, however, for the preceding season had seen a precipitate decline in both its membership and its prestige. The task of reversing this trend rested with the Repertory Committee formed in December 1869.

Feofil Tolstoy was the original chairman of the committee, and most of the other members were Conservatory professors and officials of the RMS.[71] The major exception was Alexander Serov. Tolstoy claims in his memoirs that he himself suggested that Serov be invited to participate, "despite his provocative and quarrelsome character," because he was one of the best-known musical figures in St. Petersburg.[72] There were also practical reasons for offering such a long-time opponent an honored position in the direction of the Society. His participation in selecting repertory would effectively eliminate the possibility of his continued public criticism of the RMS programs. It would also broaden the range of aesthetic viewpoints on the committee and thus, perhaps, produce concerts with appeal for a larger audience. According to Tolstoy, the committee had even attempted to expand further its range of musical positions—and, presumably, to curtail Cui's published attacks on the RMS programs—by co-opting Balakirev and Rimsky-Korsakov as well, but the board of directors rejected the move.[73] As long as Balakirev was the chief conductor for the Free Music School concerts, the RMS directors viewed him and his circle as rivals. The decline in the stature and popularity of their concerts made them willing to recognize officially their informal alliance with Serov, but they were not prepared to admit the claims to recognition and authority in St. Petersburg musical life of their chief rivals—Balakirev and his circle.[74]

Although Serov was only one of thirteen members of the RMS Repertory Committee, his position was not merely for show. Only three months after the formation of the committee, he replaced Feofil Tolstoy as chairman, thus finally receiving the recognition and honored position in the St. Petersburg RMS that he had unsuccessfully claimed for over a decade.[75] Now he could exercise what he termed "a direct and beneficial influence" on all its artistic work.[76] He thoroughly enjoyed calling on Elena Pavlovna to discuss Society business and playing the role of "a court musician from the time of Nicholas I."[77]

The eight RMS concerts for the 1870-71 season show signs of Serov's influence and the Society's willingness to expand its representation of the contemporary and Russian schools. Although Beethoven and the classical masters remained the core of the repertory, the RMS also presented the Russian premieres of two major works by Liszt, excerpts from Wagner's *Die Meistersinger,* and one concert devoted entirely to music by Russian composers: Glinka, Dargomyzhsky, Rubinstein, Rimsky-Korsakov, and a recent graduate of the St. Petersburg Conservatory, Nikolai Soloviev. The Society also performed excerpts from Serov's *Judith*[78] and announced his *Stabat Mater* but, as in the previous season, did not perform it.[79]

Balakirev's virtual absence from St. Petersburg concert life during the season of 1870-71, and the RMS concerts' increased attention to Russian and contemporary music altered the character of the press commentary on all sides. After a decade of complaining about the RMS programs, Serov finally found words of praise for the Society's repertory in his *Golos* articles.[80] Considering that he himself chaired the committee that drew up the programs, his applause seems hardly surprising. Cui also had to admit that the RMS concerts had improved greatly, but he denied the Society the ultimate credit for this improvement, ascribing it instead to his own reviews and to Balakirev's example.[81] At the end of the RMS season, Cui concluded that it had been much better than the previous year but not nearly as good as when Balakirev was principal conductor. He noted that the number of subscribers had risen slightly over the previous season, despite the reduction in the number of concerts from ten to eight for the same fifteen-ruble charge and the absence of foreign guest artists, but he declared that full success would come only when the partial reforms of that season were carried to their logical conclusion and the RMS was prepared to "devote its best efforts to the service of living, contemporary art in its best works."[82] Thus, the change in the RMS policy on repertory for the 1870-71 season ended Serov's attacks on the Society but did not silence Cui. He continued to criticize what did not suit the taste of his circle and gave credit to Balakirev for what he did.

Following the lull during the 1870-71 season, "the war between Balakirev and the Russian Musical Society was renewed: five subscription concerts of the Free Music School, with interesting programs, were announced" for the next year.[83] Balakirev worked energetically and, as two years before, became completely engrossed in his task of surpassing the RMS.[84] The programs showed Balakirev's familiar predilection for Schumann, Liszt, and Berlioz, plus the younger Russian composers, and his complete lack of interest in all pre-nineteenth century music. Soloists included Leopold Auer and Nikolai Rubinstein.[85]

With Balakirev thus resurrecting the FMS concerts just as they had existed two seasons earlier, the RMS concerts now took an entirely different direction. Instead of eight symphonic performances as in the preceding season, or ten, as in previous years, the RMS gave only five in the 1871-72 season for the fifteen-ruble membership fee,[86] but it also offered season subscriptions for the gallery, or for poorer seats on the main floor at reduced prices—three and ten rubles, respectively.[87] The most significant change in the RMS concerts, however, was in their repertory. Serov had died on January 20, 1871, depriving the RMS Repertory Committee of a powerful partisan of contemporary music, but Mikhail Azanchevsky, the new president of the board of directors of the St. Petersburg RMS, was even more bent on reforming the Society's concerts.[88] Except for a few short works selected by various soloists, no music written before the nineteenth century appeared on the programs. The major works were by Beethoven, Schumann, Liszt, Wagner, and Berlioz. No fewer than four compositions were Petersburg premieres, including Tchaikovsky's *Romeo and Juliet* overture and an excerpt from Musorgsky's *Boris Godunov.*[89] For all practical purposes, the RMS repertory had become indistinguishable from Balakirev's. Even Cui characterized the programs as "excellent". He could not find a single work "against which anything can be said."[90] He explicitly compared the RMS and FMS programs and declared that both were put together "in the same spirit, with the same orientation, . . . i.e., they are composed exclusively of beautiful, living , chiefly contemporary music."[91]

Balakirev's aesthetic viewpoint, it seems, had prevailed; the Russian Musical Society had voluntarily adopted a repertory policy identical to the one for which he had been dismissed two seasons earlier. Cui claimed this change in the RMS concerts as a moral victory for Balakirev: .

> Musical Petersburg can celebrate the complete victory over stagnation, routine, prejudice, and blind fetishism. Pure service to art and love for the beautiful, no matter where or when it is found, have prevailed. We must not forget that it was Balakirev who implemented this trend among us, that this honor belongs exclusively to him.[92]

The Balakirev circle also seemed at last on the verge of victory in the musical press. Serov, its most persistent critic, had died the previous year, and Famintsyn's music journal, *Muzykal'nyi sezon,* closed in the spring of 1871 after less than two years in existence. Just as Serov's *Muzyka i teatr* had failed for lack of public support, so, too, did Famintsyn's journal. Cui celebrated its demise in a satirical obituary that closed:

> Oh, *Muzykal'nyi sezon*! You lived out your short lifetime harmlessly, for lack of means, doing neither evil nor good; your existence was well intentioned, but you died of exhaustion and bad nourishment. Peace to your remains! They should be buried not far from *Muzyka i teatr.*[93]

Cui's claims of victory were premature, however, for in the autumn of 1871, Hermann Laroche, who was to be "the chief critical force opposed to Cui" in the 1870's,[94] moved to St. Petersburg from Moscow and became a regular music critic for *Golos.* Laroche was a graduate of the first class at the St. Petersburg Conservatory and then a professor at the Moscow Conservatory. In 1867, while still in Moscow, he had begun writing regular music reviews, and his first efforts were sufficiently successful to win the attention of both Serov and Cui in St. Petersburg. Although neither fully agreed with his aesthetic stance, both praised him for his erudition.[95] Later articles soon revealed just how sharply he differed from Cui and Balakirev in his tastes and musical principles. In 1869, for example, he devoted an entire lengthy article to defending inclusion of strict counterpoint and study of the polyphonic masters of the fifteenth and sixteenth centuries in the curriculum of the Moscow and St. Petersburg Conservatories.[96] In the same year, Laroche criticized Tchaikovsky for trying to imitate Liszt's extreme style in his symphonic poem, *Fate*. He recommended that his fellow professor from the Moscow Conservatory might escape "his false and contradictory attitude toward art" by becoming better acquainted with the great masters who had flourished when "petulant programs and formless rhapsodies were equally unknown, when musical compositions did not present such profound philosophical ideas as today, but showed more musical polish, when composers did not seek the resolution of problems of existence but always found the resolution of a dissonance."[97]

While still in Moscow, Laroche publicly criticized Balakirev and his circle, and his attacks only increased in vehemence with his arrival in the Russian capital.[98] In the spring of 1872, for example, he wrote a lengthy article for *Golos* criticizing those composers and critics who claimed that music was capable of depicting something more than a purely musical idea, and who advertised their own works as progressive while attacking the musical classics as outdated. He accused them of pandering to the unmusical masses, who found it easier to appreciate program music than an abstract symphony, and he charged that their claim to be progressive was a ploy to win the sympathy of the liberal intelligentsia.[99] No one familiar with the St. Petersburg musical scene in the 1860s could have doubted for a moment that the Balakirev circle was the target of Laroche's critical darts.

A more important setback for Balakirev in the 1871-72 season was the utter failure of his FMS concerts. The adoption by the Russian Musical Society of the repertory policy Balakirev had justified so successfully in his earlier series with the FMS may have been a moral victory for Balakirev, but it effectively eliminated the public demand for his own concerts. Even Cui admitted that the RMS programs were as interesting as those of the FMS and that Napravnik was an excellent conductor. Prices for subscriptions to the FMS concerts were cheaper, but RMS membership also provided admission to several chamber concerts.[100] Furthermore, the RMS had greater social prestige. The FMS concerts could compete, as they had two seasons earlier, but only if they offered an alternative in repertory. Cui reported that at the first FMS concert "the audience was not large, much smaller than at the concerts of the Russian Musical Society; the auditorium was half empty."[101] Nor did the situation improve noticeably later in the season. Balakirev's financial report for the first three FMS concerts showed a deficit of 863 rubles and 84 kopeks.[102] While the RMS concerts "had a significant success" and "were well attended", [103] the FMS ran out of funds after its fourth concert and had to cancel its final performance.[104]

This venture ended Balakirev's direct rivalry with the Russian Musical Society. Not only had it proven a financial failure for the Free Music School, but it was also a personal and psychological disaster for Balakirev. The competition had achieved notoriety for his circle and considerable public acceptance of the contemporary music he championed; it had even forced the Russian Musical Society to imitate his Free Music School concerts. It had not, however, won Balakirev a permanent, financially secure position in the musical life of St. Petersburg. Even Balakirev's moral victory proved fragile, for the very next season, 1872-73, the RMS, with no rival FMS concerts to consider, began to revert to its earlier, more conservative programs. Mendelssohn returned in strength, Berlioz disappeared, and the only Russians represented were Conservatory professors.[105]

Notes to Chapter VI

1.   Frid, "M.A. Balakirev," p. 34.

2.   Rubets, "Vospominaniia," 25 June 1912, p. 4.

3.   Programs for the three concerts and relevant preceding concerts appear in Liapunova, *Balakirev: letopis'*, pp. 99, 110, 113, 131, 139, 140, 152, and 155.

4.   *My Musical Life*, p. 107.

5.   Balakirev to Rimsky-Korsakov, 1 June 1869, in Rimskii-Korsakov, *Polnoe sobranie*, 5:96.

6.   Liapunova, *Balakirev: letopis'*, p. 163.

7.   "Muzykal'nye zametki," p. 2.

8.   Balakirev, *Perepiska s N. Rubinshteinom*, p. 29.

9.   Letter to his wife of 27 October 1869 in Borodin, *Pis'ma,* 1:159.

10.   For complete programs, see Liapunova, *Balakirev: letopis'*, pp. 164-68, 173.

11.   Letter of 3 November 1869 in Borodin, *Pis'ma*, 1:162.

12.   "Muzykal'nye zametki," *St.P. ved.*, 18 November 1869, p. 2.

13.   See Balakirev, *Perepiska s N. Rubinshteinom*, pp. 15-28.

14. Balakirev to N. Rubinstein, 25 September 1869, *ibid.,* p. 28.

15. Letter of 3 December 1869 in Borodin, *Pis'ma,* 1:175.

16. V. Stasov to Balakirev, 13 November 1869, in *Perepiska,* 1:274.

17. "Muzykal'nye zametki," *St.P. ved.,* 21 October 1869, p. 1.

18. L.M. Kutateladze, "E.F. Napravnik: Ocherk zhizni i deiatel'nosti" [E.F. Napravnik: a survey of his life and work], in Napravnik, *Avtobiograficheskie materialy,* p. 8.

19. Gozenpud, *Russkii opernyi teatr,* 2:38.

20. Findeizen, *Ocherk RMO,* p. 48.

21. For programs, see Findeizen, *Ocherk RMO,* appendix, pp. 10-11.

22. [Kiui], "Muzykal'nye zametki," *St.P. ved.,* 4 November 1869, p. 1.

23. Reinhold Sietz, *Aus Ferdinand Hillers Briefwechsel: Beiträge zu einer Biographie Ferdinand Hillers,* 7 vols. (Cologne: Arno Volk-Verlag, 1958-70), 3:7.

24. Balakirev to P. Tchaikovsky, 4 October 1869, in Balakirev, *Vospominaniia,* p. 138; Borodin to his wife, 3 November 1869, in Borodin, *Pis'ma,* 1:161.

25. Serov to E. Rahden, 18 April 1870, in Aleksandr Nikolaevich Serov, "Iz pisem A.N. Serova" [From the letters of A.N. Serov], *Sovetskaia muzyka,* July 1971, p. 103; Borodin to his wife, 3 November 1869, in Borodin, *Pis'ma,* 1:161.

26. Balakirev to P. Tchaikovsky, 12 November 1869, in Balakirev, *Vospominaniia,* p. 141; [Kiui], "Muzykal'nye zametki," *St.P. ved.,* 18 November 1869, p. 1.

27. "Muzykal'nye zametki," *St.P. ved.,* 4 November 1869, p. 1; 18 November 1869, pp. 1-2; 2 December 1869, pp. 1-2; 30 December 1869, p. 1; 12 March 1870, p. 1.

28. "Muzykal'nye zametki," *St.P. ved.,* 4 November 1869, p. 1.

29. "Muzykal'nye zametki," *St.P. ved.,* 18 November 1869, p. 1. See also the reviews of 2 December 1869, p. 1., and 26 February 1870, p. 1.

30. "Muzykal'nye zametki," *St.P. ved.,* 26 February 1870, p. 1.

31. "Muzykal'nye zametki," *St.P. ved.,* 4 November 1869, p. 1.

32. "Muzykal'nye zametki," *St.P. ved.,* 18 November 1869, p. 1.

33. "Muzykal'nye zametki," *St.P. ved.,* 9 May 1870, p. 1; 12 March 1870, p. 1.

34. "Muzykal'nye zametki," *St.P. ved.,* 30 December 1869, p. 2.

35. Kremlev, *Russkaia mysl' o muzyke,* 2:540.

36. Liapunova, *Balakirev: letopis',* p. 165.

37. *Ibid.,* pp. 166, 168.

38. Serov to K.I. Zvantsov, 25 October 1868, in Zvantsov, "A.N. Serov," p. 675.

39. Liapunova, *Balakirev: letopis',* pp. 166, 169.

40. Iakovlev, "K istorii 'Raika,' " p. 107.

41. Kremlev, *Russkaia mysl' o muzyke,* 2:64.

42. [Kiui], "Muzykal'nye zametki," *St.P. ved.,* 18 November 1869, p. 1; Borodin to his wife, 3 November 1869, in Borodin, *Pis'ma,* 1:161.

43. P. Tchaikovsky to his brother Anatoly, 18 November 1869, in P. Chaikovskii, *Polnoe sobranie,* 5:188.

44. "Muzykal'nye zametki," *St.P. ved.,* 4 November 1869, p. 2.

45. Letter to his wife of 16 January 1870, in Borodin, *Pis'ma,* 1:182.

46. "Muzykal'nye zametki," *St.P. ved.,* 9 May 1870, p. 1.

47. V[ladimir Vasil'evich] S[tasov], "Muzykal'nye komitet" [The musical committee], *St.P. ved.,* 1 January 1870, p. 2.

48. "Muzykal'nye zametki," *St.P. ved.,* 4 November 1870, p. 1.

49. Findeizen, *Ocherk RMO,* appendix, pp. 11-12.

50. "Muzykal'nye zametki," *St.P. ved.,* 4 November 1860, p. 1.

51. See Borodin to his wife, 3 November and 3 December 1860, in Borodin, *Pis'ma,* 1:162, 174; and [Kiui], "Muzykal'nye zametki," *St.P. ved.,* 12 March 1870, p. 1.

52. See, for example, Borodin's description of the third FMS concert in a letter to his wife of 16 November 1860 in Borodin, *Pis'ma,* 1:168.

53. Letter of 27 October 1869, *ibid.,* 1:159.

54. P. Tchaikovsky to his brother Modest, 18 November 1869, in P. Chaikovskii, *Polnoe sobranie,* 5:190.

55. Liapunova, *Balakirev: letopis',* p. 173.

56. *Ibid.,* p. 141.

57. Balakirev to P. Tchaikovsky, 1 December 1869, in Balakirev, *Vospominaniia*, p. 147.

58. V. Stasov to Balakirev, 24-25 December 1869, in *Perepiska*, 1:274-75.

59. *Ibid.*, 1:274.

60. Liapunova, *Balakirev: letopis'*, p. 172.

61. Letter of 9 May 1870 in Balakirev, *Vospominaniia*, p. 152.

62. P. Tchaikovsky to N. Rubinstein, 18 May 1870, in P. Chaikovskii, *Polnoe sobranie*, 5:217-18; Balakirev to N. Rubinstein, 19 May 1870, in Balakirev, *Perepiska s N. Rubinshteinom*, p. 35.

63. Borodin to his wife, 27 October 1869, in Borodin, *Pis'ma*, 1:159.

64. Letter of 24 September 1870 in Borodin, *Pis'ma*, 1:235.

65. Liapunova, *Balakirev: letopis'*, pp. 179-80.

66. Borodin to his wife, 24 September 1870, in Borodin, *Pis'ma*, 1:234.

67. Balakirev to N. Rubinstein, 3 September 1870, in Balakirev, *Perepiska s N. Rubinshteinom*, p. 36.

68. Borodin to his wife, 20 October 1870, in Borodin, *Pis'ma*, 1:251.

69. *My Musical Life*, p. 114.

70. Liapunova, *Balakirev: letopis'*, pp. 182, 188-89.

71. Stasov, "Muzykal'nyi komitet," p. 2.

72. "A.N. Serov," p. 373.

73. *Ibid.*, pp. 374-75.

74. In October 1870, when it was already clear that the FMS would not be presenting a subscription series that season, the RMS did invite Balakirev and Rimsky to participate in its work, but they refused. See Tolstoi, "A.N. Serov," p. 375, and Borodin to his wife, 15 October 1870, in Borodin, *Pis'ma*, 1:250.

75. F. Tolstoi, "A.N. Serov," p. 375.

76. *Izbrannye stat'i*, 1:77.

77. Repin, *Dalekoe blizkoe*, p. 340.

78. Complete programs appear in Findeizen, *Ocherk RMO*, appendix, pp. 11-12.

79.   [Kiui], "Muzykal'nye zametki," *St. P. ved.,* 23 March 1871, p. 2.

80.   [Kiui], "Muzykal'nye zametki," *St. P. ved.,* 6 January 1871, p. 1.

81.   "Muzykal'nye zametki," *St. P. ved.,* 4 November 1870, p. 1.

82.   "Muzykal'nye zametki," *St. P. ved.,* 23 March 1871, p. 2.

83.   Rimsky-Korsakov, *My Musical Life,* p. 128.

84.   Borodin to his wife, 17 October and 14 November 1871, in Borodin, *Pis'ma,* 1:308, 322.

85.   For programs see Liapunova, *Balakirev: letopis',* pp. 195-97.

86.   Findeizen, *Ocherk RMO,* appendix, pp. 12, 80-81.

87.   [Kiui], "Muzykal'nye zametki," *St. P. ved.,* 20 October 1871, p. 2.

88.   Borodin to his wife, 21 September 1871, in Borodin, *Pis'ma,* 1:295.

89.   Findeizen, *Ocherk RMO,* appendix, p. 12.

90.   "Muzykal'nye zametki," *St. P. ved.,* 20 October 1871, p. 2.

91.   "Muzykal'nye zametki," *St. P. ved.,* 11 November 1871, p. 1.

92.   *Ibid.*

93.   *Izbrannye stat'i,* p. 187.

94.   Kremlev, *Russkaia mysl' o muzyke,* 2:400.

95.   Gr. Bernandt, "Larosh—neskol'ko shtrikhov k portretu" [Laroche—several strokes for a portrait], *Sovetskaia muzyka,* January 1975, p. 112; Kiui, *Izbrannye stat'i,* pp. 132-33.

96.   *Sobranie statei,* 1:214-45.

97.   *Izbrannye stat'i,* 2:28-29.

98.   Kremlev, *Russkaia mysl' o muzyke,* 2:341-46.

99.   *Sobranie statei,* 1:319-33.

100. [Kiui], "Muzykal'nye zametki," *St. P. ved.,* 11 November 1871, p. 1.

101. "Muzykal'nye zametki," *St. P. ved.,* 4 December 1871, p. 1.

102. Liapunova, *Balakirev: letopis',* p. 196.

103. [Kiui], "Muzykal'nye zametki," *St. P. ved.,* 10 March 1872, p. 2.

104. Rimsky-Korsakov, *My Musical Life,* p. 128.

105. Complete programs appear in Findeizen, *Ocherk RMO,* appendix, p. 13.

Chapter VII

An Alternate Route to Success in Musical Life

While Balakirev was directing his major musical efforts in the late 1860s and early 1870s toward establishing himself as the leading authority in St. Petersburg's concert life, the rest of his circle set out on an alternative path to public acceptance and social prestige—composing operas. Their endeavors in this field were essentially unrelated to Balakirev's work since their success depended on their relationship with the management of the Russian Opera and on the influence of their press spokesmen, not on their access to performances at orchestral concerts. Therefore, these efforts served to widen the gap that had already begun to open between Balakirev and his original circle.

Although they did not abandon all other compositional endeavors, from early in 1868 Cui, Musorgsky, Rimsky-Korsakov, and Borodin were all seriously engaged in writing operas. Cui had always dabbled in operatic composition, but his early efforts were only performed for his friends. In 1868 he set to work in earnest on *William Ratcliffe,* which he had been composing sporadically since the early 1860s.[1] He finished the music and, with the assistance of Balakirev and Rimsky, the orchestration during that summer.[2] Having completed *Ratcliffe,* Cui began looking for a new operatic subject and finally settled on Victor Hugo's play *Angelo.* By the spring of 1871 he had several numbers of his new score ready to play for his friends.[3] Musorgsky had also been interested in opera before 1868, having begun several years earlier to set a libretto taken from Flaubert's *Salammbô.*[4] It was never finished, however, and he had only begun serious operatic composition in 1868, at first working on a musical setting of Gogol's play *The Marriage* and then beginning *Boris Godunov.*[5] The other members of Balakirev's circle had not previously shown any interest in opera composition, but they too began to think of subjects in 1868. Rimsky settled on Lev Mey's play *The Maid of Pskov* and began work on it in the summer of that year.[6] In the same year Borodin began to talk about making an opera from Mey's *Tsar's Bride* or from *The Lay of the Host of Igor.*[7] The latter subject won out, and in April 1869 Vladimir Stasov sent Borodin a complete scenario for an opera to be entitled *Prince Igor*.[8] By the fall of that year Borodin, who was the most slow-paced composer of the entire circle because of his preoccupation with his scientific work, had completed the first number of the score.[9] Even Balakirev, who had usually shown little interest in the operatic genre, gave serious consideration in the spring of 1868 to renewing work on an opera that he had begun in the early 1860s.[10] Nothing ever came of this project, however, since Balakirev became more and more involved in concert activities, but the rest of his circle persevered in their efforts to compose for the operatic stage.

The circle's sudden intense interest in writing operas in 1868 is explainable by a combination of aesthetic and practical considerations. The question of the proper direction for modern opera, especially in Russia, had always been central to their aesthetic stance simply because Glinka, their idol, was best known as an operatic composer. The conflicts and press polemics carried on with Serov over Glinka's *Ruslan*, the music dramas of Wagner, and Serov's own operas show how important this genre was for Balakirev's circle. Dargomyzhsky's desire to share his work on *The Stone Guest* with Balakirev and his followers early in 1868 undoubtedly crystallized their interest in this genre, spurring on Cui to finish *Ratcliffe* and the rest of the group to begin composing operas. Dargomyzhsky's work clearly impressed them all, especially Musorgsky, whose *Marriage* explicitly followed Dargomyzhsky's model by attempting to set an existing play, without changing a line of dialogue, to musical declamation that would retain all the inflections of natural speech.[11] After finishing only the first act Musorgsky abandoned *The Marriage* and began work on *Boris Godunov*, a project conceived in the same spirit, although it did not adhere strictly to the model of *The Stone Guest*. When Musorgsky first played Dargomyzhsky parts of *Boris*, the older composer immediately recognized the opera's kinship with his own work and declared that Musorgsky would surely surpass him as a composer of realistic opera.[12]

Practical considerations surely played a part as well in turning Balakirev's pupils to opera in the late 1860s. Despite the advances made in concert life in Russia during the preceding decade, opera remained the most popular and prestigious musical form, just as it had been in the 1850s. Serov had earned fame and a government pension from the brilliant success of *Rogneda*. This lesson was certainly not lost on the young members of Balakirev's circle. Furthermore, by 1868 signs of reform and renewal within the Russian opera troupe promised young Russian opera composers a better chance of success than ever before. To be sure, there was still no question of equality between the Italian and Russian companies. Despite full houses, the Italian company still reportedly cost the government two hundred thousand rubles in the 1868-69 season. But the Russian troupe, whose performances did not always sell out, managed to clear sixty thousand rubles that season after expenses were paid.[13] The very fact that the Russian Opera showed a profit, however, indicates that the company now enjoyed considerable public favor. Moreover, the Theater Directorate had begun to pay more attention to Russian opera. *Rogneda* had been mounted spectacularly in the fall of 1865, and a few months later Dargomyzhsky's *Rusalka* received the new production that finally won it a significant measure of popularity. In 1867 the Theater Directorate staged a new Russian opera, Vladimir Kashperov's *The Storm,* despite its very modest merits,[14] and in 1868 Glinka's *A Life for the Tsar* received a new production that elicited a most favorable review from even such an exacting critic as Vladimir Stasov.[15] Clearly, in the late 1860s "the public and the Theater Directorate began to take a greater interest in [Russian] operas and even to treat them with respect."[16]

The quality of the Russian Opera's performing forces was also improving. New singers, several of them trained at the St. Petersburg Conservatory, began to replace the older artists, who were often poor musicians.[17] By the end of the decade the leading singers received between five and ten thousand rubles a season in spite of the 1827 regulation limiting the salary of a Russian theater employee to 1,143 rubles.[18] Even more important, in 1867 Eduard Napravnik became second conductor of the Russian opera company, and two years later he took over the post of chief conductor. By all accounts he was an excellent and energetic musician. Although not himself a musical radical, he believed in the importance of producing new works by both foreign and Russian composers. Even during his tenure as assistant conductor he helped to improve the theater's performance standards and repertory; therefore, his accession to the post of chief conductor brought promise of accelerated improvement.[19]

From the beginning of his journalistic career in 1864 Cui had advocated Russian music not only in the concert hall but on the operatic stage as well. In September of that year he wrote that the Theater Directorate had only to "cast off its timid immobility and its immutable attachment to obsolete works and persons" in favor of the vital new Russian school in order to bring about a general renewal of the stagnant operatic genre.[20] Over the years he had frequently returned to the subject of Russian opera, always encouraging the Theater Directorate and public to give more support to the Russian opera troupe and particularly to Russian operas.[21] Not just any Russian opera would satisfy Cui and his friends, however, as shown by the scathing attacks he and Stasov directed at Serov's *Rogneda.* They wanted to see the Theater Directorate mount not just more Russian operas but specifically Russian operas that met their own standards of seriousness, dramatic truth, and advanced aesthetic principles—in short, the standards created by Glinka and Dargomyzhsky.

Beginning in 1868 Cui, with occasional assistance from Stasov, intensified the circle's press campaign in favor of modern Russian opera. Although Cui proclaimed that his ideal in opera was a combination of "truth" (that is, a wedding of music and text so that the former follows the content and the natural phrasing of the latter) and "beauty,"[22] he argued in favor of producing virtually *any* Russian opera. This was important, he explained, as a way of rewarding native composers and giving them stage experience.[23] "We are, of course, obliged to aid our own musical cause," he wrote, "if we wish it to develop."[24] It is surely not accidental that Cui began his campaign for the production of "any Russian opera" at the very time he and his friends began seriously to compose their own operatic works.

Although Cui advocated staging all Russian operas, he and his friends were not prepared to admit the claim of any Russian outside the group to genuine authority in the field of opera. Therefore, a Russian work by a rival composer or in a style opposed to their own was subject to sharp press criticism. Rimsky-Korsakov practically dismissed conductor Napravnik's first opera, *Nizhegorodtsy* [Men of Nizhny Novgorod], for example, in his review of its premiere late in 1868: "Mr. Napravnik's opera . . . consists for the most part of separate numbers, . . . arias, duets, trios, choruses—all written in the old routine forms. . . . But with the passage of time, the demands of taste change. It is already impossible today to write operas in such forms."[25]

Russian operas that followed the circle's "realist" precepts but not written by members of the group received harsher treatment yet. Consider, for example, *Satan's Power,* Serov's third opera, which the Russian Opera presented for the first time in the spring of 1871, shortly after Serov's death. This opera seemed to satisfy all the demands of Cui and company. It was based on a folk drama by Ostrovsky and originally conceived as "a drama of everyday life" with music "completely in the character of the peerless songs of the Russian people."[26] When Ostrovsky wanted to introduce devils and other fantastic creatures into a scene depicting the aftermath of a Shrovetide drinking bout, Serov flatly refused on the grounds that he was writing a "most realistic" work that would be spoiled by any admixture of fantasy.[27] Even Cui, in his review of the premiere, found the story the best possible subject for a modern opera and applauded Serov's abandonment of separate numbers in favor of musical declamation. Nevertheless, he attacked the opera unmercifully for its music. Although he credited some of the peasant songs and choruses with a certain liveliness and authenticity, he considered them trivial, and he termed the musical declamation that made up most of the opera "musical *rubbish.*" He even suggested that anyone could produce recitatives like Serov's simply by dipping the feet of a fly in ink, letting it walk over some sheets of blank music paper, and then adding bar lines and a text! Cui concluded that *Satan's Power* was useful for three reasons: its excellent subject would be an example to other composers; it would help prepare the public for other operas written without the conventional forms, such as Musorgsky's *Boris Godunov;* and it would finally convince the public that Serov had no taste or talent for dramatic music.[28] It seems clear that Cui did not merely want to write an unfavorable review, but that he also wanted to destroy Serov's musical reputation while simultaneously applauding his intentions, because they were identical to those of Balakirev's circle.

At the same time that the Balakirev circle was intensifying its press campaign for Russian opera and its efforts to undermine the musical authority of any Russian opera composer outside the circle, it was changing its public posture toward the Theater Directorate. Before 1868 the circle had always coupled public advocacy of Russian opera with sharp criticism of the Imperial theaters both for the obviously privileged position of the Italian Opera over its Russian counterpart and for the Russian Opera's alleged prejudice against Glinka and Dargomyzhsky.[29] In 1868, however, Cui and Stasov began to lavish praise on the Theater Directorate for the evident improvement in the status of Russian opera. Although they continued to complain about the choice of some of the Russian Opera's non-Russian repertory and to criticize the Italian company for its very existence,[30] they greeted every sign of favor for the Russian troupe or Russian opera with extravagant acclaim and encouragement. In October 1868, for example, Stasov published a special article in *Sankt-Peterburgskie vedomosti* to praise the Mariinsky Theater's "excellent" new production of *A Life for the Tsar,* but he also reminded the management that this was only the beginning of the reforms necessary for "the cause of our national opera."[31] A few months later Cui admitted that "the Directorate has already done a great deal for Russian opera," but he pointed out how much more it could do by expanding the company, spending more on salaries and sets, and introducing new Russian works.[32] In February 1871, when rumors in St. Petersburg musical circles reported that Stepan Gedeonov, the director of the Imperial theaters since 1867, would soon resign, both Cui and Stasov published articles deploring his departure. Stasov declared that Gedeonov had managed to improve the Russian opera troupe so much "that it has become unrecognizable."[33] Cui commended him for having "done so much for the Russian Opera in a very short time" and having "given it such a rational and musical direction that, if these rumors prove to be true, one begins to fear against one's will for its successful further development."[34]

Cui's and Stasov's shift in 1868 from constant criticism of the Theater Directorate to frequent praise for its work was certainly due in part to actual improvements in the status accorded Russian opera. It also coincided with the first serious interest by members of the Balakirev circle in producing operas. Certainly a policy of judicious praise was more likely to earn the good will of the theater management than one of continuous carping. The special commendations accorded Gedeonov personally strongly suggest that in fact Cui's and Stasov's praise for the Theater Directorate was at least partly a ploy to win his favor since the improvements in the Russian Opera occurred more despite him than because of him. According to Napravnik, Gedeonov preferred the Italian Opera and would not think of allowing the Russian company an equal position: "He hated the Russian Opera to the depths of his soul and used to speak of it with disdain."[35] Another figure from the theater, a Petersburg actor, writes of Gedeonov's "spite and contempt for everything Russian."[36] Both men probably overstated the case, but other contemporary figures associated with the Imperial theaters confirm that Gedeonov, after some attempts to reform the Theater Directorate immediately after he took over leadership in 1867, soon gave up any serious effort to improve the system.[37] He demonstrated his lack of concern for Russian opera and Russian musicians by his cavalier treatment of Tchaikovsky in 1869, when the latter's many efforts to get a definite decision from the director of theaters about the future of his opera *Undine* met either with unfulfilled promises or no response at all.[38] Balakirev and his friends knew of these events because Tchaikovsky wrote Balakirev a full account of them.[39] They also knew of Gedeonov's constant refusals to increase the notoriously low pay of the Russian Opera's chorus members despite Napravnik's insistence and eventual threats to resign over the issue. Cui even published a notice deploring rumors of Napravnik's imminent departure if chorus salaries were not raised,[40] yet only eleven days later he published another article praising Gedeonov for having done "extraordinarily much for Russian opera."[41] The fact that this bit of applause followed by only a few months Gedeonov's commission of an opera-ballet from the Balakirev circle[42] only underlines the element of self-interest in Cui's praise.

The Balakirev circle also employed influential friends to win productions of their own operas. Cui's *William Ratcliffe,* the first opera offered by a member of the circle to the Russian Opera management, owed its prompt acceptance in 1868 at least partly to the presence of Dargomyzhsky and, curiously, Serov on the committee assigned to review new works.[43] Dargomyzhsky of course was a close friend and associate of Balakirev and his circle; Serov, on the other hand, insisted that Cui's work be mounted even though he disliked it.[44] Presumably Serov, like Cui, also believed that *any* Russian opera deserved a production.

Ratcliffe was premiered on 14 February 1869. According to both Cui and Rimsky, the performance was excellent, especially Napravnik's conducting.[45] Rimsky reviewed his friend's opera very favorably in *Sankt-Peterburgskie vedomosti,* declaring it "a very remarkable work, which will take its place in art, along with Dargomyzhsky's *Rusalka,* just behind *Ruslan* and *A Life for the Tsar.'*[46] In fact, the review was—as Rimsky later admitted—"an unmistakable panegyric . . . springing from an honest heart, but a small critical mind."[47] It could hardly have been otherwise. Rimsky was a friend of Cui and, like the rest of the circle, had witnessed the entire composition of *Ratcliffe*. Musorgsky expressed the group's high regard for the work to Cui: "*Ratcliffe* is not only yours but also ours. He crawled out of your artistic womb before our eyes, developed, grew strong, and now goes out into the world before our very eyes. . . . How could anyone not love such a dear and fine creature!"[48]

The rest of St. Petersburg's music critics did not share this opinion. They hated *Ratcliffe* and attacked it vigorously. Feofil Tolstoy, one of the more moderate critics, explained that in fact *Ratcliffe* probably did not deserve the general condemnation it received but that the critics had used their reviews to attack the "nest," or, if you like, "small circle" of young musicians who, under the influence of Stasov, were propagating such strange ideas as that learning is dangerous to music, that Haydn and Mozart "have outlived their time," and that the entire Italian school is only "a talentless crowd." He concluded:

> From the moment when they disclosed the full essence of their false teaching and clearly displayed with crude carelessness that they were pursuing some other goals, we considered it our duty to raise our voice and to caution our young native composers as strongly as possible against the pernicious influence of Stasov's circle.[49]

Ratcliffe fared little better with the public than with the critics. The theater was filled for the premiere, but there were catcalls and some hissing.[50] Subsequent performances did not fill the auditorium, and after the eighth presentation, which was not only the least well attended of all[51] but also rather poorly performed, Cui declared in print that the public should avoid the inadequate production of his opera, which was promptly dropped from the repertory.[52] The first effort of the Balakirev circle to conquer the St. Petersburg opera world had failed. It attracted public attention to the circle's operatic principles but certainly won more disdain than respect.

The Balakirev circle next offered the St. Petersburg operatic world Dargomyzhsky's *The Stone Guest*. Although not an actual member of the circle, Dargomyzhsky had been closely associated with the group while he was working on his version of the Don Juan story, and the circle considered his "realist" approach the perfect embodiment of its operatic principles. Moreover, Dargomyzhsky had died on 5 January 1869 before finishing the score, and the task of completing it had fallen to members of Balakirev's circle. Cui, the only experienced opera composer in the group, completed the score, and Rimsky-Korsakov, already acknowledged for his skill at instrumentation, orchestrated it.[53] These tasks were completed by September 1870,[54] and the work, after lengthy and complicated negotiations with the Theater Directorate, received its first public performance a year and a half later.

The Balakirev circle naturally wanted a great success for the work to vindicate their radical principles of operatic construction. To help make this possible, they had sought to propagate sympathy for *The Stone Guest* among influential musical and intellectual figures in St. Petersburg by arranging private performances of the score for them. Those so treated included both Anton and Nikolai Rubinstein, officials of the Imperial Theater Directorate, and journalists who might help publicize the work.[55] Stasov made the purpose of such private performances perfectly clear when he wrote of his hesitation to invite Ivan Turgenev to one because he remembered Turgenev's past criticism of Glinka and Russian music generally:

> It is true that if *The Stone Guest* should have the honor to please Ivan Sergeevich, then this would even be useful to a certain extent: he might beat the drum about it not only in the press but also in all the Petersburg salons where he has so many admirers. . . . [But] is it worth the risk to call respectfully on the "great" Turgenev, to look him in the eye and await his favor [?] !!![56]

Cui and Stasov also mounted a press campaign to advertise *The Stone Guest* and to explain and justify its unorthodox style. Cui had already called it "the first conscious attempt to create a contemporary opera-drama without the slightest compromise,"[57] and less than a week before its premiere Stasov explained to his readers that one could not listen to this work "with the former operatic expectations, with the former routine operatic ideas" because *The Stone Guest* had abandoned them and begun "a new era in music—the era of realistic opera."[58] Just three days before the premiere Cui forewarned his readers that Dargomyzhsky's work contained no measured, formal melodies, no duets or ensembles, no choruses, ballet, or elaborate scenery and declared it "the fullest musical embodiment of a text ever done by anyone. . . . It is dramatic truth raised to its ideal."[59]

Despite all the efforts of Cui and Stasov and a performance that even the members of Balakirev's circle considered excellent,[60] *The Stone Guest* did not win much popularity. At its premiere on 16 February 1872 and at subsequent performances in the spring of 1872 the enthusiastic applause of its supporters was mixed with catcalls and whistling.[61] The press was even less favorable. Cui, of course, praised the opera lavishly in a lengthy review,[62] but the other critics were by no means as pleased. Laroche, for example, found the opera nothing but "a series of dry recitatives." Since such passages are usually preludes to arias or duets, he added, Dargomyzhsky's opera seems to be "an endlessly long introduction after which there turns out to be no main point, a threshold without a building, a gate standing in an open field, a mountain giving birth to a mouse."[63] Most of the other critics shared Laroche's dislike for the work, and some criticized it even more sharply.[64] After thirteen performances in two seasons *The Stone Guest* was dropped from the repertory of the Russian Opera.[65] Thus, the Balakirev circle's second operatic offering, like its predecessor, Cui's *William Ratcliffe,* won it notoriety but not success or general recognition of its aesthetic views.

The Balakirev circle's efforts on behalf of *The Stone Guest* did achieve one victory, however: revocation of the 1827 statute limiting the size of royalty payments to Russian composers to 1,143 rubles. When the Theater Directorate refused to pay Dargomyzhsky's heirs the three thousand rubles they requested for the work, Cui, in an open letter in *Sankt-Peterburgskie vedomosti,*[66] publicly raised the issue of the obvious injustice of the limitation placed on payments to Russians when foreign composers could and did receive much higher fees. Later articles by both Cui and Stasov kept the issue before the public[67] until sufficient private funds were raised to buy the score of Dargomyzhsky's opera from his heirs and present it to the Russian Opera as a gift.[68] Even though a way had thus been found to pay more than the maximum prescribed royalty for *The Stone Guest,* the question was still important to the members of the Balakirev circle. After all, they were themselves Russian composers working on operas. The Theater Directorate finally agreed to revoke the regulation, and in his review of *The Stone Guest* Cui suggested that this should be considered "one more historic service" of Dargomyzhsky's opera since it had raised the question.[69]

Between Dargomyzhsky's death and the first performance of *The Stone Guest* the Balakirev circle completed two more operas: Musorgsky's *Boris Godunov* and Rimsky's *Maid of Pskov. Boris* was submitted to the Theater Directorate in late summer or early autumn of 1870. As a first opera by a nearly unknown composer, *Boris* was subject to review by a special panel of musicians, which, when it finally convened to judge the work on 10 February 1871 rejected it.[70] The official notification did not include grounds for the decision,[71] but the memoir literature, especially Rimsky's, indicates that the committee members explained that the opera had too many choral scenes, not enough solo episodes, and no important female role. There were also complaints about musical eccentricities.[72] In part, the rejection simply reflected the committee's inability to understand and appreciate a most unconventional work of great originality. Although it contained more recognizable melodies than *The Stone Guest,* it was mainly declamatory in style, with unusually daring harmonies for 1870. Some of the committee's complaints were perfectly legitimate, however, particularly the absence of a leading female figure to provide vocal variety and the love interest without which an opera seemed unthinkable. Even Musorgsky's friends had been urging him to revise his score.[73] According to Liudmila Shestakova, Musorgsky was at her home the very evening *Boris* was rejected and, prodded by Vladimir Stasov, immediately began working on additions to the opera to satisfy both his friends and the Theater Directorate.[74]

While Musorgsky was at work on his revisions, Cui took up the cause of *Boris* in his newspaper column by challenging the validity of the judgment of the Theater Directorate's review committee. He agreed that an opera by a new composer should be reviewed before production but asserted that *Boris* had not been judged by musicians. The committee had included Napravnik; the conductors of the Russian, German, and French drama theaters, who mainly directed vaudevilles (comic plays with interpolated songs); Signor Ferrero, principal double bassist for the Italian Opera and chief of the music office of the Imperial theaters; and Herr Maurer, a retired violinist and conductor. Cui claimed that of these only Napravnik was a true musician, "sensitive to the contemporary musical movement." He appealed to his readers' nationalistic sentiments by asserting that Napravnik, the only legitimate judge, had undoubtedly supported *Boris* while "the other six members, of whom *four barely even know Russian* (Messrs. vaudeville conductors, the Italian contrabassist, and the retired German conductor) condemned a remarkable Russian opera."[75]

Musorgsky submitted his revised version of *Boris,* complete with a prominent female role and expanded solo opportunities for the other singers, to the Theater Directorate in the spring of 1872. The review committee met to consider the work in late April or May, most likely on 6 May 1872. Unfortunately, the official report of the committee has not come to light, and scholars have been forced to rely on a brief notice of *Boris's* rejection published nearly six months later in *Muzykal'nyi listok* [Musical Leaflet], the newsletter of Vasily Bessel's music publishing firm.[76] Although most writers on Musorgsky's opera have accepted this evidence of a second rejection of *Boris* by the Theater Directorate,[77] the most recent study of the subject suggests that the admittedly incomplete and often disconcertingly indirect or contradictory evidence points not to rejection but to provisional acceptance, followed by procrastination by the Theater Directorate in formally committing itself to a full production.[78] In either case, however, the presentation of the revised version of *Boris Godunov* to the Theater Directorate failed to produce a firm promise to stage the work.

Cui obviously considered the committee's decision on *Boris* a second rejection and devoted an entire article to attacking its work. He again challenged the participation of Ferrero and the drama theater conductors, arguing that they might be music-technicians but were by no means musicians. This time, however, he placed the blame for their inclusion squarely on the theater administration and behind-the-scenes intrigue:

> The decisive role of people *who do not know Russian* in passing judgment on *Russian* works can only be explained by their official relations to the Directorate. . . . it is natural that people who do not care at all about music can easily subordinate their judgment to the wishes of persons with influence over them, who, in turn, can be ruled by motives having little to do with music.

Cui raged against the injustice of allowing such a group to control not only "the fate of Russian opera but frequently the entire future of Russian composers."[79]

Meanwhile, the Balakirev circle had found a more practical method of overturning the committee's rejection of *Boris* than Cui's press campaign. In the late 1860s the circle had begun to form personal ties with a number of leading figures of the Russian Opera, including Nikolai Lukashevich, assistant director of the Imperial theaters in charge of sets and costumes at the Mariinsky Theater, and singers Yulia Platonova and Osip Petrov.[80] In the fall of 1872, several months after the Theater Directorate's second review of *Boris*, Vladimir Purgold held a musical gathering in his home featuring a complete performance of *Boris* by Musorgsky and his friends. Among the guests were Lukashevich, Platonova, and Petrov. Following this performance they decided to have at least part of the work staged at the Mariinsky Theater, despite the management's reluctance.[81] According to the practice of the time, the contracts of major singers, the conductor, and the stage director of the Russian opera troupe guaranteed each the proceeds from one performance of his or her choice. For the 1872-73 season, stage director Gennady Kondratiev demanded three scenes from Musorgsky's revised score for his benefit. After what Vladimir Stasov called "a thousand intrigues," the Theater Directorate capitulated and agreed to permit their performance.[82]

On 5 February 1873 Napravnik conducted Platonova, Petrov, and other operatic friends of the Balakirev circle in Musorgsky's public debut as an opera composer. Musorgsky and his fellow composers were extremely pleased with the performance.[83] Still more pleasing was the public response to these excerpts from *Boris*. Cui reported that the inn scene earned a standing ovation.[84] Even the critics were kinder to *Boris* than to earlier operas sponsored by the Balakirev circle.[85] Cui, of course, hailed both its dramatic intentions and, for the most part, their musical realization,[86] but this time he was not alone. Some of the staunchest critics of Musorgsky's circle and its aesthetic position were forced to bow before the musical-dramatic genius revealed in his score. Laroche, for example, found the scenes full of technical errors and violations of the rules of harmony and phrasing, but he grudgingly admitted their power and fascination:

> *Boris Godunov* is a most portentous event. This opera reveals that the circle that forms the *extreme left* of our musical world has a quality for which it has not until now been known: original intention, independent content.
>
> In union with bold and original talent the party of our musical radicals can go far without faltering.

As much as he regretted it, Laroche admitted that Musorgsky and his friends probably represented the future direction of musical development.[87]

Rimsky's *Maid of Pskov* was the last to be completed of the Balakirev circle's initial group of operatic offerings to the Russian Opera. The circle had already seen the production of *William Ratcliffe* and had been working for over a year to win productions of *The Stone Guest* and *Boris Godunov*. Thus experienced in dealing with the Theater Directorate, the circle carefully prepared the way for acceptance of its latest opera.

Rimsky completed all of *The Maid of Pskov* except the overture early in October 1871. Before submitting it to the Theater Directorate, however, he took steps to gain the backing of influential persons for its production, first writing Baron Kister, Controller of the Ministry of the Imperial Court, for his aid.[88] The circle also arranged for private performances of the opera for various artists from the Russian Opera, including conductor Napravnik.[89] Cui initiated a press campaign to encourage the Theater Directorate to accept Rimsky's opera, ending his column of 3 November 1871 with an announcement that, like Cato the Elder with his famous phrase "Carthage must be destroyed," he would end his reviews with the motto "*The Stone Guest* and *The Maid of Pskov* must be staged."[90] Furthermore, his attacks on the repertory committee for vetoing production of *Boris Godunov* placed the Theater Directorate in a position where rejection of another Russian opera, especially by a member of Balakirev's circle, would seem to justify his charges that its repertory policy was indeed anti-Russian and hopelessly conservative.

Rimsky finally submitted the score of his opera to the Theater Directorate in January 1872, and it was approved for production by the following summer.[91] Approval did not come easily, however, for the repertory committee apparently had reservations about Rimsky's opera just as it had had about *Boris Godunov*.[92] The Theater Directorate's eventual decision to stage the opera anyway seems to have been the result of other than purely artistic considerations. A letter written a few years later by the director of repertory shows that those in charge of the theaters were only too aware of the embarrassment caused by Cui's press attacks on what he called their "vaudeville committee."[93] They undoubtedly did not relish the kind of publicity they would earn in *Sankt-Peterburgskie vedomosti* if the repertory committee were allowed to forbid production of another opera by the Balakirev circle. Rimsky himself suggested another extramusical consideration that was also probably involved. Due to difficulties with the Censorship Bureau over the appearance of a Russian ruler, Ivan the Terrible, on the stage in his opera, Rimsky had applied to Nikolai Krabbe, a personal friend and minister of the navy, for assistance. The latter solicited the aid of Grand Duke Konstantin, who succeeded in having the ban on operatic depiction of tsars reigning before the house of Romanov removed. Rimsky points out in his memoirs that the Theater Directorate would probably not have dared to refuse any opera in which the grand duke was interested.[94]

In any case, the Theater Directorate agreed to mount *The Maid of Pskov;* it appeared on the stage of the Mariinsky Theater for the first time on 1 January 1873, a month before the premiere of the three scenes from *Boris Godunov.* The cast included many of the Balakirev circle's supporters from the Russian Opera—Platonova, Petrov, Daria Leonova—and Napravnik turned in his usual meticulous performance as conductor.[95] The work achieved a notable success with the public. Rimsky was called out for a bow at least once after each act and many times at the opera's conclusion.[96] *The Maid of Pskov* was performed nine more times that season; even at the last performance the auditorium was filled, and the audience called for the author to appear until the stage director announced that he was not in the theater.[97]

The critics were less kind. Even Cui expressed reservations about Rimsky's opera, but he concluded that

> except Glinka, there is not another composer whose first opera could in any way approach the merits of *The Maid of Pskov*. . . . [It] is a most gratifying occurrence in our art; it enriches our repertory with a solid and extraordinarily talented work, it serves as new proof of the seriousness of purpose, the strength of conviction, and the important future of the new Russian opera school.[98]

Other critics were considerably less impressed.[99] Laroche complained of harmonic excesses and dissonance, which gave the work "an extremely morbid character" more suitable for an opera based on Dostoevsky's *Crime and Punishment.* Although he acknowledged Rimsky's inherent talent, he charged that *The Maid of Pskov* "is infected with all the shortcomings of the musical environment in which he was trained, and several of these faults appear in extreme form."[100]

By the end of the 1872-73 season, then, the achievements of the Balakirev circle in the field of opera were as problematical as they were in the arena of St. Petersburg concert life. Three works representative of the circle and scenes from a fourth had been produced at the Mariinsky Theater. All had attracted public interest, and two had earned notable public approval. In addition, the Balakirev circle had won considerable influence within the Russian opera troupe, its campaign for abolition of the archaic regulation limiting royalty payments to Russian composers had been crowned with success, and it had even managed to have two operas accepted for production despite the disapproval of the committee that reviewed new Russian operas. Nevertheless, the circle's achievements on the operatic stage had been won only with great difficulty. It required years of effort to bring *Boris* to the stage, for example, and almost as much trouble to have *The Stone Guest* produced. Both the management of the Imperial theaters and the opera review committee remained fundamentally unsympathetic to the group. Moreover, none of the circle's operas had received significant critical support except from

Cui nor the kind of resounding public triumph once enjoyed by Serov's *Rogneda*. By 1873 the "new Russian opera school" had achieved notoriety but not popularity with the critics and opera-goers of St. Petersburg—a position not unlike that won by Balakirev himself in Petersburg concert life. The circle's struggle to obtain recognition of its music and musical aesthetics, and with it leadership of St. Petersburg musical life, was far from over.

Notes to Chapter VII

1.   Cui to V. Stasov, 3 December 1862, in Kiui, *Izbrannye pis'ma*, p. 55.

2.   Rimsky-Korsakov, *My Musical Life*, p. 96; Borodin to his wife, 25 September 1868, in Borodin, *Pis'ma*, 1:108.

3.   Stasov, *Izbrannye sochineniia*, 3:403; V. Stasov to his brother Dmitri, 6 April 1871, in Stasov, *Pis'ma k rodnym*, 1, pt. 2:70.

4.   Rimsky-Korsakov, *My Musical Life*, p. 64.

5.   Khubov, *Musorgskii*, pp. 331-32, 370.

6.   Rimsky-Korsakov, *My Musical Life*, pp. 88, 96-97.

7.   *Ibid.*, p. 86.

8.   Letter of 18 April 1869 in Sergei Dianin, *Borodin: Zhizneopisanie, materialy i dokumenty* [Borodin: a biography, materials, and documents], 2nd ed. (Moscow: Gosudarstvennoe muzykal'noe izdatel'stvo, 1960), p. 193.

9.   Borodin to his wife, 3 October 1869, in Borodin, *Pis'ma*, 1:151.

10. See Abram Akimovich Gozenpud, "Neosushchestvennyi opernyi zamysel" [An unrealized operatic idea], in Frid, *M.A. Balakirev*, pp. 362-83.

11. Musorgsky to L. Shestakova, 30 July 1868, in Musorgskii, *Literaturnoe nasledie*, 1:100.

12. Vasilii Iakovlev, "Musorgskii v vospominaniiakh i nabliudeniiakh sovremennikov" [Musorgsky in the memoirs and observations of his contemporaries], in Keldysh, *M.P. Musorgskii*, p. 138.

13. Kiui, *Izbrannye stat'i*, pp. 147-49.

14. Napravnik, *Avtobiograficheskie materialy*, pp. 44-45.

15. *Izbrannye sochineniia*, 1:188-93.

16. Stasov, *Selected Essays*, p. 77.

17. Gozenpud, *Russkii opernyi teatr*, 2:168.

18. V. Stasov to his brother Dmitri, 7 August 1870, in Stasov, *Pis'ma k rodnym*, 1, pt. 2:65; Stasov, *Izbrannye sochineniia*, 1:203-4.

19. Gozenpud, *Russkii opernyi teatr*, 2:39-40; M.V. Stanislavskii, "Eduard Frantsevich Napravnik: Monograficheskii etiud po povodu ego poluvekovogo sluzheniia russkomu muzykal'nomu iskusstvu, 1863-1913" [Eduard Frantsevich Napravnik: a monographic study of his half century of service to Russian musical art, 1863-1913], *Russkaia starina* 157 (1914):117-19.

20. *Izbrannye stat'i*, p. 37.

21. See, for example, *Izbrannye stat'i*, p. 43; " 'Rogneda,' opera g. Serova," *St.P. ved.*, 6 November 1865, p. 2; " 'Robert D'iavol' na Mariinskoi stsene" [*Robert le Diable* on the Mariinsky stage], *St.P. ved.*, 25 January 1866, p. 1; "Muzykal'nye zametki," *St.P. ved.*, 3 November 1867, p. 1.

22. *Izbrannye stat'i*, p. 144.

23. "Muzykal'nye zametki," *St.P. ved.*, 26 February 1870, p. 1.

24. "Muzykal'nyc zametki," *St.P. ved.*, 6 May 1871, p. 1; 20 October 1871, p. 1.

25. *Polnoe sobranie*, 2:15.

26. Serov to Ostrovsky, 26 May 1867, in Aleksandr Nikolaevich Ostrovskii, *A.N. Ostrovskii i russkie kompozitory: Pis'ma* [A.N. Ostrovsky and Russian composers: letters], ed. E.M. Kolosova and V. Filippova (Moscow: Gosudarstvennoe izdatel'stvo Iskusstvo, 1937), p. 106.

27. Serov to Ostrovsky, 26 June 1868, *ibid.*, p. 124.

28. "Muzykal'nye zametki," *St.P. ved.*, 24 April 1871, pp. 1-2.

29. See, for example, Stasov, *Izbrannye stat'i*, pp. 146-56; Stasov, *Izbrannye sochineniia*, 1:157; Kiui, *Izbrannye stat'i*, pp. 11, 34, 98.

30. See, for example, "Muzykal'nye zametki," *St.P. ved.*, 20 December 1869, p. 1; 16 October 1870, p. 1; Kiui, *Izbrannye stat'i*, p. 184.

31. *Izbrannye sochineniia*, 1:191-93.

32. *Izbrannye stat'i*, pp. 149-50.

33. *Izbrannye sochineniia*, 1:204.

34. "Muzykal'nye zametki," *St.P. ved.*, 10 February 1871, p. 2.

35.   "*Avtobiograficheskie materialy*, pp. 40-41.

36.   Quoted in Akademiia nauk, *Ocherki istorii Leningrada*, 2:477.

37.   See Vol'f, *Khronika s 1855*, pp. 5-6, and Konstantin Apollonovich Skal'kovskii, *V teatral'nom mire: Nabliudeniia, vospominaniia i razsuzhdeniia* [In the world of the theater: observations, memoirs, and discussions] (St. Petersburg:Tipografiia A.S. Suvorina, 1899), p. 39.

38.   P. Tchaikovsky to P. Fedorov, 6 August 1869, and to S. Gedeonov, 12 October 1869, in P. Chaikovskii, *Polnoe sobranie*, 5:167, 178.

39.   Letter of 17 November 1869, *ibid.*, 5:185.

40.   Napravnik, *Avtobiograficheskie materialy*, pp. 41-42; [Kiui], "Muzykal'nye zametki," *St.P. ved.*, 12 May 1872, p. 1.

41.   "Po povodu semi novykh russkikh oper" [Concerning seven new Russian operas], *St.P. ved.*, 23 May 1872, p. 1.

42.   Komarova, *V. Stasov*, 2:416.

43.   [Kiui], "Muzykal'nye zametki," *St.P. ved.*, 9 March 1871, p. 2.

44.   Serova, *Serovy*, pp. 136-37.

45.   Kiui, *Izbrannye stat'i*, pp. 546-47; Rimsky-Korsakov, *My Musical Life*, p. 105.

46.   *Polnoe sobranie*, 2:28-30.

47.   *My Musical Life*, p. 105.

48.   Letter of 15 August 1868 in Kiui, *Izbrannye pis'ma*, p. 505.

49.   "Muzykal'noe obozrenie," *Otechestvennye zapiski* 184 (June 1869), pt. 2, pp. 257-62.

50.   Rimskii-Korsakov, *Polnoe sobranie*, 2:30; Balakirev to N. Rubinstein, 23 February 1869, in Balakirev, *Perepiska s N. Rubinshteinom*, p. 27.

51.   A.E.M., "Istoricheskaia spravka ob operakh Kiui" [Historical information about Cui's operas], *Ezhegodnik imperatorskikh teatrov*, 1892-1893, p. 559.

52.   Shestakova, "Moi vechera," p. 123.

53.   Rimsky-Korsakov, *My Musical Life*, p. 100.

54.   Borodin to his wife, 24 September 1870, in Borodin, *Pis'ma*, 1:235.

55. Letters of 9 July 1870, 12 January 1871, and 24 April 1871 in Vladimir Vasil'evich Stasov, "Pis'ma V.V. Stasova k A.N. Molas" [V.V. Stasov's letters to A.N. Molas], *Sovetskaia muzyka,* January 1949, pp. 88-89.

56. Letter of 22 February 1871 *ibid.,* p. 89.

57. *Izbrannye stat'i,* p. 147.

58. *Izbrannye sochineniia,* 1:218.

59. "Teatr," *St.P. ved.,* 13 February 1872, p. 2.

60. Aleksandra Purgol'd, "Dnevnik A. Purgol'd" [A. Purgold's diary], *Sovetskaia muzyka,* May 1957, p. 136; Rimsky-Korsakov, *My Musical Life,* pp. 127-28.

61. Gozenpud, *Russkii opernyi teatr,* 2:313.

62. *Izbrannye stat'i,* p. 206.

63. Quoted in Kremlev, *Russkaia mysl' o muzyke,* 2:332.

64. Gozenpud, *Russkii opernyi teatr,* 2:314-16.

65. *Ibid.,* 2:313-14; Vsevelod Cheshikhin, *Istoriia russkoi opery: s 1674 po 1903 g.* [The history of Russian opera: from 1674 through 1903], 2nd rev. ed. (Moscow: P. Iurgenson, 1905), p. 220.

66. Kiui, *Izbrannye stat'i,* pp. 176-78.

67. See, for example, "Muzykal'nye zametki," *St.P. ved.,* 4 December 1870, p. 2; 10 February 1871, p. 2; Stasov, *Izbrannye sochineniia,* 1:203.

68. Editor's note to p. 178, in Kiui, *Izbrannye stat'i,* p. 587.

69. *Izbrannye stat'i,* pp. 204-5.

70. Robert William Oldani, "New Perspectives on Mussorgsky's *Boris Godunov*"(Unpublished Ph.D. dissertation, University of Michigan, 1978), p. 138.

71. Aleksandra Anatol'evna Orlova, comp., *Trudy i dni M.P. Musorgskogo: Letopis' zhizni i tvorchestva* [The works and days of M.P. Musorgsky: a chronicle of his life and work] (Moscow: Gosudarstvennoe muzykal'noe izdatel'stvo, 1963), p. 214.

72. Rimsky-Korsakov, *My Musical Life,* pp. 109-10; N. Isakhanova, "Put' k sovershenstvu" [The path to perfection], *Sovetskaia muzyka,* July 1966, p. 53; Oldani, "New Perspectives," pp. 141-43.

73. Stasov, *Izbrannye sochineniia,* 2:197.

74. "Moi vechera," p. 124.

75.   "Muzykal'nye zametki," *St.P. ved.,* 9 March 1871, p. 2.

76.   Oldani, "New Perspectives," pp. 150-51.

77.   See, for example, Khubov, *Musorgskii,* p. 384.

78.   Robert William Oldani, "Mussorgsky's *Boris Godunov* and the Russian Imperial Theaters," *Liberal Arts Review,* No. 7 (Spring 1979), pp. 10-15. The argument, though well presented, is not quite persuasive, being based too much on what does not appear in the sources and ignoring or slighting some important positive evidence for the rejection. Nevertheless, the argument for the opposing view is hardly, if at all, more persuasive.

79.   "Po povodu semi oper," *St.P. ved.,* 23 May 1872, p. 1.

80.   Rimsky-Korsakov, *My Musical Life,* p. 111; Borodin to his wife, 10 October 1869, in Borodin, *Pis'ma,* 1:152.

81.   Musorgskii, *Literaturnoe nasledie,* 1:268-69.

82.   Letter to his daughter, S.V. Medvedeva, 26 December 1873, in Stasov, *Pis'ma k rodnym,* I, pt. 2:98.

83.   Musorgsky to Napravnik, 6 February 1873, in Napravnik, *Avtobiograficheskie materialy,* pp. 294-95; Rimsky-Korsakov, *My Musical Life,* p. 133.

84.   *Izbrannye stat'i,* p. 231.

85.   See the extracts from various reviews in Orlova, *Trudy Musorgskogo,* pp. 278-88.

86.   *Izbrannye stat'i,* p. 230.

87.   Quoted in Kremlev, *Russkaia mysl' o muzyke,* 2:361-62.

88.   Rimsky-Korsakov to N. Purgold, 9 October 1871, quoted in V. Rimskii-Korsakov, "Iz semeinoi perepiski" [From the family correspondence], *Sovetskaia muzyka,* March 1969, p. 84.

89.   Borodin to his wife, 24-25 October 1871, in Borodin, *Pis'ma,* 1:310-11; Rimskii-Korsakov, *My Musical Life,* p. 127.

90.   "Muzykal'nye zametki," *St.P. ved.,* p. 2.

91.   Aleksandra Anatol'evna Orlova and V.N. Rimskii-Korsakov, comps., *Stranitsy zhizni N.A. Rimskogo-Korsakova: Letopis' zhizni i tvorchestva* [Pages of the life of N.A. Rimsky-Korsakov: a chronicle of his life and work], 4 vols. (Leningrad: Muzyka, 1970-73), 2:68, 72.

92.   Gerald Abraham, *Rimsky-Korsakov: A Short Biography* (London: Duckworth, 1945), pp. 47-48; S., "Teatr," *St.P. ved.,* 18 February 1873, p. 2.

93.   I. Gusin, "Iz istorii russkoi opery" [From the history of Russian opera], *Sovetskaia muzyka,* September 1954, pp. 75-76.

94. *My Musical Life*, pp. 125-27.

95. *Ibid.*, pp. 130-32.

96. "Teatr," *St.P. ved.*, 2 January 1873, p. 1.

97. S., "Teatr," *St.P. ved.*, 18 February 1873, p. 2.

98. *Izbrannye stat'i*, pp. 216, 218-19, 224.

99. Orlova, *Stranitsy zhizni Rimskogo*, 2:75-78.

100. Quoted in Kremlev, *Russkaia mysl' o muzyke*, 2:357.

Chapter VIII

The End of the Struggle

During the 1860s the positions of the Russian Musical Society, the Balakirev circle, and Alexander Serov, the principal parties in the rivalry for dominance of St. Petersburg musical life, altered little. Although Serov and the Balakirev circle had made tremendous advances in fame and prestige by the end of the decade, the RMS remained the most prominent purveyor of serious music and music education in the Russian capital. The Society lost its founder, Anton Rubinstein, in 1867 and then flirted with Balakirev's brand of musical modernism for two seasons, but by 1870 its concerts had reverted to their earlier style, based largely on the German classical masters. Furthermore, the St. Petersburg Conservatory had not once compromised with its critics; Nikolai Zaremba, who replaced Rubinstein as the school's director, was at least as musically conservative as his predecessor. Despite the beginnings of a rift between Balakirev and his followers, his circle remained in 1870 a relatively cohesive association of musicians with similar tastes, who presented a united front to their opponents and the rest of the musical world. Balakirev's tenure as conductor of the RMS concerts represented no compromise with the Society's conservative principles but an attempt to take over and convert the organization to his own tastes. Serov's allegiance had shifted in the 1860s, but he refused to subordinate himself to any group. His early support for the Balakirev circle had quickly changed to a posture of opposition to all the major musical institutions and figures in St. Petersburg for most of the decade. Toward the end he had allied himself with the RMS for various personal and professional reasons, but he reserved his right to criticize the Society publicly and work for change from within. Therefore, it was still possible in 1870 to distinguish three distinct currents in the musical life of St. Petersburg—currents, however, that during the first few years of the 1870s would ebb and flow so as to blur clear distinctions. The struggle for control of musical life in the Russian capital entered a new phase radically different from that of the 1860s.

The most obvious and definitive change in the parties to the musical rivalries of the 1870s was Serov's untimely death at the age of fifty-one on 20 January 1871. Since he had no dedicated followers, his death ended his influence. The Russian Musical Society, in whose camp he had been formally numbered during the last year of his life, acknowledged the association and honored Serov's passing by arranging an elaborate funeral service,[1] while the Balakirev circle marked the event with a condescending obituary by Cui[2] and a scathing review of Serov's last opera.

The changes in the Russian Musical Society in the early 1870s were less profound but more important in their lasting effects on musical life in Russia. A reform in the St. Petersburg Conservatory permanently altered the development of that institution, which had previously been preserved as a sanctuary for classical ideals even during the years when Balakirev had managed temporarily to orient the RMS concerts in a more modern direction. The turning point for the Conservatory was the retirement of its director Nikolai Zaremba in the summer of 1871 and his replacement by Mikhail Azanchevsky. As president of the board of directors of the St. Petersburg RMS he was instrumental in the adoption of decidedly unclassical repertory for the RMS concerts of the 1871-72 season. He brought a similar reforming spirit to his job as head of the Conservatory.[3]

The St. Petersburg Conservatory, in spite of its steady growth and the stabilization of its financial position under Zaremba,[4] faced two important threats to its prestige and integrity as an advanced training center for wellrounded musicians. The first resulted from the emergence and growing fame of the Balakirev circle. In the early 1860s the Conservatory could claim the participation or at least support of the most famous musicians in the city. Its leading critics were young and inexperienced composers who had few compositions of their own to support their claims that their understanding of music surpassed that to be derived from formal, academic training. By the end of the decade, however, the Balakirev circle had presented quite a number of substantial works to the musical public of St. Petersburg, and Balakirev had proven himself to be an effective conductor. The existence of this band of gifted musicians who not only were not associated with the Conservatory but also publicly disdained academic music education inevitably diminished the school's stature. Zaremba's only public answer to this challenge had been an article in Famintsyn's journal, *Muzykal'nyi sezon,* claiming that only the Conservatory could offer the full program of music education needed to form true creative musicians. As Cui sarcastically remarked, Zaremba's article essentially argued that "outside the Conservatory there is no salvation!"[5] Obviously Zaremba was not the sort of man to deal effectively with the growing reputation of the opponents of conservatory training.

The second major threat to the St. Petersburg Conservatory's integrity came from Grand Duchess Elena Pavlovna and the tsarist government. The school had been founded in the early 1860s when the Russian government was initiating a number of far-reaching reforms, including not only the famous emancipation of the serfs in 1861 but also the liberalization of educational policy. By the end of the decade, however, student unrest and an unsuccessful attempt on the life of Alexander II in 1866 by a young man who had been expelled from Kazan University for participating in student disturbances had induced the tsar to tighten controls on education. Within ten days of the assassination attempt Alexander replaced his liberal minister of education with Count Dmitry Tolstoy, a man who believed in rigid academic discipline and rigorous classical training in order to inoculate students against pernicious ideas such as socialism.[6] Shortly thereafter the tsar issued a rescript directing all those in charge of educational facilities to avoid any encouragement of independent thought in their students.[7]

The St. Petersburg Conservatory was not subject to the Ministry of Education, but the school's official patron, Grand Duchess Elena Pavlovna, undertook to bring it into line with the spirit of government educational policy by turning it into a trade school to produce skilled orchestral players for the state theaters rather than a training ground for creative artists. Adept cellists or trumpeters were always needed by some theater orchestra somewhere and would therefore become useful state employees. Composers or music historians however, fit no immediate government requirement and were likely instead to be independent figures with a higher opinion of their own importance than was good for them. Therefore, Elena Pavlovna proposed to emphasize training on orchestral instruments over all other specializations and to reduce all theoretical subjects to lecture courses involving no practical exercises.[8] Zaremba had resisted the grand duchess's projects, even submitting a report in April 1871 pointing out that such a plan would violate the Conservatory's charter, but his opposition was in vain, and he was forced to retire that summer.[9]

Mikhail Azanchevsky, Zaremba's successor, was just as opposed to Elena Pavlovna's schemes as Zaremba had been. Instead of openly challenging the grand duchess, however, he formally agreed with her proposals while simultaneously undermining them in practice. On 16 July 1871 he submitted a memorandum to her that declared that under his leadership the Conservatory would confine itself to training orchestral musicians, pianists, and singers and eliminate special theoretical classes because "such students, upon graduation from the institution, cannot practically and for their own benefit apply their knowledge."[10] In fact, Azanchevsky's reforms resulted in the rejuvenation, not elimination, of the courses in music theory and composition.

These subjects had stagnated in the hands of Zaremba because he had taught them according to thoroughly conservative methods and principles. He had not studied the new German school, Glinka, or Berlioz, and therefore he completely ignored their innovations in harmony, form, and orchestration in his theory and composition classes.[11] In his orchestra class he had spent months on one Haydn symphony or a Cherubini overture, going over each instrumental part individually while the rest of the players sat in silence.[12] Azanchevsky revitalized these courses by hiring young and talented native musicians to take over Zaremba's teaching duties.

In the fall of 1871 the Conservatory engaged Hermann Laroche as professor of music theory. Although of French ancestry, he was born and educated in Russia, had been one of the first graduates of the St. Petersburg Conservatory, and had taught theory at the Moscow Conservatory for five years. He was conservative in his aesthetic tastes but not as hidebound as Zaremba. He at least knew the work of the advanced composers of his day, he liked the music of Berlioz,[13] and he had written at great length of his admiration for Glinka and his role in creating a Russian style of composition.[14]

If hiring Laroche freshened the Conservatory's rather stale teaching of music theory, Azanchevsky's choice for Zaremba's successor as professor of composition and orchestration transformed the entire character of the institution. As one professor later wrote, "to the great astonishment of the faculty council, [Azanchevsky] suggested and even insisted on the election of Rimsky-Korsakov" to teach these subjects.[15] It is not difficult to understand the surprise of the Conservatory staff at the proposal to engage a member of the Balakirev circle, a group that had consistently challenged the Conservatory's ability to train creative artists, to teach composition and orchestration. Nevertheless, the plan offered certain advantages. Not only would it revitalize these courses, which Elena Pavlovna wished to reduce to insignificance, but it would also bridge the gap between the school and its most prominent critics and deflect charges that the St. Petersburg Conservatory was reactionary and anti-Russian.

Given the potential benefits for the Conservatory of hiring a member of the Balakirev circle, Rimsky was the obvious choice among them. Balakirev and Cui had made too many enemies with their public musical activity, Borodin was a full-time scientist who had little time for music, and Musorgsky was still almost an unknown quantity as a composer. By contrast, Rimsky had done nothing to earn himself personal enemies—aside from two controversial opera reviews—and his First Symphony, the tone poems *Sadko* and *Antar,* and some smaller pieces had all been performed successfully in St. Petersburg, several more than once. Even critics hostile to the Balakirev circle had singled him out as its most talented member.[16] All agreed that he had a special gift for colorful scoring. Thus, he seemed a reasonable choice to teach composition and orchestration even if the very idea of engaging a member of Balakirev's circle as a Conservatory professor was more than a little surprising.

On 14 July 1871 Azanchevsky sent Rimsky a formal invitation to teach "the theory of composition and orchestration" at the St. Petersburg Conservatory for a guaranteed annual salary of one thousand rubles, and Rimsky promptly accepted.[17] Although he claims in his memoirs that he hesitated to accept the offer because he considered himself unqualified due to his imperfect knowledge of music theory,[18] Rimsky had already shown an inclination for scholarship and had a reputation among his friends as the most diligent student in the group.[19] Thus, as Borodin wrote his wife, Rimsky's new post answered, "more than any other, his spiritual and musical needs."[20] The Conservatory professorship also met more practical needs for the young composer by providing him with financial security and a way of escaping the naval career he had come to dislike. Rimsky summarized the advantages of the position:

> the proposition is beneficial for me in many respects: first, for monetary considerations; second, because I will be occupied with matters that I like and for which I am best suited; third, it will be good practice for me, especially in conducting; and, finally, because it is an opportunity to establish myself eventually in the musical field and to be done with a career that I do not consider wholly honest or seemly to continue for long.[21]

Rimsky's musical colleagues, despite their vitriolic attacks, both public and private, on the Conservatory, gave their blessings to the move, for they were pleased by this recognition of their own work and the opportunity to extend their influence into that bastion of conservatism. Rimsky writes in his memoirs that Balakirev favored his acceptance in order "*to get one of his own men* into the hostile Conservatory";[22] Borodin wrote his wife that Rimsky's role as a teacher of composition would give him "the most powerful means of directing our youth onto the true path in art";[23] and Cui applauded Rimsky's appointment as a professor in *Sankt-Peterburgskie vedomosti*, hailing it as a sign that "the Conservatory repudiates its exclusive conservatism and does not reject life and movement. Given this orientation and this viewpoint, it can, of course, render the greatest aid to the cause of music here."[24]

In fact, Rimsky's engagement as a Conservatory professor marked a permanent change in the school's development. For more than a third of a century he was its principal composition teacher, and he trained dozens of musicians, including Anatoly Liadov, Anton Arensky, Mikhail Ippolitov-Ivanov, and Sergei Prokofiev.[25] The entire generation of professors teaching in the St. Petersburg Conservatory in the early twentieth century was trained in theoretical subjects in "the school of Rimsky-Korsakov."[26] Although his professorship encouraged him to undertake the kind of formal study of music theory that Balakirev had always condemned, Rimsky did not abandon many of the principles of his first teacher but instead fostered them in his own students. Thus, from 1871 the composition classes of the St. Petersburg Conservatory combined academic training with the innovative harmonies, free forms, and Russian coloration espoused by Balakirev.

Although the engagement of Laroche and Rimsky-Korsakov did much to modernize the teaching of theoretical subjects in the Conservatory, this alone could not protect the institution from Elena Pavlovna's plans to turn it into a vocational school to train orchestral musicians. In September 1872 the grand duchess announced to the directorate of the St. Petersburg RMS the imminent publication of a new charter for the Society that would transfer complete control of the St. Petersburg Conservatory from the local branch of the RMS, which had blocked her efforts, to its Chief Directorate, a body over which she had greater control. She had apparently decided to put an end to all opposition to her program. The directors of the St. Petersburg branch, led by Azanchevsky, unanimously opposed this move on the grounds that the Conservatory was founded and supported by local funds and that its direction was granted to the local RMS branch by charter. The impending battle was averted only by Elena Pavlovna's sudden death on 9 January 1873,[27] which put a stop to her scheme and removed from the St. Petersburg musical scene one of the principal figures in its rivalries of the 1860s.

The grand duchess had been patron and principal supporter of the RMS and the St. Petersburg Conservatory since their respective foundings in 1859 and 1862. She had treated these institutions almost as her private property and had done much to set their artistic direction. She had defended their conservative, classical orientation, blocked any role in the Conservatory for Balakirev when he succeeded Anton Rubinstein as the principal conductor of the RMS in 1867, and was largely responsible for his dismissal from that post in 1869 and the subsequent reversion of the Society's concerts to a more classical format. Thus, she had blocked whatever small chance there had been in 1867 for a compromise and reconciliation between the Balakirev circle and the RMS. Instead, her actions had embittered the relations of the two parties and set the stage for their continued intense rivalry into the 1870s. Now one of the greatest obstacles to cooperation between the RMS and its chief critics had vanished.

Elena Pavlovna's successor as president of the RMS and patron of the Conservatory was Grand Duke Konstantin Nikolaevich, her nephew and the brother of Alexander II. A dedicated music-lover and amateur cellist, he took a keen and active interest in the musical activities of the city.[28] Although his musical tastes and interests differed little from his aunt's, he had the discretion not to press for the transfer of control over the St. Petersburg Conservatory from the local RMS directors to the Chief Directorate. The new charter of the RMS, confirmed by the emperor on 4 June 1873, affirmed that the Society's "conservatories remain, as from their founding, under the direct authority of the local directorates."[29] Grand Duke Konstantin did bring about one farreaching change in the Society's status in the first months of his leadership—the tsar granted his petition for the title "Imperial."[30] From its founding, the RMS had been a private organization. Through Elena Pavlovna it had received some government subsidies and the legal authority to grant the rank of "free artist" to qualified graduates of the Conservatory. But neither the RMS nor the Conservatory had enjoyed official government status. All this changed, however, in 1873, and the tsarist government, for better or worse, took over ultimate supervision of the RMS as well as financial responsibility for its continued functioning.

The Balakirev circle, the third party in St. Petersburg's musical rivalries of the 1860s, also changed profoundly in the early 1870s. The group, once so closeknit and unified, began to break up. Balakirev's iron control over his pupils had already begun to weaken during the late 1860s. In the early 1870s, as he became more and more involved in his own affairs and his colleagues gained confidence and self-reliance, his leadership declined further. In the winter of 1869-70 Borodin and Rimsky-Korsakov accompanied Balakirev on a visit to Moscow, where a new acquaintance was struck both by Balakirev's "imperious treatment" of his comrades and by their willingness to assume the "air of pupils who are accustomed to obey him."[31] Very soon, however, as even Liudmila Shestakova, one of the strongest defenders of the circle's unity, admits in her memoirs, each of Balakirev's pupils "wanted to travel by his own path."[32]

Rimsky-Korsakov had begun to challenge some of his teacher's criticisms as early as 1868. Two years later he reportedly requested on one occasion that Shestakova not ask him or the others to play their pieces in the presence of Stasov, Cui, or Balakirev.[33] Apparently he had grown weary of the advice and criticism that every new composition elicited from the senior members of the circle. About the same time, he began courting his future wife,[34] which also drew him away from the common activities of his musical friends and ended once and for all any remaining need he may have felt for the almost maternal support and guidance once shown him by Balakirev. Finally, his acceptance of the Conservatory professorship provided the impetus toward complete emancipation from Balakirev and his other colleagues as well. With this step, he embarked on a path that the rest of his friends could not or would not follow.

Although Rimsky had always shown a more academic turn of mind than the rest of the circle, his conservatory duties quickly revealed his ignorance of the traditional disciplines of music theory and counterpoint. Nearly in a panic, he undertook to teach himself these subjects by intense reading and writing hundreds of exercises, managing to stay a week or two ahead of his pupils.[35]

Realizing full well that his former teacher and his musical friends could be of no help to him in this pursuit, he turned to Tchaikovsky, the one person he knew well who had received an academic musical education. Tchaikovsky later remembered that Rimsky studied "with such zeal that soon school technique became an indispensable atmosphere for him. In one summer he wrote innumerably many counterpoint exercises and sixty-four fugues." Tchaikovsky found the ten he saw "irreproachable in their own way."[36] Thus, Rimsky's responsibilities at the Conservatory not only gave him an arena for his musical interests entirely separate from Balakirev's circle, but it also led him to the very kind of academic studies that Balakirev deplored. Of the circle members, only Borodin showed any sympathy for Rimsky's immersion in counterpoint exercises and theory textbooks.[37]

Musorgsky's development in the early 1870s took a direction quite different from Rimsky's but equally destructive to the unity of the circle. Responding to a variety of influences that included Dargomyzhsky's musical innovations in *The Stone Guest*, contemporary philosophical-political currents of a somewhat radical cast, and personal experience with Russian peasant life, Musorgsky developed into a musical "populist" and "realist"— the only member of Balakirev's circle to whom these terms can be applied legitimately. His first major attempt to embody these principles in music dates to 1868 with his setting of the first act of Gogol's play *The Marriage*, during which he declared, "I am crossing the Rubicon. It is living prose in music . . . a reproduction of simple human dialects."[38] In principle, Musorgsky's effort might seem close to the operatic ideals then being advocated by Dargomyzhsky and adopted by the Balakirev circle, but in practice Musorgsky had already gone farther in this direction than the rest of the group was willing to go. Rimsky recalls that all of them were "amazed at Musorgsky's task, enthusiastic about his characterizations and many recitative phrases, but perplexed by some of his chords and harmonic progressions." Balakirev and Cui, Rimsky says, considered *The Marriage* "a mere curiosity with interesting declamatory moments."[39]

Musorgsky abandoned *The Marriage* after the first act and took up work on *Boris Godunov,* a work less radical in style but still bearing strong imprints of its author's populism and realism in the often declamatory vocal lines that reflect the inflections of spoken Russian as well as the important role given the Russian masses. This work, probably the most important artistic product of the entire Balakirev school, marked its author's artistic maturity and full independence of Balakirev's influence. Balakirev himself stated that *Boris* was composed and orchestrated entirely without his participation.[40] In fact, he did not much like it. "Balakirev the idealist" found Musorgsky's "real music not at all to his taste," Stasov remarked pointedly.[41]

Musorgsky, however, could no longer be deflected from his path by criticism from Balakirev. *Khovanshchina* and *The Fair of Sorochinsk*, the two operas on which he worked after revising *Boris*, and most of his smaller works of the 1870s reflect a continued dedication to his own understanding of musical "realism" and "populism." He came finally to dismiss the value of any technical study of music—not only the formal academic courses that Balakirev had long ridiculed but even the informal musical analysis practiced within the circle. He complained to Stasov that among his colleagues he rarely heard "living ideas, but rather school days—technique and musical vocabulary."[42] Inevitably, a deep sense of estrangement tinctured his contacts with the circle, "a persistent feeling—I cannot name it; it is the feeling you experience at the loss of a very close and dear person with whom, as they say, 'you have shared your days and whiled away your nights.' "[43]

Cui had never been on intimate terms with the junior members of Balakirev's circle, and their increasingly independent development in the early 1870s distanced him still more. Confronting the radical turn in Musorgsky, his reviews began to mix petty criticism with his usual praise of Musorgsky's originality.[44] The premiere of *Boris,* when it finally came, marked his final disillusionment with his younger colleague's path. He pronounced the opera "an immature work":

> Its immaturity appears everywhere: in the libretto, in the piling up of so many minute effects that cuts had to be made, in its enthusiasm for sound imitation, in the downgrading of artistic realism to antiartistic reality (in the first mass scene there is laughter and before the last one a hubbub without specified notes, consequently without music), and finally in a mixture of excellent musical ideas with trivial ones. There are two chief flaws in *Boris:* choppy recitatives and disjointedness of the musical ideas, which at times makes the opera like a potpourri. These faults are not the result of Mr. Musorgsky's creative weakness [but] of immaturity, of the fact that the author is not sufficiently strict in his criticism of himself, of his careless, self-satisfied, hasty composing.[45]

Musorgsky reeled from this blow: "How horrible Cui's article is! . . . Self-satisfaction!!! hasty composition! Immaturity! . . . whose? . . . whose? . . . I'd like to know."[46]

The rest of Petersburg's musical community was also stunned by Cui's *volte-face* in attacking a major work of the Balakirev circle. Many attributed it to envy of Musorgsky's success.[47] But the main reason for Cui's attack on *Boris* was more fundamental. Despite his ties to the Balakirev circle, despite his public support for "realism" in music, for the abandonment of classical forms and rules, and for a national musical style, Cui was not truly a musical radical.[48] One need only look at his *William Ratcliffe,* based on an ultra-Romantic Heine play set in Scotland and filled with formal arias and duets,[49] to appreciate how far his music differed from Musorgsky's. He had praised *The Stone Guest* and even parts of *Boris,* but Cui shrank from the full implications of musical realism as developed by Musorgsky. Just as Rimsky and Musorgsky took independent artistic paths in the early 1870s, Cui drew into himself, becoming more narrow in his tastes and opinions until he found himself no longer able to accept wholeheartedly some of the finest products of the Balakirev circle.

Of all Balakirev's principal followers from the 1860s, only Borodin remained on good terms with all the rest in the 1870s. He alone felt equally enthusiastic about the divergent directions taken by the circle members as they approached artistic maturity. He could praise Musorgsky's *Boris* as "delightful" and at the same time recommend one of Cui's "exceedingly nice little choruses" as "simply a masterpiece in the choral genre."[50] By the early 1870s Borodin was developing a distinctive and individual musical personality of his own, but he did not spurn his friends for following different paths.

The explanation of Borodin's appreciation of all his friends' work probably lies in his easy-going, tolerant nature and his view of music as an avocation rather than a vocation. His scientific and educational work often pushed music "completely in the background," at times angering his musical friends.[51] He even contemplated giving up work on his opera, *Prince Igor,* because he thought it "an enormous waste of time."[52] Composition was not an irresistible passion; music was not the focus of his life. Therefore, he was not as sensitive as Musorgsky, Rimsky, or Cui to the criticism of others or to the challenge implicit in a style different from his own.

Vladimir Stasov devoted much of his life to propagating the legend that the Balakirev circle remained united in its aesthetic outlook and tastes,[53] but by the early 1870s he could not fail to perceive the rifts developing within the group. Assessing their friends in a letter to Rimsky-Korsakov, he observed:

> Cui has passion, but he never thinks and is not capable of thinking of anything at all; he has no brains, and, furthermore, for all his talent, he is committed to absolutely nothing. Musorianin [Musorgsky] simply exceeds all bounds by virtue of talent, but his mind is rather narrow; he has no critical faculty and neither ponders nor reflects deeply on anything at all, no matter what the circumstances. Borodin is the most horrible conservative and will never take a single step forward, no matter what, but rather one hundred steps backward; he would gladly freeze everything so that nothing would move—isn't this all an oddity! What a strange collection of talented people . . . !! What a combination of gold with some sort of good-for-nothing lime or clay, what a choking of talent by eternal rubbish. Balakirev is an eagle in all things musical . . . but his Achilles' heel is a prosaic and skewed viewpoint in everything nonmusical.

Stasov praised Rimsky himself as "the most intellectual" of the circle;[54] we can only speculate about what he might have said in a letter to one of his other colleagues. Nevertheless, Stasov worked in the 1870s to maintain the group's unity, making special efforts to bring them together for music-making sessions at his or his brother Dmitri's apartment.[55]

Still, Stasov was not the type to tolerate a variety of viewpoints as did Borodin. A born crusader, he could take nothing casually. As rifts began to develop within the circle, he found himself taking sides. By 1872 he had clearly aligned himself with Musorgsky's radical ideals of musical realism and populism. Perhaps this seems surprising, considering his comments to Rimsky in the letter just quoted, but Stasov genuinely believed in realistic and nationalistic principles in art and opposed anything that hinted at formalism or scholasticism. Moreover, he greatly admired Musorgsky's native gifts. For his part, Musorgsky found Stasov a sympathetic confidant and a valuable ally. It was to him that Musorgsky poured out his indignation at Cui's review of the premiere of *Boris Godunov.*[56]

Thus, in the early 1870s Balakirev's pupils and closest friends, who had formed a close-knit group in the 1860s, began to split into factions. Musorgsky and Vladimir Stasov were linked together by their ideal of musical realism. Rimsky was occupied with his teaching at the St. Petersburg Conservatory and his own immersion in the study of music theory, harmony and counterpoint. Cui was isolated by his increasingly narrow tastes and his condescension toward Rimsky, Borodin, and Musorgsky. Borodin, although remaining on good terms with all the rest, devoted most of his time to nonmusical pursuits. Thus, by 1873 the circle, though nominally intact, had lost much of its unifying spirit and was ripe for collapse.

The fatal blow to the Balakirev circle came not from rifts among its junior members, however, but from the increasingly erratic behavior of Balakirev himself, which led finally to his abandonment of all public musical activity and complete withdrawal from the group. Balakirev had been not only the group's founder but its heart and soul. With him at its head, even the estrangement of one or two members could not have crippled the circle, but without him it lost all cohesion. None of the other members could command Balakirev's authority. After his dismissal by the RMS in the spring of 1869, however, Balakirev entered a prolonged period of emotional instability that increasingly prevented him from exercising his leadership.

Balakirev's discharge by the Russian Musical Society dealt a severe blow to both his prestige and his pocketbook. A few weeks later his father died, leaving him with full responsibility for supporting his two unmarried sisters.[57] Nevertheless, on his return to St. Petersburg after a summer in Moscow and Klin, he showed no outward signs of emotional shock. Instead he threw himself into his work for the Free Music School and its rivalry with the RMS with an almost pathological enthusiasm. Every act on the part of the opposition became an intrigue, and Balakirev started to respond in what he evidently considered to be the same spirit. Planning the first FMS subscription concert series, he warned Rimsky not to mention a word to Nikolai Rubinstein for fear he might let it slip out, "and if certain people find out ahead of time, then the whole business will be spoiled."[58] He also cautioned Tchaikovsky not to tell anyone about his project to organize a benefit for the FMS with stars of the Italian Opera because he was afraid the RMS leaders would sabotage the plan if they learned of it.[59] Considering the intensity of the rivalry between the RMS and FMS, Balakirev's suspicions may have been justified, but other evidence suggests that his extreme caution was less the result of rational judgment than a symptom of incipient paranoia. Simultaneously with the beginning of the first FMS concert series Balakirev began visiting a fortune teller in order "to learn the future fate of his concerts and of his struggle with the hated Russian Musical Society, and likewise to divine the thoughts and intentions of the persons who were at the helm of the Society."[60] Later he wrote Tchaikovsky that he had found out "from *supernatural* sources (you know from where)" that Nikolai Rubinstein would soon have a decisive battle with Elena Pavlovna, then the same "supernatural sources" warned that "some other scoundrel" besides Napravnik and Hiller would conduct some of the RMS concerts that season.[61] Balakirev, formerly an avowed believer in the materialistic philosophy popular among the radical Russian intelligentsia in the 1860s, had apparently grown so concerned with defeating the RMS and so suspicious of intrigues against himself that he had turned to mystical powers for advance warnings of danger.

Throughout the winter of 1869-70 Balakirev worked at fever pitch for the Free Music School, trying unsuccessfully to arrange some sort of spectacular benefit concert to offset FMS deficits. Then he failed in his efforts to alleviate his desperate financial straits by a solo concert in Nizhny Novgorod. Nevertheless, he seemed to bounce back from these tribulations, though his emotional resilience had clearly been strained.[62] In October 1870 he approached Borodin for information about the receiving hours at a well-known Petersburg clinic for nervous and mental disorders.[63] Balakirev had suffered from periodic headaches, fits of depression, and other nervous disorders since a severe bout of "inflammation of the brain" in 1858.[64] Presumably he was feeling similar symptoms in the fall of 1870 and therefore decided to see a specialist in mental and nervous diseases.

Balakirev's contacts with the members of his circle diminished noticeably about the same time.[65] He alone failed to attend the gathering at which *The Stone Guest* received its first public but informal performance by his colleagues and friends in December 1870.[66] Stasov reported that during February and March 1871 Balakirev would sleep all day or else play solitaire and pace his room biting his fingernails.[67] Visits to his fortune teller became more frequent.[68] Finally, he even attempted suicide.[69] Serov's sudden death on 20 January 1871 may have precipitated the crisis. Balakirev attended the funeral and just two days later confided in a letter, "I am very depressed by the death of my enemy Serov."[70]

Thus beset by depression, disappointment, and ill health, Balakirev eventually sought solace in religion. Years later he himself would write, "in 1871 I underwent a great change: from an atheist . . . I turned into a believer."[71] The event can even be dated to the period of late winter or early spring from a letter of 12 April 1871 in which Balakirev requests that his "conversion to religion" be mentioned to no one.[72] Although he had considered himself a freethinker and an atheist during the 1860s, much in his background disposed Balakirev to religion. He had been raised in a religious family who dubbed him "the bishop" for his childhood devoutness.[73] In addition, his Slavophile leanings inevitably implied a certain sympathy with the Orthodox Church, at least in its historical role in the development of Russian culture and thought. Finally, even his belief in fortune tellers suggests proximity to the brand of Orthodoxy he eventually adopted, for after his conversion he became obsessed with the idea of mystical forces, especially the power of evil spirits. He once explained to the parents of one of his piano pupils that he believed in the Devil as a personal enemy of God and saw his work not only in the sinfulness of man but also in such imperfections in God's own work as the fact that the earth revolves around the sun not in precisely 365 days but with a few excess minutes.[74] Anecdotes abound about Balakirev going up to complete strangers in church and telling them their prayers would be answered or, at other times, shouting "Get thee behind me, Satan" at someone's approach.[75] One report claimed that Balakirev believed Stasov to be possessed and was avoiding contact with his friends until he felt himself strong enough to wrestle with the Devil and exorcise him from Stasov.[76]

Although Balakirev's conversion seems to have brought relief from the terrible self-doubt and frustrations he had suffered, it did not end his psychological instability. Stasov found him completely changed—and not for the better: "Before me yesterday sat some tomb, not the former lively, energetic, restless Mily, who used to begin to rattle off all the latest news as soon as he entered a room, who used to interrogate and urge everyone onward. Now he has no interest in anyone or anything."[77] Balakirev's contacts with the members of his circle became extremely rare events. Borodin suggested in a most perceptive analysis of the situation that Balakirev was avoiding the group partly because his pride would not allow him to tolerate the independence of his now mature pupils and partly because he felt uncomfortable among people with no sympathy for his new-found religious feelings. For their part, his former associates not only distrusted Balakirev's religious fanaticism, they were angered and offended by his indifference to their musical cause as well.[78]

Regardless of his withdrawal from his musical friends, Balakirev resumed his rivalry with the RMS in the fall of 1871 and seems to have worked hard at the task, if with less enthusiasm than two years earlier. "Work is beginning for the school, and I am very glad of it," he remarked in a letter, "because I somehow feel better, more animated, and my spiritual wounds seem to be closing little by little."[79] Two weeks later Borodin reported that Balakirev was "very cheerful and working on the concerts," although in many respects he was "behaving queerly."[80] For all his efforts, Balakirev's concerts were not successful. Funds ran out completely after the fourth FMS concert, and the fifth program had to be cancelled.

This was the final blow to Balakirev. He no longer had his circle of composer-friends for support, he had not written any music in over two years, and he had been defeated utterly in his contest with the RMS. On top of that, his financial situation was worse than ever because his work for the FMS was unpaid and interfered with his source of livelihood—music lessons. By the summer of 1872 his poverty had become so great that he took a drastic step. On 6 July Balakirev, the only member of his circle who could be called a professional musician and who had devoted himself completely to musical pursuits, took a clerical job in a freight station of the Warsaw Railroad.[81] He had finally given up his quest for leadership of musical life in St. Petersburg.

Balakirev now withdrew entirely from public musical activity. He made one final appearance before his circle in December when he attended a gathering in honor of Tchaikovsky's visit to St. Petersburg. According to Musorgsky, Balakirev played "well but too nervously," and he told Shestakova and Musorgsky that he could not indulge in music as an art while forced to treat it as a trade—that is, giving piano lessons.[82] In January 1873 Borodin wrote Balakirev, urging him to end his estrangement from his friends:

> Is it possible you have left us forever? Is it possible that you will *never* visit us? Is it possible that you don't know and don't wish to know that we sincerely love you, not only as a musician but as a person? Can I believe that you actually do not have enough time to drop in on your good friends? Find time and come to visit.[83]

In March Stasov also tried his hand at bringing Balakirev back to the circle,[84] but Balakirev would not succumb to his friends' persuasions. He wrote Stasov that he would not return to giving concerts even if the opportunity arose, that he considered his railroad job preferable to giving piano lessons, which he hoped soon to be able to give up entirely, and that he could not force himself to compose anything if he did not feel the inspiration.[85] With this the break between Balakirev and his circle was complete. For many years Balakirev shunned his former pupils and neither composed nor performed publicly as a pianist or conductor.

With Balakirev gone, it was only a matter of time before the rest of the group split up. In the early 1870s the circle members had begun to follow quite different paths of development. Balakirev's departure removed the group's focal point and allowed the remaining members to drift apart. Musorgsky foresaw this as early as July 1872 when he wrote: "the past of our circle is bright—but its present is bleak: gloomy days have arrived . . . No matter how I try to drive off the annoying fly that keeps buzzing the nasty words 'gone to pieces,' it just keeps buzzing."[86]

Musorgsky's death knell for the group was a bit premature. In fact the early months of 1873 brought the Balakirev circle some of its greatest triumphs with the popular success of Rimsky's *Maid of Pskov* and the scenes from Musorgsky's *Boris Godunov*. Cui carried on his work in the press as if nothing had happened to the group, in one article proclaiming the victory of the new Russian opera school over its helpless critics,[87] in another criticizing the RMS for ignoring Russian composers, especially the members of the Balakirev circle.[88] Cui's devastating review of *Boris Godunov* early in 1874, however, exposed to all the deep rifts within the group. In 1875 another major split became public when Rimsky-Korsakov, who had taken over the directorship of the Free Music School the previous year, conducted its first concert under his leadership. The program consisted entirely of music from the Baroque and Classical eras: Haydn was the most modern composer represented. In case any of the musical public failed to notice Rimsky's apparent abandonment of the aesthetic principles for which the Balakirev circle had stood, Cui pointed it out in no uncertain terms in his reviews.[89]

Stasov labored diligently to hold the group together and to preserve a show of unity for the outside world, but it was too late.[90] A close friend of Musorgsky at the time flatly asserts in his memoirs that by 1874 the Balakirev circle "had completely broken up."[91] This did not mean that the remaining members had no contacts—they all met occasionally, Borodin remained on quite good terms with everyone, and Musorgsky and Stasov were extremely close—but even Borodin, who generally viewed every situation in the best possible light, admitted that the members now functioned as individuals more than as a single school, that great differences had developed among them, and that they did not all like one another's works.[92] In the late 1870s Balakirev resumed musical activity and contacts with his former associates, but it was too late to reconstitute the circle, and he was no longer the right man to lead it. He only succeeded in alienating Musorgsky by his patronizing instructions and angering Rimsky with his interference in the direction of the Free Music School.[93] Although all the former members of Balakirev's circle remained active in music, and three of them—Balakirev, Cui, and Rimsky-Korsakov— plus Vladimir Stasov lived well into the twentieth century, they never again formed a cohesive group, united by common goals and mutual sympathy.

Just as the first few years of the 1870s brought sweeping changes to the other two principal parties in the musical rivalries of the 1860s, so also did they alter the very essence of the Balakirev circle. Although the issues over which the earlier battles had been fought had scarcely been resolved, and no one party had yet secured control of St. Petersburg's musical life, the rivalries of the 1860s had effectively ended by 1873. Serov and Elena Pavlovna were dead. Anton Rubinstein and Balakirev had virtually withdrawn from public musical activity. The Balakirev circle had atomized into individuals preoccupied with personal rather than collective aims. While Stasov valiantly perpetuated the legend of a Mighty Handful united in the cause of nationalist music, Rimsky-Korsakov practiced a newly disciplined nationalism in that bastion of classicism and professionalism, the St. Petersburg Conservatory. The formulas and patterns of Russian musical life in the 1860s clearly would not hold in the 1870s and beyond.

Notes to Chapter VIII

1.   Zvantsov, "A.N. Serov," 681-82.

2.   "Muzykal'nye zametki," *St. P. ved.,* 10 February 1871, p. 1.

3.   Instead of the title *direktor* that Rubinstein and Zaremba had held, Azanchevsky was officially *zaveduiushchii* or manager of the school, but this was only a semantic distinction, not a practical one.

4.   Kremlev, *Leningradskaia konservatoriia,* pp. 21, 25-26; Findeizen, *Ocherk RMO,* pp. 47-48.

5.   "Musykal'nye zametki," *St. P. ved.,* 6 October 1870, p. 2.

6.   Alston, *Education and the State,* pp. 78-87.

7.   Leningrad Conservatory, *100 let,* pp. 29-30.

8.   *Ibid.*

9.   Findeizen, *Ocherk RMO,* p. 51; Kremlev, *Leningradskaia konservatoriia,* p. 26.

10.   The entire document appears in Vul'fius, *Iz istorii konservatorii,* pp. 40-45.

11.   M. Chaikovskii, *Zhizn' Chaikovskogo,* 1:163; Leningrad Conservatory, *100 let,* p. 20.

12.   Rimsky-Korsakov, *My Musical Life,* p. 119; Borodin to his wife, 21 September 1871, in Borodin, *Pis'ma,* 1:294.

13.   Rimsky-Korsakov, *My Musical Life,* p. 124.

14.   See, for example, *Glinka i ego znachenie v istorii muzyki* [Glinka and his significance in the history of music] (Moscow: Universitetskaia tipografiia, 1868), originally published as

articles in *Russkii vestnik,* October 1867, January, September, and October 1868, and reprinted in Larosh, *Izbrannye stat'i,* 1:33-157.

15. Auer, *My Long Life,* p. 152.

16. Kremlev, *Russkaia mysl' o muzyke,* 2:355-56, 528.

17. Letters quoted in Orlova, *Stranitsy zhizni Rimskogo,* 2:55.

18. *My Musical Life,* pp. 115-17.

19. Stasov to Rimsky-Korsakov, 19 April 1870, in Rimskii-Korsakov, *Polnoe sobranie,* 5:332.

20. Letter of 21 September 1871 in Borodin, *Pis'ma,* 1:293.

21. Letter to his mother of 15 July 1871, quoted in Orlova, *Stranitsy zhizni Rimskogo,* 2:55.

22. *My Musical Life,* p. 16.

23. Letter of 21 September 1871 in Borodin, *Pis'ma,* 1:294-95.

24. *Izbrannye stat'i,* p. 186.

25. Solovtsov, *Zhizn' Rimskogo-Korsakova,* p. 558. Rimsky also taught Alexander Glazunov and Igor Stravinsky but as private pupils, not Conservatory students.

26. Nikolai Fedorovich Findeizen, "50-letie S.-Peterburgskoi Konservatorii (1862-1912)" [The 50th anniversary of the St. Petersburg Conservatory (1862-1912)], *Russkaia muzykal'naia gazeta* 19, no. 51 (1912):1129.

27. Findeizen, *Ocherk RMO,* pp. 55-57.

28. See, for example, Borodin to his wife, 16 November 1869, in Borodin, *Pis'ma,* 1:168; and Joseph Joachim to his wife, 17 January 1872, in Joachim and Moser, *Briefe Joseph Joachims,* 3:88.

29. Findeizen, *Ocherk RMO,* p. 59-60.

30. Lisovskii, "Letopis' A.G. Rubinshteina," p. 618; Kremlev, *Leningradskaia konservatoriia,* p. 40.

31. Kashkin, *Stat'i o russkoi muzyke,* p. 25.

32. "Iz neizdannykh vospominanii," p. 1184.

33. Liapunova, *Balakirev: letopis',* p. 184.

34. V. Rimskii-Korsakov, "Iz semeinoi perepiski," p. 78.

35. Rimsky-Korsakov, *My Musical Life,* pp. 118-19, 150.

36.   Letter to N. von Meck of 23 December 1877 in P. Chaikovskii, *Polnoe sobranie*, 6:329.

37.   Solovtsov, *Zhizn' Rimskogo-Korsakova*, pp. 134-36.

38.   Letter to L. Shestakova, 30 July 1868, in Musorgskii, *Literaturnoe nasledie*, 1:100.

39.   *My Musical Life*, p. 100.

40.   Letter to V. Stasov of 27 March 1881 in *Perepiska*, 2:15.

41.   Letter to A. and N. Purgold of 9 July 1870 in Rimskii-Korsakov, *Polnoe sobranie*, 5:491.

42.   Letter of 13 July 1872 in Musorgskii, *Literaturnoe nasledie*, 1:136.

43.   Letter to V. Stasov of 26 December 1872 *ibid*, 1:142.

44.   See, for example, "Muzykal'nye zametki," *St. P. ved.*, 11 April 1872, p. 2.

45.   This review is unaccountably not included in Kiui, *Izbrannye stat'i*, but the bulk of it is reprinted in Orlova, *Trudy i dni Musorgskogo*, pp. 355-60.

46.   Letter to V. Stasov of 6 February 1874 in Musorgskii, *Literaturnoe nasledie*, 1:175-76.

47.   Orlova, *Trudy i dni Musorgskogo*, p. 360.

48.   Taruskin, "Opera and Drama," pp. 549-50.

49.   *Ibid.*, pp. 556-603.

50.   Letter to his wife of 20 September 1871 in Borodin, *Pis'ma*, 1:291-92.

51.   Borodin to his wife, 15 March 1871, *ibid.*, 1:205.

52.   Borodin to his wife, 4 March 1870, *ibid.*, 1:200.

53.   See, for example, *Selected Essays*, p. 109.

54.   Letter of 19 April 1870 in Rimskii-Korsakov, *Polnoe sobranie*, 5:332.

55.   See, for example, his letter to Borodin, 28 December 1871, in Dianin, *Borodin: zhizneopisanie*, p. 194.

56.   Letter of 6 February 1874 in Musorgskii, *Literaturnoe nasledie*, 1:176.

57.   Liapunova, *Balakirev: letopis'*, p. 160.

58.   Letter of 1 June 1869 in Rimskii-Korsakov, *Polnoe sobranie*, 5:96.

59.   Letter of 1 December 1869 in Balakirev, *Vospominaniia*, p. 147.

60. Rimsky-Korsakov, *My Musical Life*, p. 108.

61. Letters of 4 October and 1 December 1869 in Balakirev, *Vospominaniia*, pp. 138, 147.

62. Borodin to his wife, 20 October 1870, in Borodin, *Pis'ma*, 1:234.

63. Borodin to Balakirev, 28 October 1870, *ibid.*, 1:255.

64. Edward Garden, *Balakirev: A Critical Study of His Life and Music* (New York: St. Martin's Press, 1967), p. 40; Frid, "M.A. Balakirev," p. 17.

65. Borodin's voluminous correspondence with his wife from 1869 through 1871 mentions dozens of musical gatherings attended by various members of the group, but beginning in late 1870 Balakirev was conspicuously absent. See Borodin, *Pis'ma*, 1:99-323.

66. Borodin to his wife, 16 December 1870, in Borodin, *Pis'ma*, 1:283.

67. Letter of 22 February 1871 in V. Stasov, "Pis'ma k A.N. Molas," p. 89.

68. Liapunova, *Balakirev: letopis'*, p. 189.

69. Editor's introduction to Balakirev and V. Stasov, *Perepiska*, 1:15.

70. Letters to Vladimir Zhemchuzhnikov of 22 and 23 January 1871 in Balakirev, *Vospominaniia*, pp. 103-4.

71. Letter to Jan Kollar, 27 May 1900, quoted in Liapunova, *Balakirev: letopis'*, pp. 195-96.

72. Letter to V. Zhemchuzhnikov in Balakirev, *Vospominaniia*, p. 105.

73. Frid, "M.A. Balakirev," p. 26.

74. M.V. Volkonskaia, "Za 38 let: otryvki iz neizdannykh vospominanii; posviashchaiutsia pamiati Miliia Alekseevicha Balakireva" [38 years: excerpts from unpublished memoirs; dedicated to the memory of Mily Alexeevich Balakirev], *Russkaia starina* 153 (1913):98-99.

75. *Ibid.*, p. 97.

76. V. Stasov to his daughter, S.V. Medvedeva, 11 October 1872, in Stasov, *Pis'ma k rodnym*, 1, pt. 2:92.

77. Stasov to Rimsky-Korsakov, 17 April 1871, in Rimskii-Korsakov, *Polnoe sobranie*, 5:341.

78. Letter to his wife of 24-25 October 1871 in Borodin, *Pis'ma*, 1:311-13.

79. Letter to V. Zhemchuzhnikov, 4 October 1871, in Balakirev, *Vospominaniia*, p. 106.

80. Letter to his wife, 17 October 1871, in Borodin, *Pis'ma*, 1:308.

81. Liapunova, *Balakirev: letopis'*, p. 198.

82.   Musorgsky to V. Stasov, 26 December 1872, in Musorgskii, *Literaturnoe nasledie,* 1:142-43.

83.   Letter of 14 January 1873 in Borodin, *Pis'ma,* 2:23.

84.   V. Stasov to Balakirev, 15 March 1873, in Vladimir Vasil'evich Stasov, *Pis'ma k deiateliam russkoi kul'tury* [Letters to Russian cultural figures], ed. N.D. Chernikova, 2 vols. (Moscow: Izdatel'stvo Akademii Nauk SSSR, 1962-67), 1:99-100.

85.   Letter of 15 March 1873 in *Perepiska,* 1:285-86.

86.   Letter to L. Shestakova of 11 July 1872 in Musorgskii, *Literaturnoe nasledie,* 1:133.

87.   *Izbrannye stat'i,* p. 233.

88.   "Muzykal'nye zametki," *St. P. ved.,* 17 February 1873, p. 1.

89.   Solovtsov, *Zhizn' Rimskogo-Korsakova,* pp. 127-28.

90.   Olkhovsky, "Vladimir Stasov," p. 223.

91.   Arsenii Arkad'evich Golenishchev-Kutuzov, "Vospominaniia o M.P. Musorgskom" [Memoirs about M.P. Musorgskii], in M.V. Ivanov-Boretskii, ed., *Muzykal'noe nasledstvo: Sbornik materialov po istorii muzykal'noi kul'tury v Rossii* [Musical heritage: a collection of materials on the history of musical culture in Russia] (Moscow: Gosudarstvennoe muzykal'noe izdatel'stvo, 1935), p. 23.

92.   Letter to L. Karmalina, 1 June 1876, in Borodin, *Pis'ma,* 2:107-8.

93.   Garden, *Balakirev,* pp. 108, 111.

Conclusion

The turbulent history of musical life in St. Petersburg from 1859 to 1873 explored here remains one of the most consequential chapters in modern Russian cultural history. Its character and importance have been distorted, however, by the persistent power of the Romantic notion that serious composers are pure servants of art unsullied by personal ambition, by a general acceptance in the twentieth century of the validity of nationalist principles, at least in cultural matters, and by the later prominence of the Balakirev circle. Modern historians and musicologists have been only too willing to see the contest exclusively as a clash of ideals and principles. This in turn has virtually guaranteed the members of the Balakirev circle favorable treatment, for they claimed to be the champions of national values, a cause that is now usually viewed with approbation, and because their eventual recognition as Russia's most talented musicians of the 1860s has seemed to give them greater claim than Anton Rubinstein or Serov to be considered true "idealist-artists" in the mold of the Romantic stereotype.

A favorable view of the Balakirev circle has been encouraged further by the work of their principal publicists, Vladimir Stasov and César Cui. Stasov devoted his life to fostering what he considered Russian national art. A recent study of his role in promoting the work of the Russian painters known as the "Peredvizhniki" has shown how he shaped their image as a narrowly conceived national school and eventually persuaded both the Russian intelligentsia and the painters themselves to accept this view.[1] He did much the same for the Balakirev circle, publicizing them within Russia as a unified band of selfless artists working exclusively to create and foster Russian national music. Cui spread the same message abroad with his book *La Musique en Russie,* which was published in Paris in 1880. As the first general study of Russian music in a Western European language, this work had enormous influence on the Western view of the rivalry between the Balakirev circle and the Russian Musical Society. In it Cui portrayed his own camp as a united group of progressive artists "seeking neither profit nor success but stimulated only by a great love of art, by the fire of its ideals."[2] This is the myth that has continued to dominate both Russian and Western literature on the Balakirev circle to the present. Some musicologists have admitted that the members of the circle ceased to be a united band with common ideals and goals once they achieved artistic maturity,[3] but the purity of their motives or the correctness of their ideals have not been called into question.

Against such idealized competition, Anton Rubinstein and Alexander Serov have not fared very well. Neither wrote music of the stature of the best works of the Balakirev circle; therefore, according to the Romantic image of the true artist, their motives are more subject to suspicion than are those of Balakirev and his followers. Furthermore, neither Rubinstein nor Serov was as fortunate as the Balakirev circle in winning long-term favorable publicity. Serov wrote copiously for the press, of course, but after his death in 1871 no one took up the task of keeping his name and works before the public. Rubinstein rarely wrote for publication, and he never had a public spokesman with the talent or tenacity of Vladimir Stasov. Rubinstein had the additional handicap of having opposed national values in art. Although at least one Soviet scholar has attempted to portray him as a secret supporter of Russian national music, his effort to endow Rubinstein with traits now in favor in the Soviet Union is not convincing.[4] The majority of other scholars, East and West, depict him as a champion of sterile cosmopolitanism, unable to appreciate the new, "progressive," national development of music. Historians have thus tended to ignore the part that both Rubinstein and Serov played in Russia's musical development in the 1860s or else to treat them as retrograde and narrow-minded, perhaps even unscrupulous, enemies of the noble and progressive Balakirev circle.

This study has demonstrated the inaccuracy and inadequacy of the traditional interpretations of this period in Russian musical history. The rivalries simply cannot be explained wholly in terms of differences of opinion and taste. The leaders of the Russian Musical Society, Serov, and the members of Balakirev's circle all espoused high principles, but they worked to popularize their ideals as much for their personal benefit as for any selfless cause. Their efforts to win public support for their various musical ideologies were linked intimately with their own ambitions to carve out musical careers. Much of the heat of the battle among Serov, the Balakirev circle, and the Russian Musical Society resulted not from the friction of ideologies but from the keen competition for the very few opportunities for even the most gifted Russian musician to achieve success in St. Petersburg. The intense personal dislike that developed among the chief competitors for leadership of musical activity in the Russian capital added fuel to the flames. Personality conflicts, envy, and unvarnished prejudice all combined to embitter the relations of the leading figures.

In so far as the rivalries of the 1860s had an ideological basis, they centered mainly around the question of musical modernism, not nationalism. The national issue was valuable for winning support from certain circles of St. Petersburg society, but it was of little importance in determining the membership of any particular party or predicting whose music would win its support. The Russian Musical Society under Anton Rubinstein did not shun Russian music, nor did the Balakirev circle always support it.

Viewed in this light, the contest between the Russian Musical Society, Serov, and the Balakirev circle appears in an entirely new perspective. It ceases to be a struggle of nationalism against cosmopolitanism, liberalism against conservatism, good against evil, and becomes instead a rivalry between talented and ambitious men intent on building careers in music. Faced with the obstacles of a poorly developed public musical life controlled by a conservative government bureaucracy and a musical public that was at best indifferent to music by native composers, these men all had to employ every means available to further their own positions. All the parties relied heavily on the influence of highly-placed friends and partisan criticism in the press to win recognition from the government and support from the public. None of the parties could risk compromising for long with rival factions; the stakes were too high and the chances of success already too small.

Ironically, the efforts of Rubinstein, Balakirev, and the other figures discussed in this study produced greater benefits for their successors and Russian musical culture in general than for themselves. They all achieved considerable public notice, but it was often unfavorable. Rubinstein's career as director of the RMS and the St. Petersburg Conservatory was cut short by his disputes with other leaders of the Society, Balakirev never achieved a position as prestigious or secure as Rubinstein's, and Serov was unable to parlay the outstanding success of his opera *Rogneda* into a permanent appointment in St. Petersburg's musical life. Nevertheless, their labors in the 1860s revolutionized Russian musical culture. Rubinstein, through the Russian Musical Society, brought about the professionalization of music in Russia. He not only made it possible for Russians to acquire advanced music education at home, he also won government recognition of music as a profession equal to painting, architecture, or acting. At the same time, Balakirev and his circle developed the various elements that have become known collectively as the Russian national style of composition and that first won Russian music international renown. It was the combination of these two developments that allowed Russia to achieve autonomy in the world of music in the last third of the nineteenth century. Until 1860 foreign composers and performers dominated musical life in Russia. Even the few native composers of secular art music for the most part imitated Western models. By the 1870s, however, the country had acquired the means to train its own musicians and a distinctive school of composition that could make a valuable contribution to world music. In conjuction, these two factors resulted in Russia's emergence in the late nineteenth and the twentieth centuries as the producer of dozens of composers and performing artists of international caliber. Thus, the work of the Balakirev circle and the Russian Musical Society gave birth to one of the most important musical traditions of the modern world.

Nevertheless, this was probably achieved more in spite of than because of the rivalries discussed in this study. Neither Balakirev nor Serov would accept the value of professional music education, and the leaders of the Russian Musical Society were slow to acknowledge the importance of the new music being created by their severest critics. Instead, each party did its best to denigrate and defeat the others. Certainly the heat of the battle attracted attention to all the groups and stimulated them to intense activity, but it also channeled a great deal of energy into unproductive polemics and contests and won all the parties a certain amount of public distrust for their obvious biases. The greatest casualty of all from St. Petersburg's musical rivalries of the 1860s was undoubtedly Balakirev himself. Although he resumed musical work in the late 1870s, both composing and conducting, he never recovered fully from the nervous breakdown he suffered in the early 1870s at least in part due to the strain of his struggle with the Russian Musical Society. His enormous gifts as a composer, teacher, and conductor were never again as fully applied as they were in the 1860s; he never again played a central role in St. Petersburg's musical life. Thus, while the rivalries of the 1860s brought to the fore the two trends that were to produce the great school of Russian music, they also probably delayed the very fruitful combination of professionalism and a distinctive national style that eventually won Russian music international fame, and the struggle contributed to the premature end of the promising career of one of Russia's most talented musicians.

Despite this high price, the parties to the rivalries made impressive gains and accomplished much considering the circumstances under which they worked. Aside from artistic achievements, capped by Musorgsky's *Boris Godunov,* one cannot help but be struck by their success in changing the organizational structure and government regulation of musical life in the Russian capital. In the face of the conservative, supposedly immovable, Russian bureaucracy, these private citizens, on their own initiative, managed to found concert societies and music schools, to modify the legal requirements for the privileged status of "free artist" to include musicians, and to rescind the 1827 regulations limiting royalties and payments to Russian musicians by the state theaters. Without government encouragement and sometimes even against direct government opposition, these men expanded the scope and resources of musical life in the Russian capital, forced the public and the government to take Russian music seriously, and made music a respectable, legally recognized profession. This, perhaps, rather than any supposed reflection of the conflict between Slavophiles and Westernizers, is the most significant part of the story of the musical rivalries of the 1860s for a general understanding of nineteenth-century Russian history. Indeed, the question of nationalism was not essential to the contest among Serov, the Balakirev circle, and the RMS. Theirs was not a rivalry of Slavophile versus Westernizer, regardless of the superficial similarities. It was, however, part of the general revival of Russian society after the stultifying reign of Nicholas I. For the first time in many years private citizens of the Russian Empire had the opportunity to speak out for change, to undertake new public projects, to affect directly the development of Russian society. Without such opportunities, the musical rivalries would have been impossible; with them, native musicians were able to carve out positions for themselves in St. Petersburg and thus begin the process of Russianizing musical life in Russia.

Notes to the Conclusion

1. Elizabeth Valkenier, *Russian Realist Art: The State and Society: The Peredvizhniki and Their Tradition* (Ann Arbor, Mich.: Ardis, 1977), pp. 52-62.

2. *La Musique en Russie,* pp.70-79, 111-12.

3. See, for example, Iurii Vsevolodovich Keldysh, "Musorgskii i problema nasledstva proshlogo" [Musorgsky and the problem of the legacy of the past], in Keldysh, *M.P. Musorgskii,* p. 8; Calvocoressi, *Masters of Russian Music,* pp. 112-13.

4. Barenboim, *A.G. Rubinshtein, passim.*

Bibliography

This book is based on published sources because I was denied placement in the Soviet Union, by the Soviet authorities, for the International Research and Exchanges Board fellowship I received to undertake archival research. Fortunately, the array of printed documents, criticism, letters, and memoirs is very extensive, and the secondary literature is enormous.

Sources

Asaf'ev, Boris Vladimirovich [Igor' Glebov]. *Anton Grigor'evich Rubinshtein v ego muzykal'noi deiatel'nosti i otzyvakh sovremennikov* [Anton Grigorievich Rubinstein in his musical activity and reviews of his contemporaries]. Moscow: Gosudarstvennoe izdatel'stvo, Muzykal'nyi sektor, 1929.

Auer, Leopold, *My Long Life in Music*. New York: Frederick A. Stokes, 1923.

Balakirev, Milii Alekseevich. "Avtobiograficheskie zametki M.A. Balakireva (Iz pisem ego k N. Findeizenu 1903 i 1907 g.)" [Autobiographical notes of M.A. Balakirev (from his letters to N. Findeizin of 1903 an 1907)]. *Russkaia muzykal'naia gazeta* 17, no. 41 (1910):861-62.

———. "Iz perepiski M.A. Balakireva" [From the correspondence of M.A. Balakirev]. *Russkaia muzykal'naia gazeta* 18, no. 38-39 (1911):749-54, 777-83.

———. *Perepiska s N.G. Rubinshteinom i s M.P. Beliaevym* [Correspondence with N.G. Rubinstein and M.P. Beliaev]. Edited by V.A. Kiselev. Moscow: Gosudarstvennoe muzykal'noe izdatel'stvo, 1956.

———. "Pis'ma M.A. Balakireva k A.P. Arsen'evu" [M.A. Balakirev's letters to A.P. Arseniev]. *Russkaia muzykal'naia gazeta* 17, no. 41-42 (1911):867-74, 897-902.

———. *Vospominaniia i pis'ma* [Memoirs and letters]. Edited by Emiliia Lazarevna Frid. Leningrad: Gosudarstvennoe muzykal'noe izdatel'stvo, 1962.

Balakirev, Milii Alekseevich, and Stasov, Vladimir Vasil'evich. *Perepiska* [Correspondence]. Edited by Anastasiia Sergeevna Liapunova. 2 vols. Moscow: Muzyka, 1970-1971.

Berlioz, Hector. *A Selection from His Letters*. Edited by Humphrey Searle. New York: Harcourt Brace & World, 1966.

Bessel', Vasilii Vasil'evich. "Moi vospominaniia ob Antone Grigor'eviche Rubinshteine" [My memoirs about Anton Grigorievich Rubinstine]. *Russkaia starina* 94 (1898):351-74.

Boborykin, Petr. *Vospominaniia* [Memoirs]. Edited by E. Vilenskaia and L. Roitberg. 2 vols. Moscow: Khudozhestvennaia literatura, 1965.

Borodin, Aleksandr Porfir'evich. *Pis'ma A.P. Borodina* [Letters of A.P. Borodin]. Edited by Sergei Dianin. 4 vols. Moscow: Gosudarstvennoe izdatel'stvo, Muzykal'nyi sektor, 1927/28-1950.

Borodina, Al. "Moe vospominanie ob A.S. Dargomyzhskom" [My memoirs about A.S. Dargomyzhsky]. *Russkaia starina* 165 (1916):25-44.

Bychkov, I.A., compiler, "Iz perepiski kniazia V.F. Odoevskogo" [From the correspondence of Prince V.F. Odoevsky]. *Russkaia starina* 17 (1877):372-85, 705-16; 18 (1877):367-78, 569-90; 19 (1877):151-66, 413-42.

Chaikovskii, Petr Il'ich. *Muzykal'no-kriticheskie stat'i* [Musico-critical articles]. Second edition. Edited by Vasilii Iakovlev. Moscow: Gosudarstvennoe muzykal'noe izdatel'stvo, 1953.

————. *Polnoe sobranie sochinenii* [Complete writings]. Moscow: Gosudarstvennoe muzykal'noe izdatel'stvo, 1959-

Cui, César. See Kiui, Tsezar.

Dargomyzhskii, Aleksandr Sergeevich. "Aleksandr Sergeevich Dargomyzhskii: Materialy dlia ego biografii, 1813-1869" [Alexander Sergeevich Dargomyzhsky: materials for his biography, 1813-1869]. Compiled by Vladimir Vasil'evich Stasov. *Russkaia starina* 12 (1875):339-58, 565-74, 797-811; 13 (1875):101-10, 259-66, 416-35.

————. *Izbrannye pis'ma* [Selected letters]. Edited by M.S. Pekelis. Moscow: Gosudarstvennoe muzykal'noe izdatel'stvo, 1952.

Dianin, Sergei. *Borodin: Zhizneopisanie, materialy i dokumenty* [Borodin: a biography, materials and documents]. Second edition. Moscow: Gosudarstvennoe muzykal'noe izdatel'stvo, 1960.

Glinka, Mikhail Ivanovich. *Literaturnoe nasledie* [Literary legacy]. Edited by V.M. Bogdanov-Berezovskii. 2 vols. Leningrad: Gosudarstvennoe muzykal'noe izdatel'stvo, 1952-1953.

————. *Memoirs*. Translated by Richard B. Mudge. Norman, Oklahoma: University of Oklahoma Press, 1963.

Golenishchev-Kutuzov, Arsenii Arkad'evich. "Vospominaniia o M.P. Musorgskom" [Memoirs about M.P. Musorgsky]. In M.V. Ivanov-Boretskii, editor. *Muzykal'noe nasledstvo: Sbornik materialov po istorii muzykal'noi kul'tury v Rossii* [Musical heritage: a collection of materials on the history of musical culture in Russia], pp. 13-30. Moscow: Gosudarstvennoe muzykal'noe izdatel'stvo, 1935.

Gusin, I. "Iz istorii russkoi opery" [From the history of Russian opera]. *Sovetskaia muzyka,* September 1954, pp. 75-77.

Hiller, Ferdinand. *Erinnerungsblatter.* Cologne: M. Dumont-Schauberg, 1884.

Iakovlev, Vasilii, editor. *Dni i gody P.I. Chaikovskogo: Letopis' zhizni i tvorchestva* [The days and years of P.I. Tchaikovsky: a chronicle of his life and work]. Moscow: Gosudarstvennoe muzykal'noe izdatel'stvo, 1940.

————. "Musorgskii v vospominaniiakh i nabliudeniiakh sovremennikov" [Musorgsky in the memoirs and observations of his contemporaries]. In Iurii Vsevolodovich Keldysh and Vasilii Iakovlev, editors. *M.P. Musorgskii: K piatidesiatiletiiu so dnia smerti, 1881-1931: Stat'i i materialy* [M.P. Musorgsky: on the fiftieth anniversary of the day of his death, 1881-1931: articles and materials], pp. 106-66. Moscow: Gosudarstvennoe muzykal'noe izdatel'stvo, 1932.

"Iz zabytykh pisem i vospominanii" [From forgotten letters and memoirs], *Sovetskaia muzyka,* December 1966, pp. 101-8.

Joachim, Johannes, and Moser, Andreas, compilers. *Briefe von und an Joseph Joachim.* 3 vols. Berlin: Julius Bard, 1911-1913.

Kashkin, Nikolai Dmitrievich. *Stat'i o russkoi muzyke i muzykantakh* [Articles about Russian music and musicians]. Edited by S.I. Shlifshtein. Moscow: Gosudarstvennoe muzykal'noe izdatel'stvo, 1953.

————. *Vospominaniia o P.I. Chaikovskom* [Memoirs about P.I. Tchaikovsky]. Moscow: P. Iurgenson, 1896.

Kiui, Tsezar. *Izbrannye pis'ma* [Selected letters]. Edited by I.L. Gusin. Leningrad: Gosudarstvennoe muzykal'noe izdatel'stvo, 1952.

————. *Izbrannye stat'i* [Selected articles]. Edited by I.L. Gusin. Leningrad: Gosudarstvennoe muzykal'noe izdatel'stvo, 1952.

_____ . "Muzykal'nye zametki" [Musical notes]. *Sankt-Peterburgskie vedomosti*, 1864-1873.

Kropotkin, Peter. *Memoirs of a Revolutionist*. New York: Horizon Press, 1968.

Kruglikov, S.N. "Vospominaniia ob A.P. Borodine, zapisannye S.N. Kruglikovym" [Reminiscences about A.P. Borodin, recorded by S.N. Kruglikov]. *Muzykal'noe nasledstvo: Sborniki po istorii muzykal'noi kul'tury SSSR* [Musical legacy: collections on the history of musical culture in the U.S.S.R.] 4 vols. Moscow: Gosudarstvennoe muzykal'noe izdatel'stvo, 1962-1976. 3:241-52.

L[alaev], M. [S.] "Ital'ianskaia opera v Peterburge: Sezon 1861-1862 goda" [The Italian Opera in Petersburg: the season of 1861-1862]. *Sovremennik* (Sovremennoe obozrenie) 91 (January-February 1862):51-82.

_____ . "Ital'ianskaia opera v Peterburge: Sezon 1862-1863 goda" [The Italian Opera in Petersburg: the season of 1862-1863]. *Sovremennik* (Sovremennoe obozrenie) 94 (January-February 1863):199-227.

Larosh, German Avgustovich. "Anton Grigor'evich Rubinshtein: v vospominaniiakh byv. uchenika Spb. konservatorii" [Anton Grigorievich Rubinstein: in the memoirs of a former student of the St. Petersburg Conservatory]. *Russkaia starina* 64 (1889):589-600.

_____ . *Glinka i ego znachenie v istorii muzyki* [Glinka and his significance in the history of music]. Moscow: Universitetskaia tipografiia, 1868.

_____ . *Izbrannye stat'i* [Selected articles]. Edited by Abram Akimovich Gozenpud. 5 vols. Leningrad: Muzyka, 1974- .

_____ . *Sobranie muzykal'no-kriticheskikh statei* [Collected musico-critical articles]. 2 vols. Moscow: Muzykal'no-Teoreticheskaia Biblioteka v Moskve and Gosudarstvennoe muzykal'noe izdatel'stvo, 1913-1922.

_____ . "Vospominaniia o P.I. Chaikovskom" [Memoirs about P.I. Tchaikovsky]. In V.V. Protopopov, editor. *Vospominaniia o P.I. Chaikovskom*. Moscow: P. Iurgenson, 1896.

Leonova, Dar'ia Mikhailovna. "Vospominaniia artistki imperatorskikh teatrov D.M. Leonovoi" [Memoirs of D.M. Leonova, artist of the Imperial theaters]. *Istoricheskii vestnik* 43 (1891):120-44, 326-51, 632-59; 44 (1891):73-85.

Liapunova, Anastasiia Sergeevna, and Iazovitskaia, E.E., compilers. *Milii Alekseevich Balakirev: Letopis' zhizni i tvorchestva* [Mily Alexeevich Balakirev: a chronicle of his life and work]. Leningrad: Muzyka, 1967.

Lomakin, Gavriil Iakimovich. "Avtobiograficheskie zapiski, s primechaniiami V.V. Stasova" [Autobiographical notes, with annotations by V.V. Stasov]. *Russkaia starina* 49 (1886):645-66; 50 (1886):311-26, 675-89; 51 (1886):467-85.

M—ch, B. "Russkoe muzykal'noe obshchestvo (K izdateliu Severnoi Pchely)" [The Russian Musical Society (to the editor of *Severnaia pchela*)]. *Severnaia pchela*, 19 May 1861, pp. 453-54.

Musorgskii, Modest Petrovich. *Literaturnoe nasledie* [Literary legacy]. Edited by M.S. Pekelis. 2 vols. Moscow: Muzyka, 1971-1972.

Napravnik, Eduard Frantsevich. *Avtobiograficheskie tvorcheskie materialy, dokumenty, pis'ma* [Autobiographical creative materials, documents, letters]. Edited by Iurii Vsevolodovich Keldysh. Leningrad: Gosudarstvennoe muzykal'noe izdatel'stvo, 1959.

Nazimova, Mar'ia Grigor'evna. "Dvor Velikoi Kniagini Eleny Pavlovny (1865-1867)" [The court of Grand Duchess Elena Pavlovna (1865-1867)]. *Russkii arkhiv* 37, pt. 3 (1899):311-18.

Nikitenko, Aleksandr Vasil'evich. *Dnevnik* [Diary]. Edited by I.Ia. Aizenshtok. 3 vols. Leningrad: Gosudarstvennoe izdatel'stvo khudozhestvennoi literatury, 1955-1956.

Obolenskii, Dmitrii Aleksandrovich. "Moi vospominaniia o Velike Kniagine Elene Pavlovne" [My memoirs about Grand Duchess Elena Pavlovna]. *Russkaia starina* 137 (1909):503-28; 138 (1909):37-62, 260-77.

Odoevskii, Vladimir Fedorovich. "Dnevnik V.F. Odoevskogo, 1859-69 gg." [The diary of V.F. Odoevsky, 1859-69]. *Literaturnoe nasledstvo* 22/24 (1935).

————— . *Muzykal'no-literaturnoe nasledie* [Musico-literary legacy]. Edited by G.B. Bernandt. Moscow: Gosudarstvennoe muzykal'noe izdatel'stvo, 1956.

Onnore, Irina Ivanovna. "Odinnadtsat' let v teatre (Iz vospominanii artisticheskoi zhizni Iriny Ivanovny Onnore, byvshei pevitsy Imperatorskogo Moskovskogo teatra, nyne professora peniia v Peterburge)" [Eleven years in the theater (from the memoirs of the artistic life of Irina Ivanovna Onnore, former singer at the Imperial Moscow Theater, now a professor of singing in Petersburg)]. *Russkaia starina* 141 (1910):95-108, 543-54; 149 (1912):160-72, 316-26.

Orlova, Aleksandra Anatol'evna, compiler. *Trudy i dni M.P. Musorgskogo: Letopis' zhizni i tvorchestva* [The works and days of M.P. Musorgsky: a chronicle of his life and work]. Moscow: Gosudarstvennoe muzykal'noe izdatel'stvo, 1963.

Orlova, Aleksandra Anatol'evna, and Rimskii-Korsakov, V.N., compilers. *Stranitsy zhizni N.A. Rimskogo-Korsakova: Letopis' zhizni i tvorchestva* [Pages on the life of N.A. Rimsky-Korsakov: a chronicle of his life and work]. 4 vols. Leningrad: Muzyka, 1970-1973.

Ostrovskii, Aleksandr Nikolaevich. *A.N. Ostrovskii i russkie kompozitory: Pis'ma* [A.N. Ostrovsky and Russian composers: letters]. Edited by E.M. Kolosova and V. Filippova. Moscow: Gosudarstvennoe muzykal'noe izdatel'stvo, 1937.

Otchet Russkogo muzykal'nogo obshchestva za 1862-1863 god [The annual report of the Russian Musical Society for 1862-1863]. St. Petersburg, 1864.

Patkul', Adjutant General. Report on the arrest of A.N. Serov at Alexander Lazarev's concert of 26 March 1861. *Russkii arkhiv* 21, pt. 3 (1883):202-3.

Protopopov, V.V., editor. *Vospominaniia o P.I. Chaikovskom* [Memoirs about P.I. Tchaikovsky]. Moscow: Gosudarstvennoe muzykal'noe izdatel'stvo, 1962.

Purgol'd, Aleksandra. "Dnevnik A. Purgol'd" [A. Purgold's diary]. *Sovetskaia muzyka*, May 1957, pp. 134-38.

R[appaport], M. Weekly music and theater reviews in *Syn otechestva* from June through December 1860.

Repin, Il'ia. *Dalekoe blizkoe* [Remote nearness]. Edited by Kornei Ivanovich Chukovskii. Moscow: Izdatel'stvo Akademii khudozhestv SSSR, 1960.

Rimskii-Korsakov, Nikolai Andreevich. *Polnoe sobranie sochinenii* [Complete writings]. Moscow: Gosudarstvennoe muzykal'noe izdatel'stvo, 1955- .

Rimskii-Korsakov, V. "Iz semeinoi perepiski" [From the family correspondence]. *Sovetskaia muzyka*, March 1969, pp. 76-85.

Rimsky-Korsakov, Nikolay Andreyevich. *My Musical Life.* Translated from the 5th revised Russian edition by Judah A. Joffe, edited by Carl Van Vechten. 3rd revised English edition. New York: Alfred A. Knopf, 1942.

R[ozenberg], M.B. "Anton Grigor'evich Rubinshtein: Zametki k ego biografii" [Anton Grigorievich Rubinstein: notes on his biography]. *Russkaia starina* 64 (1889):579-87.

Rubets, Aleksandr Ivanovich. "Vospominaniia o pervykh godakh Peterburgskoi konservatorii" [Memoirs about the first years of the St. Petersburg Conservatory]. *Novoe vremia*, 7 May 1912, p. 4; 21 May 1912, p. 3; 4 June 1912, p. 4; 11 June 1912, p. 4; 25 June 1912, p. 4.

Rubinshtein, Anton Grigor'evich. "Avtobiograficheskie rasskazy (1829-1889)" [Autobiographical accounts (1829-1889)]. In Lev Aronovich Barenboim. *Anton Grigor'evich Rubinshtein: Zhizn', artisticheskii put', tvorchestvo, muzykal'no-obshchestvennaia deiatel'nost'* [Anton Grigorievich Rubinstein: life, artistic course, creative work, musico-social activity]. 2 vols. Leningrad: Gosudarstvennoe muzykal'noe izdatel'stvo, 1957-1962. 1:399-421; 2:451-61.

————— . *Izbrannye pis'ma* [Selected letters]. Edited by Lev Aronovich Barenboim. Moscow: Gosudarstvennoe muzykal'noe izdatel'stvo, 1954.

Serov, Aleksandr Nikolaevich. "Aleksandr Nikolaevich Serov: Materialy dlia ego biografii, 1820-1871" [Alexander Nikolaevich Serov: materials for his biography, 1820-1871]. *Russkaia starina* 13 (1875):581-602; 14 (1876):328-39, 492-501; 15 (1876):130-43, 348-63, 853-70; 16 (1876):132-46; 17 (1877):787-810; 18 (1877):145-59, 363-68, 513-30, 683-98; 19 (1877):101-12; 20 (1878):335-46. 523-34; 21 (1878):151-76.

_____. "Iz pisem A.N. Serova"[From the letters of A.N. Serov]. *Sovetskaia muzyka*, July 1971, pp. 102-5.

_____. *Izbrannye stat'i* [Selected articles]. Edited by Georgii Khubov. 2 vols. Moscow: Gosudarstvennoe muzykal'noe izdatel'stvo, 1950-1957.

_____. "Pis'ma A.N. Serova k Iu.F. Abaze" [A.N. Serov's letters to Iu.F. Abaza]. *Biriuch petrogradskikh gosudarstvennykh akademicheskikh teatrov: Sbornik statei* [The herald of the Petrograd state academic theaters: a collection of articles], 2 (1920):242-56.

_____. "Pis'ma A.N. Serova k kniaziu Odoevskomu"[A.N. Serov's letters to Prince Odoevsky]. *Muzykal'naia starina: Sbornik statei i materialov dlia istorii muzyki v Rossii* [Musical antiquity: a collection of articles and materials on the history of music in Russia]. 4 (1907):118-41.

_____. *Pis'ma Aleksandra Nikolaevicha Serova k ego sestre S.N. Diu-Tour (1845-1861 gg.)* [Alexander Nikolaevich Serov's letters to his sister S.N. Du Tour(1845-1861)]. St. Petersburg: Tipografiia N. Findeizena, 1896.

_____. "Pis'ma k M. Balakirevu" [Letters to M. Balakirev]. *Sovetskaia muzyka*, May 1953, pp. 68-75.

_____. "Pis'ma k V.V. i D.V. Stasovym"[Letters to V.V. and D.V. Stasov]. In *Muzykal'noe nasledstvo: Sborniki po istorii muzykal'noi kul'tury SSSR*[Musical legacy: collections on the history of musical culture in the U.S.S.R.]. 4 vols. Moscow: Gosudarstvennoe muzykal'noe izdatel'stvo, 1962-1976. 1:11-312; 2, pt. 1:44-267; 3:27-207.

_____. "Pis'ma k V. Zhukovoi" [Letters to V. Zhukova]. *Sovetskaia muzyka*, August 1954, pp. 59-77.

_____. "Pis'mo A.N. Serova"[A letter of A.N. Serov]. *Russkii arkhiv* 52, pt. 1 (1914):449-54.

Serova, Valentina. *Serovy Aleksandr Nikolaevich i Valentin Aleksandrovich: Vospominaniia* [The Serovs, Alexander Nikolaevich and Valentin Alexandrovich: memoirs]. St. Petersburg: Izdatel'stvo "Shipovnik," 1914.

Shestakova, Liudmila Ivanovna. "Iz neizdannykh vospominanii o novoi russkoi shkole" [From unpublished memoirs about the new Russian school]. *Russkaia muzykal'naia gazeta* 20, nos, 51-52 (1913):1180-86.

_____. "Mikhail Ivanovich Glinka: V vospominaniiakh ego sestry L.I. Shestakovoi"[Mikhail Ivanovich Glinka: in the memoirs of his sister L.I. Shestakova]. *Russkaia starina* 44 (1884):593-604.

_____. "Moi vechera"[My soirées]. *Ezhegodnik imperatorskikh teatrov*, 1893-1894, appendix 2, pp. 119-40.

_____. "Poslednie gody zhizni i konchina M.I. Glinki: Vospominaniia sestry ego, L.I. Shestakovoi, 1854-1857"[The last years of the life and the death of M.I. Glinka: memoirs of his sister, L.I. Shestakova, 1854-1857]. *Russkaia starina* 2 (1870, 3rd ed.):410-31.

Sietz, Reinhold. *Aus Ferdinand Hillers Briefwechsel: Beiträge zu einer Biographie Ferdinand Hillers*. 7 vols. Cologne: Arno Volk-Verlag, 1958-1970.

Skal'kovskii, Konstantin Apollonovich. *V teatral'nom mire: Nabliudeniia, vospominaniia i razsuzhdeniia* [In the world of the theater: observations, memoirs, and discussions]. St. Petersburg: Tipografiia A.S. Suvorina, 1899.

_____. *Vospominaniia molodosti (Po moriu zhiteiskomu) 1843-1869*[Reminiscences of youth (on the sea of life) 1843-1869]. St. Petersburg: Tipografiia A.S. Suvorina, 1906.

Sokolov, Vladimir Timofeevich. "Aleksandr Sergeevich Dargomyzhskii v 1856-1869 gg." [Alexander Sergeevich Dargomyzhsky in 1856-1869]. *Russkaia starina* 46 (1885):339-66.

_____. "Iz moikh vospominanii" [From my memoirs]. *Istoricheskii vestnik* 37 (1889):528-49.

Starchevskii, Al'bert Vikent'evich. "Kompozitor A.N. Serov (Iz vospominanii)"[The composer A.N. Serov (from my memoirs)]. *Nabliudatel'* 7, no. 3 (March 1888):147-73.

Stasov, Vladimir Vasil'evich. *Izbrannye sochineniia (Zhivopis', Skul'ptura, Muzyka)* [Selected writings (painting, sculpture, music)]. Edited by E.D. Stasova, *et al.* 3 vols. Moscow: Iskusstvo, 1952.

_____ . *Izbrannye stat'i o muzyke* [Selected articles on music]. Leningrad: Gosudarstvennoe muzykal'noe izdatel'stvo, 1949.

_____ . "Mikhail Ivanovich Glinka: Novye materialy dlia ego biografii" [Mikhail Ivanovich Glinka: new materials for his biography]. *Russkaia starina* 61 (1889):387-400.

_____ . "Muzykal'nyi komitet" [The musical committee]. *Sankt-Peterburgskie vedomosti*, 1 January 1870, p. 2.

_____ . *Pis'ma k deiateliam russkoi kul'tury* [Letters to Russian cultural figures]. Edited by N.D. Chernikova. 2 vols. Moscow: Izdatel'stvo Akademii Nauk SSSR, 1962-1967.

_____ . *Pis'ma k rodnym* [Letters to relations]. Edited by Iurii Vsevolodovich Keldysh *et al.* 3 vols. Moscow: Gosudarstvennoe muzykal'noe izdatel'stvo, 1953-1962.

_____ . "Pis'ma V.V. Stasova k A.N. Molas" [V.V. Stasov's letters to A.N. Molas]. *Sovetskaia muzyka*, January 1949, pp. 86-91.

_____ . *Selected Essays on Music.* Translated by Florence Jonas. New York: Frederick A. Praeger, 1968.

_____ . "Zamechaniia na stat'iu g. Rubinshteina" [Remarks on Mr. Rubinstein's article]. *Severnaia pchela,* 24 February 1861, pp. 181-82.

Tchaikovskii, Petr Il'ich. See Chaikovskii, Petr Il'ich.

Timofeev, Grigorii. "M.A. Balakirev v Prage: Iz ego perepiski" [M.A. Balakirev in Prague: from his correspondence]. *Sovremennyi mir,* June 1911, pp. 147-86.

Tiutcheva, Anna Fedorovna. *Pri dvore dvukh imperatorov: Dnevnik 1855-1882* [At the court of two emperors: a diary 1855-1882]. Translated by E.V. Ger'e, edited by S.V. Bakhrushin. Moscow: Izdanie M. i S. Sabashnikovykh, 1929.

Tolstoi, Feofil Matveevich. "Aleksandr Nikolaevich Serov, 1820-1871 gg.: Vospominaniia Feofila Matveevicha Tolstogo" [Alexander Nikolaevich Serov, 1820-1871: memoirs of Feofil Matveevich Tolstoy]. *Russkaia starina* 9 (1874):339-80.

_____ . "K voprosu ob uprazdnenii, v vidakh ekonomicheskikh i patrioticheskikh ital'ianskoi opery i dramaticheskoi frantsuzskoi truppy" [On the question of abolishing the Italian Opera and the French drama troupe on economic and patriotic grounds]. *Severnaia pchela,* 22 February 1863, p. 197.

_____ . "Muz. obozrenie" [Musical review]. *Otechestvennye zapiski* 184, pt. 2 (1869):257-69.

_____ . "Neskol'ko slov o pervom predstavlenii opery 'Iudif' "[A few words about the first performance of *Judith*]. *Severnaia pchela,* 19 May 1863, p. 525.

_____ . "Zamechatel'nye iavleniia v Russkom muzykal'nom mire" [Remarkable events in the Russian musical world]. *Severnaia pchela,* 13 March 1863, p. 273.

_____ . "Zapadnaia reklama, perenesennaia na russkuiu pochvu" [Western publicity transferred to Russian soil]. *Severnaia pchela,* 14 May 1863, pp. 505-6.

Tumanina, N.V., editor. *Vospominaniia o Moskovskoi konservatorii* [Memoirs about the Moscow Conservatory]. Moscow: Muzyka, 1966.

Volkonskaia, M.V. "Za 38 let: Otryvki iz neizdannykh vospominanii; posviashchaiutsia pamiati Miliia Alekseevicha Balakireva" [38 years: excerpts from unpublished memoirs; dedicated to the memory of Mily Alexeevich Balakirev]. *Russkaia starina* 153 (1913):83-99, 301-17, 516-27; 154 (1913):107-21; 106 (1913):70-79, 251-57, 518-25; 157 (1914):175-96; 158 (1914):312-32.

Vul'fius, Pavel Aleksandrovich, editor. *Iz istorii Leningradskoi konservatorii: Materialy i dokumenty, 1862-1917* [From the history of the Leningrad Conservatory: materials and documents, 1862-1917]. Leningrad: Muzyka, 1964.

Wagner, Richard. *Mein Leben.* Edited by Martin Gregor-Dellin. 2 vols. Munich: Paul List Verlag, 1969.

Zvantsov, Konstantin Ivanovich. "Aleksandr Nikolaevich Serov v 1857-1871 gg.: Vospominaniia o nem i ego pis'ma" [Alexander Nikolaevich Serov, 1857-1871: memoirs about him, and his letters]. *Russkaia starina* 59 (1888):343-84, 647-82.

Secondary Literature

Abraham, Gerald. *Rimsky-Korsakov: A Short Biography*. London: Duckworth, 1945.

————. *Studies in Russian Music*. London: William Reeves, 1935.

Abramovskii, G., "Opera Serova 'Rogneda' " [Serov's opera *Rogneda*]. *Sovetskaia muzyka*, December 1976, pp. 92-101.

Akademiia nauk SSSR. Institut istorii. *Ocherk istorii Leningrada* [A survey of the history of Leningrad]. 6 vols. Moscow: Izdatel'stvo Akademii Nauk SSSR, 1955-1970.

Alston, Patrick L. *Education and the State in Tsarist Russia*. Stanford: Stanford University Press, 1969.

Amburger, Erik. *Geschichte der Behördenorganisation Russlands von Peter dem grossen bis 1917*. Leiden: E.J. Brill, 1966.

Asaf'ev, Boris Vladimirovich [Igor' Glebov]. "Iz zabytykh stranits russkoi muzyki" [From the forgotten pages of Russian music]. In A.N. Rimskii-Korsakov, editor. *Muzykal'naia letopis': Stat'i i materialy* [Musical chronicle: articles and materials]. 3 vols. Petrograd: Mysl', 1922-1925. 1:61-78.

Barenboim, Lev Aronovich. *Anton Grigor'evich Rubinshtein: Zhizn', artisticheskii put', tvorchestvo, muzykal'no-obshchestvennaia deiatel'nost'* [Anton Grigorievich Rubinstein: life, artistic course, creative work, musico-social activity]. 2 vols. Leningrad: Gosudarstvennoe muzykal'noe izdatel'stvo, 1957-1962.

Barzun, Jacques. *Berlioz and the Romantic Century*. 2 vols. Boston: Little, Brown and Company, 1950.

Bernandt, Gr. "Larosh: Neskol'ko shtrikhov k portretu" [Laroche: Several strokes for a portrait]. *Sovetskaia muzyka*, January 1975, pp. 110-15.

Bernatskii, V.A. "Iz zolotogo veka ital'ianskoi opery v Peterburge" [From the golden age of Italian opera in Petersburg]. *Russkaia starina* 168 (1916):17-24, 276-83, 434-56.

Brown, David. *Tchaikovsky: The Early Years 1840-1874*. New York: Norton, 1978.

Calvocoressi, Michel D. *A Survey of Russian Music*. Westport, Conn.: Greenwood Press, 1974. A reprint of the 1944 edition by Penguin Books, Middlesex, England.

Calvocoressi, Michel D., and Abraham, Gerald. *Masters of Russian Music*. New York: Tudor Publishing Company, 1944.

Chaikovskii, Modest Il'ich. *Zhizn' Petra Il'icha Chaikovskogo* [The life of Piotr Ilyich Tchaikovsky]. 3 vols. Moscow: P. Iurgenson, 1900-1902.

Cheshikhin, Vsevolod. *Istoriia russkoi opery: s 1674 po 1903 g.* [The history of Russian opera: from 1674 through 1903]. Second revised edition. Moscow: P. Iurgenson, 1905.

Clarkston, Jesse D. *A History of Russia*. Second edition. New York: Random House, 1969.

Cui, César. *La Musique en Russie*. Paris: Librarie Sandoz et Fischbacher, 1880. Reprinted in 1974 by Zentralantiquariat der Deutschen Demokratischen Republic, Leipzig.

Dement'ev, A.G.; Zapadov, A.V., and Cherepakhov, M.S., editors. *Russkaia periodicheskaia pechat' (1702-1894): Spravochnik* [The Russian periodical press (1702-1894): a guide]. Moscow: Gosudarstvennoe izdatel'stvo politicheskoi literatury, 1959.

Dianin, Sergei. *Borodin*. Translated by Robert Lord. London: Oxford University Press, 1963.

Druskin, Mikhail Semenovich. "Peterburg—Petrograd—Leningrad." *Sovetskaia muzyka*, July 1957, pp. 17-25.

Entsiklopedicheskii muzykal'nyi slovar' [The encyclopedic musical dictionary]. Second edition, revised and enlarged. Moscow: Izdatel'stvo "Sovetskaia entsiklopediia," 1966.

Findeizen, Nikolai Fedorovich. *Ocherk deiatel'nosti S.-Peterburgskogo otdeleniia imperator skogo Russkogo Muzykal'nogo Obshchestva (1859-1909)* [A survey of the work of the St. Petersburg branch of the Imperial Russian Musical Society (1859-1909)]. St. Petersburg: Tipografiia Glavnogo Upravleniia Udelov, 1909.

————. *Ocherki po istorii muzyki v Rossii: S drevneishikh vremen do kontsa XVIII veka* [A survey of the history of music in Russia: from earliest times to the end of the eighteenth century]. 2 vols. Moscow: Muzykal'nyi sektor Gosudarstvennogo izdatel'stva, 1928-1929.

————. "50-letie S. Peterburgskoi konservatorii (1862-1912)" [The 50th anniversary of the St. Petersburg Conservatory (1862-1912)]. *Russkaia muzykal'naia gazeta* 19, no. 51 (1912):1122-33.

Florinsky, Michael T. *Russia: A Short History.* New York: The Macmillan Co., 1964.

Frid, Emiliia Lazarevna. "Milii Alekseevich Balakirev (1837-1910)." In Emiliia Lazarevna Frid, editor. *Milii Alekseevich Balakirev: Issledovaniia i stat'i* [Mily Alexeevich Balakirev: research and articles]. Leningrad: Gosudarstvennoe muzykal'noe izdatel'stvo, 1961.

Garden, Edward. *Balakirev: A Critical Study of His Life and Music.* New York: St. Martin's Press, 1967.

Gatsiskii, A.S. "Aleksandr Dmitrievich Ulybyshev." *Russkii arkhiv* 24, pt. 1 (1886):55-68.

Gordeeva, Evgeniia Mikhailovna. *Moguchaia kuchka* [The mighty handful]. Second, enlarged edition. Moscow: Muzyka, 1966.

Gozenpud, Abram Akimovich. *Muzykal'nyi teatr v Rossii ot istokov do Glinki* [Musical theater in Russia from its beginnings to Glinka]. Leningrad: Gosudarstvennoe muzykal'noe izdatel'stvo, 1959.

————. "Neosushchestvlennyi opernyi zamysel" [An unrealized operatic idea]. In Emiliia Lazarevna Frid, editor. *Milii Alekseevich Balakirev: Issledovaniia i stat'i* [Mily Alexeevich Balakirev: research and articles], pp. 362-83. Leningrad: Gosudarstvennoe muzykal'noe izdatel'stvo, 1961.

————. "Opernoe tvorchestvo A.N. Serova" [The operatic creations of A.N. Serov]. *Sovetskaia muzyka,* July 1971, pp. 91-102.

————. *Russkii opernyi teatr XIX veka* [The Russian opera theater in the nineteenth century]. 3 vols. Leningrad: Muzyka, 1969-1973.

Grout, Donald Jay. *A History of Western Music.* Third edition. New York: Norton, 1980.

Iakovlev, Vasilii. "K istorii 'Raika' i 'Klassika' " [On the history of "The Peepshow" and "The Classicist"]. *Sovetskaia muzyka,* June 1967, pp. 103-7.

Isakhanova, N. "Put' k sovershenstvu" [The path to perfection]. *Sovetskaia muzyka,* July 1966, pp. 51-60.

Ivanov, M. "Pervoe desiatiletie postoiannogo ital'ianskogo teatra v Peterburge v XIX veka (1843-1853 gg.)" [The first decade of the permanent Italian theater in St. Petersburg in the nineteenth century (1843-1853)]. *Ezhegodnik imperatorskikh teatrov,* 1893-1894, appendix 2, pp. 55-95.

Keldysh, Iurii Vsevolodovich. "Musorgskii i problema nasledstva proshlogo" [Musorgsky and the problem of the legacy of the past]. In Iurii Vsevolodovich Keldysh and Vasilii Iakovlev, editors. *M.P. Musorgskii: K piatidesiatiletiiu so dnia smerti, 1881-1931: Stat'i i materialy* [M.P. Musorgsky: on the fiftieth anniversary of the day of his death, 1881-1931: articles and materials]. Moscow: Gosudarstvennoe muzykal'noe izdatel'stvo, 1932.

Khubov, Georgii. *Musorgskii.* Moscow: Muzyka, 1969.

————. *Zhizn' A. Serova* [The life of A. Serov]. Moscow: Gosudarstvennoe muzykal'noe izdatel'stvo, 1950.

Kiui, Tsezar. See Cui, César.

Komarova, Varvara Dmitrievna [Vladimir Karenin]. *Vladimir Stasov: Ocherk ego zhizni i deiatel'nosti* [Vladimir Stasov: a survey of his life and work]. 2 vols. Leningrad: Mysl', 1927.

Korabel'nikova, L. "Stroitel' muzykal'noi Moskvy" [The builder of musical Moscow]. *Sovetskaia muzyka,* June 1960, pp. 80-87.

Kremlev, Iulii Anatol'evich. *Leningradskaia gosudarstvennaia konservatoriia, 1862-1937* [Leningrad State Conservatory, 1862-1937]. Moscow: Gosudarstvennoe muzykal'noe izdatel'stvo, 1938.

_____ . *Russkaia mysl' o muzyke* [Russian thought on music]. 3 vols. Leningrad: Gosudarstvennoe muzykal'noe izdatel'stvo, 1954-1960.

Kutateladze, L.M. "E.F. Napravnik: Ocherk zhizni i deiatel'nosti" [E.F. Napravnik: a survey of his life and work]. In Eduard Frantsevich Napravnik. *Avtobiograficheskie tvorcheskie materialy, dokumenty, pis'ma* [Autobiographical creative materials, documents, letters]. Edited by Iurii Vsevolodovich Keldysh. Leningrad: Gosudarstvennoe muzykal'noe izdatel'stvo, 1959.

Lang, Paul Henry. *Music in Western Civilization.* New York: Norton, 1941.

Lebedev, Andrei Konstantinovich, and Solodovnikov, Aleksandr Vasil'evich. *Vladimir Vasil'evich Stasov: Zhizn' i tvorchestvo* [Vladimir Vasilievich Stasov: life and works]. Moscow: Iskusstvo, 1976.

Leningrad Conservatory. *100 let Leningradskoi konservatorii: Istoricheskii ocherk* [100 years of the Leningrad Conservatory: a historical survey]. Leningrad: Gosudarstvennoe muzykal'noe izdatel'stvo, 1962.

Levasheva, Ol'ga Evgen'evna; Keldysh, Iurii Vsevolodovich, and Kandinskii, Aleksei Ivanovich. *Istoriia russkoi muzyki* [The history of Russian music]. Second edition. 2 vols. Moscow: Muzyka, 1973- .

Liapunov, Sergei Mikhailovich, and Liapunova, Anastasiia Sergeevna. "Molodye gody Balakireva" [Balakirev's young years]. In Milii Alekseevich Balakirev. *Vospominaniia i pis'ma* [Memoirs and letters]. Edited by Emiliia Lazarevna Frid. Leningrad: Gosudarstvennoe muzykal'noe izdatel'stvo, 1962.

Liapunova, Anastasiia Sergeevna. "Glinka i Balakirev." *Sovetskaia muzyka,* February 1953, pp. 75-81.

Lincoln, W. Bruce. "The Circle of the Grand Duchess Yelena Pavlovna, 1847-1861." *Slavonic and East European Review* 48, no. 3 (July 1970):373-87.

_____ . *Nicholas I, Emperor and Autocrat of All the Russias.* Bloomington: Indiana University Press, 1978.

Lisovskii, N.M. "Letopis' sobytii v zhizni i deiatel'nosti A.G. Rubinshteina: S ukazaniem na otzyvy i stat'i o nem i ego proizvedeniiakh v russkoi pechati, 1829-1889" [A chronicle of events in the life and work of A.G. Rubinstein: with references to reviews and articles about him and his works in the Russian press, 1829-1889]. *Russkaia starina* 64 (1889):601-32.

Livanova, Tamara Nikolaevna. *Russkaia muzykal'naia kul'tura XVIII veka v ee sviazakh s literaturoi, teatrom i bytom: Issledovaniia i materialy* [Russian musical culture of the eighteenth century in connection with literature, theater and daily life: research and materials]. 2 vols. Moscow: Gosudarstvennoe muzykal'noe izdatel'stvo, 1952-1953.

Livanova, Tamara Nikolaevna, and Vinogradova, O.A., compilers. *Muzykal'naia bibliografiia russkoi periodicheskoi pechati XIX veka* [A musical bibliography of the Russian periodical press in the XIX century]. Moscow: "Sovetskii kompozitor," 1960- .

Loesser, Arthur. *Men, Women and Pianos: A Social History.* New York: Simon and Schuster, 1954.

M, A.E. "Istoricheskaia spravka ob operakh Kiui" [Historical information about Cui's operas]. *Ezhegodnik imperatorskikh teatrov,* 1892-1893, p. 559.

Marchesi, Gustavo. "The Years of La Forza del Destino." *Verdi,* no. 4 (1961):313-58; no. 5 (1962):1033-87; no. 6 (1966).1995-2059.

Mercy-Argenteau, Marie Clothilde de. *César Cui: Esquisse critique.* Paris: Librairie Fischbacher, 1888.

Miliukov, Pavel Nikolaevich. *Ocherk po istorii russkoi kul'tury* [A survey of the history of Russian culture]. 3 vols. Jubilee edition. Paris: Izdatel'stvo "Sovremennyia zapiski," 1931.

Muzykal'noe nasledstvo: Sborniki po istorii muzykal'noi kul'tury SSSR [Musical legacy: collections on the history of musical culture in the U.S.S.R.]. 4 vols. Moscow: Gosudarstvennoe muzykal'noe izdatel'stvo, 1962-1976.

Oldani, Robert William, "Mussorgsky's *Boris Godunov* and the Russian Imperial Theaters." *Liberal Arts Review,* no. 7 (Spring 1979):6-24.

———. "New Perspectives on Mussorgsky's *Boris Godunov.*" Unpublished Ph.D. dissertation, University of Michigan, 1978.

Olkhovsky, George Andrew. "Vladimir Stasov and His Quest for Russian National Music." Unpublished Ph.D. dissertation, Georgetown University, 1968.

Pintner, Walter M. "The Social Characteristics of the Early Nineteenth-Century Russian Bureaucracy." *Slavic Review* 29, no. 3 (September 1970):429-43.

Raynor, Henry. *A Social History of Music: From the Middle Ages to Beethoven.* New York: Schocken Books, 1972.

Rimskii-Korsakov,A.N., editor. *Muzykal'naia letopis': Stat'i i materialy* [Musical chronicle: articles and materials]. 3 vols. Petrograd: Mysl', 1922-1925.

Savelova, Z. "Musorgskii v krugu ego lichnykh znakomstv: Materialy k biografii"[Musorgsky in the circle of his personal acquaintances: materials for his biography]. In Iurii Vsevolodovich Keldysh and Vasilii Iakovlev, editors. *M.P. Musorgskii: K piatidesiatiletiiu so dnia smerti, 1881-1931: Stat'i i materialy* [M.P. Musorgsky: on the fiftieth anniversary of the day of his death, 1881-1931: articles and materials], pp. 167-88. Moscow: Gosudarstvennoe muzykal'noe izdatel'stvo, 1932.

Seaman, Gerald R. *History of Russian Music: Volume I, From Its Origins to Dargomyzhsky.* New York: Praeger, 1967.

Seroff, Victor I. *The Mighty Five: The Cradle of Russian National Music.* New York: Allen, Towne and Heath, Inc., 1948.

Shteinberg, Anna. "U istokov russkoi mysli o muzyke"[At the sources of Russian thought about music]. *Sovetskaia muzyka,* October 1967, pp. 73-82.

Sokhor, Arnol'd Naumovich. "Stranitsy tvorcheskoi druzhby" [Pages of creative friendship]. *Sovetskaia muzyka,* May 1960, pp. 61-67.

Solovtsov, Anatolii Aleksandrovich. *Zhizn' i tvorchestvo N.A. Rimskogo-Korsakova* [The life and work of N.A. Rimsky-Korsakov]. Moscow: Muzyka, 1964.

Spisok russkikh povremennykh izdanii s 1703 po 1899 god s svedeniiami ob ekzempliarakh, prinadlezhashchikh biblioteke imperatorskoi akademii nauk [A list of Russian periodical publications from 1703 to 1899 with information about copies belonging to the library of the Imperial Academy of Sciences]. St. Petersburg: Tipografiia imperatorskoi akademii nauk, 1901.

Stanislavskii, M.V. "Eduard Frantsevich Napravnik: Monograficheskii etiud po povodu ego poluvekovogo sluzheniia russkomu muzykal'nomu iskusstvu, 1863-1913" [Eduard Frantsevich Napravnik: a monographic study of his half century of service to Russian musical art, 1863-1913]. *Russkaia starina* 157 (1914):114-31.

Swan, Alfred J. *Russian Music and Its Sources in Chant and Folk-Song.* London: John Baker, 1973.

Taneev, Sergei. "Publichnye kontserty i baly v stolitsakh" [Public concerts and balls in the capitals]. *Russkii arkhiv* 23, pt. 2 (1885):442-46.

Taruskin, Richard. "Glinka's Ambiguous Legacy and the Birth Pangs of Russian Opera." *Nineteenth Century Music* 1 (November 1977):142-62.

———. "Opera and Drama in Russia: The Preachment and Practice of Operatic Esthetics in the Eighteen Sixties." Unpublished Ph.D. dissertation, Columbia University, 1975.

———. "Realism as Preached and Practiced: The Russian Opera Dialogue." *The Musical Quarterly* 56 (July 1970):431-54.

Tchaikovskii, Modest Il'ich. See Chaikovskii, Modest Il'ich.

Timofeev, Grigorii. "M.A. Balakirev: Na osnovanii novykh materialov"[M.A. Balakirev: on the basis of new materials]. *Russkaia mysl',* June 1912, pp. 38-62; July 1912, pp. 55-81.

Valkenier, Elizabeth. *Russian Realist Art: The State and Society: The Peredvizhniki and Their Tradition.* Ann Arbor, Michigan: Ardis, 1977.

Vol'f, A.I. *Khronika Peterburgskikh teatrov s kontsa 1826 do nachala 1855 goda* [A chronicle of the Petersburg theaters from the end of 1826 to the beginning of 1855]. 2 vols. St. Petersburg: R. Golike, 1877.

————. *Khronika Peterburgskikh teatrov s kontsa 1855 do nachala 1881 goda.* [A chronicle of the Petersburg theaters from the end of 1855 to the beginning of 1881]. St. Petersburg, 1884.

Weber, William. *Music and the Middle Class: The Social Structure of Concert Life in London, Paris and Vienna.* New York: Holmes & Meier Publishers. 1975.

Young, Percy M. *The Concert Tradition: From the Middle Ages to the Twentieth Century.* London: Routledge and Kegan Paul, 1965.

Index

Yaroslavl, 82
Yusupov, Prince Nikolai, 174

Zabel, Albert Heinrich, 41
Zaremba, Nikolai: aesthetic principles
    and taste in music; 41, 42, 162-63,

211; and Balakirev, 81; and the
Russian Musical Society, 145, 147,
152, 211, 226 n.6; and the St.
Petersburg Conservatory, 41, 145,
211-214